Writing for Vaudeville

by

Brett Page

The Echo Library 2007

Published by

The Echo Library

Echo Library
131 High St.
Teddington
Middlesex TW11 8HH

www.echo-library.com

Please report serious faults in the text to complaints@echo-library.com

ISBN 978-1-4068-2313-4

INTRODUCTION

It falls to the lot of few men in these days to blaze a new trail in Bookland. This Mr. Brett Page has done, with firmness and precision, and with a joy in every stroke that will beget in countless readers that answering joy which is the reward of both him who guides and him who follows. There is but one word for a work so penetrating, so eductive, so clear—and that word is *masterly*. Let no one believe the modest assertion that "Writing for Vaudeville" is "less an original offering than a compilation." I have seen it grow and re-grow, section by section, and never have I known an author give more care to the development of his theme in an original way. Mr. Page has worked with fidelity to the convictions gained while himself writing professionally, yet with deference for the opinions of past masters in this field. The result is a book quite unexcelled among manuals of instruction, for authority, full statement, analysis of the sort that leads the reader to see what essentials he must build into his own structures, and sympathetic helpfulness throughout. I count it an honor to have been the editorial sponsor for a pioneer book which will be soon known everywhere.

J. BERG ESENWEIN

CHAPTER I

THE WHY OF THE VAUDEVILLE ACT

1. THE Rise of Vaudeville

A French workman who lived in the Valley of the Vire in the fourteenth or fifteenth century, is said to be vaudeville's grandparent. Of course, the child of his brain bears not even a remote resemblance to its descendant of to-day, yet the line is unbroken and the relationship clearer than many of the family trees of the royal houses. The French workman's name was Oliver Bassel, or Olivier Basselin, and in his way he was a poet. He composed and sang certain sprightly songs which struck the popular fancy and achieved a reputation not only in his own town but throughout the country.

Bassel's success raised the usual crop of imitators and soon a whole family of songs like his were being whistled in France. In the course of time these came to be classed as a new and distinct form of musical entertainment. They were given the name of "Val-de-Vire" from the valley in which Bassel was born. This name became corrupted, into "vaux-de-vire" in the time of Louis XVI, and was applied to all the popular or topical songs sung on the streets of Paris. Then the aristocrats took up these songs and gave entertainments at their country seats. To these entertainments they gave the name of "vaux-de-ville," the last syllable being changed to honor Bassel's native town [1] And gradually the x was dropped and the word has remained through the years as it is to-day.

As the form of entertainment advanced, the word vaudeville expanded in meaning. It came to comprise not only a collection of songs, but also acrobatic feats and other exhibitions. Having no dramatic sequence whatever, these unrelated acts when shown together achieved recognition as a distinct form of theatrical entertainment. As "vaudeville"—or "variety"—this form of entertainment became known and loved in every country of the world.

Vaudeville was introduced into this country before 1820, but it did not become a common form of entertainment until shortly before the Civil War when the word 'variety' was at once adopted and became familiar as something peculiarly applicable to the troubled times. The new and always cheerful entertainment found the reward of its optimism in a wide popularity. But as those days of war were the days of men, vaudeville made its appeal to men only. And then the war-clouds passed away and the show business had to reestablish itself, precisely as every other commercial pursuit had to readjust itself to changed conditions.

Tony Pastor saw his opportunity. On July 31, 1865, he opened "Tony Pastor's Opera House" at 199-201 Bowery, New York. He had a theory that a vaudeville entertainment from which every objectionable word and action were

---

[1] Another version relates that these songs were sung on the Pont Neuf in Paris, where stands the Hotel de Ville, or City Hall, and thus the generic name acquired the different termination.

taken away, and from which the drinking bar was excluded, would appeal to women and children as well as men. He knew that no entertainment that excluded women could long hold a profitable place in a man's affections. So to draw the whole family to his new Opera House, Tony Pastor inaugurated clean vaudeville[2]. Pastor's success was almost instantaneous. It became the fashion to go to Pastor's Opera House and later when he moved to Broadway, and then up to Fourteenth Street, next to Tammany Hall, he carried his clientele with him. And vaudeville, as a form of entertainment that appealed to every member of the home circle, was firmly established—for a while.

For Pastor's success in New York did not at first seem to the average vaudeville manager something that could be duplicated everywhere. A large part of the profits of the usual place came from the sale of drinks and to forego this source of revenue seemed suicidal. Therefore, vaudeville as a whole continued for years on the old plane. "Variety" was the name—in England vaudeville is still called "variety"—that it held even more widely then. And in the later seventies and the early eighties "variety" was on the ebb-tide. It was classed even lower than the circus, from which many of its recruits were drawn.

Among the men who came to vaudeville's rescue, because they saw that to appear to the masses profitably, vaudeville must be clean, were F. F. Proctor in Philadelphia, and B. F. Keith in Boston. On Washington Street in Boston, B. F. Keith had opened a "store show." The room was very small and he had but a tiny stage; still he showed a collection of curiosities, among which were a two-headed calf and a fat woman. Later on he added a singer and a serio-comic comedian and insisted that they eliminate from their acts everything that might offend the most fastidious. The result was that he moved to larger quarters and ten months later to still more commodious premised.

Continuous vaudeville—"eleven o'clock in the morning until eleven at night"—had its birth on July 6, 1885. It struck the popular fancy immediately and soon there was hardly a city of any importance that did not possess its "continuous" house. From the "continuous" vaudeville has developed the two-performances-a-day policy, for which vaudeville is now so well known.

The vaudeville entertainment of this generation is, however, a vastly different entertainment from that of even the nineties. What it has become in popular affection it owes not only to Tony Pastor, F. F. Proctor, or even to B. F. Keith— great as was his influence—but to a host of showmen whose names and activities would fill more space than is possible here. E. F. Albee, Oscar Hammerstein, S. Z. Poli, William Morris, Mike Shea, James E. Moore, Percy G. Williams, Harry Davis, Morris Meyerfeld, Martin Beck, John J. Murdock, Daniel F. Hennessy,

---

[2] In the New York Clipper for December 19, 1914, there is an interesting article: "The Days of Tony Pastor," by Al. Fostelle, an old-time vaudeville performer, recounting the names of the famous performers who played for Tony Pastor in the early days. It reads like a "who's who" of vaudeville history. Mr. Fostelle, has in his collection a bill of an entertainment given in England in 1723, consisting of singing, dancing, character impersonations, with musical accompaniment, tight-rope walking, acrobatic feats, etc.

Sullivan and Considine, Alexander Pantages, Marcus Loew, Charles E. Kohl, Max Anderson, Henry Zeigler, and George Castle, are but a few of the many men living and dead who have helped to make vaudeville what it is.

From the old variety show, made up of a singer of topical songs, an acrobatic couple, a tight-rope walker, a sidewalk "patter" pair, and perhaps a very rough comedy sketch, there has developed a performance that sometimes includes as many as ten or twelve acts, each one presented by an artist whose name is known around the world. One of the laments of the old vaudeville performers is that they have a place in vaudeville no more. The most famous grand opera singers and the greatest actors and actresses appear in their room. The most renowned dramatists write some of its playlets. The finest composers cut down their best-known works to fit its stage, and little operas requiring forty people and three or four sets of scenery are the result. To the legitimate [3] stage vaudeville has given some of its successful plays and at least one grand opera has been expanded from a playlet. To-day a vaudeville performance is the best thought of the world condensed to fit the flying hour.

2. Of What a Vaudeville Show is Made

There is no keener psychologist than a vaudeville manager. Not only does he present the best of everything that can be shown upon a stage, but he so arranges the heterogeneous elements that they combine to form a unified whole. He brings his audiences together by advertising variety and reputations, and he sends them away aglow with the feeling that they have been entertained every minute. His raw material is the best he can buy. His finished product is usually the finest his brain can form. He engages Sarah Bernhardt, Calve, a Sir James M. Barrie playlet, Ethel Barrymore, and Henry Miller. He takes one of them as the nucleus of a week's bill. Then he runs over the names of such regular vaudevillians as Grace La Rue, Nat Wills, Trixie Friganza, Harry Fox and Yansci Dollie, Emma Carus, Sam and Kitty Morton, Walter C. Kelly, Conroy and LeMaire, Jack Wilson, Hyams and McIntyre, and Frank Fogarty. He selects two or maybe three of them. Suddenly it occurs to him that he hasn't a big musical "flash" for his bill, so he telephones a producer like Jesse L. Lasky, Arthur Hopkins or Joe Hart and asks him for one of his fifteen- or twenty-people acts. This he adds to his bill. Then he picks a song-and-dance act and an acrobatic turn. Suddenly he remembers that he wants—not for this show, but for some future week—Gertrude Hoffman with her big company, or Eva Tanguay all by herself. This off his mind, the manager lays out his show—if it is the standard nine-act bill—somewhat after the following plan, as George A. Gottlieb, who books Keith's Palace Theatre, New York, shows— probably the best and certainly the "biggest" vaudeville entertainments seen in this country—has been good enough to explain.

---

[3] *Legitimate* is a word used in the theatrical business to distinguish the full-evening drama, its actors, producers, and its mechanical stage from those of burlesque and vaudeville. Originally coined as a word of reproach against vaudeville, it has lost its sting and is used by vaudevillians as well as legitimate actors and managers.

"We usually select a 'dumb act' for the first act on the bill. It may be a dancing act, some good animal act, or any act that makes a good impression and will not be spoiled by the late arrivals seeking their seats. Therefore it sometimes happens that we make use of a song-and-dance turn, or any other little act that does not depend on its words being heard.

"For number two position we select an interesting act of the sort recognized as a typical 'vaudeville act.' It may be almost anything at all, though it should be more entertaining than the first act. For this reason it often happens that a good man-and-woman singing act is placed here. This position on the bill is to 'settle' the audience and to prepare it for the show.

"With number three position we count on waking up the audience. The show has been properly started and from now on it must build right up to the finish. So we offer a comedy dramatic sketch—a playlet that wakens the interest and holds the audience every minute with a culminative effect that comes to its laughter-climax at the 'curtain,' or any other kind of act that is not of the same order as the preceding turn, so that, having laid the foundations, we may have the audience wondering what is to come next.

"For number four position we must have a 'corker' of an act—and a 'name.' It must be the sort of act that will rouse the audience to expect still better things, based on the fine performance of the past numbers. Maybe this act is the first big punch of the show; anyway, it must strike home and build up the interest for the act that follows.

"And here for number five position, a big act, and at the same time another big name, must be presented. Or it might be a big dancing act—one of those delightful novelties vaudeville likes so well. In any event this act must be as big a 'hit' as any on the bill. It is next to intermission and the audience must have something really worth while to talk over. And so we select one of the best acts on the bill to crown the first half of the show.

"The first act after intermission, number six on the bill, is a difficult position to fill, because the act must not let down the carefully built-up tension of interest and yet it must not be stronger than the acts that are to follow. Very likely there is chosen a strong vaudeville specialty, with comedy well to the fore. Perhaps a famous comedy dumb act is selected, with the intention of getting the audience back in its seats without too many conspicuous interruptions of what is going on on the stage. Any sort of act that makes a splendid start-off is chosen, for there has been a fine first half and the second half must be built up again—of course the process is infinitely swifter in the second half of the show—and the audience brought once more into a delighted-expectant attitude.

"Therefore the second act after intermission—number seven—must be stronger than the first. It is usually a full-stage act and again must be another big name. Very likely it is a big playlet, if another sketch has not been presented earlier on the bill. It may be a comedy playlet or even a serious dramatic playlet, if the star is a fine actor or actress and the name is well known. Or it may be anything at all that builds up the interest and appreciation of the audience to welcome the 'big' act that follows. "For here in number eight position—next to closing, on a nine-act bill—the comedy hit of the show is usually placed. It is one of the acts for which the audience has been waiting. Usually it is one of the famous 'single' man or 'single' women acts that vaudeville has made such favorites.

"And now we have come to the act that closes the show. We count on the fact that some of the audience will be going out. Many have only waited to see the chief attraction of the evening, before hurrying off to their after-theatre supper and dance. So we spring a big 'flash.' It must be an act that does not depend for its success upon being heard perfectly. Therefore a 'sight' act is chosen, an animal act maybe, to please the children, or a Japanese troupe with their gorgeous kimonos and vividly harmonizing stage draperies, or a troupe of white-clad trapeze artists flying against a background of black. Whatever the act is, it must be a showy act, for it closes the performance and sends the audience home pleased with the program to the very last minute.

"Now all the time a booking-manager is laying out his show, he has not only had these many artistic problems on his mind, but also the mechanical working of the show. For instance, he must consider the actual physical demands of his stage and not place next each other two full-stage acts. If he did, how would the stage hands change the scenery without causing a long and tedious wait? In vaudeville there must be no waits. Everything must run with unbroken stride. One act must follow another as though it were especially made for the position. And the entire show must be dovetailed to the split seconds of a stop-watch.

"Therefore it is customary to follow an 'act in One' (See below) with an act requiring Full Stage. Then after the curtain has fallen on this act, an act comes on to play in One again. A show can, of course, start with a full-stage act, and the alternation process remains the same. Or there may be an act that can open in One and then go into Full Stage—after having given the stage hands time to set their scenery—or vice versa, close in One. Briefly, the whole problem is simply this—acts must be arranged not only in the order of their interest value, but also according to their physical demands.

"But there is still another problem the manager must solve. 'Variety' is vaudeville's paternal name—vaudeville must present a *varied* bill and a show consisting of names that will tend to have a box-office appeal. No two acts in a show should be alike. No two can be permitted to conflict. 'Conflict' is a word that falls with ominous meaning on a vaudeville performer's or manager's ears, because it means death to one of the acts and injury to the show as a whole. If two famous singing 'single' women were placed on the same bill, very likely there would be odious comparisons—even though they did not use songs that were alike. And however interesting each might be, both would lose in interest. And yet, sometimes we do just this thing—violating a minor rule to win a great big box-office appeal.

"Part of the many sides of this delicate problem may be seen when you consider that no two 'single' singing acts should be placed next each other—although they may not conflict if they are placed far apart on the bill. And no two 'quiet' acts may be placed together. The tempo of the show must be maintained—

and because tragic playlets, and even serious playlets, are suspected of 'slowing up a show,' they are not booked unless very exceptional."

These are but a few of the many sides of the problem of what is called "laying out a show." A command of the art of balancing a show is a part of the genius of a great showman. It is a gift. It cannot be analyzed. A born showman lays out his bill, not by rule, but by feeling.

3. The Writer's Part in a Vaudeville Show

In preparing the raw material from which the manager makes up his show, the writer may play many parts. He may bear much of the burden of entertainment, as in a playlet, or none of the responsibility, as in the average dumb act. And yet, he may write the pantomimic story that pleases the audience most. Indeed, the writer may be everything in a vaudeville show, and always his part is an important one.

Of course the trained seals do not need a dramatist to lend them interest, nor does the acrobat need his skill; but without the writer what would the actress be, and without the song-smith, what would the singer sing? And even the animal trainer may utilize the writer to concoct his "line of talk." The monologist, who of all performers seems the most independent of the author, buys his merriest stories, his most up-to-the-instant jests, ready-made from the writer who works like a marionette's master pulling the strings. The two-act, which sometimes seems like a funny impromptu fight, is the result of the writer's careful thinking. The flirtatious couple who stroll out on the stage to make everyone in the audience envious, woo Cupid through the brain of their author. And the musical comedy, with its strong combination of nearly everything; is but the embodied flight of the writer's fancy. In fact, the writer supplies much of the life-blood of a vaudeville show. Without him modern vaudeville could not live.

Thus, much of the present wide popularity of vaudeville is due to the writer. It is largely owing to the addition of his thoughts that vaudeville stands to-day as a greater influence—because it has a wider appeal—than the legitimate drama in the make-believe life of the land. Even the motion pictures, which are nearer the eyes of the masses, are not nearer their hearts. Vaudeville was the first to foster motion pictures and vaudeville still accords the motion picture the place it deserves on its bills. For vaudeville is the amusement weekly of the world—it gathers and presents each week the best the world affords in entertainment. And much of the best comes from the writer's brain.

Because mechanical novelties that are vaudeville-worth-while are rare, and because acrobats and animal trainers are of necessity limited by the frailties of the flesh, and for the reason that dancers cannot forever present new steps, it remains for the writer to bring to vaudeville the never-ceasing novelty of his thoughts. New songs, new ideas, new stories, new dreams are what vaudeville demands from the writer. Laughter that lightens the weary day is what is asked for most.

It is in the fulfilling of vaudeville's fine mission that writers all over the world are turning out their best. And because the mission of vaudeville is fine, the writing of anything that is not fine is contemptible. The author who tries to turn his talents to base uses—putting an untrue emphasis on life's false values, picturing situations that are not wholesome, using words that are not clean—deserves the fate of failure that awaits him. As E. F. Albee, who for years has been a controlling force in vaudeville, wrote: [4]"We have no trouble in keeping vaudeville clean and wholesome, unless it is with some act that is just entering, for the majority of the performers are jealous of the respectable name that vaudeville has to-day, and cry out themselves against besmirchment by others."

Reality and truth are for what the vaudeville writer strives. The clean, the fine, the wholesome is his goal. He finds in the many theatres all over the land a countless audience eager to hear what he has to say. And millions are invested to help him say it well.

---

[4] "The Future of the Show Business," by E. F. Albee, in The Billboard for December 19, 1914.

CHAPTER II

SHOULD YOU TRY TO WRITE FOR VAUDEVILLE?

"I became a writer," George Bernard Shaw once said, "because I wanted to get a living without working for it—I have since realized my mistake." Anyone who thinks that by writing for vaudeville he can get a living without working for it is doomed to a sad and speedy awakening.

If I were called upon to give a formula for the creation of a successful vaudeville writer, I would specify: The dramatic genius of a Shakespere, the diplomatic craftiness of a Machiavelli, the explosive energy of a Roosevelt, and the genius-for-long-hours of an Edison: mix in equal proportions, add a dash of Shaw's impudence, all the patience of Job, and keep boiling for a lifetime over the seething ambition of Napoleon.

In other—and less extreme—words, if you contemplate writing for vaudeville for your bread and butter, you must bring to the business, if not genius, at least the ability to think, and if not boundless energy, at any rate a determination never to rest content with the working hours of the ordinary professions.

If you suppose that the mere reading of this book is going to make you able to think, permit me gently to disillusion you; and if you are imbued with the flattering faith that after studying these chapters you will suddenly be able to sit down and write a successful playlet, monologue, two-act, musical comedy libretto, or even a good little "gag," in the words of classic vaudeville—forget it! All this book can do for you—all any instruction can do—is to show you the right path, show precisely *how* others have successfully essayed it, and wish you luck. Do you remember the brave lines of W. E. Henley, the blind English poet:

> Out of the night that covers me,
> Black as the pit from pole to pole,
> I thank whatever gods may be
> For my unconquerable soul.

And again in the same poem, "Invictus":

> I am the master of my fate:
> I am the captain of my soul.

There sings the spirit that will carry a writer to success in vaudeville or in any other line of writing; and it is this inspired attitude you should assume toward the present book of instruction.

These chapters, carefully designed and painstakingly arranged, contain information and suggestions which, if studied and applied by the right person, will help him to a mastery of vaudeville writing. But they should be viewed not as laying down rules, only as being suggestive. This book cannot teach you how to write—with its aid you may be able to teach yourself.

Are you the sort of person likely to make a success of writing for vaudeville? You, alone, can determine. But the following discussion of some of the elements of equipment which anyone purposing to write for vaudeville should possess, may help you find the answer.

1. Experience in Other Forms of Writing Valuable

Let us suppose that you have been engaged in writing for a newspaper for years. You started as a reporter and because of your unusual ability in the handling of political news have made politics your specialty. You have been doing nothing but politics until politics seems to be all you know. Suddenly the sporting editor falls ill, and at the moment there is no one to take his place but you. Your assistant takes over your work and you are instructed to turn out a daily page of sporting news.

If you knew nothing at all about writing you would find the task nearly impossible to accomplish. But you do know how to write and therefore the mere writing does not worry you. And your experience as a special writer on politics has taught you that there are certain points all special newspaper work has in common and you apply your knowledge to the task before you.

Still you are seriously handicapped for a time because you have been thinking in terms of politics. But soon, by turning all your energy and ability upon your new subject, you learn to think in terms of sport. And, if you are a better thinker and a better writer than the old sporting editor, it won't be long before you turn out a better sporting page than he did. If you were the owner of the newspaper, which, in the emergency, would you choose to be your sporting editor: the untried man who has never demonstrated his ability to write, the reporter who has no knowledge of special writing, or the trained writer who has mastered one specialty and, it may reasonably be supposed, will master another quickly? The same care you would exercise in choosing another man to work for you, you should exercise in choosing your own work for yourself.

Do you know how to write? Do you write with ease and find pleasure in the work? If you do, class yourself with the reporter.

What success have you had in writing fiction? Have you written successful novels or short-stories? If you have, class yourself with the special writer. Did you ever write a play? Was your full-evening play accepted and successful? If you have written a play and if your play was a success, class yourself with the sporting editor himself—but as one who has made a success in only one specialty in the realm of sport.

For, those who have had some success in other forms of writing—even the successful playwright—and those who never have written even a salable joke, all have to learn the slightly different form of the vaudeville act.

But, having once learned the form and become perfectly familiar with vaudeville's peculiar requirements, the dramatist and the trained fiction writer will outstrip the untrained novice. Remember that the tortoise was determined, persistent, and energetic.

2. Ability to Think in Drama and Technical Knowledge of the Stage Required

The dramatist and the trained fiction writer possess imagination, they think in plots, they have learned how to picture vivid, dramatic incidents, and they know a story when it comes up and taps them on the shoulder. Furthermore, they know where to look for ideas, and how to twist them to plot uses. In every one of these points of special knowledge both the dramatist and the trained fiction writer have the advantage over the untrained novice, for the essence of all vaudeville writing lies in plot—which is story—arrangement.

But there is a wide difference between being able to think in a story-plot and in drama, and in this the playwright who has produced a full-evening play has the advantage over even the trained fiction writer when it comes to applying his dramatic knowledge to vaudeville. Precisely what the difference is, and what drama itself is—especially that angle of the art to be found in vaudeville—will be taken up and explained as clearly as the ideas admit of explanation, in the following pages. But not on one page, nor even in a whole chapter, will the definition of drama be found, for pulsating life cannot be bound by words. However, by applying the rules and heeding the suggestions herein contained, you will be able to understand the "why" of the drama that you feel when you witness it upon the stage. The ability to think in drama means being able to see drama and bring it fresh and new and gripping to the stage.

Of course drama is nothing more than story presented by a different method than that employed in the short-story and the novel. Yet the difference in methods is as great as the difference between painting and sculpture. Indeed the novel-writer's methods have always seemed to me analogous to those employed by the painter, and the dramatist's methods similar to those used by the sculptor. And I have marvelled at the nonchalant way in which the fiction writer often rushes into the writing of a play, when a painter would never think of trying to "sculpt" until he had learned at least some of the very different processes employed in the strange art-form of sculpture. The radical difference between writing and playwrighting [5] has never been popularly understood, but some day it will be comprehended by everybody as clearly as by those whose business it is to make plays.

An intimate knowledge of the stage itself is necessary for success in the writing of plays. The dramatist must know precisely what means, such as scenery, sound-effects, and lights—the hundred contributing elements of a purely mechanical nature at his command— he can employ to construct his play to mimic reality. In the present commercial position of the stage such knowledge is absolutely necessary, or the writer may construct an act that cannot possibly win a production, because he has made use of scenes that are financially out of the question, even if they are artistically possible.

---

[5] Note the termination of the word *playwright*. A "wright" is a workman in some mechanical business. Webster's dictionary says: "Wright is used chiefly in compounds, as, figuratively, playwright." It is significant that the playwright is compelled to rely for nearly all his effects upon purely mechanical means.

This is a fundamental knowledge that every person who would write for the stage must possess. It ranks with the "a b c" course in the old common school education, and yet nearly every novice overlooks it in striving after the laurel wreaths of dramatic success that are impossible without it. And, precisely in the degree that stage scenery is different from nature's scenes, is the way people must talk upon the stage different from the way they talk on the street. The method of stage speech—*what* is said, not *how* it is said—is best expressed in the definition of all art, which is summed up in the one word "suppression." Not what to put in, but what to leave out, is the knowledge the playwright—in common with all other artists—must possess. The difference in methods between writing a novel and writing a play lies in the difference in the scenes and speeches that must be left out, as well as in the descriptions of scenery and moods of character that everyone knows cannot be expressed in a play by words.

Furthermore, the playwright is working with *spoken*, not *written*, words, therefore he must know something about the art of acting, if he would achieve the highest success. He must know not only how the words he writes will sound when they are spoken, but he must also know how he can make gestures and glances take the place of the volumes they can be made to speak.

Therefore of each one of the different arts that are fused into the composite art of the stage, the playwright must have intimate knowledge. Prove the truth of this statement for yourself by selecting at random any play you have liked and inquiring into the technical education of its author. The chances are scores to one that the person who wrote that play has been closely connected with the stage for years. Either he was an actor, a theatrical press agent, a newspaper man, a professional play-reader for some producer, or gained special knowledge of the stage through a dramatic course at college or by continual attendance at the theatre and behind the scenes. It is only by acquiring *special* knowledge of one of the most difficult of arts that anyone may hope to achieve success.

3. A Familiar Knowledge of Vaudeville and its Special Stage Necessary

It is strange but true that a writer able to produce a successful vaudeville playlet often writes a successful full-evening play, but that only in rare instances do full-evening dramatists produce successful vaudeville playlets. Clyde Fitch wrote more than fifty-four long plays in twenty years, and yet his "Frederic Lemaitre," used by Henry Miller in vaudeville, was not a true vaudeville playlet—merely a short play—and achieved its success simply because Fitch wrote it and Miller played it with consummate art.

The vaudeville playlet and the play that is merely short, are separate art forms, they are precisely and as distinctly different as the short-story and the story that is merely short. It is only within the last few years that Brander Matthews drew attention to the artistic isolation of the short-story; and J. Berg Esenwein, in his very valuable work[6], established the truth so that all might read and know it. For

---

[6] Writing the Short-Story, by J. Berg Esenwein, published uniform with this volume, in, "The Writer's Library."

years I have contended for the recognition of the playlet as an art form distinct from the play that is short.

And what is true of the peculiar difference of the playlet form is, in a lesser measure, true of the monologue, the two-act, and the one-act musical comedy. They are all different from their sisters and brothers that are found as integral parts of full-evening entertainments.

To recognize these forms as distinct, to learn what material [7]best lends itself to them and how it may be turned into the most natural and efficient form, requires a special training different from that necessary for the writing of plays for the legitimate stage.

But not only is there a vast difference between the material and the art forms of the legitimate and the vaudeville stage, there is also a great difference in their playing stages. The arrangements of the vaudeville stage, its lights and scenery, are all unique, as are even the playing spaces and mechanical equipment.

Therefore the author must know the mechanical aids peculiar to his special craft, as well as possess a familiar knowledge of the material that vaudeville welcomes and the unique forms into which that material must be cast.

4. What Chance Has the Beginner?

The "gentle reader" who has read thus far certainly has not been deterred by the emphasis—not undue emphasis, by the way—placed on the value of proved ability in other forms of writing to one who would write for vaudeville. That he has not been discouraged by what has been said—if he is a novice—proves that he is not easily downcast. If he has been discouraged—even if he has read this far simply from curiosity—proves that he is precisely the person who should not waste his time trying to write for vaudeville. Such a person is one who ought to ponder his lack of fitness for the work in hand and turn all his energies into his own business. Many a good clerk, it has been truly said, has been wasted in a poor writer.

But, while emphasis has been laid upon the value of training in other forms of literary work, the emphasis has been placed not on purely literary skill, but on the possession of ideas and the training necessary to turn the ideas to account. It is "up to" the ambitious beginner, therefore, to analyze the problem for himself and to decide if he possesses the peculiar qualifications that can by great energy and this special training place him upon a par with the write who has made a success in other forms of literary work. For there is a sense in which no literary training is really necessary for success in vaudeville writing.

If the amateur has an imaginative mind, the innate ability to see and turn to his own uses an interesting and coherent story, and is possessed of the ability to think in drama, and, above all, has the gift of humor, he can write good vaudeville material, even if he has not education or ability to write an acceptable poem,

---

[7] The word *material* in vaudeville means manuscript material. To write vaudeville material is to write monologues and playlets and the other forms of stage speech used in vaudeville acts.

article or short-story. In other words, a mastery of English prose or verse is not necessary for success in vaudeville writing. Some of the most successful popular songs, the most successful playlets, and other vaudeville acts, have been written by men unable to write even a good letter.

But the constant advancement in excellence demanded of vaudeville material, both by the managers and the public, is gradually making it profitable for only the best-educated, specially-trained writers to undertake this form of work. The old, illiterate, rough-and-ready writer is passing, in a day when the "coon shouter" has given the headline-place to Calve and Melba, and every dramatic star has followed Sarah Bernhardt into the "two-a-day." [8]

Nevertheless, in this sense the novice needs no literary training. If he can see drama in real life and feels how it can be turned into a coherent, satisfying story, he can learn how to apply that story to the peculiar requirements of vaudeville. But no amount of instruction can supply this inborn ability. The writer himself must be the master of his fate, the captain of his own dramatic soul.

---

[8] The *two-a-day* is stage argot for vaudeville. It comes from the number of performances the actor "does," for in vaudeville there are two shows every day, six or seven days a week.

CHAPTER III

THE VAUDEVILLE STAGE AND ITS DIMENSIONS

To achieve success in any art the artist must know his tools and for what purposes they are designed. Furthermore, to achieve the highest success, he must know what he cannot do as well as what he can do with them.

The vaudeville stage—considered as a material thing—lends itself to only a few definite possibilities of use, and its scenery, lights and stage-effects constitute the box of tools the vaudeville writer has at his command.

I. THE PHYSICAL PROPORTIONS OF THE VAUDEVILLE STAGE

The footlights are the equator of the theatre, separating the "front of the house," or auditorium, from the "back of the house," or stage. The frame through which the audience views the stage is the "proscenium arch." Flat against the stage side of the arch run the "house curtain" and the asbestos curtain that are raised at the beginning and lowered at the end of the performance.

That portion of the stage which lies between the curving footlights and a line drawn between the bases of the proscenium arch is called the "apron." The apron is very wide in old-fashioned theatres, but is seldom more than two or three feet wide in recently built houses.

1. One

Back of the proscenium arch—four feet or more behind it—you have noticed canvas-covered wings painted in neutral-toned draperies to harmonize with every sort of curtain, and you have noticed that they are pushed forward or drawn back as it is found necessary to widen or make narrow the stage opening. These first wings, called "tormentors," [9]extend upward from the floor—anywhere from 18 to 25 feet,—to the "Grand Drapery" and "Working Drapery," or first "border," which extend and hang just in front of them across the stage and hide the stage-rigging from the audience. The space lying between the tormentors and a line drawn between the bases of the proscenium arch is called "One."

It is in One that monologues, most "single acts"—that is, acts presented by one person—and many "two-acts"—acts requiring but two people—are played.

Behind the tormentors is a curtain called the "olio," which fulfills the triple purpose of hiding the rest of the stage, serving as scenery for acts in One and often as a curtain to raise and lower on acts playing in the space back of One.

2. Two

Five, or six, or even seven feet behind the tormentors you have noticed another set of wings which—extending parallel with the tormentors—serve to

---

[9] No one of the score I have asked for the origin of the word *tormentor* has been able to give it. They all say they have asked old-time stage-carpenters, but even they did not know.

mask the rest of stage. The space between these wings and the line of the olio is called "Two."

In Two, acts such as flirtation-acts—a man and a woman playing lover-like scenes—which use scenery or small "props," and all other turns requiring but a small playing space, are staged.

3. Three

An equal number of feet back of the wings that bound Two, are wings that serve as boundaries for "Three."

In Three, playlets that require but shallow sets, and other acts that need not more than twelve feet for presentation, are played.

4. Four or Full Stage

Behind the wings that bound Three are another pair of wings, set an equal number of feet back, which serve as the boundaries of "Four." But, as there are rarely more than four entrances on any stage, Four is usually called "Full Stage."

In Full Stage are presented all acts such as acrobatic acts, animal turns, musical comedies, playlets and other pretentious acts that require deep sets and a wide playing space.

5. Bare Stage

Sometimes the very point of a playlet depends upon showing not the conventional stage, as it is commonly seen, but the real stage as it is, unset with scenery; therefore sometimes the entire stage is used as the playing stage, and then in the vernacular it is called "Bare Stage." [10]

On the opposite page is a diagram of the stage of Keith's Palace Theatre, New York City. A comparison of the preceding definitions with this diagram should give a clear understanding of the vaudeville playing stage.

II. THE WORKING DEPARTMENTS OF THE VAUDEVILLE STAGE

At audience-right—or stage-left—flat against the extended wall of the proscenium arch in the First Entrance (to One) there is usually a signal-board equipped with push buttons presided over by the stage-manager. The stage-manager is the autocrat behind the scenes. His duty is to see that the program is run smoothly without the slightest hitch or wait between acts and to raise and lower the olio, or to signal the act-curtain up or down, on cues. [11]

A *cue* is a certain word or action regarded as the signal for some other speech or action by another actor, or the signal for the lights to change or a bell to ring or something to happen during the course of a dramatic entertainment.

[diagram]

---

[10] The New Leader, written by Aaron Hoffman and played for so many years by Sam Mann & Company, is an excellent example of a Bare Stage act.
[11] The New Leader, written by Aaron Hoffman and played for so many years by Sam Mann & Company, is an excellent example of a Bare Stage act.

STAGE-DIAGRAM OF THE PALACE THEATRE, NEW YORK

The author wishes to express his thanks to Mr. Elmer F. Rogers, house-manager, and Mr. William Clark, stage-manager, respectively, of the Palace Theatre, for the careful measurements from which this diagram was drawn.

When an act is ready to begin, the stage-manager pushes a button to signal the olio up or raises it himself—if, that drop is worked from the stage—and on the last cue he pushes another button to signal the curtain down, or lowers it himself, as the case may be. He keeps time on the various acts and sees that the performers are ready when their turn arrives. Under the stage-manager are the various departments to which the working of scenery and effects are entrusted.

A *drop* is the general name for a curtain of canvas—painted to represent some scene and stretched on a batten—a long, thick strip of wood—pocketed in the lower end to give the canvas the required stability. *Sets of lines* are tied to the upper batten on which the drop is tied and thus the drop can be raised or lowered to its place on the stage. There are sets of lines in the rear boundaries of One, Two, Three and Four, and drops can be *hung* on any desired set.

1. The Stage-Carpenter and His Flymen and Grips

As a rule the stage-manager is also the stage-carpenter. As such he, the wizard of scenery, has charge of the men, and is able to erect a palace, construct a tenement, raise a garden or a forest, or supply you with a city street in an instant.

Up on the wall of the stage, just under a network of iron called the "gridiron"—on which there are innumerable pulleys through which run ropes or "lines" that carry the scenery—there is, in the older houses, a balcony called the "fly-gallery." Into the fly-gallery run the ends of all the lines that are attached to the counter-weighted drops and curtains; and in the gallery are the flymen who pull madly on these ropes to lift or lower the curtains and drops when the signal flashes under the finger of the stage-manager at the signal-board below. But in the newer houses nearly all drops and scenery are worked from the stage level, and the fly-gallery—if there is one—is deserted. When a "set" is to be made, the stage-carpenter takes his place in the centre of the stage and claps his hands a certain number of times to make his men understand which particular set is wanted—if the sequence of the sets has not yet been determined and written down for the flymen to follow in definite order. Then the flymen lower a drop to its place on the stage and the "grips" push out the "flats" that make the wall of a room or the wings that form the scenery of a forest—or whatever the set may be.

2. The Property-Man and His Assistants

Into the mimic room that the grips are setting comes the Property-man—"Props," in stage argot—with his assistants, who place in the designated positions the furniture, bric-a-brac, pianos, and other properties, that the story enacted in this room demands.

After the act has been presented and the curtain has been rung down, the order to "strike" is given and the clearers run in and take away all the furniture and properties, while the property-man substitutes the new furniture and properties that are needed. This is done at the same time the grips and fly men are changing the scenery. No regiment is better trained in its duties. The property-man of the average vaudeville theatre is a hard-worked chap. Beside being an expert in properties, he must be something of an actor, for if there is an "extra man" needed in a playlet with a line or two to speak, it is on him that the duty falls. He must be ready on the instant with all sorts of effects, such as glass-crashes and wood-crashes, when a noise like a man being thrown downstairs or through a window is required, or if a doorbell or a telephone-bell must ring at a certain instant on a certain cue, or the noise of thunder, the wash of the sea on the shore, or any one of a hundred other effects be desired.

3. The Electrician

Upon the electrician fall all the duties of Jove in the delicate matter of making the sun to shine or the moon to cast its pale rays over a lover's scene. Next to the stage-manager's signal-board, or in a gallery right over it, or perhaps on the other side of the stage, stands the electric switch-board. From here all the stage lights and the lights in the auditorium and all over the front of the house are operated.

From the footlights with their red and white and blue and vari-tinted bulbs, to the borders that light the scenery from above, the bunch-lights that shed required lights through windows, the grate-logs, the lamps and chandeliers that light the mimic rooms themselves, and the spot-light operated by the man in the haven of the gallery gods out front, all are under the direction of the electrician who sits up in his little gallery and makes the moonlight suddenly give place to blazing sunlight on a cue.

It is to the stage-manager and the stage-carpenter, the property-man and the electrician, that are due the working of the stage miracles that delight us in the theatres.

III. THE SCENERY OF THE VAUDEVILLE STAGE

In the ancient days before even candles were invented—the rush-light days of Shakespere and his predecessors—plays were presented in open court-yards or, as in France, in tennis-courts in the broad daylight. A proscenium arch was all the scenery usually thought necessary in these outdoor performances, and when the plays were given indoors even the most realistic scenery would have been of little value in the rush-lit semi-darkness. Then, indeed, the play was the thing. A character walked into the STORY and out of it again; and "place" was left to the imagination of the audience, aided by the changing of a sign that stated where the story had chosen to move itself.

As the centuries rolled along, improvements in lighting methods made indoor theatrical presentations more common and brought scenery into effective use. The invention of the kerosene lamp and later the invention of gas brought enough light upon the stage to permit the actor to step back from the footlights into a wider working-space set with the rooms and streets of real life. Then with the electric light came the scenic revolution that emancipated the stage forever from enforced gloomy darkness, permitted the actor's expressive face to be seen farther back from the footlights, and made of the proscenium arch the frame of a picture.

"It is for this picture-frame stage that every dramatist is composing his plays," Brander Matthews says; "and his methods are of necessity those of the picture-frame stage; just as the methods of the Elizabethan dramatic poet were of necessity those of the platform stage." And on the same page: The influence of the realistic movement of the middle of the nineteenth century imposed on the stage-manager the duty of making every scene characteristic of the period and of the people, and of relating the characters closely to their environment." [12]

On the vaudeville stage to-day, when all the sciences and the arts have come to the aid of the drama, there is no period nor place, nor even a feeling of atmosphere, that cannot be reproduced with amazing truth and beauty of effect. Everything in the way of scenery is artistically possible, from the squalid room of the tenement-dweller to the blossoming garden before the palace of a king—but artistic possibility and financial advisability are two very different things.

If an act is designed to win success by spectacular appeal, there is no doubt that it is good business for the producer to spend as much money as is necessary to make his effects more beautiful and more amazing than anything ever before seen upon the stage. But even here he must hold his expenses down to the minimum that will prove a good investment, and what he may spend is dependent on what the vaudeville managers will pay for the privilege of showing that act in their houses.

But it is not worth spectacular acts that the vaudeville writer has particularly to deal. His problem is not compounded of extravagant scenery, gorgeous properties, trick-scenes and light-effects. Like Shakespere, for him the play—the story—is the thing. The problem he faces is an embarrassment of riches. With everything artistically possible, what is financially advisable?

1. The Successful Writer's Attitude toward Scenery

The highest praise a vaudevillian can conjure up out of his vast reservoir of enthusiastic adjectives to apply to any act is, "It can be played in the alley and knock 'em cold." In plain English he means, the STORY is so good that it doesn't require scenery.

Scenery, in the business of vaudeville—please note the word "business"—has no artistic meaning. If the owner of a dwelling house could rent his property with the rooms unpapered and the woodwork unpainted, he would gladly do so and pocket the saving, wouldn't he? In precisely the same spirit the vaudeville-act owner would sell his act without going to the expense of buying and transporting scenery, if he could get the same price for it. To the vaudevillian scenery is a business investment.

Because he can get more money for his act if it is properly mounted in a pleasing picture, the vaudeville producer invests in scenery. But he has to figure closely, just as every other business man is compelled to scheme and contrive in

---

[12] The Study of the Drama, Brander Matthews.

dollars and cents, or the business asset of scenery will turn into a white elephant and eat up all his profits.

Jesse L. Lasky, whose many pleasing musical acts will be remembered, had many a near-failure at the beginning of his vaudeville-producing career because of his artistic leaning toward the beautiful in stage setting. His subsequent successes were no less pleasing because he learned the magic of the scenery mystery. Lasky is but one example, and were it not that the names of vaudeville acts are but fleeting memories, dimmed and eclipsed by the crowded impressions of many acts seen at one sitting, there might be given an amazing list of beautiful little entertainments that have failed because of the transportation cost of the scenery they required.

When a producer is approached with a request to read a vaudeville act he invariably asks, "What scenery?" His problem is in two parts:

1. He must decide whether the merits of the act, itself, justify him in investing his money in scenery on the gamble that the act will be a success.

2. If the act proves a success, can the scenery be transported from town to town at so low a cost that the added price he can get for the act will allow a gross profit large enough to repay the original cost of the scenery and leave a net profit?

An experience of my own in producing a very small act—small enough to be in the primary class—may be as amusing as it is typical. My partners and I decided to put out a quartet. We engaged four good singers, two of them men, and two women. I wrote the little story that introduced them in a humorous way and we set to work rehearsing. At the same time the scenic artist hung three nice big canvases on his paint frames and laid out a charming street-scene in the Italian Quarter of Anywhere, the interior of a squalid tenement and the throne room of a palace.

The first drop was designed to be hung behind the Olio—for the act opened in One—and when the Olio went up, after the act's name was hung out, the lights dimmed to the blue and soft green of evening in the Quarter. Then the soprano commenced singing, the tenor took up the duet, and they opened the act by walking rhythmically with the popular ballad air to stage-centre in the amber of the spot-light. When the duet was finished, on came the baritone, and then the contralto, and there was a little comedy before they sang their first quartet number.

Then the first drop was lifted in darkness and the scene changed to the interior of the squalid tenement in which the pathos of the little story unfolded, and a characteristic song was sung. At length the scene changed to the throne room of the palace, where the plot resolved itself into happiness and the little opera closed with the "Quartet from Rigoletto."

The act was a success; it never received less than five bows and always took two encores. But we paid three hundred and fifty dollars for those miracles of drops, my partners and I, and we used them only one week.

In the first place, the drops were too big for the stage on which we "tried out" the act. We could not use them there and played before the house street-drop and in the house palace set. The act went very well. We shipped the drops at length-rates—as all scenery is charged for by expressmen and railroads—to the next town. There we used them and the act went better. It was a question whether the bigger success was due to the smoother working of the act or to the beautiful drops.

The price for which the act was playing at that breaking-in period led me to ponder the cost of transporting the drops in their rolled-up form on the battens. Therefore when I was informed that the stage in the next town was a small one, I had a bright idea. I ordered the stage-carpenter to take the drops from their battens, discard the battens, and put pockets on the lower ends of the drops and equip the upper ends with tie ropes so the drops could be tied on the battens used in the various houses. The drops would then fit small or large stages equally well and could be folded up into a small enough space to tuck in a trunk and save all the excess transportation charges.

Of course the drops folded up all right, but they unfolded in chips of scaled-off paint. In the excitement, or the desire to "take a chance," I had not given a thought to the plain fact that the drops were not aniline. They were doomed to chip in time anyway, and folding only hastened their end. Still, we received just as much money for the act all the time we were playing it, as though we had carried the beautiful drops.

Now comes the third lesson of this incident: Although we were precisely three hundred and sixty-eight dollars "out" on account of the drops, we really saved money in the end because we were forced to discard them. The local union of the International Association of Theatrical Stage Employees—Stage Hands' Union, for short—tried to assess me in the town where we first used the drops, for the salary of a stage-carpenter. According to their then iron-clad rule, before which managers had to bow, the scenery of every act carrying as many as three drops on battens had to be hung and taken down by the act's own stage-carpenter—at forty dollars a week. They could not collect from such an act today because the rules have been changed, but our act was liable, under the old rules, and I evaded it only by diplomacy. But even to-day every act that carries a full set of scenery—such as a playlet requiring a special set—must carry its own stage-carpenter.

Therefore, to the problem of original cost and transportation expense, now add the charge of forty dollars a week against scenery—and an average of five dollars a week extra railroad fare for the stage-carpenter—and you begin to perceive why a vaudeville producer asks, when you request him to read an act: "What scenery?"

There is no intention of decrying the use of special scenery in vaudeville. Some of the very best and most profitable acts, even aside from great scenic one-act dramas like "The System," [13]would be comparatively valueless without their individual sets. And furthermore the use of scenery, with the far-reaching possibilities of the special set in all its beauty and—on this side of the water—hitherto unrealized effectiveness, has not yet even approached its noon. Together

---

[13] See Appendix.

with the ceaseless advance of the art of mounting a full-evening play on the legitimate stage [14] will go the no less artistic vaudeville act. But, for the writer anxious to make a success of vaudeville writing, the special set should be decried. Indeed, the special set ought not to enter into the writer's problem at all.

No scenery can make up for weakness of story. Rather, like a paste diamond in an exquisitely chased, pure gold setting, the paste story will appear at greater disadvantage: because of the very beauty of its surroundings. The writer should make his story so fine that it will sparkle brilliantly in any setting.

The only thought that successful vaudeville writers give to scenery is to indicate in their manuscripts the surroundings that "relate the characters closely to their environment."

It requires no ability to imagine startling and beautiful scenic effects that cost a lot of money to produce—that is no "trick." The vaudeville scenery magic lies in making use of simple scenes that can be carried at little cost—or, better still for the new writer, in twisting the combinations of drops and sets to be found in every vaudeville house to new uses.

---

[14] The Theatre of To-Day, Hiram Kelly Moderwell's book on the modern theatre, will repay reading by anyone particularly interested in the special set and its possibilities.

CHAPTER IV

THE SCENERY COMMONLY FOUND IN VAUDEVILLE THEATRES

1. THE Olio

In every vaudeville theatre there is an Olio and, although the scene which it is designed to represent may be different in each house, the street Olio is common enough to be counted as universally used. Usually there are two drops in "One," either of which may be the Olio, and one of them is likely to represent a street, while the other is pretty sure to be a palace scene.

2. Open Sets

Usually in Four—and sometimes in Three—there are to be found in nearly every vaudeville theatre two different drops, which with their matching wings [15] form the two common "open sets"—or scenes composed merely of a rear drop and side wings, and not boxed in.

The Wood Set consists of a drop painted to represent the interior of a wood or forest, with wings painted in the same style. It is used for knock-about acts, clown acts, bicycle acts, animal turns and other acts that require a deep stage and can play in this sort of scene.

The Palace Set, with its drop and wings, is painted to represent the interior of a palace. It is used for dancing acts, acrobats and other acts that require a deep stage and can appropriately play in a palace scene.

3. The Box Sets

A "box set" is, as the name implies, a set of scenery that is box-shaped. It represents a room seen through the fourth wall, which has been removed. Sometimes with a, ceiling-piece, but almost invariably with "borders"—which are painted canvas strips hanging in front of the "border-lights" to mask them and keep the audience from seeing the ropes and pulleys hanging from the gridiron—the box set more nearly mimics reality than the open set, which calls upon the imagination of the audience to supply the realities that are entirely lacking or only hinted at.

The painted canvas units which are assembled to make the box set are called "flats." A flat is a wooden frame about six feet six inches wide and from twelve to eighteen feet long, covered with canvas and, of course, painted with any scene desired. It differs from a wing in being only one-half the double frame; therefore it cannot stand alone.

Upon the upper end of each flat along the unpainted outer edge there is fastened a rope as long as the flat. Two-thirds of the way up from the bottom of the corresponding edge of the matching flat there is a "cleat," or metal strip, into

---

[15] A *wing* is a double frame of wood covered with painted canvas and set to stand as this book will when its covers are opened at right angles to each other.

which the rope, or "lash-line" is snapped. The two flats are then drawn tight together so that their edges match evenly and the lash-line is lashed through the framework to hold the flats firmly together.

While one flat may be a painted wall, the next may contain a doorway and door, another a part of an ornamental arch, and still another a window, so, when the various flats are assembled and set, the box set will have the appearance of a room containing doors and windows and even ornamental arches. The most varied scenes can thus be realistically set up.

In the rear of open doors there are usually wings, or perhaps flats, [16] painted to represent the walls of hallways and adjoining rooms and they are called "interior backings." Behind a door supposed to open out into the street or behind windows overlooking the country, there are hung, or set, short drops or wings painted to show parts of a street, a garden, or a country-side, and these are called "exterior backings."

The Centre-door Fancy is the most common of the box sets. Called "fancy," because it has an arch with portieres and a rich-looking backing, and because it is supposed to lead into the other palatial rooms of the house, this set can be used for a less pretentious scene by the substitution of a matched door for the arch.

In this plainer form it is called simply *The Parlor Set*. Sometimes a parlor set is equipped with a French window, but this should not be counted on. But there are usually a grate and mantelpiece, and three doors. The doors are designed to be set, one in the rear wall, and one in each of the right and left walls. A ceiling-piece is rarely found, but borders are always to be had, and a chandelier is customary.

The Kitchen Set is, as the name implies, less pretentious than the changeable parlor set. It usually is equipped with three doors, possesses matching borders, may have an ordinary window, and often has a fireplace panel.

Slightly altered in appearance, by changing the positions of the doors and the not very common substitution of a "half-glass door" in the rear wall, the kitchen set does duty as *The Office Set*.

It is in these two box sets—changed in minor details to serve as four sets—that the vaudeville playlet is played.

On the following pages will be found eight diagrams showing how the stock or house box sets can be set in various forms. A study of these will show how two different acts using the same house set can be given surroundings that appear absolutely different. These diagrams should prove of great help to the playlet writer who wishes to know how many doors he may use, where they are placed and how his act will fit and play in a regulation set of scenery.

---

[16] When flats are used as backings they are made stable by the use of the *stage-brace*, a device made of wood and capable of extension, after the manner of the legs of a camera tripod. It is fitted with double metal hooks on one end to hook into the wooden cross-bar on the back of the flat and with metal eyes on the other end through which *stage-screws* are inserted and screwed into the floor of the stage.

INTRODUCTION TO DIAGRAMS

The following diagrams, showing the scenic equipment of the average vaudeville theatre, have been specially drawn for this volume and are used here by courtesy of the Lee Lash Studios, New York. As they are drawn to a scale of one-eighth of an inch to the foot, the precise size of the various scenes may be calculated.

The diagrams are based on the average vaudeville stage, which allows thirty or thirty-two feet between tormentors. The proscenium arch *may* be much greater, but the average vaudeville stage will set the tormentors about thirty feet apart. All vaudeville stage settings are made back of the tormentor line.

At the tormentor line there will be, of course, a Grand Drapery and Working Drapery which will mask the first entrance overhead.

There will be either a set of borders for each scene, or else the borders will be painted to use with any scene, to mask the stage rigging. The borders are usually hung from six to seven feet apart, so that in planning a scene this should be considered. In a few of the larger houses, a ceiling-piece is found, but, as has been said, this is so rare it should not be counted on.

Most houses have a floor cloth, and medallion or carpet, in addition to the properties hereafter described. Reference to the diagrams will show that the tormentors have a "flipper," which runs to the proscenium arch wall; in the flipper is usually a door or a curtained opening for the entrances and exits of acts in One.

If you will combine with the diagrams shown these elements which cannot be diagrammed, you will have a clear idea of the way in which any scene is constructed. Then if you will imagine the scene you have in mind as being set up on a stage like that of the Palace Theatre, shown in the last chapter, you will have a working understanding of the vaudeville stage.

WHAT THE DIAGRAMS INCLUDE

A well-ordered vaudeville stage, as has been described, possesses Drops for use in One, one or more Fancy Interiors, a Kitchen Set, and Exterior Sets. The Drops in One are omitted from these diagrams, because they would be represented merely by a line drawn behind the tormentors.

The Fancy Interiors may include a Light Fancy, a Dark Fancy, an Oak Interior, and a Plain Chamber set. As the differences are largely of painting, the usual Centre-door Fancy is taken as the basis for the variations—five different ways of setting it are shown.

Two out of the many different ways of setting the Kitchen Set are given.

The Exterior Set allows little or no variation; the only thing that can be done is to place balustrades, vases, etc., in different positions on the stage; therefore but one diagram is supplied.

DIAGRAM I.—FANCY INTERIOR No. 1

Showing the usual method of setting a "Fancy." It may be made shallower by omitting a wing on either side.

DIAGRAM II.—FANCY INTERIOR No. 2

The double arch is thrown from the centre to the side, the landscape drop being used to back the scene—the drop may be seen through the window on stage-left. The window of the Fancy Interior is always of the French type, opening full to the floor.

DIAGRAM III.—FANCY INTERIOR No. 3

This is a deeper and narrower set, approximating more closely a room in an ordinary house. The double arch at the rear may be backed with an interior backing or a conservatory backing. If the interior backing is used, the conservatory backing may be used to back the single four-foot arch at stage-left.

DIAGRAM IV.—FANCY INTERIOR No. 4

This shows the double arch flanked by a single arch on each side, making three large openings looking out on the conservatory drop.

DIAGRAM V.—FANCY INTERIOR No. 5

The fireplace is here brought into prominence by setting it in a corner with two "jogs" on each side. The window is backed with a landscape or garden drop as desired.

DIAGRAM VI.—KITCHEN SET No. 1

This arrangement of a Kitchen Set makes use of three doors, emphasizing the double doors in the centre of rear wall, which open out on an interior backing or a wood or garden drop. In this and the following setting a small window can be fitted into the upper half of either of the single doors.

DIAGRAM VII.—KITCHEN SET No. 2

Two doors only are used in this setting; the double doors, in the same relative position as in the preceding arrangement, open out on a wood or landscape backing. The fireplace is brought out on stage-right. The single door on stage-left opens on an interior backing.

DIAGRAM VIII.—WOOD OR GARDEN SET

Many theatres have two sets of Exterior wings—one of Wood Wings and one of Garden Wings. In some houses the Wood Wings are used with the Garden Drop, set vases and balustrades being used to produce the garden effect, as shown here. Some theatres also have a Set House and Set Cottage, which may be placed on either side of the stage; each has a practical door and a practical window. With the Set House and Set Tree slight variations of exterior settings may be contrived.

4. Properties

In the argot of the stage the word "property" or "prop" means any article—aside from scenery—necessary for the proper mounting or presentation of a play.

A property may be a set of furniture, a rug, a pair of portieres, a picture for the wall, a telephone, a kitchen range or a stew-pan—indeed, anything a tall that is not scenery, although serving to complete the effect and illusion of a scene.

Furniture is usually of only two kinds in a vaudeville playhouse. There is a set of parlor furniture to go with the parlor set and a set of kitchen furniture to furnish the kitchen set. But, while these are all that are at the immediate command of the property-man, he is usually permitted to exchange tickets for the theatre with any dealer willing to lend needed sets of furniture, such as a desk or other office equipment specially required for the use of an act.

In this way the sets of furniture in the property room may be expanded with temporary additions into combinations of infinite variety. But, it is wise not to ask for anything out of the ordinary, for many theatre owners frown upon bills for hauling, even though the rent of the furniture may be only a pair of seats.

For the same reason, it is unwise to specify in the property-list— which is a printed list of the properties each act requires—anything in the way of rugs that is unusual. Though some theatres have more than two kinds of rugs, the white bear rug and the carpet rug are the most common. It is also unwise to ask for pictures to hang on the walls. If a picture is required, one is usually supplied set upon an easel.

Of course, every theatre is equipped with prop telephones and sets of dishes and silver for dinner scenes. But there are few vaudeville houses in the country that have on hand a bed for the stage, although the sofa is commonly found.

A buffet, or sideboard, fully equipped with pitchers and wine glasses, is customary in every vaudeville property room. And champagne is supplied in advertising bottles which "pop" and sparkle none the less realistically because the content is merely ginger ale.

While the foregoing is not an exhaustive list of what the property room of a vaudeville theatre may contain, it gives the essential properties that are commonly found. Thus every ordinary requirement of the usual vaudeville act can be supplied.

The special properties that an act may require must be carried by the act. For instance, if a playlet is laid in an artist's studio there are all sorts of odds and ends that would lend a realistic effect to the scene. A painter's easel, bowls of paint brushes, a palette, half-finished pictures to hang on the walls, oriental draperies, a model's throne, and half a dozen rugs to spread upon the floor, would lend an atmosphere of charming bohemian realism.

Special Sound-Effects fall under the same common-sense rule. For, while all vaudeville theatres have glass crashes, wood crashes, slap-sticks, thunder sheets, cocoanut shells for horses' hoof-beats, and revolvers to be fired off-stage, they could not be expected to supply such little-called-for effects as realistic battle sounds, volcanic eruptions, and like effects.

If an act depends on illusions for its appeal, it will, of course, be well supplied with the machinery to produce the required sounds. And those that do not depend on exactness of illusion can usually secure the effects required by calling on the drummer with his very effective box-of-tricks to help out the property-man.

5. The Lighting of the Vaudeville Stage

At the electrical switchboard centre all the lights of the theatre, as well as those of the stage itself. Presided over by the electrician, the switchboard, so far as the stage and its light effects are concerned, commands two classes of lights. The first of these is the arc light and the second the electric bulb.

The Spot-lights are the lamps that depend upon the arc for their illumination. If you have ever sat in the gallery of any theatre, and particularly of a vaudeville theatre, you certainly have noticed the very busy young man whose sole purpose in life appears to be to follow the heroine around the stage with the focused spot of light that shines like a halo about her. The lamp with which he accomplishes this difficult feat is appropriately called a "spot-light." While there are often spot-lights on the electrician's "bridge," as his balcony is called, the gallery out front is the surest place to find the spot-light.

The Footlights are electric bulbs dyed amber, blue, and red— or any other special shade desired—beside the well-known white, set in a tin trough sunk in the stage and masked to shine only upon the stage. By causing only one group of colors to light, the electrician can secure all sorts of variations, and with the aid of "dimmers" permit the lights to shine brilliantly or merely to glow with faint radiance.

The Border-lights are electric bulbs of varying colors set in tin troughs a little longer than the proscenium opening and are suspended above the stage behind the scenery borders. They shine only downward. There are border-lights just in front of the drops in One, Two, Three and Four, and they take the names of "first border-light," "second border-light," and so on from the drops they illuminate.

Strip-lights are electric bulbs set in short strips of tin troughs, that are equipped with hooks by which they can be hung behind doors and out-of-the-way dark places in sets to illuminate the backings.

A Bunch-light is a box of tin set on a standard, which can be moved about the stage the length of its electric cord, and has ten or twelve electric bulbs inside that cast a brilliant illumination wherever it is especially desired. Squares of gelatine in metal frames can be slipped into the grooves in front of the bunch-light to make the light any color or shade desired. These boxes are especially valuable in giving the effect of blazing sunlight just outside the doors or windows of a set, or to shine through the windows in the soft hue of moonlight.

Grate Logs are found in nearly every vaudeville house and are merely iron painted to represent logs of wood, inside of which are concealed lamps that shine up through red gelatine, simulating the glow of a wood fire shining in the fireplace under the mantelpiece usually found in the centre-door-fancy set.

Special Light-effects have advanced so remarkably with the science of stage illumination that practically any effect of nature may be secured. If the producer wishes to show the water rippling on the river drop there is a "ripple-lamp" at his command, which is a clock-actuated mechanism that slowly revolves a ripple glass in front of a "spot-lamp" and casts a realistic effect of water rippling in the moonlight.

By these mechanical means, as well as others, the moon or the sun can be made to shine through a drop and give the effect of rising or of setting, volcanos can be made to pour forth blazing lava and a hundred other amazing effects can be obtained. In fact, the modern vaudeville stage is honeycombed with trapdoors and overhung with arching light-bridges, through which and from which all manner of lights can be thrown upon the stage, either to illuminate the faces of the actors with striking effect, or to cast strange and beautiful effects upon the scenery. Indeed, there is nothing to be seen in nature that the electrician cannot reproduce upon the stage with marvellous fidelity and pleasing effect.

But the purpose here, as in explaining all the other physical departments of the vaudeville stage, is not to tell what has been done and what can be done, interesting and instructive as such a discussion would be, but to describe what is usually to be found in a vaudeville theatre. The effects that are at ready command are the only effects that should interest anyone about to write for vaudeville. As was emphasized in the discussion of scenery, the writer should not depend for success on the unusual. His aim should be to make use of the common stage-effects that are found on every vaudeville stage—if, indeed, he depends on any effects at all.

Here, then, we have made the acquaintance of the physical proportions and aspects of the vaudeville stage and have inquired into all the departments that contribute to the successful presentation of a vaudeville entertainment. We have examined the vaudeville writer's tool-box and have learned to know the uses for which each tool of space, scenery, property, and light is specially designed. And by learning what these tools can do, we have also learned what they cannot do.

Now let us turn to the plans and specifications—called manuscripts— that go to make up the entertaining ten or forty minutes during which a vaudeville act calls upon these physical aids to make it live upon the mimic stage, as though it were a breathing reality of the great stage of life.

CHAPTER V

THE NATURE OF THE MONOLOGUE

THE word monologue comes from the combination of two Greek words, *monos*, alone, and *legein*, to speak. Therefore the word monologue means "to speak alone"—and that is often how a monologist feels. If in facing a thousand solemn faces he is not a success, no one in all the world is more alone than he.

It appears easy for a performer to stroll into a theatre, without bothersome scenery, props, or tagging people, and walk right out on the stage alone and set the house a-roar. But, like most things that appear easy, it is not. It is the hardest "stunt" in the show business, demanding two very rare things: uncommon ability in the man, and extraordinary merit in the monologue itself.

To arrive at a clear understanding of what a monologue is, the long way around through the various types of "talking singles" may be the shortest cut home to the definition.

1. Not a Soliloquy.

The soliloquy of the by-gone days of dramatic art was sometimes called a monologue, because the person who spoke it was left alone upon the stage to commune with himself in spoken words that described to the audience what manner of man he was and what were the problems that beset him. Hamlet's "To be or not to be," perhaps the most famous of soliloquies, is, therefore, a true monologue in the ancient sense, for Hamlet spoke alone when none was near him. In the modern sense this, and every other soliloquy, is but a speech in a play. There is a fundamental reason why this is so: A monologue is spoken *to the audience*, while in a soliloquy (from the Latin *solus*, alone, *loqui*, to talk) the actor communes *with himself* for the "benefit" of the audience.

2. Not Merely an Entertainment by One Person

There are all sorts of entertaining talking acts in vaudeville presented by a single person. Among them are the magician who performs his tricks to the accompaniment of a running fire of talk which, with the tricks themselves, raises laughter; and the person who gives imitations and wins applause and laughter by fidelity of speech, mannerisms and appearance to the famous persons imitated. Yet neither of these can be classed as a monologist, because neither depends upon speech alone to win success.

3. Not a Disconnected String of Stories

Nor, in the strictest vaudeville sense, is a monologue merely a string of stories that possesses no unity as a whole and owns as its sole reason of being that of amusement and entertainment. For instance, apropos of nothing whatever an entertainer may say:

> I visited Chinatown the other evening and took dinner in one of the charming Oriental restaurants there. The first dish I ordered was called Chop Suey. It was fine. They make it of several kinds of

vegetables and meats, and one dark meat in particular hit my taste. I wanted to find out what it was, so I called the waiter. He was a solemn-looking Chinaman, whose English I could not understand, so I pointed to a morsel of the delicious dark meat and, rubbing the place where all the rest of it had gone, I asked:
"Quack-quack?"
The Chink grinned and said:
"No. No. Bow-wow."

Before the laughter has subsided the entertainer continues:

That reminds me of the deaf old gentleman at a dinner party who was seated right next to the prettiest of the very young ladies present. He did his best to make the conversation agreeable, and she worked hard to make him understand what she said. But finally she gave it up in despair and relapsed into a pained silence until the fruit was passed. Then she leaned over and said:
"Do you like bananas?"

A smile of comprehension crept over the deaf old man's face and he exclaimed:
"No, I like the old-fashioned night-gowns best."

And so, from story to story the entertainer goes, telling his funny anecdotes for the simple reason that they are funny and create laughter. But funny as they are, they are disconnected and, therefore, do not meet the requirement of unity of character, which is one of the elements of the pure monologue.

4. Not a Connected Series of Stories Interspersed With Songs and the Like

If the entertainer had told the stories of the Chinaman and the deaf old gentleman as though they had happened to a single character about whom all the stories he tells revolve, his act and his material would more nearly approach the pure monologue form. For instance:

Casey's a great fellow for butting into queer places to get a bite to eat. The other evening we went down to Chinatown and in one of those Oriantal joints that hand out Chop Suey in real china bowls with the Jersey City dragoons on 'em, we struck a dish that hit Casey just right.

"Mither av Moses," says Casey, "this is shure the atein fer ye; but what's thot dilicate little tid-bit o' brown mate?"
"I don't know," says I.
"Oi'll find out," says Casey. "Just listen t'me spake that heathen's language."
"Here, boy," he hollers, "me likee, what you call um?"

The Chink stares blankly at Casey. Casey looks puzzled, then he winks at me. Rubbing his hand over the place where the rest of the meat had gone, he says:
"Quack-quack?"
A gleam shot into the Chink's almond eyes and he says:
"No. No. Bow-wow."

It took seven of us to hold Casey, he felt that bad. But that wasn't a patchin' to the time we had dinner with a rich friend o' ours and Casey was seated right next to the nicest little old lady y'ever saw.
. . .

And so on until the banana story is told, with Casey the hero and victim of each anecdote.

But an entertainer feels no necessity of making his entire offering of related anecdotes only. Some monologists open with a song because they want to get the audience into their atmosphere, and "with" them, before beginning their monologue. The song merely by its melody and rhythm helps to dim the vividness of impression left by the preceding act and gives the audience time to quiet down, serving to bridge the psychic chasm in the human mind that lies between the relinquishing of one impression and the reception of the next.

Or the monologist may have a good finishing song and knows that he can depend on it for an encore that will bring him back to tell more stories and sing another song. So he gives the orchestra leader the cue, the music starts and off he goes into his song.

Or he may have some clever little tricks that will win applause, or witty sayings that will raise a laugh, and give him a chance to interject into his offering assorted elements of appeal that will gain applause from different classes of people in his audience. Therefore, as his purpose is to entertain, he sings his song, performs his tricks, tells his witty sayings, or perhaps does an imitation or two, as suits his talent best. And a few end their acts with serious recitations of the heart-throb sort that bring lumps into kindly throats and leave an audience in the satisfied mood that always comes when a touch of pathos rounds off a hearty laugh.

But by adding to his monologue unrelated offerings the monologist becomes an "entertainer," an "impersonator," or whatever title best describes his act. If he stuck to his stories only and told them all on a single character, his offering would be a monologue in the sense that it observes the unity of character, but still it would not be a pure monologue in the vaudeville sense as we now may define it—though a pure monologue might form the major part of his "turn."

II. WHAT A MONOLOGUE IS

Having seen in what respects other single talking acts—the soliloquy, the "talking single" that has no unity of material, the disconnected string of stories, and the connected series of stories interspersed with songs—differ from the pure monologue, it will now be a much simpler task to make plain the elements that compose the real vaudeville monologue.

The real monologue possesses the following eight characteristics:
1. It is performed by one person.
2. It is humorous.
3. It possesses unity of character.
4. It is not combined with songs, tricks or any other entertainment form.
5. It takes from ten to fifteen minutes to deliver.

6. It is marked by compression.
7. It is distinguished by vividness.
8. It follows a definite form of construction.

Each of these eight characteristics has either been mentioned already or will be taken up in detail later, so now we can combine them into a single paragraphic definition:

> The pure vaudeville monologue is a humorous talk spoken by one person, possesses unity of character, is not combined with any other entertainment form, is marked by compression, follows a definite form of construction and usually requires from ten to fifteen minutes for delivery.

It must be emphasized that because some single talking acts do not meet every one of the requirements is no reason for condemning them[17]. They may be as fine for entertainment purposes as the pure monologue, but we must have some standard by which to work and the only true standard of anything is its purest form. Therefore, let us now take up the several parts that make up the pure monologue as a whole, and later we shall consider the other monologue variations that are permissible and often desirable.

Mr. Fogarty won The New York Morning Telegraph contest to determine the most popular performer in vaudeville in 1912, and was elected President of "The White Rats"—the vaudeville actors' protective Union—in 1914. [end footnote]

If you have not yet turned to the appendix and read Aaron Hoffman's "The German Senator" do so now. (See Appendix.) It will be referred to frequently to illustrate structural points.

III. THE MONOLOGUE'S NOTABLE CHARACTERISTICS

1. Humor

All monologues, whether of the pure type or not, possess one element in common—humor. I have yet to hear of a monologist who did not at least try to be funny. But there are different types of monologic humor.

"Each eye," the Italians say, "forms its own beauty," so every nation, every section, and each individual forms its own humor to suit its own peculiar risibilities. Still, there are certain well-defined kinds of stories and classes of points in which we Americans find a certain delight.

What these are the reader knows as well as the writer and can decide for himself much better than I can define them for him. Therefore, I shall content myself with a mere mention of the basic technical elements that may be of suggestive help.

---

[17] Frank Fogarty, "The Dublin Minstrel," one of the most successful monologists in vaudeville, often opens with a song and usually ends his offering with a serious heart-throb recitation. By making use of the song and serious recitation Mr. Fogarty places his act in the "entertainer" class, but his talking material is, perhaps, the best example of the "gag"-anecdotal-monologue to be found in vaudeville.

(a) *The Element of Incongruity.* "The essence of all humor," it has been said, "is incongruity," and in the monologue there is no one thing that brings better laugh-results than the incongruous. Note in the Appendix the closing point of "The German Senator." Could there be any more incongruous thing than wives forming a Union?

(b) *Surprise.* By surprise is meant leading the audience to believe the usual thing is going to happen, and "springing" the unusual—which in itself is often an incongruity, but not necessarily so.

(c) *Situation.* Both incongruity and surprise are part and parcel of the laughter of a situation. For instance; a meeting of two people, one of whom is anxious to avoid the other—a husband, for instance, creeping upstairs at three A. M. meeting his wife—or both anxious to avoid each other—wife was out, too, and husband overtakes wife creeping slowly up, doing her best not to awaken him, each supposing the other in bed and asleep. The laughter comes because of what is said at that particular moment in that particular situation—"and is due," Freud says, "to the release from seemingly unpleasant and inevitable consequences."

(d) *Pure Wit.* Wit exists for its own sake, it is detachable from its context, as for example:

>And what a fine place they picked out for Liberty to stand. With Coney Island on one side and Blackwell's Island on the other. [18]

(e) *Character.* The laughable sayings that are the intense expression at the instant of the individuality of the person voicing them, is what is meant by the humor of character. For instance: the German Senator gets all "balled up" in his terribly long effort to make a "regular speech," and he ends:

>We got to feel a feeling of patriotic symptoms—we got to feel patriotic symp—symps—you got to feel the patri—you can't help it, you got to feel it.

These five suggestions—all, in the last analysis, depending on the first, incongruity—may be of assistance to the novice in analyzing the elements of humor and framing his own efforts with intelligence and precision.

In considering the other elemental characteristics of the monologue, we must bear in mind that the emphasizing of humor is the monologue's chief reason for being.

2. Unity of Character

Unity of character does not mean unity of subject—note the variety of subjects treated in "The German Senator"—but, rather, the singleness of impression that a monologue gives of the "character" who delivers it, or is the hero of it.

The German Senator, himself, is a politician "spouting," in a perfectly illogical, broken-English stump speech, about the condition of the country and the reason why things are so bad. Never once do the various subjects stray far beyond their connection with the country's deplorable condition and always they

---

[18] The German Senator. See Appendix.

come back to it. Furthermore, not one of the observations is about anything that a politician of his mental calibre would not make. Also the construction of every sentence is in character. This example is, of course, ideal, and the precision of its unity of character one of the great elements of a great monologue.

Next to humor, unity of character is the most important requirement of the monologue. Never choose a subject, or write a joke, that does not fit the character delivering the monologue. In other words, if you are writing a pure monologue, do not, just because it is humorous, drag in a gag [19] or a point [20] that is not in character or that does not fit the subject. Make every turn of phrase and every word fit not only the character but also the subject.

3. Compression

We have long heard that "brevity is the soul of wit," and certainly we realize the truth in a hazy sort of way, but the monologue writer should make brevity his law and seven of his ten commandments of writing. Frank Fogarty, who writes his own gags and delivers them in his own rapid, inimitable way, said to me:

"The single thing I work to attain in any gag is brevity. I never use an ornamental word, I use the shortest word I can and I tell a gag in the fewest words possible. If you can cut out one word from any of my gags and not destroy it, I'll give you five dollars, and it'll be worth fifty to me to lose it. "You can kill the whole point of a gag by merely an unnecessary word. For instance, let us suppose the point of a gag is 'and he put the glass there'; well, you won't get a laugh if you say, 'and then he picked the glass up and put it there.' Only a few words more—but words are costly.

"Take another example. Here's one of my best gags, a sure-fire laugh if told this way:

"O'Brien was engaged by a farmer to milk cows and do chores. There were a hundred and fifty cows, and three men did the milking. It was hard work, but the farmer was a kind-hearted, progressive man, so when he went to town and saw some milking-stools he bought three and gave 'em to the men to sit down on while at work. The other two men came back delighted, but not O'Brien. At last he appeared, all cut-up, and holding one leg of the stool.

"'What's the matter?' said the farmer.

"'Nothing, only I couldn't make the cow sit down on it.'

"When I tell it this way it invariably gets a big laugh. Now here's the way I once heard a 'chooser' [21] do it.

"'O'Brien came to this country and looked around for work. He couldn't get a job until at last a friend told him that a farmer up in the country wanted a man to milk cows. So O'Brien got on a trolley car and went out to the end of the line, took a side-door pullman from there, was ditched and had to walk the rest of the

---

[19] A *gag* is the vaudeville term for any joke or pun.
[20] A *point* is the laugh-line of a gag, or the funny observation of a monologue.
[21] *Chooser*—one who chooses some part of another performer's act and steals it for his own use.

way to the farm. But at last he got to the farmer's place and asked him for the job.

""Sure I can use you," said the farmer, "here's a milk pail and a milking-stool. Take 'em and go out and milk the cows in the barn."

"Now O'Brien didn't know how to milk a cow, he'd never milked a cow in his whole life, but he needed a job so he didn't tell the farmer he hadn't ever milked a cow. He took the pail and the milking-stool and went out to the barn. After half an hour he came back to the farm house all cut-up, and he had one leg of the milking-stool in his hand.

""What's the matter?" asked the farmer, "How'd you get all cut up—been in a fight or something?"

""No," said O'Brien, "I couldn't get the cow to sit on it.""

"See the difference? There's only one right way to tell any gag and that's to make it brief, little—like the works of a watch that'll fit in a thin watch case and be better and finer than a big turnip of a pocket clock."

So, then, each point and gag in a monologue is told in the fewest, shortest words possible and the monologue, as a whole, is marked by compression. Remember, "brevity is the soul of wit"—never forget it.

4. Vividness

If a successful monologue writer has in mind two gags that are equally funny he will invariably choose the one that can be told most vividly—that is, the one that can be told as if the characters themselves were on the stage. For instance, the words, "Here stood John and there stood Mary," with lively, appropriate gestures by the monologist, make the characters and the scene seem living on the stage before the very eyes of the audience. That is why the monologist illustrates his points and gags with gestures that picturize.

Every gag and every point of great monologues are told in words that paint pictures. If the gag is supposititious, and the direct right-here-they-stood method cannot be used, the point is worded so strikingly, and is so comically striking in itself, that the audience sees—visualizes—it. [22]

Unlike the playlet, the monologue does not have flesh-and-blood people on the stage to act the comic situation. The way a point or gag is constructed, the words used, the monologist's gestures, and his inflections, must make the comic situation live in vivid pictures.

Therefore, in selecting material the monologue writer should choose those gags and points that can be told in pictures, and every word he uses should be a picture-word.

5. Smoothness and Blending

A monologue—like the thin-model watch mentioned—is made up of many parts. Each part fits into, the other—one gag or point blends perfectly into the following one—so that the entire monologue seems not a combination of many

---

[22] Walter Kelly, "The Virginia Judge," offers a fine example of the monologist who makes his words picturize. He "puts his stories over" almost without a gesture.

different parts, but a smoothly working, unified whole.

Count the number of different points there are in "The German Senator" and note how each seemingly depends on the one before it and runs into the one following; you will then see what is meant by blending. Then read the monologue again, this time without the Panama Canal point—plainly marked for this exposition—and you will see how one part can be taken away and still leave a smoothly reading and working whole.

It is to careful blending that the monologue owes its smoothness. The ideal for which the writer should strive is so to blend his gags and points that, by the use of not more than one short sentence, he relates one gag or point to the next with a naturalness and inevitableness that make the whole perfectly smooth.

We are now, I think, in a position to sum up the theory of the monologue. The pure vaudeville monologue, which was defined as a humorous talk spoken by one person, possesses unity of character, is not combined with any other entertainment form, is marked by compression, follows a definite form of construction, and usually requires from ten to fifteen minutes for delivery. Humor is its most notable characteristic; unity of the character delivering it, or of its "hero," is its second most important requirement. Each point, or gag, is so compressed that to take away or add even one word would spoil its effect; each is expressed so vividly that the action seems to take place before the eyes of the audience. Finally, every point leads out of the preceding point so naturally, and blends into the following point so inevitably, that the entire monologue is a smooth and perfect whole.

CHAPTER VI

WRITING THE MONOLOGUE

I. CHOOSING A THEME

Before an experienced writer takes up his pencil he has formed definitely in his mind just what he is going to write about—that is the simple yet startling difference between the experienced writer and the novice. Not only does the former know what his subject is, but he usually knows how he is going to treat it, and even some striking phrases and turns of sentences are ready in his mind, together with the hundreds of minute points which, taken together, make up the singleness of impression of the whole.

But just as it is impossible for the human mind—untrained, let us say, in the art of making bricks—to picture at a glance the various processes through which the clay passes before it takes brick form, so it is identically as impossible for the mind of the novice to comprehend in a flash the various purposes and half-purposes that precede the actual work of writing anything.

True as this is of writing in general, it seems to me particularly true of writing the monologue, for the monologue is one of those precise forms of the art of writing that may best be compared to the miniature, where every stroke must be true and unhesitating and where all combine unerringly to form the composite whole.

In preparing monologue material the writer usually is working in the *sounds* of spoken—and mis-spoken—words, and the humor that lies in the twisting of ideas into surprising conclusions. He seldom deliberately searches for a theme—more often some laugh-provoking incident or sentence gives him an idea and he builds it into a monologue with its subject for the theme.

1. Themes to Avoid

Anything at all in the whole range of subjects with which life abounds will lend itself for a monologue theme—provided the writer can without straining twist it to the angle of humor; but propriety demands that nothing blatantly suggestive shall be treated, and common sense dictates that no theme of merely local interest shall be used, when the purpose of the monologue is to entertain the whole country. Of course if a monologue is designed to entertain merely a certain class or the residents of a certain city or section only, the very theme—for instance, some purely local happening or trade interest—that you would avoid using in a monologue planned for national use, would be the happiest theme that could be chosen. But, as the ambitious monologue writer does not wish to confine himself to a local or a sectional subject and market, let us consider here only themes that have universal appeal.

II. A FEW THEMES OF UNIVERSAL INTEREST

| Politics | Woman Suffrage |
| Love | Drink |

Marriage	Baseball
Woman's Dress	Money

While there are many more themes that can be twisted to universal interest—and anyone could multiply the number given—these few are used in whole or in part in nearly every successful monologue now being presented. And, they offer to the new writer the surest ground to build a new monologue. That they have all been done before is no reason why they should not be done again: the new author has only to do them better—and a little different. It is all a matter of fresh vision. What is there in any art that is really new—but treatment?

Do not make the fatal mistake of supposing that these few themes are the only themes possessing universal interest. Anything in the whole wide world may be the subject for a monologue, when transmuted by the magic of common sense and uncommon ability into universal fun.

III. HOW TO BEGIN TO WRITE

As a monologue is a collection of carefully selected and smoothly blended points or gags, with a suitable introduction to the routine[23]—each point and gag being a complete, separate entity, and the introduction being as truly distinct—the monologue writer, unlike the playlet writer, may begin to write anywhere. He may even write the last point or gag used in the routine before he writes the first. Or he may write the twelfth point before he writes either the first one or the last one. But usually, he writes his introduction first.

1. The Introduction

A monologue introduction may be just one line with a point or a gag that will raise a snicker, or it may be a long introduction that stamps the character as a "character," and causes amusement because it introduces the entire monologue theme in a bright way.

An example of the short introduction is:

"D'you know me friend Casey? He's the guy that put the sham in shamrock," then on into the first gag that stamps Casey as a sure-'nuff "character," with a giggle-point to the gag.

The very best example of the long introduction being done on the stage today is the first four paragraphs of "The German Senator." The first line, "My dear friends and falling Citizens," stamps the monologue unquestionably as a speech. The second line, "My heart fills up with vaccination to be disabled," declares the mixed-up character of the oration and of the German Senator himself, and causes amusement. And the end of the fourth paragraph—which you will note is one

---

[23] *Routine*—the entire monologue; but more often used to suggest its arrangement and construction. A monologue with its gags and points arranged in a certain order is one routine; a different routine is used when the gags or points are arranged in a different order. Thus *routine* means *arrangement*. The word is also used to describe the arrangement of other stage offerings—for instance, a dance: the same steps arranged in a different order make a new "dance routine."

long involved sentence filled with giggles—raises the first laugh.

Nat Wills says the introduction to the gag-monologue may often profitably open with a "local"—one about the town or some local happening—as a local is pretty sure to raise a giggle, and will cause the audience to think the monologist "bright" and at least start their relations off pleasantly. He says: "Work for giggles in your introduction, but don't let the audience get set—with a big laugh—until the fifth or sixth joke."

The introduction, therefore, is designed to establish the monologist with the audience as "bright," to stamp the character of the "character" delivering it—or about whom the gags are told—and to delay a big laugh until the monologist has "got" his audience.

2. The Development

The "point," you will recall, we defined as the funny observation of a pure monologue—in lay-conversation it means the laugh line of a joke; and "gag" we defined as a joke or a pun. For the sake of clearness let us confine "point" to a funny observation in a monologue, and "gag" to a joke in a connected series of stories.

It is impossible for anyone to teach you how to write a really funny point or a gag. But, if you have a well-developed sense of humor, you can, with the help of the suggestions for form given here and the examples of humor printed in the appendix, and those you will find in the funny papers and hear along the street or on the stage, teach yourself to write saleable material. All that this chapter can hope to do for you is to show you how the best monologue writes and the most successful monologists work to achieve their notable results, and thus put you in the right path to accomplish, with the least waste of time and energy, what they have done.

Therefore, let us suppose that you know what is humorous, have a well-developed sense of humor, and can produce really funny points and gags. Now, having your points and gags clearly framed in mind and ready to set down on paper, you naturally ask, How shall I arrange them? In what order shall I place them to secure the best effect for the whole monologue?

Barrett Wendell, professor of English at Harvard University, [24]has suggested an effective mechanical aid for determining the clearest and best arrangement of sentences and paragraphs in English prose, and his plan seems especially adapted to help the monologue writer determine a perfect routine. Briefly his method may be paraphrased thus:

Have as many cards or slips of paper as you have points or gags. Write only one point or gag on one card or slip of paper. On the first card write "Introduction," and always keep that card first in your hand. Then take up a card and read the point or gag on it as following the introduction, the second card as the second point or gag, and so on until you have arranged your monologue in an effective routine.

---

[24] English Composition, page 165.

Then try another arrangement. Let us say the tenth joke in the first routine reads better as the first joke. All right, place it in your new arrangement right after the introduction. Perhaps the fourteenth point or gag fits in well after the tenth gag—fine, make that fourteenth gag the second gag; and so on through your cards until you have arranged a new routine.

Your first arrangement can invariably be improved—maybe even your seventh arrangement can be made better; very good, by shuffling the cards you may make as many arrangements as you wish and eventually arrive at the ideal routine. And by keeping a memorandum of preceding arrangements you can always turn back to the older routine—if that appears the best after all other arrangements have been tried.

But what is really the ideal arrangement of a monologue? How may you know which routine is really the best? Frankly, you cannot *know* until it has been tried out on an audience many, many times—and has been proved a success by actual test. Arranging a routine of untried points and gags on paper is like trying to solve a cut-out puzzle with the key-piece missing. Only by actually trying out a monologue before an audience and fitting the points and gags to suit the monologist's peculiar style (indeed, this is the real work of writing a monologue and will be described later on) can you determine what really is the best routine. And even then another arrangement may "go" better in another town. Still there are a few suggestions—a very few—that can be given here to aid the beginner.

Like ocean waves, monologic laughs should come in threes and nines—proved, like most rules, by exceptions. Note the application of this rule in "The German Senator."

Study the arrangement of the points in this great monologue and you will see that each really big point is dependent on several minor points that precede it to get its own big laugh. For instance, take the following point:

And if meat goes any higher, it will be worth more than money.
Then there won't be any money.
Instead of carrying money in your pocket, you'll carry meat around.
A sirloin steak will be worth a thousand dollar bill.
When you go down to the bank to make a deposit, instead of giving the cashier a thousand dollar bill, you'll slip him a sirloin steak.
If you ask him for change, he'll give you a hunk of bologny.

The first line blends this point with the preceding one about the high cost of eggs. The second line awakens interest and prepares for the next, "Instead of carrying money in your pocket, you'll carry meat around," which is good for a grin. The next line states the premise necessary for the first point-ending "—you'll slip him a sirloin steak," which is always good for a laugh. Then the last line, "If you ask him for change, he'll give you a hunk of bologny," tops the preceding laugh.

From this example you see what is meant by monologic laughs coming in threes and nines. The introduction of each new story—the line after the blend-line—should awaken a grin, its development cause a chuckle, and the point-line itself raise a laugh.

Each new point should top the preceding point until with the end of that particular angle or situation, should come a roar of honest laughter. Then back to the grin, the chuckle, and on to the laugh again, building up to the next big roar.

With the end of the monologue should come complete satisfaction in one great burst of laughter. This, of course, is the ideal.

3. How and Where to End

A monologue should run anywhere from ten to fifteen minutes. The monologist can vary his playing time at will by leaving out points and gags here and there, as necessity demands, so the writer should supply at least a full fifteen minutes of material in his manuscript.

"How shall I time my manuscript?" is the puzzling problem the new writer asks himself. The answer is that it is very difficult to time a monologue exactly, because different performers work at different speeds and laughs delay the delivery and, therefore, make the monologue run longer. But here is a very rough counting scale that may be given, with the warning that it is far from exact:

For every one hundred and fifteen to one hundred and forty words count one minute for delivery. This is so inexact, depending as it does on the number of laughs and the monologist's speed of delivery, that it is like a rubber ruler. At one performance it may be too long, at another too short.

Having given a full fifteen minutes of material, filled, let us hope, with good points made up of grins, chuckles and laughs, now choose your very biggest laugh-point for the last. When you wrote the monologue and arranged it into the first routine, that biggest laugh may have been the tenth, or the ninth, or the fifteenth, but you have spotted it unerringly as the very biggest laugh you possess, so you blend it in as the final laugh of the completed monologue.

It may now be worth while thus to sum up the ideal structure:

A routine is so arranged that the introduction stamps the monologist as bright, and the character he is impersonating or telling about as a real "character." The first four points or gags are snickers and the fifth or sixth is a laugh. [25]Each point or gag blends perfectly into the ones preceding and following it. The introduction of each new story awakens a grin, its development causes a chuckle, and the point-line itself raises a laugh. The final point or gag rounds the monologue off in the biggest burst of honest laughter.

IV. BUILDING A MONOLOGUE BEFORE AN AUDIENCE

When a writer delivers the manuscript of a monologue to a monologist his work is not ended. It has just begun, because he must share with the monologist the pains of delivering the monologue before an audience. Dion Boucicault once said, "A play is not written, but rewritten." True as this is of a play, it is, if possible, even more true of a monologue.

Of course, not all beginners can afford to give this personal attention to

---

[25] It is true that some monologists strive for a laugh on the very first point, but to win a big laugh at once is very rare.

staging a monologue, but it is advisable whenever possible. For, points that the author and the monologist himself were sure would "go big," "die," while points and gags that neither thought much of, "go big." It is for precisely this purpose of weeding out the good points and gags from the bad that even famous monologists "hide away," under other names, in very small houses for try-outs. And while the monologist is working on the stage to make the points and gags "get over," the author is working in the audience to note the effect of points and finding ways to change a phrase here and a word there to build dead points into life and laughter. Then it is that they both realize that Frank Fogarty's wise words are true: "There is only one way to tell a gag. If you can cut one word out from any of my gags I'll give you five dollars, for it's worth fifty to me. Words are costly."

Some entire points and gags will be found to be dead beyond resurrection, and even whole series of gags and points must be cast away and new and better ones substituted to raise the golden laughs. So the monologue is changed and built performance after performance, with both the monologist and the author working as though their very lives depended on making it perfect.

Then, when it is "set" to the satisfaction of both, the monologist goes out on the road to try it out on different audiences and to write the author continually for new points and gags. It may be said with perfect truth that a monologue is never finished. Nat Wills, the Tramp Monologist, pays James Madison a weekly salary to supply him with new jokes every seventh day. So, nearly every monologist retains the author to keep him up to the minute with material, right in the forefront of the laughter-of-the-hour.

V. OTHER SINGLE TALKING ACT FORMS

The discussion of the monologue form has been exhaustive, for the pure monologue holds within itself all the elements of the other allied forms. The only difference between a pure monologue and any other kind is in the addition of entertainment features that are not connected gags and points. Therefore, to cover the field completely it is necessary only to name a few of the many different kinds of single talking acts and to describe them briefly.

The most common talking singles—all of whom buy material from vaudeville writers—are:

(a) *The Talking Magician*—who may have only a few little tricks to present, but who plays them up big because he sprinkles his work with laughter-provoking points.

(b) *The "Nut Comedian"*—who does all manner of silly tricks to make his audience laugh, but who has a carefully prepared routine of "nut" material.

(c) *The Parody Monologist*—who opens and closes with funny parodies on the latest song hits and does a monologue routine between songs.

(d) *The "Original Talk"* Impersonator—who does impersonations of celebrities, but adds to his offering a few clever points and gags.

VI. A FINAL WORD

Before you seek a market [26] for your monologue, be sure that it fulfills all the requirements of a monologue and that it is the very best work you can do. Above all, make sure that every gag or point you use is original with you, and that the angle of the subject you have selected for your theme is honestly your own. For if you have copied even one gag or point that has been used before, you have laid your work open to suspicion and yourself to the epithet of "chooser."

The infringer—who steals gags and points bodily—can be pursued and punished under the copyright law, but the chooser is a kind of sneak thief who works gags and points around to escape taking criminal chances, making his material just enough different to evade the law. A chooser damages the originator of the material without himself getting very far. No one likes a chooser; no one knowingly will have dealings with a chooser. Call a vaudeville man a liar and he may laugh at you—call him a chooser and you'll have to fight him.

There are, of course, deliberate choosers in the vaudeville business, just as there are "crooks" in every line of life, but they never make more than a momentary success. Here is why they invariably fail:

When you sit in the audience, and hear an old gag or point, you whisper, "Phew, that's old," or you give your companion a knowing look, don't you? Well, half the audience is doing the very same thing, and they, like you, receive the impression that all the gags are old, and merely suppose that they haven't heard the other ones before.

The performer, whose bread and butter depends on the audience thinking him bright, cannot afford to have anything ancient in his routine. Two familiar gags or points will kill at least twenty-five percent of his applause. He may not get even one bow, and when audiences do not like a monologist well enough to call him out for a bow, he might as well say good-by to his chances of getting even another week's booking. Therefore the performer watches the material that is offered him with the strained attention of an Asiatic potentate who suspects there is poison in his breakfast food. He not only guards against old gags or points, but he takes great care that the specific form of the subject of any routine that he accepts is absolutely new.

Some of the deliberate choosers watch the field very closely and as soon as anyone strikes a new vein or angle they proceed to work it over. But taking the same subject and working around it—even though each gag or point is honestly new—does not and cannot pay. Even though the chooser secures some actor willing to use such material, he fails ultimately for two reasons: In the first place, the copier is never as good as the originator; and, in the second place, the circuit managers do not look with favor upon copy-acts.

As the success of the performer depends on his cleverness and the novelty of his material, in identically the same way the success of a vaudeville theatre lies in the cleverness and novelty of the acts it plays. Individual house managers, and therefore circuit managers, cannot afford to countenance copy-acts. For this

---

[26] See Chapter XXIV, Manuscripts and Markets.

two-act and but one "does" the monologue, you will notice in reading "The Art of Flirtation," that the two-act depends a surprising lot on "business" [28] to punch home its points and win its laughs. This is the first instance in our study of vaudeville material in which "acting" [29] demands from the writer studied consideration.

So large a part does the element of business play in the success of the two-act that the early examples of this vaudeville form were nearly all built out of bits of business. And the business was usually of the "slap-stick" kind.

3. What Slap-Stick Humor Is

Slap-stick humor wins its laughs by the use of physical methods, having received its name from the stick with which one clown hits another.

A slap-stick is so constructed that when a person is hit a light blow with it, a second piece of wood slaps the first and a surprisingly loud noise, as of a hard blow, is heard. Children always laugh at the slap-stick clowns and you can depend upon many grown-ups, too, going into ecstasies of mirth.

Building upon this sure foundation, a class of comedians sprang up who "worked up" the laughter by taking advantage of the human delight in expectation. For instance: A man would lean over a wall and gaze at some distant scene. He was perfectly oblivious to what was going on behind him. The comedy character strolled out on the stage with a stick in his hand. He nearly walked into the first man, then he saw the seat of the man's trousers and the provokingly tempting mark they offered. In the early days of the use of the slap-stick, the comedian would have spanked the man at once, got one big laugh and have run off the stage in a comic chase. In the later days the comedian worked up his laugh into many laughs, by spacing all of his actions in the delivery of the blow.

As soon as the audience realized that the comedian had the opportunity to spank the unsuspecting man, they laughed. Then the comedian would make elaborate preparations to deliver the blow. He would spit on his hands, grasp the stick firmly and take close aim—a laugh. Then he would take aim again and slowly swing the stick over his shoulder ready to strike—a breathless titter. Down would come the stick—and stop a few inches short of the mark and the comedian would say: "It's a shame to do it!" This was a roar, for the audience was primed to laugh and had to give vent to its expectant delight. A clever comedian could do this twice, or even three times, varying the line each time. But usually on the third preparation he would strike—and the house would be convulsed.

In burlesque they sometimes used a woman for the victim, and the laughter was consequently louder and longer. It is an interesting commentary on the

---

[28] *Business* means any movement an actor makes on the stage. To walk across the stage, to step on a man's toes, to pick up a telephone, to drop a handkerchief, or even to grimace—if done to drive the spoken words home, or to "get over" a meaning without words—are all, with a thousand other gestures and movements, *stage business*.

[29] Acting is action. It comprises everything necessary to the performing of a part in a play and includes business.

advancement of all branches of the stage in recent years that even in burlesque such extreme slap-stick methods are now seldom used. In vaudeville such an elemental bit of slap-stick business is rarely, if ever, seen. Happily, a woman is now never the victim.

But it was upon such "sure-fire" [30] bits of business that the early vaudeville two-acts—as well as many other acts—depended for a large percentage of their laughs. It mattered little what were the lines they spoke. They put their trust in business—and invariably won. But their business was always of the same type as that "bit" [31] of spanking the unsuspecting man. It depended for its humor on the supposed infliction of pain. It was always physical—although by no means always even remotely suggestive.

Because such acts did not depend on lines but on slap-stick humor, they became known as slap-stick acts. And because these vaudeville two-acts—as we have elected to call them—were usually presented by two men and worked in One, in front of a drop that represented a street, they were called "sidewalk comedian slap-stick acts."

Their material was a lot of jokes of the "Who was that lady I saw you with last night?"—"She weren't no lady, she was my wife," kind. Two performers would throw together an act made up of sure-fire comedy bits they had used in various shows, interpolate a few old "gags"—and the vaudeville writer had very little opportunity.

But to-day—as a study of "The Art of Flirtation" will show—wit and structural skill in the material itself is of prime importance. Therefore the writer is needed to supply vaudeville two-acts. But even to-day business still plays a very large part in the success of the two-act. It may even be considered fundamental to the two-act's success. Therefore, before we consider the structural elements that make for success in writing the two-act, we shall take up the matter of two-act business.

4. The "Business" of the Two-Act

The fact that we all laugh—in varying degrees—at the antics of the circus clown, should be sufficient evidence of the permanence of certain forms of humor to admit of a belief in the basic truth that certain actions do in all times find a humorous response in all hearts. Certain things are fundamentally funny, and have made our ancestors laugh, just as they make us laugh and will make our descendants laugh.

"There's no joke like an old joke," is sarcastically but nevertheless literally true. There may even be more than a humorous coincidence—perhaps an unconscious recognition of the sure-firedness of certain actions—in the warnings received in childhood to "stop that funny business."

---

[30] Any act or piece of business or line in a speech that can be depended on to win laughter at every performance is called *sure-fire*.

[31] Anything done on the stage may be called a *bit*. A minor character may have only a *bit*, and some one part of a scene that the star may have, may be a *bit*. The word is used to describe a successful little scene that is complete in itself.

5. Weber and Fields on Sure-Fire Business

However this may be, wherever actors foregather and talk about bits of stage business that have won and always will win laughs for them, there are a score or more points on which they agree. No matter how much they may quarrel about the effectiveness of laugh-bits with which one or another has won a personal success—due, perhaps, to his own peculiar personality—they unite in admitting the universal effectiveness of certain good old stand-bys.

Weber and Fields—before they made so much money that they retired to indulge in the pleasant pastime of producing shows—presented probably the most famous of all the sidewalk comedian slap-stick acts. [32] They elevated the slap-stick sidewalk conversation act into national popularity and certainly reduced the business of their performance to a science—or raised it to an art. In an article entitled "Adventures in Human Nature," published in The Associated Sunday Mazagines for June 23, 1912, Joe Weber and Lew Fields have this to say about the stage business responsible, in large measure, for the success of their famous two-act:

> The capitalizing of the audiences' laughter we have set down in the following statistics, ranged in the order of their value. An audience will laugh loudest at these episodes:
> (1) When a man sticks one finger into another man's eye.
> (2) When a man sticks two fingers into another man's eyes.
> (3) When a man chokes another man and shakes his head from side to side.
> (4) When a man kicks another man.
> (5) When a man bumps up suddenly against another man and knocks him off his feet.
> (6) When a man steps on another man's foot.
>
> Human nature—as we have analyzed it, with results that will be told you by the cashier at our bank—will laugh louder and oftener at these spectacles, in the respective order we have chronicled them, than at anything else one might name. Human nature here, as before, insists that the object of the attacks—the other man—be not really hurt.
>
> Now, let us tell you how we arrived at our conclusions. The eye is the most delicate part of the body. If a man, therefore, pokes his two forefingers into the eyes of another man *without hurting them*, then human nature will make you scream with mirth; not at the sight of the poking of the fingers into the other man's eyes (as you who have seen us do this trick night in and night out have imagined), but because you get all the sensations of such a dangerous act without there being any actual pain involved in the case of the man you were

---

[32] The great success of the return of Weber and Fields to vaudeville in 1915-16, with excerpts from their old successes, is only one more proof of the perennial value of sure-fire business.

watching. You laugh because human nature tells you to. You laugh because the man who had the fingers stuck into his eyes might have been hurt badly, but wasn't.

The greatest laughter, the greatest comedy, is divided by a hair from the greatest tragedy. Always remember that! As the chance of pain, the proportion of physical misery, the proportion of tragedy, becomes diminished (see the other items in the table), so does the proportion of laughter become less and less. We have often tried to figure out a way to do something to the other's kneecap—second in delicacy only to the eye—but the danger involved is too great. Once let us figure out the trick, however, and we shall have capitalized another item that may be listed high in our table. Here is how you can verify the truth of our observations yourself:

You have seen those small imitation tacks made of rubber. Exhibit one, put it on a chair, ask a stranger to sit down—and everybody who is in on the joke will scream with mirth. Try it with a real tack, and everybody will take on a serious face and will want to keep the man from sitting down.

6. What George M. Cohan Has to Say

George M. Cohan spent his boyhood on the vaudeville stage as one of "The Four Cohans." In collaboration with George J. Nathan, Mr. Cohan published in McClure's Magazine for November, 1913, an article entitled "The Mechanics of Emotion." Here is what he has to say about some bits of business that are sure-fire laughs: [33]

> Here, then, are a few of the hundred-odd things that you constantly laugh at on the stage, though, when you see them in cold type, you will probably be ashamed of doing so.
> (1) Giving a man a resounding whack on the back under the guise of friendship. The laugh in this instance may be "built up" steadily in a climacteric way by repeating the blow three times at intervals of several minutes.
> (2) A man gives a woman a whack on the back, believing in an absent-minded moment that the woman (to whom he is talking) is a man.
> (3) One character steps on the sore foot of another character, causing the latter to jump with pain.
> (4) The spectacle of a man laden with many large bundles.
> (5) A man or a woman starts to lean his or her elbow on a table or the arm of a chair, the elbow slipping off abruptly and suddenly precipitating him or her forward.
> (6) One character imitating the walk of another character, who is

---

[33] These sure-fire bits of business should be considered as being equally effective when used in any form of stage work. Some of them, however, lend themselves most readily to the vaudeville two-act.

walking in front of him and cannot see him.
(7) A man consuming a drink of considerable size at one quick gulp.
(8) A character who, on entering an "interior" or room scene, stumbles over a rug. If the character in point be of the "dignified" sort, the power of this laugh provoker is doubled.
(9) Intoxication in almost any form. [34]
(10) Two men in heated conversation. One starts to leave. Suddenly, as if fearing the other will kick him while his back is turned, this man bends his body inward (as if he actually had been kicked) and sidles off.
(11) A man who, in trying to light his cigar or cigarette, strikes match after match in an attempt to keep one lighted. If the man throws each useless match vigorously to the floor with a muttered note of vexation the laughter will increase.
(12) The use of a swear-word. [35]
(13) A man proclaims his defiance of his wife while the latter is presumably out of hearing. As the man is speaking, his wife's voice is heard calling him. Meekly he turns and goes to her. This device has many changes, such as employer and employee. All are equally effective.
(14) A pair of lovers who try several times to kiss, and each time are interrupted by the entrance of some one or by the ringing of the doorbell or telephone-bell or something of the sort.
(15) A bashful man and a not-bashful woman are seated on a bench or divan. As the woman gradually edges up to the man, the man just as gradually edges away from her.

All these "laugh-getters" are known to the experienced as "high class"; that is, they may all be used upon the legitimate stage. On the burlesque and vaudeville stages devices of a somewhat lower intellectual plane have established a permanent standing An authority on this phase of the subject is Mr. Frederick Wyckoff, who catalogues the following as a few of the tricks that make a vaudeville audience laugh:

Open your coat and show a green vest, or pull out your shirt front and expose a red undershirt. Another excellent thing to do is to wear a shirt without sleeves and pull off your coat repeatedly. [36]

---

[34] Intoxication, however, must never be revolting. To be welcomed, it must always be funny; in rare instances, it may be pathetic.

[35] The use of swear-words is prohibited in most first-class vaudeville theatres. On the walls of every B. F. Keith Theatre is posted this notice: "The use of 'Damn' and 'Hell' is forbidden on the stage of this theatre. If a performer cannot do without using them, he need not open here."

[36] Such ancient methods of winning laughs, however, belong to vaudeville yesterdays. It should be remembered that Mr. Nathan, who bore the labor of writing this excellent

Ask the orchestra leader if he is married.

Have the drummer put in an extra beat with the cymbals, then glare at him.

Always use an expression which ends with the query, "Did he not?" Then say, "He did not."

The men who elaborated this kind of thing into a classic are Messrs. Weber and Fields. They are the great presiding deities of "slap-stick" humor. They have capitalized it to enormous financial profit. They claim that Mr. Fields' favorite trick of poking his forefinger periodically in Mr. Weber's eye is worth a large fortune in itself. A peculiarity of this kind of humor is that it finds its basis in the inflicting of pain. A painful situation apparently contains elements of the ridiculous so long as the pain is not actually of a serious nature. Here, too, the stage merely mirrors life itself. We laugh at the person who falls on the ice, at the man who bumps against a chair or table in the dark, at the headache of the "morning after," at the boy who eats green apples and pays the abdominal penalty, at the woman whose shoes are so tight they hurt her, at the person who is thrown to the floor by a sudden lurch of a street-car, and at the unfortunate who sits on a pin. A man chasing his rolling hat in the street makes everybody laugh.

The most successful tricks or jokes are all based on the idea of pain or embarrassment. Tacks made of rubber, matches that explode or refuse to light, exploding cigars or cigarettes, fountain-pens that smear ink over the fingers immediately they are put to use, "electric" bells with pins secreted in their push buttons, and boutonnieres that squirt water into the face of the beholder, are a few familiar examples.

Here, then, we have the bits of business that three of the ablest producers of the legitimate stage—all graduates from vaudeville, by the way—agree upon as sure-fire for the vaudeville two-act. Paradoxically, however, they should be considered not as instructive of what you should copy, but as brilliant examples of what you should avoid. They belong more to vaudeville's Past than to its Present. Audiences laughed at them yesterday—they may not laugh at them tomorrow. If you would win success, you must invent new business in the light of the old successes. The principles underlying these laugh-getters remain the same forever.

7. Sure-Fire Laughs Depend upon Action and Situation, Not on Words

If you will read again what Weber and Fields have to say about their adventures in human nature, you will note that not once do they mention the lines with which they accompanied the business of their two-act. Several times they mention situation—which is the result of action, when it is not its cause—but the

---

article, is blessed with a satirical soul—which, undoubtedly, is the reason why he is so excellent and so famous a dramatic critic.

words by which they accompanied those actions and explained those situations they did not consider of enough importance to mention. Every successful two-act, every entertainment-form of which acting is an element—the playlet and the full-evening play as well—prove beyond the shadow of a doubt that what audiences laugh at—what you and I laugh at—is not words, but actions and situations.

Later on, this most important truth—the very life-blood of stage reality—will be taken up and considered at greater length in the study of the playlet. But it cannot be mentioned too often. It is a vital lesson that you must learn if you would achieve even the most fleeting success in writing for the stage in general and vaudeville in particular.

But by action is not meant running about the stage, or even wild wavings of the arms. *There must be action in the idea—in the thought*—even though the performers stand perfectly still.

So it is not with words, witty sayings, funny observations and topsy-turvy language alone that the writer works, when he constructs a vaudeville two-act. It is with clever ideas, expressed in laughable situations and actions, that his brain is busy when he begins to marshal to his aid the elements that enter into the preparation of two-act material.

CHAPTER VIII

THE STRUCTURAL ELEMENTS OF TWO-ACT MATERIAL

IT is very likely that in your study of "The German Senator" and "The Art of Flirtation," there has crossed your mind this thought: Both the monologue and the two-act are composed of points and gags. The only difference—besides the merely physical difference of two persons delivering the gags and the greater amount of business used to "get them over"[37]—lies in the way the gags are constructed. The very same gags—twisted just a little differently—would do equally well for either the monologue or the two-act.

I. THE INDIVIDUAL TWIST OF THE TWO-ACT

There is just enough truth in this to make it seem an illuminating fact. For instance, take the "janitor point" in "The German Senator." We may imagine the characters of a two-act working up through a routine, and then one saying to the other:

> A child can go to school for nothing, and when he grows up to be a man and he is thoroughly educated he can go into the public school and be a teacher and get fifty dollars a month.

The other swiftly saying:

> And the janitor gets ninety-five.

There would be a big laugh in this arrangement of this particular gag, without a doubt. But only a few points of "The German Senator" could be used for a two-act, with nearly as much effect as in the monologue form. For instance, take the introduction. Of course, that is part and parcel of the monologue form, and therefore seems hardly a fair example, yet it is particularly suggestive of the unique character of much monologic material.

But take the series of points in "The German Senator," beginning: "We were better off years ago than we are now." Picture the effect if one character said:

Look at Adam in the Garden of Eat-ing.

2nd
Life to him was a pleasure.

1st
There was a fellow that had nothing to worry about.

2nd
Anything he wanted he could get.

1st

---

[37] To *get over* a vaudeville line or the entire act, means to make it a success—to make it get over the foot-lights so that the audience may see and appreciate it, or "get" it.

But the old fool had to get lonesome.

>2nd

And that's the guy that started all our trouble etc. etc. etc.

Even before the fourth speech it all sounded flat and tiresome, didn't it? Almost unconsciously you compared it with the brighter material in "The Art of Flirtation." But, you may say: "If the business had been snappy and funny, the whole thing would have raised a laugh."

How could business be introduced in this gag—without having the obvious effect of being lugged in by the heels? Business, to be effective, must be the body of the material's soul. The material must suggest the business, so it will seem to be made alive by it. It must be as much the obvious result of the thought as when your hand would follow the words, "I'm going to give you this. Here, take it."

Herein lies the reason why two-act material differs from monologic material. Experience alone can teach you to "feel" the difference unerringly.

Yet it is in a measure true that some of the points and gags that are used in many monologues—rarely the anecdotal gag, however, which must be acted out in non-two-act form—would be equally effective if differently treated in the two-act. But often this is not due so much to the points themselves as to the fault of the writer in considering them monologic points.

The underlying cause of many such errors may be the family likeness discernible in all stage material. Still, it is much better for the writer fully to recompense Peter, than to rob Peter to pay Paul inadequately.

Nevertheless, aside from the "feel" of the material—its individual adaptability—there is a striking similarity in the structural elements of the monologue and the two-act. Everything in the chapter on "The Nature of the Monologue" is as true of the two-act as of the monologue, if you use discrimination. Refer to what was said about humor, unity of character, compression, vividness, smoothness and blending, and read it all again in the light of the peculiar requirements of the two-act. They are the elements that make for its success.

II. THINKING OUT THE TWO-ACT

The two-act—like all stage material in which acting plays a part—is not written; it is constructed. You may write with the greatest facility, and yet fail in writing material for the vaudeville stage. The mere wording of a two-act means little, in the final analysis. It is the action behind the words that suggests the stage effect. It is the business—combined with the acting—that causes the audience to laugh and makes the whole a success. So the two-act, like every other stage form, must—before it is written—be thought out.

In the preceding chapter, you read of the elements that enter into the construction of a two-act. They are also some of the broad foundation elements which underlie, in whole or in part, all other stage-acting—material. A few of the two-act elements that have to do more particularly with the manuscript construction have been reserved for discussion in the paragraphs on development. In this chapter we shall consider what you must have before you even begin to think out your two-act—your theme.

1. Selecting a Theme

Imitation may be the sincerest flattery, but it is dangerous for the imitator. And yet to stray too far afield alone is even more hazardous. Successful vaudeville writers are much like a band of Indians marching through an enemy's country—they follow one another in single file, stepping in each other's footprints. In other words, they obey the rules of their craft, but their mental strides, like the Indians' physical footsteps, are individual and distinct.

2. Fundamental Themes

Experience has taught effective writers that certain definite themes are peculiarly adaptable to two-act form and they follow them. But success comes to them not because they stick to certain themes only—they win because they vary these fundamental themes as much as they can and still remain within the limits of proved theatrical success.

(a) *The Quarrel Theme.* Search my memory as diligently as I may, I cannot now recall a single successful two-act that has not had somewhere in its routine a quarrel, while many of the most successful two-acts I remember have been constructed with a quarrel as their routine motives.

With this observation in mind, re-read "The Art of Flirtation" and you will discover that the biggest laughs precede, arise from, or are followed by quarrels. Weber and Fields in their list of the most humorous business, cite not only mildly quarrelsome actions, but actually hostile and seemingly dangerous acts. The more hostile and the more seemingly dangerous they are, the funnier they are. Run through the Cohan list and you will discover that nearly every bit of business there reported is based on a quarrel, or might easily lead to a fight.

(b) *The "Fool" Theme.* To quote again from Weber and Fields:

> There are two other important items in human nature that we have capitalized along with others to large profit. Human nature, according to the way we analyzed it, is such a curious thing that it will invariably find cause for extreme mirth in seeing some other fellow being made a fool of, no matter who that fellow may be, and in seeing a man betting on a proposition when he cannot possibly win. We figured it out, in the first place, that nothing pleased a man much more than when he saw another man being made to look silly in the eyes of others.
>
> For example, don't you laugh when you observe a dignified looking individual strutting down the street wearing a paper tail that has been pinned to his coat by some mischievous boys? [38]

Note how the "fool" theme runs all through "The Art of Flirtation." Go to see as many two-acts as you can and you will find that one or another of the

---

[38] From the Weber and Fields article already quoted.

characters is always trying to "show up" the other.

(c) *The "Sucker" Theme.*

As for the quirk in human nature that shows great gratification at the sight of a man betting on something where he is bound to be the loser: in inelegant language, this relates simply to the universal impulse to laugh at a "sucker." It is just like standing in front of a sideshow tent after you have paid your good money, gone in, and been "stung," and laughing at everyone else who pays his good money, comes out, and has been equally "stung." You laugh at a man when he loses the money he has bet on a race that has already been run when the wager has been posted. You laugh at a man who bets a man ten dollars "receive" is spelled "recieve," when you have just looked at the dictionary and appreciate that he hasn't a chance. . . . Comedy that lives year after year—no matter whether you choose to call it "refined" or not—never comes to its exploiters by accident. The intrinsic idea, the germ, may come accidentally; but the figuring out of the elaboration and execution of the comedy takes thinking and a pretty fair knowledge of your fellow men. [39]

Although there are very many two-acts—among them "The Art of Flirtation"—which do not make use of this third fundamental theme, there are a great many that depend for their biggest laughs upon this sure-fire subject.

In common with the "fool" theme, the "sucker" theme lends itself to use as a part or bit of a two-act. And both these themes are likely to be interspersed with quarrels.

There are, of course, other themes that might be classed with these three fundamental themes. But they tend to trail off upon doubtful ground. Therefore, as we are considering only those that are on incontrovertible ground, let us now turn our attention to the act themes which we will call:

3. Subject Themes

What can you bring to the vaudeville stage in the way of themes that are new? That is what you should ask yourself, rather than to inquire what has already been done.

Anything that admits of treatment on the lines of the two-act as it has been spread before you, offers itself as a subject theme. In the degree that you can find in it points that are bright, clever, laughter-provoking and business-suggestive, does it recommend itself to you as a theme.

Here is the merest skimming of the themes of the two-acts presented in one large city during one week:

Flirting: done in a burlesque way. Our own example, "The Art of Flirtation."

Quarrelsome musicians in search of a certain street. One is always wrong. Gags all on this routine subject.

Getting a job: "sucker" theme. One character an Italian politician, the other

---

[39] From the Weber and Fields article.

an Italian laborer.

Wives: one man is boss at home, the other is henpecked. Furthermore, the wives don't agree. Quarrel theme.

Old times: two old schoolmates meet in the city. One a "fly guy," the other a simple, quiet country fellow. "Fool" theme, in the old days and the present.

Note the variety of subjects treated. If my memory serves me correctly, everyone of these acts had a quarrel either as its entire subject, or the usual quarrels developed frequently in the routine. These quarrels, as in most two-acts, were fundamental to much of their humor. But no two of the acts had the same subject theme.

It would seem, then, that in thinking out the two-act, the author would do well to avoid every theme that has been used—if such a thing is humanly possible, where everything seems to have been done—and to attempt, at least, to bring to his two-act a new subject theme.

But if this is impossible, the writer should bring to the old theme a new treatment. Indeed, a new treatment with all its charm of novelty will make any old theme seem new. One of the standard recipes for success in any line of endeavor is: "Find out what somebody else has done, and then do that thing—better." And one of the ways of making an old theme appear new, is to invest it with the different personalities of brand new characters.

III. TWO-ACT CHARACTERS

From the time when vaudeville first emerged as a commanding new form of entertainment, distinct from its progenitor, the legitimate stage, and its near relatives, burlesque and musical comedy, there have been certain characters indissolubly associated with the two-act. Among them are the Irish character, or "Tad"; the German, or "Dutch," as they are often misnamed; the "black-face," or "Nigger"; the farmer, or "Rube"; the Swedish, or "Swede"; the Italian, or "Wop"; and the Hebrew, or "Jew."

Not much chance for a new character, you will say—but have you thought about the different combinations you can make? There is a wealth of ready humor waiting not only in varying combinations, but in placing the characters in new businesses. For example, doesn't a "Jew" aviator who is pestered by an insurance agent or an undertaker, strike you as offering amusing possibilities?

But don't sit right down and think out your two-act on the lines of the combination I have suggested on the spur of the moment. Others are sure to be ahead of you. You can only win success with new characters that are all your own. Then you are likely to be the first in the field.

As a final warning, permit the suggestion that bizarre combinations of characters very probably will be difficult to sell. Make your combinations within the limits of plausibility, and use characters that are seen upon the stage often enough to be hailed with at least a pleasant welcome.

IV. THE TWO CHARACTER PARTS
"Comedy" and "Straight"

The characters of the two-act are technically called the "comedian" and the "straight-man." The comedian might better be called the "laugh-man," just as the straight is more clearly termed the "feeder."

In the early days of the business the comedian was always distinguishable by his comedy clothes. One glance would tell you he was the comical cuss. The straight-man dressed like a "gent," dazzling the eyes of the ladies with his correct raiment. From this fact the names "comedian" and "straight" arose.

But today you seldom can tell the two apart. They do not dress extravagantly, either for comedy or for fashion effect. They often dress precisely alike—that is, so far as telling their different characters is concerned. Their difference in wealth and intelligence may be reflected in their clothes, but only as such differences would be apparent in real life. Indeed, the aim today is to mimic reality in externals, precisely as the real characters themselves are impersonated in every shade of thought and artistic inflection of speech. There are, to be sure, exceptions to this modern tendency.

The original purposes of their stage names, however, remain as true today as they did when the two-act first was played. The comedian has nearly all the laugh lines and the straight-man feeds him.

Not only must you keep the characters themselves pure of any violation of their unity, but you must also see to it that every big laugh is given to the comedian. If the comedian is the one "getting the worst of it"—as is almost invariably the case—he must get the worst of it nearly every time. But that does not influence the fact that he also gets almost all the laugh lines.

Note the working out of the laugh lines in "The Art of Flirtation." You will see that only on the rarest of occasions does the straight-man have a funny line given him.

The only time the feeder may be given a laugh line, is when the laugh is what is called a "flash-back." For example, take the point in "The Art of Flirtation" beginning:

>COMEDIAN
>And does she answer?

>STRAIGHT
>She's got to; it says it in the book.

>COMEDIAN
>Does she answer you with a handkerchief?

>STRAIGHT
>Yes, or she might answer you with an umbrella.

This is a flash-back. But, the comedian gets a bigger laugh on the next line—worked up by a gesture:

>COMEDIAN Over the head.

Or take this form of the flash-back, which may seem an even

clearer example:

> COMEDIAN
> Oh, I know how to be disagreeable to a lady. You ought to hear me talk to my wife.
>
> STRAIGHT
> To your wife? Any man can be disagreeable to his wife. But think—,

and so on into the introduction to the next point. It is always a safe rule to follow that whenever you give the straight-man a flash-back, top it with a bigger laugh for the comedian. How many flash-backs you may permit in your two-act, depends upon the character of the material, and also varies according to the bigness of the roars that the business adds to the comedian's laughs. No stated rule can be given you. In this, as in everything else, you must carve your own way to win your own business.

CHAPTER IX

PUTTING THE TWO-ACT ON PAPER

YOU have selected your theme, chosen your characters, thought out every angle of business, and mapped nearly all of your points, as well as your big laugh-lines: now you are ready to put your two-act on paper. Before "taking your pen in hand," stop for a moment of self-analysis.

You can now determine how likely you are to succeed as a writer of the two-act, by this simple self-examination:

How much of my two-act have I thought out clearly so that it is playing before my very eyes?

If you have thought it all out, so that every bit of business moves before your eyes, as every point rings in your ears, you are very likely to turn out an acceptable two-act—if you have not played a "chooser's" part, and your points are real points.

But do not imagine because you are positive that you have thought everything out beforehand, and now have come to writing it down, that your job of thinking is ended. Not at all; there are a few things still to be thought out, while you are writing.

I. WHERE TO BEGIN

As in the monologue—because your material is made up of points—you may begin nearly anywhere to write your two-act. And like the monologue, you need not have a labored formal introduction.

The Introduction

Still, your introduction is no less comprehensively informing because it has not the air of formality. If your characters by their appearance stamp themselves for what they are, you may trust complete characterization—as you should in writing every form of stage material—to what each character does and says.

But in your very first line you should subtly tell the audience, so there cannot possibly be any mistake, what your subject is.

Why are those two men out there on the stage?
What is the reason for their attitude toward each ther?
If they are quarreling, why are they quarreling?
If they are laughing, why are they laughing?

But don't make the mistake of trying to tell too much. To do that, would be to make your introduction draggy. You must make the audience think the characters are bright—precisely as the introduction of the monologue is designed to make the audience think the monologist is bright. Write your introduction in very short speeches. Show the attitude of the characters clearly and plainly, as the first speech of our two-act example shows the characters are quarreling:

STRAIGHT

Say, whenever we go out together you always got a kick coming. What's the matter with you?

Then get into your subject-theme quickly after you have given the audience time to get acquainted and settled, with the memory of the preceding act dimmed in their minds by the giggle-points of your introduction.

The introduction of the two-act is designed to stamp the characters as real characters, to establish their relations to each other, to give the audience time to settle down to the new "turn," to make them think the performers are "bright" and to delay the first big laugh until the psychological moment has come to spring the initial big point of the subject theme, after the act has "got" the audience.

II. THE DEVELOPMENT

It would seem needless to repeat what has already been stated so plainly in the chapters on the monologue, that no one can teach you how to write excruciatingly funny points and gags, and that no one can give you the power to originate laughter-compelling situations. You must rise or fall by the force of your own ability.

There are, however, two suggestions that can be given you for the production of a good two-act. One is a "don't," and the other a "do." Don't write your points in the form of questions and answers. The days of the "Why did the chicken cross the road?"—"Because she wanted to get on the other side" sort of two-act, is past. Write all your points in conversational style.

Never write:

What were you doing at Pat's dinner lathering your face with a charlotte russe?

Write it:

So you were down at Pat's house for dinner, and you went and lathered your face with a charlotte russe—I saw you.

Of course when a legitimate question is to be asked, ask it. But do not deliberately throw your points into question form. Your guide to the number of direct queries you would use should be the usual conversational methods of real life.

Your subject, of course, in a large measure determines how many questions you need to ask. For instance, if your theme is one that develops a lot of fun through one character instructing the other, a correspondingly large number of questions naturally would be asked. But, as "The Art of Flirtation" plainly shows, you can get a world of fun out of even an instruction theme, without the use of a wearying number of inquiries. The two-act fashion today is the direct, conversational style.

Now for the second suggestion:

Although some exceedingly successful two-acts have been written with many themes scattered through their twelve or more minutes, probably a larger number have won success through singleness of subject. A routine with but one subject worked up to its most effective height is often more likely to please.

Furthermore, for the reason that the two-act is breaking away from the offering that is merely pieced together out of successful bits—precisely as that class of act struggled away from the old slap-stick turn—the single-routine now finds readier sale. The present tendency of the two-act seems to be to present clever characterization—and so to win by artistic acting, as before it won by cruder methods.

Therefore, strive for unity of routine. Treat but one subject and amplify that one subject with singleness of purpose.

The point, or the gag, of a two-act is very much like that of the monologue. In so far as construction is concerned—by this I mean laugh-wave construction—they are identical. Study "The Art of Flirtation," and you will see how little laughs precede big laughs and follow after, mounting into still bigger laughs that rise into roars of laughter.

1. Introducing a Point

If you were telling a joke to a friend you would be sure to tell him in your very first sentence all the things he would need in order to understand the point of the joke, wouldn't you? You would take great care not to leave out one salient bit of information that would make him see the joke plainly—you would be as logical as though you were trying to sell him a bill of goods. Take the same attitude toward each point that you introduce into your two-act. Remember, you are wholesaling your "jokes" to the comedians, who must retail them to their audiences. Therefore, introduce each new point as clearly and as briefly as you can.

Let us take a point from "The Art of Flirtation" and see how it is constructed. The very first line the straight-man speaks when he comes out on the stage unmistakably declares his relation to the comedian. When he shows the book, he explains precisely what it is. And while laugh after laugh is worked out of it, the precise things that the book teaches are made clear.

> STRAIGHT
> No. It ain't ten cent love. It's fine love. (Opens book) See—here is the destructions. Right oil the first page you learn something. See—how to flirt with a handkerchief.
>
> COMEDIAN
> Who wants to flirt with a handkerchief? I want to flirt with a woman.
>
> STRAIGHT
> Listen to what the book says. To a flirter all things have got a language. According to this book flirters can speak with the eye, with the fan, with the cane, with the umbrella, with the handkerchief, with anything; this book tells you how to do it.

COMEDIAN
For ten cents.

Note that the straight-man does not say, "with the eye, cane, umbrella—" and so on through the list. He says "With the eye, with the fan, with the cane—." There can be no mistake—as there might be if the items were enumerated swiftly. Each one is given importance by the "with the eye, with the fan." The words "with the" lend emphasis and a humorous weight.

STRAIGHT
Shut up. Now when you see a pretty woman coming along who wants to flirt with you, what is the first thing a man should do?

COMEDIAN
Run the other way.

STRAIGHT
No, no. This is the handkerchief flirtation. . . .

You see precisely what the subject of this particular point is because it is stated in unmistakable words.

STRAIGHT
.As soon as a pretty woman makes eyes at you, you put your hands in your pockets.

COMEDIAN
And hold on to your money.

Now this is a big laugh at every performance—a sure-fire laugh when it is well done. Note that it is the fourth line the comedian has after the specific point introduction, ". . .See—how to flirt with a handkerchief?" Now the line "Who wants to flirt with a handkerchief? I want to flirt with a woman," is not intended to be a real laugh-line. It serves as an audience settler, gives emphasis to the explanation of just what the book tells and helps to blend into the next line.

There's a first laugh on, "For ten cents." A bigger laugh comes on, "Run the other way." And the bigest—in this point-division— on the third laugh line "And hold on to your money."

2. Blending into the Following Point

When you have a big laugh, you must make the next line carry you on smoothly into the succeeding lint. It matters not whether the points are all related to the same general subject or not—although we are considering here only the single-routine two-act—you must take great care that each point blends into the following one with logical sequence.

The line, "Who wants to flirt with a handkerchief? I want to flirt with a woman," helps in the blending of the point division we have just examined.

The straight man's line following the big laugh line in that point division,

"No, you take out your handkerchief," (biz.[40]) is another example of the blend-line. And it is the very first introduction of the peculiar style of business that makes of "The Art of Flirtation" so funny an act.

3. The Use of Business
Let us continue in the examination of this example.

> COMEDIAN
> Suppose you ain't got a handkerchief?

> STRAIGHT
> Every flirter must have a handkerchief. It says it in the book. Now you shake the handkerchief three times like this. (Biz) Do you know what that means?

> COMEDIAN
> (Biz. of shaking head.)

> STRAIGHT
> That means you want her to give you—

> COMEDIAN
> Ten cents.

The reason why these two words come with such humorous effect, lies in two causes. First, "ten cents" has been used before with good laugh results—as a "gag line," you recall—and this is the comedian's magical "third time" use of it. It is a good example of the "three-sequence mystery" which Weber and Fields mentioned, and which has been used to advantage on the stage for many, many years.

Second, the comedian had refused to answer the straight-man's question. He simply stood there and shook his head. It was the very simple business of shaking his head that made his interruption come as a surprise and gave perfect setting for the "gag-line."

Read the speeches that follow and you will see how business is used. Note particularly how the business makes this point stand out as a great big laugh:

> STRAIGHT
> ...Den you hold your handkerchief by the corner like dis.

> COMEDIAN
> Vat does that mean?

> STRAIGHT

---

[40] *Biz.* is often used in vaudeville material for *bus.*, the correct contraction of *business*.

Meet me on the corner.

                    COMEDIAN

Och, dat's fine. (Takes handkerchief). . . Den if you hold it dis way, dat means (biz.): "Are you on the square?"

This line reads even funnier than many laughs in the act that are bigger, but its business cannot be explained in words. It seems funnier to you because you can picture it. You actually see it, precisely as it is done.

Then the next line blends it into the next point, which is clearly introduced with a grin—is developed into a laugh, a bigger laugh by effective business, and then into a roar.

Point after point follows—each point topping the preceding point—until the end of the two-act is reached in the biggest laugh of all.

III. HOW AND WHERE TO END

The business of the two-act, which secures its effects by actions that are often wholly without words, makes the two-act more difficult to time than a monologue. Furthermore, even if the time-consuming bits of business were negligible, the precise timing of a two-act by the author is not really necessary.

Precisely as a monologist can vary the length of his offering by leaving out gags, the two-act performers can shorten their offering at will—by leaving out points. Hence it is much better to supply more points than time will permit to delivery in the finished performance, than to be required to rewrite your material to stretch the subject to fill out time. All you need do is to keep the two-act within, say, twenty minutes. And to gauge the length roughly, count about one hundred and fifteen words to a minute.

Therefore, having arranged your points upon separate cards, or slips of paper, and having shuffled them about and tried them all in various routines to establish the best, choose your very biggest laugh for the last. [41]Wherever that biggest laugh may have been in the sample routines you have arranged, take it out and blend it in for your final big roar.

Remember that the last laugh must be the delighted roar that will take the performers off stage, and bring them back again and again for their bows.

IV. MAKING THE MANUSCRIPT A STAGE SUCCESS

The manuscript of a two-act is only a prophecy of what *may* be. It *may* be a good prophecy or a bad prognostication—only actual performance before an audience can decide. As we saw in the monologue, points that the author thought would "go big"—"die"; and unexpectedly, little grins waken into great big laughs. There is no way of telling from the manuscript.

When you have finished your two-act you must be prepared to construct it all over again in rehearsal, and during all the performances of its try-out weeks. Not only must the points be good themselves, they must also fit the performers like

---

[41] See description of card system, Chapter VI, section III.

the proverbial kid gloves.

More two-acts—and this applies to all other stage-offerings as well—have started out as merely promising successes, than have won at the first try-out. For this reason, be prepared to work all the morning rehearsing, at the matinee and the night performances, and after the theatre is dark, to conjure giggle points into great big laughs, and lift the entire routine into the success your ability and the performers' cleverness can make it.

Even after it has won its way into a contract and everybody is happy, you must be prepared to keep your two-act up-to-the-minute. While it is on the road, you must send to the performers all the laughs you can think of—particularly if you have chosen for your theme one that demands constant furbishing to keep it bright.

V. OTHER TWO-ACT FORMS

It is with direct purpose that the discussion of the two-act has been confined to the kind of act that Weber and Fields made so successful—and of which Mr. Hoffman's "The Art of Flirtation" is a more up-to-date, mild and artistic form. There are other forms of the two-act, of course, but the kind of two-act we have discussed is peculiarly typical of two-act material. It holds within itself practically all the elements of the two-act that the writer has to consider. It is only necessary now to describe the other forms briefly.

By "pure two-act form," I mean the two-act that is presented without songs, tricks, or any other entertainment elements. Yet many of the most successful two-acts open with a song, introduce songs or parodies into the middle of their dialogue, or close with a song or some novelty.

Do not imagine that a two-act in which songs are introduced cannot be precisely as good as one that depends upon its talk alone. It may be an even better act. If it pleases the audience better, it is a better act. Remember that while we have been discussing the two-act from the writer's view-point, it is the applause of the audience that stamps every act with the final seal of approval. But, whether a two-act makes use of songs or tricks or anything else, does not change the principles on which all two-act points and gags are constructed.

The more common talking two-acts are:

1. The Sidewalk Conversation or Gag Act

This form may or may not open and close with songs, and depends upon skillfully blended, but not necessarily related, gags and jokes.

2. The Parody Two-Act

This sort of act opens and closes with parodies on the latest song-hits, and uses talk for short rests and humorous effect between the parodies by which the act makes its chief appeal.

3. The Singing Two-Act

This type makes its appeal not by the use of songs, but because the voices are very fine. Such an act may use a few gags and unrelated jokes—perhaps of the "nut" variety—to take the act out of the pure duet class and therefore offer wider appeal.

4. The Comedy Act for Two Women

Such acts may depend on precisely the same form of routine the pure talking two-act for men uses. Of course, the treatment of the subject themes is gentler and the material is all of a milder character.

5. The Two-Act with Plot Interest

Acts of this character make use of a comedy, burlesque, melodramatic or even a dramatic plot. This form of sketch seldom rises into the playlet class. It is a two-act merely because it is played by two persons. Often, however, this form of the two-act uses a thread of plot on which to string its business and true two-act points. It may or may not make use of songs, parodies, tricks or other entertainment elements. We have now come to a form of two-act which is of so popular a nature that it requires more than passing mention. This is

6. The Flirtation Two-Act

Usually presented with songs making their appeal to sentiment, almost always marked by at least one change of costume by the woman, sometimes distinguished by a special drop and often given more than a nucleus of plot, this very popular form of two-act sometimes rises into the dignity of a little production. Indeed, many two-acts of this kind have been so successful in their little form they have been expanded into miniature musical comedies[42].

(a) *Romance* is the chief source of the flirtation two-act's appeal. It is the dream-love in the heart of every person in the audience which makes this form of two-act "go" so well. Moonlight, a girl and a man—this is the recipe.

(b) *Witty Dialogue* that fences with love, that thrusts, parries and—surrenders, is what makes the flirtation two-act "get over." It is the same kind of dialogue that made Anthony Hope's "Dolly Dialogues" so successful in their day, the sort of speeches which we, in real life, think of afterward and wish we had made.

(c) *Daintiness of effect* is what is needed in this form of two-act. Dialogue and business, scenery, lights and music all combine to the fulfillment of its purpose. The cruder touches of other two-act forms are forgotten and the entire effort is concentrated on making an appeal to the "ideal." Turn to the Appendix, and read "After the Shower," and you will see how these various elements are unified. This famous flirtation two-act has been chosen because it shows practically all the elements we have discussed.

---

[42] See Chapter XXX, The One-Act Musical Comedy.

CHAPTER X

THE PLAYLET AS A UNIQUE DRAMATIC FORM

THE playlet is a very definite thing—and yet it is difficult to define. Like the short-story, painting as we know it today, photography, the incandescent lamp, the telephone, and the myriad other forms of art and mechanical conveniences, the playlet did not spring from an inventor's mind full fledged, but attained its present form by slow growth. It is a thing of life—and life cannot be bounded by words, lest it be buried in the tomb of a hasty definition.

To attempt even the most cautious of definitions without having first laid down the foundations of understanding by describing some of the near-playlet forms to be seen on many vaudeville bills would, indeed, be futile. For perhaps the surest way of learning what a thing is, is first to learn what it is not. Confusion is then less likely to creep into the conception, and the definition comes like a satisfactory summing up of familiar points that are resolved into clear words.

I. NEAR-DRAMATIC FORMS WHICH PRECEDED THE VAUDEVILLE PLAYLET

Even in the old music hall days, when a patron strolled in from a hard day's work and sat down to enjoy an even harder evening's entertainment, the skit or sketch or short play which eventually drifted upon the boards—where it was seen through the mists of tobacco smoke and strong drink—was *the* thing. The admiration the patrons had for the performers, whom they liberally treated after the show, did not prevent them from actively driving from the stage any offering that did not possess the required dramatic "punch." [43] They had enjoyed the best of everything else the music hall manager could obtain for their amusement and they demanded that their bit of a play be, also, the very best of its kind.

No matter what this form of entertainment that we now know by the name of vaudeville may be called, the very essence of its being is variety. "Topical songs"—we call their descendants "popular songs"—classic ballads, short concerts given on all sorts of instruments, juggling, legerdemain, clowning, feats of balancing, all the departments of dancing and of acrobatic work, musical comedy, pantomime, and all the other hundred-and-one things that may be turned into an amusing ten or twenty minutes, found eager welcome on the one stage that made it, and still makes it, a business to present the very newest and the

---

[43] It is worthy of note in this connection that many of the dramatic and particularly the comedy offerings seen in the music halls of twenty years ago, and in the "Honkitonks" of Seattle and other Pacific Coast cities during the Alaskan gold rush, have, expurgated, furnished the scenarios of a score of the most successful legitimate dramas and comedies of recent years. Some of our greatest legitimate and vaudeville performers also came from this humble and not-to-be-boasted-of school. This phase of the growth of the American drama has never been written. It should be recorded while the memories of "old timers" are still fresh.

very best of everything. To complete its claim to the title of variety, to separate itself from a likeness to the circus, to establish itself as blood brother of the legitimate stage, and, most important of all, to satisfy the craving of its audiences for *drama*, vaudeville tried many forms of the short play before the playlet was evolved to fill the want.

Everything that bears even the remotest likeness to a play found a place and had a more or less fleeting—or lasting—popularity. And not only was every form of play used, but forms of entertainment that could not by reason of their very excellencies be made to fill the crying want, were pressed into service and supplied with ill-fitting plots in the vain attempt.

Musical acts, whose chief appeal was the coaxing of musical sounds from wagon tires, drinking glasses, and exotic instruments, were staged in the kitchen set. And father just home from work would say, "Come, daughter, let's have a tune." Then off they would start, give their little entertainment, and down would come the curtain on a picture of never-to-be-seen domestic life. Even today, we sometimes see such a hybrid act.

Slap-stick sidewalk conversation teams often would hire an author to fit them with a ready-made plot, and, pushed back behind the Olio into a centre-door fancy set, would laboriously explain why they were there, then go through their inappropriate antics and finish with a climax that never "climaxed." All kinds of two-acts, from the dancing pair to the flirtatious couple, vainly tried to give their offerings dramatic form. They did their best to make them over into little plays and still retain the individual elements that had won them success.

The futility of such attempts it took years to realize. It was only when the stock opening, "I expect a new partner to call at the house today in answer to my advertisement (which was read for a laugh) and while I am waiting for him I might as well practice my song," grew so wearisome that it had to be served with a special notice in many vaudeville theatres, that these groping two-acts returned to the pure forms from which they never should have strayed. But even today you sometimes see such an act—with a little less inappropriate opening—win, because of the extreme cleverness of the performers.

II. DRAMATIC FORMS FROM WHICH THE PLAYLET EVOLVED

Among the dramatic forms—by which I mean acts depending on dialogue, plot and "acting" for appeal—that found more or less success in vaudeville, were sketches and short plays (not playlets) using either comedy, farce, or dramatic plots, and containing either burlesque or extravaganza. Let us take these dramatic forms in their order of widest difference from the playlet and give to each the explanatory word it deserves.

1. Extravaganza Acts

Extravaganza is anything out of rule. It deals comically with the impossible and the unreal, and serves its purpose best when it amazes most. Relying upon physical surprises, as well as extravagant stage-effects, the extravaganza act may be best explained, perhaps, by naming a famous example—"Eight Bells." The

Byrne Brothers took the elements of this entertainment so often into vaudeville and out of it again into road shows that it is difficult to remember where it originated. The sudden appearances of the acrobatic actors and their amazing dives through seemingly solid doors and floors, held the very essence of extravaganza. Uncommon nowadays even in its pure form, the extravaganza act that tries to ape the play form is seldom if ever seen.

2. Burlesque Acts

Burlesque acts, however, are not uncommon today and are of two different kinds. First, there is the burlesque that is travesty, which takes a well-known and often serious subject and hits off its famous features in ways that are uproariously funny. "When Caesar Sees Her," took the famous meeting between Cleopatra and Marc Antony and made even the most impressive moment a scream. [44]And Arthur Denvir's "The Villain Still Pursued Her" (See Appendix), an exceptionally fine example of the travesty, takes the well-remembered melodrama and extracts laughter from situations that once thrilled.

Second, there are the acts that are constructed from bits of comedy business and depend for their success not on dialogue, but on action. Merely a thread of plot holds them together and on it is strung the elemental humor of the comedy bits, which as often as not may be slap-stick. The purpose being only to amuse for the moment, all kinds of entertainment forms may be introduced. One of the most successful examples of the burlesque tab, [45]James Madison's "My Old Kentucky Home" (See Appendix), serves as the basic example in my treatment of this vaudeville form.

3. Short Plays

Short plays, as the name implies, are merely plays that are short. They partake of the nature of the long play and are simply short because the philosophic speeches are few and the number of scenes that have been inserted are not many. The short play may have sub-plots; it may have incidents that do not affect the main design; its characters may be many and some may be introduced simply to achieve life-like effect; and it usually comes to a leisurely end after the lapse of from twenty minutes to even an hour or more.

Again like the full-evening play, the one-act play that is merely short paints its characters in greater detail than is possible in the playlet, where the strokes are made full and broad. Furthermore, while in the playlet economy of time and

---

[44] In musical comedy this is often done to subjects and personalities of national interest. The Ziegfeld perennial Follies invariably have bits that are played by impersonators of the national figure of the moment. Sometimes in musical revues great dramatic successes are travestied, and the invariable shouts of laughter their presentation provokes are an illuminating exemplification of the truth that between tragedy and comedy there is but a step.

[45] *Tab* is short for tabloid. There may be tabloid musical comedies—running forty minutes or more—as well as *burlesque tabs*.

attention are prime requisites, in the short play they are not; to take some of the incidents away from the short play might not ruin it, but to take even one incident away from a playlet would make it incomplete.

For many years, however, the following tabloid forms of the legitimate drama were vaudeville's answer to the craving of its audiences for drama.

(a) *Condensed Versions, "Big" Scenes and Single Acts of Long Plays.* For example— an example which proves three points in a single instance: the need for drama in vaudeville, vaudeville's anxiety for names, and its willingness to pay great sums for what it wants—Joseph Jefferson was offered by F. F. Proctor, in 1905, the then unheard-of salary of $5,000 a week for twelve consecutive weeks to play "Bob Acres" in a condensed version of "The Rivals." Mr. Jefferson was to receive this honorarium for himself alone, Mr. Proctor agreeing to furnish the condensed play, the scenery and costumes, and pay the salaries of the supporting cast. The offer was not accepted, but it stood as the record until Martin Beck paid Sarah Bernhardt the sum of $7,500 a week for herself and supporting players during her famous 1913 tour of the Orpheum Circuit. In recent years nearly every legitimate artist of national and international reputation has appeared in vaudeville in some sort of dramatic vehicle that had a memory in the legitimate.

But that neither a condensed play, nor one "big" scene or a single act from a long play, is not a playlet should be apparent when you remember the impression of inadequacy left on your own mind by such a vehicle, even when a famous actor or actress has endowed it with all of his or her charm and wonderful art.

(b) *The Curtain-Raiser.* First used to supplement or preface a short three-act play so as to eke out a full evening's entertainment, the little play was known as either an "afterpiece" or a "curtain-raiser"; usually, however, it was presented before the three-act drama, to give those who came early their full money's worth and still permit the fashionables, who "always come late," to be present in time to witness the important play of the evening. Then it was that "curtain-raiser" was considered a term of reproach. But often in these days a curtain-raiser, like Sir James M. Barrie's "The Twelve Pound Look," proves even more entertaining and worth while than the ambitious play it precedes.

That Ethel Barrymore took "The Twelve Pound Look" into vaudeville does not prove, however, that the curtain-raiser and the vaudeville playlet are like forms. As in the past, the curtain-raiser of today usually is more kin to the long play than to the playlet. But it is nevertheless true that in some recent curtain-raisers the compact swiftness and meaningful effect of the playlet form has become more apparent—they differ from the vaudeville playlet less in form than in legitimate feeling.

Historically, however, the curtain-raiser stands in much the same position in the genealogy of the playlet that the forms discussed in the preceding section occupy. As in the other short plays, there was no sense of oneness of plot and little feeling of coming-to-the-end that mark a good playlet.

Therefore, since the short play could not fully satisfy the vaudeville patron's natural desire for drama, the sketch held the vaudeville stage unchallenged until the playlet came.

4. Vaudeville Sketches

The vaudeville sketch in the old days was almost anything you might care to name, in dramatic form. Any vaudeville two-act that stepped behind the Olio and was able to hold a bit of a plot alive amid its murdering of the King's English and its slap-stick ways, took the name of "a sketch." But the "proper sketch," as the English would say—the child of vaudeville and elder half-brother to the playlet—did not make use of other entertainment forms. It depended on dialogue, business and acting and a more or less consistent plot or near-plot for its appeal. Usually a comedy—yet sometimes a melodrama—the vaudeville sketch of yesterday and of today rarely makes plot a chief element. The *story* of a sketch usually means little in its general effect. The general effect of the sketch is—general. That is one of the chief differences between it and the playlet.

The purpose of the sketch is not to leave a single impression of a single story. It points no moral, draws no conclusion, and sometimes it might end quite as effectively anywhere before the place in the action at which it does terminate. It is built for entertainment purposes only, and furthermore, for entertainment purposes that end the moment the sketch ends. When you see a sketch you carry away no definite impression, save that of entertainment, and usually you cannot remember what it was that entertained you. Often a sketch might be incorporated into a burlesque show or a musical comedy and serve for part of an act, without suffering, itself, in effect. [46]And yet, without the sketch of yesterday there would be no playlet today.

(a) *The Character Sketch.* Some sketches, like Tom Nawn's "Pat and the Geni," and his other "Pat" offerings, so long a famous vaudeville feature, are merely character sketches. Like the near-short-story character-sketch, the vaudeville sketch often gives an admirable exposition of character, without showing any change in the character's heart effected by the incidents of the story. "Pat" went through all sorts of funny and startling adventures when he opened the brass bottle and the Geni came forth, but he was the very same Pat when he woke up and found it all a dream. [47]

Indeed, the vaudeville sketch was for years the natural vehicle and "artistic reward" for clever actors who made a marked success in impersonating some particular character in burlesque or in the legitimate. The vaudeville sketch was

---

[46] Not so many years ago, a considerable number of vaudeville sketches were used in burlesque; and vice versa, many sketches were produced in burlesque that afterward had successful runs in vaudeville. Yet they were more than successful twenty-minute "bits," taken out of burlesque shows. They had a certain completeness of form which did not lose in effect by being transplanted.

[47] The Ryan and Richfield acts that have to do with Haggerty and his society-climbing daughter Mag, may be remembered. For longer than my memory runs, Mag Haggerty has been trying to get her father into society, but the Irish brick-layer will never "arrive." The humor lies in Haggerty's rich Irishness and the funny mistakes he always makes. The "Haggerty" series of sketches and the "Pat" series show, perhaps better than any others, the closeness of the character-sketch short-story that is often mistaken for the true short-story, to the vaudeville sketch that is so often considered a playlet.

written around the personality of the character with which success had been won and hence was constructed to give the actor opportunity to show to the best advantage his acting in the character. And in the degree that it succeeded it was and still is a success—and a valuable entertainment form for vaudeville.

(b) *The Narrative Sketch.* Precisely as the character sketch is not a playlet, the merely narrative sketch is not a true playlet. No matter how interesting and momentarily amusing or thrilling may be the twenty-minute vaudeville offering that depends upon incident only, it does not enlist the attention, hold the sympathy, or linger in the memory, as does the playlet.

Character revelation has little place in the narrative sketch, a complete well-rounded plot is seldom to be found, and a change in the relations of the characters rarely comes about. The sketch does not convince the audience that it is complete in itself—rather it seems an incident taken out of the middle of a host of similar experiences. It does not carry the larger conviction of reality that lies behind reality.

(1) *The Farce Sketch.* Nevertheless such excellent farce sketches as Mr. and Mrs. Sydney Drew, Rice and Cohen, Homer Mason and Margaret Keeler, and other sterling performers have presented in vaudeville, are well worth while. The fact that many of the minor incidents that occur in such finely amusing sketches as Mason and Keeler's "In and Out" [48] do not lend weight to the ending, but seem introduced merely to heighten the cumulative effect of the farce-comedy, does not prove them, or the offering, to be lacking in entertainment value for vaudeville. Rather, the use of just such extraneous incidents makes these sketches more worth while; but the introduction of them and the dependence upon them, for interest, does mark such offerings as narrative sketches rather than as true playlets.

(2) *The Straight Dramatic and Melodramatic Sketch.* In identically the same way the introduction into one-act dramas and melodramas of "bits" that are merely added to heighten the suspense and make the whole seem more "creepy," without having a definite—an inevitable—effect upon the ending makes and marks them as narrative dramas and melodramas and not true playlet forms.

From the foregoing examples we may now attempt

5. A Definition of a Vaudeville Sketch

> A Vaudeville Sketch is a simple narrative, or a character sketch, presented by two or more people, requiring usually about twenty minutes to act, having little or no definite plot, developing no vital change in the relations of the characters, and depending on effective incidents for its appeal, rather than on the singleness of effect of a problem solved by character revelation and change.

It must be borne in mind that vaudeville is presenting today all sorts of sketches, and that nothing in this definition is levelled against their worth. All that has been attempted so far in this chapter has been to separate for you the various

---

[48] By Porter Emerson Brown, author of *A Fool There Was*, and other full-evening plays.

forms of dramatic and near-dramatic offerings to be seen in vaudeville. A good sketch is decidedly worth writing. And you should also remember that definitions and separations are dangerous things. There are vaudeville sketches that touch in one point or two or three the peculiar requirements of the playlet and naturally, in proportion as these approach closely the playlet form, hair-splitting separations become nearly, if not quite, absurd.

Furthermore, when an experienced playwright sits down to write a vaudeville offering he does not consider definitions. He has in his mind something very definite that he plans to produce and he produces it irrespective of definitions. He is not likely to stop to inquire whether it is a sketch or a playlet. [49]The only classifications the professional vaudeville writer considers, are failures and successes. He defines a success by the money it brings him.

But today there is a force abroad in vaudeville that is making for a more artistic form of the one-act play. It is the same artistic spirit that produced out of short fiction the short-story. This age has been styled the age of the short-story and of vaudeville—it is, indeed, the age of the playlet.

The actor looking for a vaudeville vehicle today is not content with merely an incident that will give him the opportunity to present the character with which he has won marked success on the legitimate stage. Nor is he satisfied with a series of incidents, however amusing or thrilling they may be. He requires an offering that will lift his work into a more artistic sphere. He desires a little play that will be remembered after the curtain has been rung down.

This is the sort of vehicle that he must present to win success in vaudeville for any length of time. While vaudeville managers may seem content to book an act that is not of the very first rank, because it is played by someone whose ability and whose name glosses over its defects, they do not encourage such offerings by long contracts. Even with the most famous of names, vaudeville managers—reflecting the desires of their audiences—demand acceptable playlets.

III. HOW THE VAUDEVILLE SKETCH AND THE PLAYLET DIFFER

Edgar Allan Woolf, one of the day's most successful playlet writers who has won success year after year with vaudeville offerings that have been presented by some of the most famous actors of this country and of England, said when I asked him what he considered to be the difference between the sketch and the playlet:

"There was a time when the vaudeville sketch was moulded on lines that presented less difficulties and required less technique of the playwright than does the playlet of today. The curtain generally rose on a chambermaid in above-the-ankle skirts dusting the furniture as she told in soliloquy form that her master and mistress had sent for a new butler or coachman or French teacher. How the butler, coachman or French teacher might make her happier was not disclosed.

---

[49] In discussing this, Arthur Hopkins said: "When vaudeville presents a very good dramatic offering, 'playlet' is the word used to describe it. If it isn't very fine, it is called a 'sketch.'"

"Then came a knock on the door, followed by the elucidating remark of the maid, 'Ah, this must be he now.' A strange man thereupon entered, who was not permitted to say who he was till the piece was over or there would have been no piece. The maid for no reason mistook him for the butler, coachman or French teacher, as the case may have been, and the complications ensuing were made hilarious by the entrance of the maid's husband who, of course, brought about a comedy chase scene, without which no 'comedietta' was complete. Then all characters met—hasty explanations—and 'comedy curtain.'

"Today, all these things are taboo. A vaudeville audience resents having the 'protiasis' or introductory facts told them in monologue form, as keenly as does the 'legitimate' audience. Here, too, the actor may not explain his actions by 'asides.' And 'mistaken identity' is a thing of the past.

"Every trivial action must be thoroughly motivated, and the finish of the playlet, instead of occurring upon the 'catabasis,' or general windup of the action, must develop the most striking feature of the playlet, so that the curtain may come down on a surprise, or at least an event toward which the entire action has been progressing.

"But the most important element that has developed in the playlet of today is the problem, or theme. A little comedy that provokes laughter yet means nothing, is apt to be peddled about from week to week on the 'small time' and never secure booking in the better houses. In nearly all cases where the act has been a 'riot' of laughter, yet has failed to secure bookings, the reason is to be found in the fact that it is devoid of a definite theme or central idea.

"The booking managers are only too eager to secure playlets—and now I mean precisely the *playlet*—which are constructed to develop a problem, either humorous or dramatic. The technique of the playlet playwright is considered in the same way that the three-act playwright's art of construction is analyzed by the dramatic critic."

IV. WHAT A PLAYLET IS

We have seen what the playlet is not. We have considered the various dramatic and near-dramatic forms from which it differs. And now, having studied its negative qualities, I may assemble its positive characteristics before we embark once more upon the troubled seas of definition. The true playlet is marked by the following ten characteristics:

1—A clearly motivated opening—not in soliloquy form.
2—A single definite and predominating problem or theme.
3—A single preeminent character.
4—Motivated speeches.
5—Motivated business and acting.
6—Unity of characters.
7—Compression.
8—Plot.
9—A finish that develops the most striking feature into a surprise—or is an event toward which every speech and every action has been progressing.

10—Unity of impression [50]

Each of these characteristics has already been discussed in our consideration of the dramatic forms—either in its negative or positive quality—or will later be taken up at length in its proper place. Therefore, we may hazard in the following words

A Definition of a Playlet

A Playlet is a stage narrative taking usually about twenty minutes to act, having a single chief character, and a single problem which predominates, and is developed by means of a plot so compressed and so organized that every speech and every action of the characters move it forward to a finish which presents the most striking features; while the whole is so organized as to produce a single impression.

You may haunt the vaudeville theatres in a vain search for a playlet that will embody all of these characteristics in one perfect example. [51]But the fact that a few playlets are absolutely perfect technically is no reason why the others should be condemned. Remember that precise conformity to the rules here laid down is merely academic perfection, and that the final worth of a playlet depends not upon adherence to any one rule, or all—save as they point the way to success—but upon how the playlet as a whole succeeds with the audience.

Yet there will be found still fewer dramatic offerings in vaudeville that do not conform to some of these principles. Such near-playlets succeed not because they evade the type, but mysteriously in spite of their mistakes. And as they conform more closely to the standards of what a playlet should be, they approach the elements that make for lasting success.

But beyond these "rules"—if rules there really are—and far above them in the heights no rules can reach, lies that something which cannot be defined, which breathes the breath of life into words and actions that bring laughter and tears. Rules cannot build the bridge from your heart to the hearts of your audiences. Science stands abashed and helpless before the task. All that rules can suggest, all that science can point out—is the way others have built their bridges

For this purpose only, are these standards of any value to you.

---

[50] See page 30, Writing the Short-Story, by J. Berg Esenwein, published in "The Writer's Library," uniform with this volume. Note the seven characteristics of the short-story and compare them with the playlet's ten characteristics. You will find a surprising similarity between the short-story and the playlet in some points of structure. A study of both in relation to each other may give you a clearer understanding of each.

[51] Study the playlet examples in the Appendix and note how closely each approaches technical perfection.

CHAPTER XI

KINDS OF PLAYLET

THE kind of playlet is largely determined by its characters and their surroundings, and on these there are practically no limits. You may have characters of any nationality; you may treat them reverently, or—save that you must never offend—you may make them as funny as you desire; you may give them any profession that suits your purpose; you may place them in any sort of house or on the open hills or in an air-ship high in the sky; you may show them in any country of the earth or on the moon or in the seas under the earth—you may do anything you like with them. Vaudeville wants everything—everything so long as it is well and strikingly done. Therefore, to attempt to list the many different kinds of playlet to be seen upon the vaudeville stage would, indeed, be a task as fraught with hazard as to try to classify minutely the divers kinds of men seen upon the stage of life. And of just as little practical value would it be to have tables showing the scores of superficial variations of character, nationality, time and place which the years have woven into the playlets of the past.

In the "art" of the playlet there are, to be sure, the same three "schools"—more or less unconsciously followed in nearly every vaudeville instance—which are to be found in the novel, the short-story, painting, and the full-length play. These are, of course, realism, romance, and idealism. [52]These distinctions, however, are—in vaudeville—merely distinctions without being valuable differences. You need never give thought as to the school to which you are paying allegiance in your playlet; your work will probably be neither better nor worse for this knowledge or its lack. Your playlet must stand on its own legs, and succeed or fail by the test of interest. Make your playlet grip, that is the thing.

But do not confuse the word "romance," as it is used in the preceding paragraph, with love. Love is an emotional, not a technical element, and consorts equally well with either romance or realism in writing. Love might be the heading of one of those tables we have agreed not to bother with. Into everything that is written for vaudeville love may stray. Or it may not intrude, if your purpose demands that love stay out. Yet, like the world, what would vaudeville be, if love were left out? And now we come to those broad types of playlet which you should recognize instinctively. Unless you do so recognize them—and the varying

---

[52] Should you wish to dally with the mooted question of the difference between realism and romanticism—in the perplexing mazes of which many a fine little talent has been snuffed out like a flickering taper in a gust of wind—there are a score or more volumes that you will find in any large library, in which the whole matter is thrashed out unsatisfactorily. However, if you wish to spend a half-hour profitably and pleasantly, read Robert Louis Stevenson's short chapter, A Note on Realism, to be found in his suggestive and all-too-few papers on The Art of Writing. In the collection of his essays entitled Memories and Portraits will be found an equally delightful and valuable paper, A Gossip on Romance. A brief technical discussion will also be found in Writing the Short-Story, by J. Berg Esenwein, pp. 64 67.

half-grounds that lie between, where they meet and mingle quite as often as they appear in their pure forms—you will have but little success in writing the playlet.

In considering the broad types of playlet you should remember that words are said to *denote* definitely the ideas they delineate, and to *connote* the thoughts and emotions they do not clearly express but arouse in the hearer or reader. For example, what do "farce," "comedy," "tragedy" and "melodrama" *connote* to you? What emotions do they suggest? This is an important matter, because all great artistic types are more or less fully associated with a mood, a feeling, an atmosphere.

Webster's dictionary gives to them the following denotations, or definitions:

Farce: "A dramatic composition, written without regularity, and differing from comedy chiefly in the grotesqueness, extravagance and improbability of its characters and incidents; low comedy."

Arthur Denvir's "The Villain Still Pursued Her" is one of the best examples of the travesty vaudeville has produced. [53] James Madison's "My Old Kentucky Home" is a particularly fine example of burlesque in tabloid form.

Comedy: "A dramatic composition or representation, designed for public amusement and usually based upon laughable incidents, or the follies or foibles of individuals or classes; a form of the drama in which humor and mirth predominate, and the plot of which usually ends happily; the opposite of tragedy."

Edgar Allan Woolf's "The Lollard" is an exceptionally good example of satirical comedy. [54]

Tragedy: "A dramatic composition, representing an important event or a series of events in the life of some person or persons in which the diction is elevated, the movement solemn and stately, and the catastrophe sad; a kind of drama of a lofty or mournful cast, dealing with the dark side of life and character." Richard Harding Davis's "Blackmail" is a notable example of tragedy. [55]

Melodrama: "A romantic [connoting love] play, generally of a serious character, in which effect is sought by startling incidents, striking situations, exaggerated sentiment and thrilling denouement, aided by elaborate stage effects. The more thrilling passages are sometimes accentuated by musical accompaniments, the only surviving relic of the original musical character of the melodrama."

Taylor Granville's "The System" is one of the finest examples of pure melodrama seen in vaudeville. [56]

There are, of course, certain other divisions into which these four basic kinds of playlet—as well as the full-length play—may be separated, but they are more or less false forms. However, four are worthy of particular mention:

The Society Drama: The form of drama in which a present-day story is told, and the language, dress and manners of the actors are those of polite modern society.

---

[53] These two acts have been chosen to show the difference between two of the schools of farce.
[54] See Appendix.
[55] See Appendix.
[56] Written by Taylor Granville, Junie MacCree and Edward Clark; see Appendix.

[57]You will see how superficial the distinction is, when you realize that the plot may be farcical, comic, tragic or melodramatic.

The same is true of

The Problem Drama: The form of drama dealing with life's "problems"—of sex, business, or what not.[58]

And the same is likewise true of

The Pastoral-Rural Drama: The form of drama dealing with rustic life.[59]

And also of

The Detective Drama: [60]The form of drama dealing with the detection of crime and the apprehension of the criminal. I cannot recollect a detective playlet—or three-act play, for that matter—that is not melodramatic. When the action is not purely melodramatic, the lines and the feeling usually thrill with melodrama. [61]"The System," which is a playlet dealing with the detection of detectives, is but one example in point.

Here, then, we have the four great kinds of playlet, and four out of the many variations that often seem to the casual glance to possess elemental individuality.

Remember that this chapter is merely one of definitions and that a definition is a description of something given to it after—not before—it is finished. A definition is a tag, like the label the entomologist ties to the pin after he has the butterfly nicely dead. Of questionable profit it would be to you, struggling to waken your playlet into life, to worry about a definition that might read "Here Lies a Polite Comedy."

Professor Baker says that the tragedies of Shakespere may have seemed to the audiences of their own day "not tragedies at all, but merely more masterly specimens of dramatic story-telling than the things that preceded them." [62]If Shakespere did not worry about the precise labels of the plays he was busy writing and producing, you and I need not. Forget definitions—forget everything but your playlet and the grip, the thrill, the punch, the laughter of your plot.

To sum up: The limits of the playlet are narrow, its requirements are exacting, but within those limits and those requirements you may picture anything you possess the power to present. Pick out from life some incident, character, temperament—whatever you will—and flash upon it the glare of the vaudeville

---

[57] As the dramas of the legitimate stage are more often remembered by name than are vaudeville acts, I will mention as example of the society drama Clyde Fitch's The Climbers. This fine satire skirted the edge of tragedy.

[58] Ibsen's Ghosts; indeed, nearly every one of the problem master's plays offer themselves as examples of the problem type.

[59] The long play Way Down East is a fine example of the pastoral—or rural—drama of American life.

[60] Mr. Charlton Andrews makes a series of interesting and helpful discriminations among the several dramatic forms, in his work The Technique of Play Writing, published uniform with this volume in "The Writer's Library."

[61] Sherlock Holmes, William Gillette's masterly dramatization of Sir Arthur Conan Doyle's famous detective stories, is melodramatic even when the action is most restrained.

[62] Development of Shakespere as a Dramatist, by Prof. Baker of Harvard University.

spot-light; breathe into it the breath of life; show its every aspect and effect; dissect away the needless; vivify the series of actions you have chosen for your brief and trenchant crisis; lift it all with laughter or touch it all with tears. Like a searchlight your playlet must flash over the landscape of human hearts and rest upon some phase of passion, some momentous incident, and make it stand out clear and real from the darkness of doubt that surrounds it.

CHAPTER XII

HOW PLAYLETS ARE GERMINATED

WHERE does a playlet writer get his idea? How does he recognize a playlet idea when it presents itself to him? How much of the playlet is achieved when he hits on the idea? These questions are asked successful playlet writers every day, but before we proceed to find their answers, we must have a paragraph or two of definition.

I. THE THEME-PROBLEM AND ITS RANGE

Whenever the word "problem" is used—as, "the problem of a playlet"—I do not mean it in the sense that one gathers when he hears the words "problem play"; nothing whatever of sex or the other problems of the day is meant. What I mean is grasped at first glance better, perhaps, by the word "theme." Yet "theme" does not convey the precise thought I wish to associate with the idea.

A theme is a subject—that much I wish to convey—but I choose "problem" because I wish to connote the fact that the theme of a playlet is more than a subject: it is precisely what a problem in mathematics is. Given a problem in geometry, you must solve it—from its first statement all the way through to the "Q.E.D." Each step must bear a plain and logical relation to that which went before and what follows. Your playlet theme is your problem, and you must choose for a theme or subject only such a problem as can be "proved" conclusively within the limits of a playlet.

Naturally, you are inclined to inquire as a premise to the questions that open this chapter, What are the themes or subjects that offer themselves as best suited to playlet requirements? In other words, what make the best playlet problems? Here are a few that present themselves from memory of playlets that have achieved exceptional success:

A father may object to his son's marrying anyone other than the girl whom he has chosen for him, but be won over by a little baby—"Dinkelspiel's Christmas," by George V. Hobart.

A slightly intoxicated young man may get into the wrong house by mistake and come through all his adventures triumphantly to remain a welcome guest—"In and Out," by Porter Emerson Brown.

A "crooked" policeman may build up a "system," but the honest policemen will hunt him down, even letting the lesser criminal escape to catch the greater—"The System," by Taylor Granville, Junie MacCree and Edward Clark.

Youth that lies in the mind and not in the body or dress may make a grandmother act and seem younger than her granddaughter—"Youth," by Edgar Allan Woolf.

A foolish young woman may leave her husband because she has "found him out," yet return to him again when she discovers that another man is no better than he is—"The Lollard," by Edgar Allan Woolf.

A man may do away with another, but escape the penalty because of the flawless method of the killing—"Blackmail," by Richard Harding Davis.

A wide range of themes is shown in even these few playlets, isn't there? Yet the actual range of themes from which playlet problems may be chosen is not even suggested. Though I stated the problems of all the playlets that were ever presented in vaudeville, the field of playlet-problem possibilities would not be even adequately suggested. Anything, everything, presents itself for a playlet problem—if you can make it human, interesting and alive.

What interests men and women? Everything, you answer. Whatever interests you and your family, and your neighbor and his family, and the man across the street and his wife's folks back home—is a subject for a playlet. Whatever causes you to stop and think, to laugh or cry, is a playlet problem. "Art is life seen through a personality," is as true of the playlet as of any other art form.

Because some certain subject or theme has never been treated in a playlet, does not mean that it cannot be. It simply means that that particular subject has never yet appealed to a man able to present it successfully. Vaudeville is hungering for writers able to make gripping playlets out of themes that never have been treated well. To such it offers its largest rewards. What do you know better than anyone else—what do you feel keener than anyone else does—what can you present better than anyone else? That is the subject you should choose for *your* playlet problem.

And so you see that a playlet problem is not merely just "an idea"; it is a subject that appeals to a writer as offering itself with peculiar credentials—as the theme that he should select. It is anything at all—anything that you can make *your own* by your mastery of its every angle.

1. What Themes to Avoid

(a) *Unfamiliar Themes.* If a subject of which you have not a familiar knowledge presents itself to you, reject it. Imagine how a producer, the actors and an audience—if they let the thing go that far—would laugh at a playlet whose premises were false and whose incidents were silly, because untrue. Never give anyone an opportunity to look up from a manuscript of yours and grin, as he says: "This person's a fool; he doesn't know what he's writing about."

(b) *"Cause" Themes.* Although more powerful than the "stump" or the pulpit today, and but little less forceful than the newspaper as a means of exposing intolerable conditions and ushering in new and better knowledge, the stage is not the place for propaganda. The public goes to the theatre to be entertained, not instructed—particularly is this true of vaudeville—and the writer daring enough to attempt to administer even homeopathic doses of instruction, must be a master-hand to win. Once in a generation a Shaw may rise, who, by a twist of his pen, can make the public think, while he wears a guileful smile as he propounds philosophy from under a jester's cap; but even then his plays must be edited—as some of Shaw's are—of all but the most dramatic of his belligerently impudent notions.

If you have a religious belief, a political creed, a racial propagandum—in short, a "cause"—either to defend or to forward, don't write it in a drama. The legitimate stage might be induced to present it, if someone were willing to pay the theatre's losses, but vaudeville does not want it. Choose any form of presentation—a newspaper article, a magazine story, anything at all—save a playlet for polemic or "cause" themes.

(c) *Hackneyed Themes.* What has been "done to death" in vaudeville? You know as well as the most experienced playlet-writer, if you will only give the subject unbiased thought. What are the things that make you squirm in your seat and the man next you reach for his hat and go out? A list would fill a page, but there are two that should be mentioned because so many playlets built upon them are now being offered to producers without any hope of acceptance. There is the "mistaken identity" theme, in which the entire action hinges on one character's mistaking another for someone else—one word spoken in time would make the entire action needless, but the word is never spoken—or there would be no playlet. And the "henpecked husband," or the mistreated wife, who gets back at the final curtain, is a second. Twenty years hence either one of these may be the theme of the "scream" of the season, for stage fashions change like women's styles, but, if you wish your playlet produced today, don't employ them.

(d) *Improper Themes.* Any theme that would bring a blush to the cheek of your sister, of your wife, of your daughter, you must avoid. No matter how pure your motive might be in making use of such a theme, resolutely deny it when it presents itself to you. The fact that the young society girl who offered me a playlet based on, to her, an amazing experience down at the Women's Night Court—where she saw the women of the streets brought before the judge and their "men" paying the fines—was a clean-minded, big-hearted girl anxious to help better conditions, did not make her theme any cleaner or her playlet any better.

Of course, I do not mean that you must ignore such conditions when your playlet calls for the use of such characters. I mean that you should not base your playlet entirely on such themes—you should never make such a theme the chief reason of your playlet's being.

2. What Themes to Use

You may treat any subject or play upon any theme, whatsoever it may be, provided it is not a "cause," is not hackneyed, is not improper for its own sake and likely to bring a blush to the cheeks of those you love, *is* familiar to you in its every angle, and is a subject that forms a problem which can be proved conclusively within the requirements of a playlet.

II. WHERE PLAYLET WRITERS GET THEIR IDEAS

1. The Three Forms of Dramatic Treatment

It is generally accepted by students of the novel and the short-story that there are three ways of constructing a narrative:

(a) Characters may be fitted with a story.
(b) A sequence of events may be fitted with characters.
(c) An interesting atmosphere may be expressed by characters and a sequence

of events.

In other words, a narrative may be told by making either the characters or the events or the atmosphere peculiarly and particularly prominent.

It should be obvious that the special character of vaudeville makes the last-named—the story of atmosphere—the least effective; indeed, as drama is action—by which I mean a clash of wills and the outcome—no audience would be likely to sit through even twenty minutes of something which, after all, merely results in a "feeling." Therefore the very nature of the pure story of atmosphere eliminates it from the stage; next in weakness of effect is the story of character; while the strongest—blood of its blood and bone of its bone—is the story of dramatic events. This is for what the stage is made and by which it lives. To be sure, character and atmosphere both have their places in the play of dramatic action, but for vaudeville those places must be subordinate.

These last two ways of constructing a story will be taken up and discussed in detail later on, in their proper order; they are mentioned here to help make clear how a playwright gets an idea.

2. Themes to fit Certain Players

It is not at all uncommon for a playlet writer to be asked to fit some legitimate star, about to enter vaudeville, with a playlet that shall have for its hero or its heroine the particular character in which the star has had marked success.[63] And often a man and wife who have achieved a reputation in vaudeville together will order a new playlet that shall have characters modeled on the lines of those in the old playlet. Or, indeed, as I have know in many instances, three performers will order a playlet in which there must be characters to fit them all. When a writer receives such an order it would seem that at least a part of his task is already done for him; but this is not the case, he still must seek that most important things—a story.

3. Themes Born in the Mind of the Writer

The beginner, fortunately, is not brought face to face with this problem; he is foot-free to wander wherever his fancy leads. And yet he may find in his thoughts a character or two who beg to serve him so earnestly that he cannot deny them. So he takes them, knowing them so well that he is sure he can make them live— and he constructs a story around them.

Or there may first pop into his mind a story in its entirety, full fledged, with beginning, middle and ending—that is; thoroughly motivated in every part and equipped with characters that live and breathe. Unhappily this most fortunate of

---

[63] In precisely the same way writers of the full-evening play for the legitimate stage are forever fashioning vehicles for famous stars. The fact that the chief consideration is the star and that the play is considered merely as a "vehicle" is one of the reasons why our plays are not always of the best. Where you consider a personality greater than a story, the story is likely to suffer. Can you name more than one or two recent plays so fashioned that have won more than a season's run?

occurrences usually happens only in the middle of the night, when one must wake up next morning and sadly realize it was but a dream.

4. The Newspaper as a Source of Ideas.

A playwright, let us say, reads in the newspapers of some striking characters, or of an event that appeals to him as funny or as having a deep dramatic import. There may be only a few bald lines telling the news. features of the story in one sentence, or there may be an entire column, discussing the case from every angle. Whatever it is, the bit of news appeals to him, and maybe of all men to him only, so he starts *thinking* about the possibilities it offers for a playlet.

5. Happenings of which the Playwright is Told or Which Occur under his Notice

Some striking incident rises out of the life about the playwright and he sees it or hears about it, and straightway comes the thought: This is a playlet idea. A large number of playlets have been germinated so.

6. Experiences that Happen to the Playwright

Some personal experience which wakens in the mind of the playwright the thought, Here's something that'll make a good playlet, is one of the fruitful sources of playlet-germs.

But however the germ idea comes to him—whether as a complete story, or merely as one striking incident, or just a situation that recommends itself to him as worth while fitting with a story—he begins by turning it over in his mind and casting it into dramatic form.

III. A SUPPOSITITIOUS EXAMPLE OF GERM-DEVELOPMENT

For the purpose of illustration, let us suppose that Taylor Granville, who conceived the idea of "The System," had read in the New York newspapers about the Becker case and the startling expose of the alleged police "system" that grew out of the Rosenthal murder, here is how his mind, trained to vaudeville and dramatic conventions, might have evolved that excellent melodramatic playleet. [64]

In this connection it should be emphasized that the Becker case did not make The System a great playlet; the investigation of the New York Police Department only gave it the added attraction of timeliness and, therefore, drew particular attention to it. Dozens of other playlets and many long plays that followed The System on the wave of the same timely interest failed. Precisely as Within the Law, Bayard Veiller's great play, so successful for the Selwyn Company, was given a striking timeliness by the Rosenthal murder, The System reaped merely the brimming harvest of lucky accident. And like Within the Law, this great playlet would be as successful today as it was then—because it is "big" in itself. [end footnote]

The incidents of "the Becker Case" were these: Herman Rosenthal, a gambler

---

[64] As a matter of fact, Mr. Granville had the first draft of the playlet in his trunk many months before the Rosenthal murder occurred, and Mr. MacCree and Mr. Clark were helping him with the final revisions when the fatal shot was fired.

of notorious reputation, one day went to District Attorney Whitman with the story that he was being hounded by the police—at the command of a certain Police Lieutenant. Rosenthal asserted that he had a story to tell which would shake up the New York Police Department. He was about to be called to testify to his alleged story when he was shot to death in front of the Metropole Hotel on Forty-third Street and the murderer or murderers escaped in an automobile. Several notorious underworld characters were arrested, charged with complicity in the murder, and some, in the hope, it has been said, of receiving immunity, confessed and implicated Police Lieutenant Becker, who was arrested on the charge of being the instigator of the crime. [65]These are the bare facts as every newspaper in New York City told them in glaring headlines at the time. Merely as incidents of a striking story, Mr. Granville would, it is likely, have turned them over in his mind with these thoughts:

"If I take these incidents as they stand, I'll have a grewsome ending that'll 'go great' for a while—if the authorities let me play it—and then the playlet will die with the waning interest. There isn't much that's dramatic in a gambler shown in the District Attorney's Office planning to 'squeal,' and then getting shot for it, even though the police in the playlet were made to instigate the murder. It'd make a great 'movie,' perhaps, but there isn't enough time in vaudeville to go through all the motions: I've got to recast it into drama.

"I must 'forget' the bloody ending, too—it may be great drama, but it isn't good vaudeville. The two-a-day wants the happy ending, if it can get it.

"And even if the Becker story's true in every detail, Rosenthal isn't a character with whom vaudeville can sympathize—I'll have to get a lesser offender, to win sympathy—a 'dip's' about right— 'The Eel.'

"There isn't any love-interest, either—where's the girl that sticks to him through thick and thin? I'll add his sweetheart, Goldie. And I'll give The Eel more sympathy by making Dugan's motive the attempt to win her.

"Then there's got to be the square Copper—the public knows that the Police force is fundamentally honest—so the Department has got to clean itself up, in my playlet; fine, there's McCarthy, the honest Inspector."

Here we have a little more, perhaps, than a bare germ idea, but it is probably the sort of thing that came into Mr. Granville's mind with the very first thought of "The System." Even more might have come during the first consideration of his new playlet, and—as we are dealing now not with a germ idea only but primarily with how a playwright's mind works—let us follow his supposititious reasoning further:

"All right; now, there's got to be an incident that'll give Dugan his chance to 'railroad' The Eel, and a money-society turn is always good, so we have Mrs. Worthington and the necklace, with Goldie, the suspected maid, who casts suspicion on The Eel. Dugan 'plants' it all, gets the necklace himself, tries to lay it

---

[65] Becker's subsequent trial, conviction, sentence to death and execution occurred many months later and could not have entered into the playwright's material, therefore they are not recounted here.

to The Eel, and win Goldie besides—but a dictograph shows him up. Now a man-to-man struggle between Dugan and The Eel for good old melodrama. The Eel is losing, in comes the Inspector and saves him—Dugan caught—triumph of the honest police—and Goldie and The Eel free to start life anew together. That's about it—for a starter, anyway.

"Re-read these dramatic incidents carefully, compare them with the incidents of the suggestive case as the newspapers reported them, and you will see not only where a playwright may get a germ idea, but how his mind works in casting it into stage form.

The first thing that strikes you is the dissimilarity of the two stories; the second, the greater dramatic effectiveness of the plot the playlet-writer's mind has evolved; third, that needless incidents have been cut away; fourth, that the very premise of the story, and all the succeeding incidents, lead you to recognize them in the light of the denouement as the logical first step and succeeding steps of which the final scene is inevitably the last; fifth, however many doubts may hover around the story of the suggesting incident, there is no cloud of doubt about the perfect justice of the stage story; and, sixth, that while you greet the ending of the suggesting story with a feeling of repugnance, the final scene of the stage story makes the whole clearly, happily and pleasantly true—truer than life itself, to human hearts which forever aspire after what we sometimes sadly call "poetic justice."

Now, in a few short paragraphs, we may sum up the answer to the question which opens this chapter, and answer the other two questions as well. A playlet writer may get the germ of a playlet idea: from half-ideas suggested by the necessity of fitting certain players; directly from his own imagination; from the newspapers; from what someone tells him, or from his observation of incidents that come under his personal notice; from experiences that happen to him—in fact, from anywhere.

IV. HOW A PLAYLET WRITER RECOGNIZES A PLAYLET IDEA

A playlet writer recognizes that the character or characters, the incident or incidents, possess a funny, serious or tragic *grip*, and the fact that he, himself, is gripped, is evidence that a playlet is *"there,"* if—IF—he can trust his own dramatic instinct. A playlet writer recognizes an idea as a playlet idea, because he is able so to recognize such an idea; there is no escape from this: YOU MUST POSSESS DRAMATIC INSTINCT [66] to recognize playlet ideas and write playlets.

V. HOW MUCH OF THE PLAYLET IS ACHIEVED WITH THE IDEA

No two persons in this world act alike, and certainly no two persons think alike. How much of a playlet is achieved when the germ idea is found and recognized, depends somewhat upon the idea—whether it is of characters that must be fitted with a story, a series of incidents, or one incident only—but more upon the writer. I have known playlets which were the results of ideas that

---

[66] See the following chapter on "The Dramatic—the Vital Element of Plot."

originated in the concepts of clever final situations, the last two minutes of the playlet serving as the incentive to the construction of the story that led inevitably up to the climax. I have also known playlets whose big scenes were the original ideas—the opening and finish being fitted to them. One or two writers have told me of playlets which came almost entirely organized and motivated into their minds with the first appearance of the germ idea. And others have told me of the hours of careful thinking through which they saw, in divers half-purposes of doubt, the action and the characters emerge into a definite, purposeful whole.

What one writer considers a full-fledged germ idea, may be to another but the first faint evidence that an idea may possibly be there. The skilled playlet-writer will certainly grasp a germ idea, and appraise its worth quicker than the novice can. In the eager acceptance of half-formed ideas that speciously glitter, lies the pitfall which entraps many a beginner. Therefore, engrave on the tablets of your resolution this determination and single standard:

> Never accept a subject as a germ idea and begin to write a playlet until you have turned its theme over in your mind a sufficient length of time to establish its worth beyond question. Consider it from every angle in the light of the suggestions in this chapter, and make its characters and its action as familiar to you as is the location of every article in your own room. Then, when your instinct for the dramatic tells you there is no doubt that here is the germ idea of a playlet, state it in one short sentence, and consider that statement as a problem that must be solved logically, clearly and conclusively, within the requirements of the playlet form.

With the germ idea the entire playlet may flood into the writer's mind, or come in little waves that rise continually, like the ever advancing tide, to the flood that touches high-water mark. But, however complete the germ idea may be, it depends upon the writer alone whether he struggles like a novice to keep his dramatic head above water, or strikes out with the bold, free strokes of the practised swimmer.

CHAPTER XIII

THE DRAMATIC—THE VITAL ELEMENT OF PLOT

WHAT the dramatic is—no matter whether it be serious or comic in tone—requires some consideration in a volume such as this, even though but a brief discussion is possible and only a line of thought may be pointed out.

This discussion is placed here in the sequence of chapters, because it first begins to trouble the novice after he has accepted his germ idea, and before he has succeeded in casting it into a stage story. Indeed, at that moment even the most self-sure becomes conscious of the demands of the dramatic. Yet this chapter will be found to overlap some that precede it and some that follow—particularly the chapter on plot structure, of which this discussion may be considered an integral part—as is the case in every attempt to put into formal words, principles separate in theory, but inseparable in application.

In the previous chapter, the conscious thought that precedes even the acceptance of a germ idea was insisted on—it was "played up," as the stage phrase terms a scene in which the emotional key is pitched high—with the purpose of forcing upon your attention the prime necessity of thinking out—not yet writing—the playlet. Emphasis was also laid on the necessity for the possession of dramatic instinct—a gift far different from the ability to think—by anyone who would win success in writing this most difficult of dramatic forms. But now I wish to lay an added stress—to pitch even higher the key of emphasis—on one fundamental, this vital necessity: Anyone who would write a playlet must possess in himself, as an instinct—something that cannot be taught and cannot be acquired—the ability to recognize and grasp the dramatic.

No matter if you master the technic by which the great dramatists have built their plays, you cannot achieve success in writing the playlet if you do not possess an innate sense of what is dramatic. For, just as a man who is tone-deaf [67] might produce musical manuscripts which while technically faultless would play inharmoniously, so the man who is drama-blind might produce "perfect" playlet manuscripts that would play in dramatic discords.

1. What Dramatic Instinct Is

When you witness a really thrilling scene in a play you find yourself sitting on the edge of your seat; you clench your hands until the nails sink into your flesh; tears roll down your cheeks at other scenes, until you are ashamed of your emotion and wipe them furtively away; and you laugh uproariously at still other scenes. But your quickened heart-beats, your tears, and your laughter are, however, no evidence that you possess dramatic instinct—they are a tribute to the possession of that gift in the person who wrote the play. So do not confuse appreciation—the ultimate result of another's gift—with the ability to create: they

---

[67] Not organically defective, as were the ears of the great composer, Beethoven, but tone-deaf, as a person may be color-blind.

are two very different things.

No more does comprehension of a dramatist's methods—a sort of detached and often cold appreciation—indicate the possession of gifts other than those of the critic.

> Dramatic instinct is the ability to see the dramatic moments in real life; to grasp the dramatic possibilities; to pick out the thrills, the tears and the laughter, and to lift these out from the mass and set them—combined, coherent and convincing—in a story that seems truer than life itself, when unfolded on the stage by characters who are more real than reality. [68]

Elizabeth Woodbridge in her volume, The Drama, says: "It is in finding the mean between personal narrowness which is too selective, and photographic impersonality that is not selective at all, that the individuality of the artist, his training, and his ideals, are tested. It is this that determines how much his work shall possess of what we may call poetic, or artistic, truth." [end footnote]

Yet, true as it is that dramatic ability inevitably shines through finished drama when it is well played upon the stage, there are so many determining factors of pleasing theme, acting, production and even of audience—and so many little false steps both in manuscript and presentation; which might be counted unfortunate accident—that the failure of a play is not always a sure sign that the playwright lacks dramatic instinct. If it were, hardly one of our successful dramatists of today would have had the heart to persevere—for some wrote twenty full-evening plays before one was accepted by a manager, and then plodded through one or more stage failures before they were rewarded with final success. If producing managers could unerringly tell who has dramatic instinct highly developed and who has it not at all, there would be few play failures and the show-business would cease to be a gamble that surpasses even horse-racing for hazard.

Not only is it impossible for anyone to weigh the quantity or to assay the quality of dramatic instinct—whether in his own or another's breast—but it is as nearly impossible for anyone to decide from reading a manuscript whether a play will succeed or fail. Charles Frohman is reported to have said: "A man who could pick out winners would be worth a salary of a million dollars a year."

And even when a play is put into rehearsal the most experienced men in the business cannot tell unerringly whether it will succeed or fail before an audience. An audience—the heart of the crowd, the intellect of the mass, whatever you wish to call it—is at once the jury that tries a play and the judge who pronounces sentence to speedy death or a long and happy life. It is an audience, the "crowd," that awards the certificate of possession of dramatic instinct. [69]

From three of the ablest critics of the "theatre crowd" I quote a tabloid

---

[68] Arniel in his Journal says: "The ideal, after all, is truer than the real; for the ideal is the eternal element in perishable things; it is their type, their sum, their 'raison d'etre,' their formula in the book of the Creator, and therefore at once the most exact and the most condensed expression of them."

[69] [four paragraphs:]

statement:

"The theatre is a function of the crowd," says Brander Matthews, "and the work of the dramatist is conditioned by the audience to which he meant to present it. In the main, this influence is wholesome, for it tends to bring about a dealing with themes of universal interest. To some extent, it may be limiting and even harmful—but to what extent we cannot yet determine in our present ignorance of that psychology of the crowd which LeBon has analyzed so interestingly."

Here is M. LeBon's doctrine neatly condensed by Clayton Hamilton: "The mental qualities in which men differ from one another are the acquired qualities of intellect and character; but the qualities in which they are one are basic passions of the race. A crowd, therefore, is less intellectual and more emotional than the individuals that compose it. It is less reasonable, less judicious, less disinterested, more credulous, more primitive, more partisan; and hence, a man, by the mere fact that he forms a part of an organized crowd, descends several rungs on the ladder of civilization. Even the most cultured and intellectual of men, when he forms an atom of a crowd, loses consciousness of his acquired mental qualities, and harks back to his primal nakedness of mind. The dramatist, therefore, because he writes for the crowd, writes for an uncivilized and uncultivated mind, a mind richly human, vehement in approbation, violent in disapproval, easily credulous, eagerly enthusiastic, boyishly heroic, and carelessly thinking."

And Clayton Hamilton himself adds that, ". . .both in its sentiments and in its opinions, the crowd is hugely commonplace. It is incapable of original thought and of any but inherited emotion. It has no speculation in its eyes. What it feels was felt before the flood; and what it thinks, its fathers thought before it. The most effective moments in the theatre are those that appeal to commonplace emotions—love of women, love of home, love of country, love of right, anger, jealousy, revenge, ambition, lust and treachery."

[end footnote]

2. What "Good Drama" Is

By what standards, then, do producers decide whether a play has at least a good chance of success? How is it possible for a manager to pick a successful play even once in a while? Why is it that managers do not produce failures all the time?

Leaving outside of our consideration the question of changeable fashions in themes, and the commercial element (which includes the number of actors required, the scenery, costumes and similar factors), let us devote our attention, as the manager does, to the determining element—the story.

Does the story grip? Does it thrill? Does it lure to laughter? Does it touch to tears? Is it well constructed—that is, does it interest every minute of the time? Is every word, is every action, thoroughly motivated? Is the dialogue fine? Are the characters interesting, lovable, hateable, laughable, to be remembered? Does it state its problem clearly, so that everyone can comprehend it, develop its angle absorbingly, and end, not merely stop, with complete satisfaction? Could one little scene be added, or even one little passage be left out, without marring the whole? Is it true to life—truer than life? If it is all this, it is good drama.

Good drama is therefore more than plot. It is more than story plus characters, dialogue, acting, costumes, scenery—it is more than them all combined. Just as a man is more than his body, his speech, his dress, his movings to and fro in the scenes where he plays out his life, and even more than his deeds, so is a play more than the sum of all its parts. Every successful play, every great playlet, possesses a soul—a character, if you like—that carries a message to its audiences by means which cannot be analyzed.

But the fact that the soul of a great play cannot be analyzed does not prevent some other dramatist from duplicating the miracle in another play. And it is from a study of these great plays that certain mechanics of the drama—though, of course, they cannot explain the hidden miracle—have been laid down as laws.

3. What is Dramatic?

These few observations upon the nature of drama, which have scarcely been materially added to since Aristotle laid down the first over two thousand years ago, will be taken up and discussed in their relation to the playlet in the chapter on plot construction. Here they have no place, because we are concerned now not with *how* the results are obtained, but with *what they are*.

Let us approach our end by the standard definition route. The word "drama" is defined by Webster as, "A composition in poetry or prose, or both, representing a picture of human life, arranged for action, and having a plot, developed by the words and actions of its characters, which culminates in a final situation of human interest. It is usually designed for production on the stage, with the accessories of costumes, scenery, music, etc."

"Dramatic," is defined as, "Of or pertaining to the drama; represented by action; appropriate to or in the form of a drama; theatrical. Characterized by the force and fidelity appropriate to the drama."

In this last sentence we have the first step to what we are seeking: anything to be dramatic must be forceful, and it also must be faithful to life. And in the preceding sentence, "dramatic... is theatrical," we have a second step.

But what is "forceful," and why does Webster define anything that is dramatic as "theatrical"? To define one shadow by the name of another shadow is not making either clearer. However, the necessary looseness of the foregoing definitions is why they are so valuable to us—they are most suggestive.

If the maker of a dictionary, [70]hampered by space restrictions, finds it necessary to define "dramatic" by the word "theatrical," we may safely assume that theatrical effect has a foundation in the very heart of man. How many times have you heard someone say of another's action, "Oh, he did that just for theatrical effect"? Instantly you knew that the speaker was accusing the other of a desire to impress you by a carefully calculated action, either of the fineness of his

---

[70] Webster's Dictionary was chosen because it is, historically, closely associated with American life, and therefore would seem to reflect the best American thought upon the peculiar form of our own drama.

own character or of the necessity and righteousness of your doing what he suggested so forcefully. We need not go back several thousand years to Aristotle to determine what is dramatic. In the promptings of our own hearts we can find the answer. [71]

What is dramatic, is not what falls out as things ordinarily occur in life's flow of seemingly disconnected happenings; it is what occurs with precision and purpose, and with results which are eventually recognizable as being far beyond the forces that show upon its face. In an illuminating flash that reveals character, we comprehend what led up to that instant and what will follow. It is the revealing flash that is dramatic. Drama is a series of revealing flashes.

"This is not every-day life," we say, "but *typical* life—life as it would be if it were compactly ordered—life purposeful, and leading surely to an evident somewhere."

And, as man's heart beats high with hope and ever throbs with justice, those occurrences that fall out as he would wish them are the ones he loves the best; in this we find the reason for "poetic justice"—the "happy ending." For, as "man is of such stuff as dreams are made of," so are his plays made of his dreams. Here is the foundation of what is dramatic.

Yet, the dramatic ending may be unhappy, if it rounds the play out with big and logical design. Death is not necessarily poignantly sad upon the stage, because death is life's logical end. And who can die better than he who dies greatly? [72]Defeat, sorrow and suffering have a place as exquisitely fitting as success, laughter and gladness, because they are inalienable elements of life. Into every life a little sadness must come, we know, and so the lives of our stage-loves may be "draped with woe," and we but love them better.

Great souls who suffer, either by the hand of Fate, or unjustly through the machinations of their enemies, win our sympathy for their sorrows and our admiration by their noble struggles. If Fate dooms them, there may be no escape, and still we are content; but if they suffer by man's design, there must be escape from sorrow and defeat through happiness to triumph—for, if it were not so, they would not be great. The heart of man demands that those he loves upon the stage succeed, or fail greatly, because the hero's dreams are our dreams—the hero's life is ours, the hero's sorrows are our own, and because they are ours, the hero must triumph over his enemies.

---

[71] Shelley, in his preface to Cenci, says: "The highest moral purpose aimed at in the highest species of the drama is the teaching of the human heart, through its sympathies and antipathies, the knowledge of itself."

[72] "The necessity that tragedy and the serious drama shall possess an element of greatness or largeness—call it nobility, elevation, what you will—has always been recognized. The divergence has come when men have begun to say what they meant by that quality, and—which is much the same thing—how it is to be attained. Even Aristotle, when he begins to analyze methods, sounds, at first hearing, a little superficial." Elizabeth Woodbridge, The Drama, pp. 23-24.

4. The Law of the Drama

Thus, for the very reason that life is a conflict and because man's heart beats quickest when he faces another man, and leaps highest when he conquers him, the essence of the dramatic is—conflict. Voltaire in one of his letters said that every scene in a play should represent a combat. In "Memories and Portraits," Stevenson says: "A good serious play must be founded on one of the passionate cruces of life, where duty and inclination come nobly to the grapple." Goethe, in his "William Meister" says: "All events oppose him [the hero] and he either clears and removes every obstacle out of his path, or else becomes their victim." But it was the French critic, Ferdinand Brunetiere, who defined dramatic law most sharply and clearly, and reduced it to such simple terms that we may state it in this one free sentence: (Drama is a struggle of wills and its outcome.")

In translating and expounding Brunetiere's theory, Brander Matthews in his "A Study of the Drama" condenses the French critic's reasoning into these illuminating paragraphs:

"It [the drama] must have some essential principle of its own. If this essential principle can be discovered, then we shall be in possession of the sole law of the drama, the one obligation which all writers for the stage must accept. Now, if we examine a collection of typical plays of every kind, tragedies and melodramas, comedies and farces, we shall find that the starting point of everyone of them is the same. Some one central character wants something; and this exercise of volition is the mainspring of the action. . . . In every successful play, modern or ancient, we shall find this clash of contending desires, this assertion of the human will against strenuous opposition of one kind or another.

"Brunetiere made it plain that the drama must reveal the human will in action; and that the central figure in a play must know what he wants and must strive for it with incessant determination. . . .Action in the drama is thus seen to be not mere movement or external agitation; it is the expression of a will which knows itself.

"The French critic maintained also that, when this law of the drama was once firmly grasped, it helped to differentiate more precisely the several dramatic species. If the obstacles against which the will of the hero has to contend are insurmountable, Fate or Providence or the laws of nature—then there is tragedy, and the end of the struggle is likely to be death, since the hero is defeated in advance. But if these obstacles are not absolutely insurmountable, being only social conventions and human prejudices, then the hero has a chance to attain his desire,—and in this case, we have the serious drama without an inevitably fatal ending. Change this obstacle a little, equalize the conditions of the struggle, set two wills in opposition—and we have comedy. And if the obstacle is of still a lower order, merely an absurdity of custom, for instance, we find ourselves in farce."

Here we have, sharply and brilliantly stated, the sole law of drama—whether it be a play in five acts requiring two hours and a half to present, or a playlet taking but twenty minutes. This one law is all that the writer need keep in mind as the great general guide for plot construction.

Today, of course, as in every age when the drama is a bit more virile than in the years that have immediately preceded it, there is a tendency to break away from conventions and to cavil at definitions. This is a sign of health, and has in the past often been the first faint stirring which betokened the awakening of the drama to greater uses. In the past few years, the stage, both here and abroad, has been throbbing with dramatic unrest. The result has been the presentation of oddities—a mere list of whose names would fill a short chapter—which have aimed to "be different." And in criticising these oddities—whose differences are more apparent than real—critics of the soundness and eminence of Mr. William Archer in England, and Mr. Clayton Hamilton in America, have taken the differences as valid ground for opposing Brunetiere's statement of the law of the drama.

Mr. Hamilton, in his thought-provoking "Studies in Stage-craft," takes occasion to draw attention to the fact that Brunetiere's statement is not as old as Aristotle's comments on the drama. Mr. Hamilton seemingly objects to the eagerness with which Brunetiere's statement was accepted when first it was made, less than a quarter century ago, and the tenacity with which it has been held ever since; while acknowledging its general soundness he denies its truth, more on account of its youth, it would seem, than on account of the few exceptions that "prove it," putting to one side, or forgetting, that its youth is not a fault but a virtue, for had it been stated in Aristotle's day, Brunetiere would not have had the countless plays from which to draw its truth, after the fruitful manner of a scientist working in a laboratory on innumerable specimens of a species. Yet Mr. Hamilton presents his criticism with such critical skill that he sums it all up in these judicial sentences:

"...But if this effort were ever perfectly successful, the drama would cease to have a reason for existence, and the logical consequence would be an abolition of the theatre.... But on the other hand, if we judge the apostles of the new realism less by their ultimate aims than by their present achievements, we must admit that they are rendering a very useful service by holding the mirror up to many interesting contrasts between human characters which have hitherto been ignored in the theatre merely because they would not fit into the pattern of the well-made play."

As to the foremost critical apostle of the "new realism"—which seeks to construct plays which begin anywhere and have no dramatic ending and would oppose the force of wills by a doubtfully different "negation of wills"—let us now turn to Mr. William Archer and his very valuable definition of the dramatic in his "Play-Making":

"The only really valid definition of the dramatic is: any representation of imaginary personages which is capable of interesting an average audience assembled in a theatre.... Any further attempt to limit the term 'dramatic' is simply the expression of an opinion that such-and-such forms of representation will not be found to interest an audience; and this opinion may always be rebutted by experiment."

Perhaps a truer and certainly as inclusive an observation would be that the word "dramatic," like the words "picturesque" and "artistic," has one meaning that is historical and another that is creative or prophetic. To say of anything that it is dramatic is to say that it partakes of the nature of all drama that has gone before, for "ic" means "like." But dramatic does not mean only this, it means besides, as Alexander Black expresses it, that "the new writer finds all the world's dramatic properties gathered as in a storehouse for his instruction. Under the inspiration of the life of the hour, the big man will gather from them what is dramatic today, and the bigger man will see, not only what was dramatic yesterday and what is dramatic today, but what will be dramatic tomorrow and the day after tomorrow."

Now these admirably broad views of the drama and the dramatic are presented because they are suggestive of the unrestricted paths that you may tread in selecting your themes and deciding on your treatment of them in your playlets. True, they dangerously represent the trend of "individualism," and a master of stagecraft may be individual in his plot forms and still be great, but the novice is very likely to be only silly. So read and weigh these several theories with care. Be as individual as you like in the choice of a theme—the more you express your individuality the better your work is likely to be—but in your treatment tread warily in the footprints of the masters, whose art the ages have proved to be true. Then you stand less chance of straying into the underbrush and losing yourself where there are no trails and where no one is likely to hear from you again.

5. The Essence of the Dramatic lies in Meaning, not in Movement or in Speech

But clear and illuminating as these statements of the law of the drama are, one point needs slight expansion, and another vital point, not yet touched upon, should be stated, in a volume designed not for theory but for practice.

The first is, "Action in the drama is thus seen to be not mere movement or external agitation; it is the expression of a will which knows itself." Paradoxical as it may seem, action that is dramatic is not "action," as the word is commonly understood. Physical activity is not considered at all; the action of a play is not acting, but plot—story. Does the story move—not the bodies of the actors, but the merely mental recounting of the narrative? As the French state the principle in the form of a command, "Get on with the story! Get on!" This is one-half of the playwright's action problem.

The other half—the other question—deals, not with the story itself, but with how it is made to "get on." How it is told in action—still mental and always mental, please note—is what differentiates the stage story from other literary forms like the novel and the short-story. It must be told dramatically or it is not a stage story; and the dramatic element must permeate its every fibre. Not only must the language be dramatic—slang may in a given situation be the most dramatic language that could be used—and not only must the quality of the story itself be dramatic, but the scene-steps by which the story is unfolded must scintillate with the soul of the dramatic—revealing flashes.

To sum up, the dramatic, in the final analysis, has nothing whatever to do with characters moving agitatedly about the stage, or with moving at all, because the dramatic lies not in what happens but in what the happening means. Even a murder may be undramatic, while the mere utterance of the word "Yes," by a paralyzed woman to a paralyzed man may be the most dramatic thing in the world. Let us take another instance: Here is a stage—in the centre are three men bound or nailed to crosses. The man at the left turns to the one in the middle and sneers:

"If you're a god, save yourself and us."

The one at the left interrupts,

"Keep quiet! We're guilty, we deserve this, but this Man doesn't."

And the Man in the centre says,

"This day shalt thou be with me in paradise."

Could there be anything more dramatic than that? [73]

To carry this truth still further, let me offer two examples out of scores that might be quoted to prove that the dramatic may not even depend upon speech.

In one of Bronson Howard's plays, a man the police are after conspires with his comrades to get him safely through the cordon of guards by pretending that he is dead. They carry him out, his face covered with a cloth. A policeman halts them—not a word is spoken—and the policeman turns down the cover from the face. Dramatic as this all is, charged as it is with meaning to the man there on the stretcher and to his comrades, there is even more portentous meaning in the facial expression of the policeman as he reverently removes his helmet and motions the bearers to go on—the man has really died.

The movements are as simple and unagitated as one could imagine, and not one word is spoken, yet could you conceive of anything more dramatic? Again, one of the master-strokes in Bulwer-Lytton's "Richelieu" is where the Cardinal escapes from the swords of his enemies who rush into his sleeping apartments to slay him, by lying down on his bed with his hands crossed upon his breast, and by his ward's lover (but that instant won to loyalty to Richelieu) announcing to his fellow conspirators that they have come too late—old age has forestalled them, "Richelieu is dead."

6. Comedy is Achieved in the Same Dramatic Way

The only difference between the sublime and the ridiculous is the proverbial step. The sad and the funny are merely a difference of opinion, of viewpoint. Tragedy and comedy are only ways of looking at things. Often it is but a difference of to whom the circumstance happens, whether it is excruciatingly funny or unutterably sad. If you are the person to whom it happens, there is no argument about it—it is sad; but the very same thing happening to another person would be—funny.

Take for example, the everyday occurrence of a high wind and a flying hat: If

---

[73] Do not attempt to stage this sacred scene. However, Ran Kennedy, who wrote The Servant in the House, did so at Winthrop Ames' Little Theatre, New York, in an evening of one-act plays, with surprising results.

the hat is yours, you chase it with unutterable thoughts—not the least being the consciousness that hundreds may be laughing at you—and if, just as you are about to seize the hat, a horse steps on it, you feel the tragedy of going all the way home without a hat amid the stares of the curious, and the sorrow of having to spend your good money to buy another.

But let that hat be not yours but another's and not you but somebody else be chasing it, and the grins will play about your mouth until you smile. Then let the horse step on the hat and squash it into a parody of a headgear, just as that somebody else is about to retrieve it—and you will laugh outright. As Elizabeth Woodbridge in summing up says, "the whole matter is seen to be dependent on perception of relations and the assumption of a standard of reference."

Incidentally the foregoing example is a very clear instance of the comic effect that, like the serious or tragic effect, is achieved without words. Any number of examples of comedy which secure their effect without action will occur to anyone, from the instance of the lackadaisical Englishman who sat disconsolately on the race track fence, and welcomed the jockey who had ridden the losing horse that had swept away all his patrimony, with these words: "Aw, I say, what detained you?" [74] to the comedy that was achieved without movement or words in the expressive glance that the owner of the crushed headgear gave the guileless horse.

Precisely as the tragic and the serious depend for their best effects upon character-revealing flashes and the whole train of incidents which led up to the instant and lead away from it, does the comic depend upon the revealing flash that is the essence of the dramatic, the veritable soul of the stage.

7. Tragedy, the Serious, Comedy, and Farce, all Depend on their Dramatic Meaning in the Minds of the Audience

No matter by what technical means dramatic effect is secured, whether by the use of words and agitated movement, or without movement, or without words, or sans both, matters not; the illuminating flash which reveals the thought behind it all, the meaning to the characters and their destiny—in which the audience is breathlessly interested because they have all unconsciously taken sides—is what makes the dramatic. Let me repeat: It is not the incident, whatever it may be, that is dramatic, but the illuminating flash that reveals to the minds of the audience the *meaning* of it.

Did you ever stand in front of a newspaper office and watch the board on which a baseball game, contested perhaps a thousand miles away, is being played with markers and a tiny ball on a string? There is no playing field stretching its cool green diamond before that crowd, there are no famous players present, there is no crowd of adoring fans jamming grand stand and bleachers; there is only a small board, with a tiny ball swaying uncertainly on its string, an invisible man to operate it, markers to show the runs, and a little crowd of hot, tired men and

---

[74] It would seem needless to state categorically that the sources of humor, and the technical means by which comedy is made comic, have no place in the present discussion. We are only concerned with the flashes by which comedy, like tragedy, is revealed.

office boys mopping their faces in the shadeless, dirty street. There's nothing pretty or pleasant or thrillingly dramatic about this.

But wait until the man behind the board gets the flashes that tell him that a Cravath has knocked the ball over the fence and brought in the deciding run in the pennant race! Out on the board the little swaying ball flashes over the mimic fence, the tiny piece of wood slips to first and chases the bits of wood that represent the men on second and third—*home*! "Hurray! Hurray!! Hurray!!!" yell those weary men and office boys, almost bursting with delight. Over what? Not over the tiny ball that has gone back to swaying uncertainly on its string, not over the tiny bits of board that are now shoved into their resting place, not even over those runs—but over what those runs *mean*!

And so the playlet writer makes his audience go wild with delight— not by scenery, not by costumes, not by having famous players, not by beautifully written speeches, not even by wonderful scenes that flash the dramatic, but by what those scenes in the appealing story *mean* to the characters and their destiny, whereby each person in the audience is made to be as interested as though it were to *him* these things were happening with all their *dramatic meaning* of sadness or gladness.

However, it is to the dramatic artist only that ability is given to breathe nobility into the whole and to charge the singleness of effect with a vitality which marks a milestone in countless lives.

In this chapter we have found that the essence of drama is conflict— a clash of wills and its outcome; that the dramatic consists in those flashes which reveal life at its significant, crucial moments; and that the dramatic method is the way of telling the story with such economy of attention that it is comprehended by means of those illuminating flashes which both reveal character and show in an instant all that led up to the crisis as well as what will follow.

Now let us combine these three doctrines in the following definition, which is peculiarly applicable to the playlet:

> Drama—whether it be serious or comic in tone—is a representation of reality arranged for action, and having a plot which is developed to a logical conclusion by the words and actions of its characters and showing a single situation of big human interest; the whole is told in a series of revealing flashes of which the final illuminating revelation rounds out the entire plot and leaves the audience with a single vivid impression.

Finally, we found that the physical movements of the characters often have nothing to do with securing dramatic effect, and that even words need not of necessity be employed. Hence dramatic effect in its final analysis depends upon what meaning the various minor scenes and the final big situation have for the characters and their destinies, and that this dramatic effect depends, furthermore, upon the big broad meaning which it bears to the minds of the audience, who have taken sides and feel that the chief character's life and destiny represent their own, or what they would like them to be, or fear they might be. In the next chapter we shall see how the dramatic spirit is given form by plot structure.

CHAPTER XIV

THE STRUCTURAL ELEMENTS OF PLOT

IN the chapter on the germ idea we saw that the theme or subject of a playlet is a problem that must be solved with complete satisfaction. In this chapter we shall see how the problem—which is the first creeping form of a plot—is developed and expanded by the application of formal elements and made to grow into a plot. At the same time we shall see how the dramatic element of plot—discussed in the preceding chapter—is given form and direction in logical expression.

I. WHAT IS A PLAYLET PLOT?

You will recall that our consideration of the germ idea led us farther afield than a mere consideration of a theme or subject, or even of the problem—as we agreed to call the spark that makes the playlet go. In showing how a playlet writer gets an idea and how his mind works in developing it, we took the problem of "The System" and developed it into a near-plot form. It may have seemed to you at the time that the problem we assumed for the purpose of exposition was worked out very carefully into a plot, but if you will turn back to it now, you will realize how incomplete the elaboration was—it was no more complete than any germ idea should be before you even consider spending time to build it into a playlet.

Let us now determine definitely what a playlet plot is, consider its structural elements and then take one of the fine examples of a playlet in the Appendix and see how its plot is constructed.

The plot of a playlet is its story. It is the general outline, the plan, the skeleton which is covered by the flesh of the characters and clothed by their words. If the theme or problem is the heart that beats with life, then the scenery amid which the animated body moves is its habitation, and the dramatic spirit is the soul that reveals meaning in the whole.

To hazard a definition:

> A playlet plot is a sequence of events logically developed out of a theme or problem, into a crisis or entanglement due to a conflict of the characters' wills, and then logically untangled again, leaving the characters in a different relation to each other—changed in themselves by the crisis.

Note that a mere series of incidents does not make a plot—the presence of crisis is absolutely necessary to plot. If the series of events does not develop a complication that changes the characters in themselves and in their relations to each other, there can be no plot. If this is so, let us now take the sequence of events that compose the story of "The Lollard" [75] and see what constitutes them a plot. I shall

---

[75] Edgar Allan Woolf's fine satirical comedy to be found in the Appendix.

not restate its story, only repeat it in the examination of its various points[76].

The coming of Angela Maxwell to Miss Carey's door at 2 A.M.—unusual as is the hour—is just an event; the fact that Angela has left her husband, Harry, basic as it is, is but little more than an event; the entrance of the lodger, Fred Saltus, is but another event, and even Harry Maxwell's coming in search of his wife is merely an event—for if Harry had sat down and argued Angela out of her pique, even though Fred were present, there would have been no complication, save for the cornerstone motive of her having left him. If this sequence of events forms merely a mildly interesting narrative, what, then, is the complication that weaves them into a plot?

The answer is, in Angela's falling in love with Fred's broad shoulders, wealth of hair and general good looks—this complication develops the crisis out of Harry's wanting Angela. If Harry hadn't cared, there would have been no drama—the drama comes from Harry's wanting Angela when Angela wants Fred; Angela wants something that runs counter to Harry's will—*there* is the clash of wills out of which flashes the dramatic.

But still there would be no plot—and consequently no playlet—if Harry had acknowledged himself beaten after his first futile interview with Angela. The entanglement is there—Harry has to untangle it. He has to win Angela again—and how he does it, on Miss Carey's tip, you may know from reading the playlet. But, if you have read it, did you realize the dramatic force of the unmasking of Fred—accomplished without (explanatory) words, merely by making Fred run out on the stage and dash back into his room again? *There* is a fine example of the revealing flash! This incident—made big by the dramatic—is the ironical solvent that loosens the warp of Angela's will and prepares her for complete surrender. Harry's entrance in full regimentals—what woman does not love a uniform?— is merely the full rounding out of the plot that ends with Harry's carrying his little wife home to happiness again.

But, let us pursue this examination further, in the light of the preceding chapter. There would have been no drama if the *meaning* of these incidents had not—because Angela is a "character" and Harry one, too—been inherent in them. There would have been no plot, nothing of dramatic spirit, if Harry had not been made by those events to realize his mistake and Angela had not been made to see that Harry was "no worse" than another man. It is the *change* in Harry and the *change* in Angela that changes their relations to each other—therein lies the essence of the plot. [77]

---

[76] As a side light, you see how a playlet theme differs from a playlet plot. You will recall that in the chapter on "The Germ Idea," the theme of The Lollard was thus stated in terms of a playlet problem: "A foolish young woman may leave her husband because she has 'found him out,' yet return to him when she discovers that another man is no better than he is." Compare this brief statement with the full statement of the plot given hereafter.

[77] Unfortunately, the bigger, broader meaning we all read into this satire of life, cannot enter into our consideration of the structure of plot. It lies too deep in the texture of the playwright's mind and genius to admit of its being plucked out by the roots for critical

Now, having determined what a plot is, let us take up its structural parts and see how these clearly understood principles make the construction of a playlet plot in a measure a matter of clear thinking.

II. THE VITAL PARTS OF THE PLOT

We must swerve for a moment and cut across lots, that we may touch every one of the big structural elements of plot and relate them with logical closeness to the playlet, summing them all up in the end and tying them closely into—what I hope may be—a helpful definition, on the last page of this chapter.

The first of the structural parts that we must consider before we take up the broader dramatic unities, is the seemingly obvious one that *a plot has a beginning, a middle and an ending.*

There has been no clearer statement of this element inherent in all plots, than that made by Aristotle in his famous twenty-century old dissection of tragedy; he says:

"Tragedy is an imitation of an action, that is complete and whole, and of a certain magnitude (not trivial). . . . A whole is that which has a beginning, middle and end. A beginning is that which does not itself follow anything by causal necessity, but after which something naturally is or comes to be. An end, on the contrary, is that which itself naturally follows some other thing, either by necessity or in the regular course of events, but has nothing to follow it. A middle is that which naturally follows something as some other thing follows it. A well-constructed plot, therefore, must neither begin nor end at haphazard, but conform to the type here described." [78]

Let us state the first part of the doctrine in this way:

1. The Beginning Must State the Premises of the Problem Clearly and Simply

Although life knows neither a beginning nor an end—not your life nor mine, but the stream of unseparate events that make up existence—a work of art, like the playlet, must have both. The beginning of any event in real life may lie far back in history; its immediate beginnings, however, start out closely together and distinctly in related causes and become more indistinctly related the farther back they go. Just where you should consider the event that is the crisis of your playlet has its beginning, depends upon how you want to tell it—in other words, it depends upon you. No one can think for you, but there are one or two observations upon the nature of plot-beginnings that may be suggestive.

In the first place, no matter how carefully the dramatic material has been severed from connection with other events, it cannot be considered entirely

---

examination. The bigger meaning is there—we all see it, and recognize that it stamps The Lollard as good drama. Each playwright must work out his own meanings of life for himself and weave them magically into his own playlets; this is something that cannot be added to a man, that cannot be satisfactorily explained when seen, and cannot be taken away from him.

[78] Aristotle, Poetics VII.

independent. By the very nature of things, it must have its roots in the past from which it springs, and these roots—the foundations upon which the playlet rises—must be presented to the audience at the very beginning.

If you were introducing a friend of yours and his sister and brother to your family, who had never met them before, you would tell which one was your particular friend, what his sister's name was, and his brother's name, too, and their relationship to your friend. And, if the visit were unexpected, you would—naturally and unconsciously—determine how they happened to come and how long you might have the pleasure of entertaining them; in fact, you would fix every fact that would give your family a clear understanding of the event of their presence. In other words, you would very informally and delicately establish their status, by outlining their relations to you and to each other, so that your family might have a clear understanding of the situation they were asked to face.

This is precisely what must be done at the very beginning of a playlet—the friends, who are the author's characters, must be introduced to his interested family, the audience, with every bit of information that is necessary to a clear understanding of the playlet's situation. These are the roots from which the playlet springs—the premise of its problem. Precisely as "The Lollard" declares in its opening speeches who Miss Carey is and who Angela Maxwell is, and that Angela is knocking at Miss Carey's door at two o'clock in the morning because she has left Harry, her husband, after a quarrel the roots of which lie in the past, so every playlet must state in its very first speeches, the "whos" and "whys"—the premises—out of which the playlet logically develops.

The prologue of "The Villain Still Pursued Her" is an excellent illustration of this point. When this very funny travesty was first produced, it did not have a prologue. It began almost precisely as the full-stage scene begins now, and the audience did not know whether to take it seriously or not. The instant he watched the audience at the first performance, the author sensed the problem he had to face. He knew, then, that he would have to tell the next audience and every other that the playlet is a farce, a roaring travesty, to get the full value of laughter that lies in the situations. He pondered the matter and saw that if the announcement in plain type on the billboards and in the program that his playlet was a travesty was not enough, he would have to tell the audience by a plain statement from the stage before his playlet began. So he hit upon the prologue that stamps the act as a travesty in its very first lines, introduces the characters and exposes the roots out of which the action develops so clearly that there cannot possibly be any mistake. And his reward was the making over of an indifferent success into one of the most successful travesties in vaudeville.

This conveying to the audience of the knowledge necessary to enable them to follow the plot is technically known as "exposition." It is one of the most important parts of the art of construction—indeed, it is a sure test of a playwright's dexterity. While there are various ways of offering preliminary information in the long drama—that is, it may be presented all at once in the opening scene of the first act, or homeopathically throughout the first act, or some minor bits of necessary information may be postponed even until the opening of the second act—there is only one way of presenting the information necessary to the understanding of the playlet: It must all be compressed into the very first speeches of the opening scene.

The clever playlet writer is advertised by the ease—the simplicity—with which he condenses every bit of the exposition into the opening speeches. You are right in the middle of things before you realize it and it is all done so skillfully that its straightforwardness leaves never a suspicion that the simplicity is not innate but manufactured; it seems artless, yet its artlessness is the height of art. The beginning of a playlet, then, must convey to the audience every bit of information about the characters and their relations to each other that is necessary for clear understanding. Furthermore, it must tell it all compactly and swiftly in the very first speeches, and by the seeming artlessness of its opening events it must state the problem so simply that what follows is foreshadowed and seems not only natural but inevitable.

2. The Middle Must Develop the Problem Logically and Solve the Entanglement in a "Big" Scene

For the purpose of perfect understanding, I would define the "middle" of a playlet as that part which carries the story on from the indispensable introduction to and into the scene of final suspense—the climax—in which the chief character's will breaks or triumphs and the end is decided. In "The Lollard" this would be from the entrance of Fred Saltus and his talk with Angela, to Miss Carey's exposure of Fred's "lollardness," which breaks down Angela's determination by showing her that her husband is no worse than Fred and makes it certain that Harry has only to return to his delightful deceptions of dress to carry her off with him home.

(a) *The "Exciting Force."* The beginning of the action that we have agreed to call the middle of a playlet, is technically termed "the exciting force." The substance of the whole matter is this: Remember what your story is and tell it with all the dramatic force with which you are endowed.

Perhaps the most common, and certainly the very best, place to "start the trouble"—to put the exciting force which arouses the characters to conflict—is the very first possible instant after the clear, forceful and foreshadowing introduction. The introduction has started the action of the story, the chief characters have shown what they are and the interest of the audience has been awakened. Now you must clinch that interest by having something happen that is novel, and promises in the division of personal interests which grow out of it to hold a punch that will stir the sympathies legitimately and deeply.

(b) *The "Rising Movement."* This exciting force is the beginning of what pundits call "the rising movement"—in simple words, the action which from now on increases in meaning vital to the characters and their destinies. What happens, of course, depends upon the material and the treatment, but there is one point that requires a moment's discussion here, although closely linked with the ability to seize upon the dramatic—if it is not, itself, the heart of the dramatic. This important point is, that in every story set for the stage, there are certain

(c) *Scenes that Must be Shown.* From the first dawn of drama until today, when the motion pictures are facing the very same necessity, the problem that has vexed playwrights most is the selection of what scenes must be shown. These all-important scenes are the incidents of the story or the interviews between characters that cannot be recounted by other characters. Call them dramatic scenes, essential scenes, what you will, if they are not shown actually happening, but are described by dialogue—the interest of the audience will lag and each person from the first seat in the orchestra to the last bench in the gallery will be disappointed and dissatisfied. For instance:

If, instead of Fred Saltus' appearing before the audience and having his humorously thoughtless but nevertheless momentous talk with Angela *in which Angela falls in love with him*, the interview had been told the audience by Miss Carey, there would have been no playlet. Nearly as important is the prologue of "The Villian Still Pursued Her"; Mr. Denvir found it absolutely necessary to show those characters to the audience, so that they might see them with their own eyes in their farcical relations to each other, before he secured the effect that made his playlet. Turn to "The System" and try to find even one scene there shown that could be replaced by narrative dialogue and you will see once more how important are the "scenes that must be shown."

One of the all-rules-in-one for writing drama that I have heard, though I cannot now recall what playwright told me, deals with precisely this point. He expressed it this way: "First tell your audience what you are going to do, then show it to them happening, and then tell 'em it has happened!" You will not make a mistake, of course, if you show the audience those events in which the dramatic conflict enters. The soul of a playlet is the clash of the wills of the characters, from which fly the revealing flashes; a playlet, therefore, loses interest for the audience when the scenes in which those wills clash and flash revealingly are not shown.

It is out of such revealing scenes that the rising movement grows, as Freytag says, "with a progressive intensity of interest." But, not only must the events progress and the climax be brought nearer, but the scenes themselves must broaden with force and revealing power. They must grow until there comes one big scene—"big" in every way—somewhere on the toes of the ending, a scene next to the last or the last itself.

(d) *The Climax.* Here is where the decisive blow is struck in a moment when the action becomes throbbing and revealing in every word and movement. In "The Lollard" it is when Fred makes his revealing dash through the room—this is the dramatic blow which breaks Angela's infatuation. It is the crowning point of the crowning scene in which the forces of the playlet culminate, and the "heart wallop"—as Tom Barry calls it[79]—is delivered and the decision is won and made.

---

[79] Vaudeville Appeal and the "Heart Wallop," by Tom Barry, author of The Upstart and Brother Fans, an interesting article in The Dramatic Mirror of December 16, 1914. For this and other valuable information I wish to acknowledge my indebtedness and to

Whatever this decision may be and however it is won and made, the climax must be first of all a real climax—it must be "big," whether it be a comedy scream or the seldom-seen tragic tear. Big in movement and expression it must be, depending for effect not on words but on the revealing flash; it must be the summit of the action; it must be the event toward which the entire movement has been rising; it must be the fulfillment of what was foreshadowed; it must be keen, quick, perfectly logical and *flash* the illuminating revelation, as if one would say, "Here, this is what I've kept you waiting for—my whole reason for being." Need I say that such a climax will be worth while?

And now, as the climax is the scene toward which every moment of the playlet—from the first word of the introduction and the first scene-statement of the playlet's problem—has been motivated, and toward which it has risen and culminated, so also the climax holds within itself the elements from which develops the ending.

3. The Ending Must Round the Whole Out Satisfyingly.

For the purpose of clearness, let me define the ending of a playlet as a scene that lies between the climax or culminating scene—in which the audience has been made to feel the coming-to-an-end effect—and the very last word on which the curtain descends. If you have ever watched a sailor splicing a rope, you will know what I mean when I say that the worker, reaching for the loose ends to finish the job off neatly, is like the playlet writer who reaches here and there for the playlet's loose ends and gathers them all up into a neat, workmanlike finish. The ending of a playlet must not leave unfulfilled any promises of the premise, but must fulfill them all satisfyingly.

The characteristics of a good playlet ending—besides the completeness with which the problem has been "proved" and the satisfyingness with which it all rounds out—are terseness, speed and "punch." If the climax is a part of the playlet wherein words may not be squandered, the ending is the place where words—you will know what I mean—may not be used at all. Everything that must be explained must be told by means which reach into the spectator's memory of what has gone before and make it the positive pole of the battery from which flash the wireless messages from the scene of action. As Emerson defined character as that which acts by mere presence without words, let me define the ending of a playlet as that which acts without words by the simple bringing together of the characters in their new relations.

The climax has said to the audience, "Here, this is what I've kept you waiting for—my whole reason for being," therefore the ending cannot dally—it must run swiftly to the final word. There is no excuse for the ending to linger over anything at all—the shot has been fired and the audience waits only for the smoke to clear away, that it may see how the bull's-eye looks. The swifter you can blow the smoke away, show them that you've hit the bull's-eye dead in the centre, and bow

---

express my thanks to The Dramatic Mirror and its courteous Vaudeville Editor, Frederick James Smith.

yourself off amid their pleased applause, the better your impression will be.

Take these three examples:

When Fred Saltus dashes revealingly across the stage and back into his room again, "The Lollard's" climax is reached; and as soon as Angela exclaims "What 'a lollard' *that* is!" there's a ring at the door bell and in comes Harry to win Angela completely with his regimentals and to carry her off and bring the curtain down— *in eight very short speeches.*

In "The System," the climax arrives when the honest Inspector orders Dugan arrested and led away. Then he gives "The Eel" and Goldie their freedom and exits with a simple "Good Night"—and the curtain comes down—*all in seven speeches.*

The climax of "Blackmail" seems to come when Fallon shoots Mohun and Kelly breaks into the room—to the curtain it is *seven speeches*. But the real climax is reached when Kelly shouts over the telephone "Of course, in self-defense, you fool, *of course*, in self-defense." This is—*the last speech.*

Convincing evidence, is this not, of the speed with which the curtain must follow the climax?

And so we have come, to this most important point—the "finish" or "the curtain," as vaudeville calls it. The very last thing that must be shown, and the final word that must be said before the curtain comes down, are the last loose ends of the plot which must be spliced into place—the final illuminating word to round out the whole playlet humanly and cleverly. "The Lollard" goes back to Miss Carey's sleep, which Angela's knock on the door interrupted: "Now, thank Gawd, I'll get a little sleep," says Miss Carey as she puts out the light. A human, an everyday word it is, spoken like a reminiscent thrill—and down comes the curtain amid laughter and applause. A fine way to end.

But not the only way—let us examine "The System."

"Well, we're broke again," says Goldie tearfully. "We can't go West now, so there's no use packing." Now, note the use of business in the ending, and the surprise. The Eel goes stealthily to the window L, looks out, and pulls the dictograph from the wall. Then he comes down stage to Goldie who is sitting on the trunk and has watched him. He taps her on the shoulder, taking Dugan's red wallet out of his pocket. "Go right ahead and pack," says The Eel, while Goldie looks astonished and begins to laugh. The audience, too, look astonished and begin to laugh when they see that red wallet. It is a surprise—a surprise so cleverly constructed that it hits the audience hard just above the laughter-and-applause-belt— a surprise that made the act at least twenty-five per cent better than it would have been without it. And from it we may now draw the "rules" for the use of that most helpful and most dangerous element, surprise in the vaudeville finish:

Note first, that it was entirely logical for The Eel to steal the wallet—he is a pickpocket. Second, that the theft of the wallet is not of trivial importance to Goldie's destiny and to his—they are "broke" and they must get away; the money solves all their problems. And third, note that while The Eel's possession of the wallet is a surprise, the wallet itself is *not* a surprise—it has first played a most important part in the tempting of Goldie and has been shown to the audience not once but many times; and its very color—red—makes it instantly recognizable; the spectators know what it contains and what its contents mean to the destinies of both The Eel and Goldie—it is only that The Eel has it, that constitutes the surprise.

Now I must sound a warning against striving too hard after a surprise finish. The very nature of many playlets makes it impossible to give them such a curtain. If you have built up a story which touches the heart and brings tears to the eyes, and then turn it all into a joke, the chances are the audience will feel that their sympathies have been outraged, and so the playlet will fail. For instance, one playlet was ruined because right on top of the big, absorbing climax two of the characters who were then off stage stuck their heads in at the door and shouted at the hero of the tense situation, "April Fool."

Therefore, the following may be considered as an important "rule"; a playlet that touches the heart should never end with a trick or a surprise. [80]

Now, let me sum up these four elements of surprise:

> A surprise finish must be fitting, logical, vitally important, and revealingly dramatic; if you cannot give a playlet a surprise-finish that shall be all of these four things at once, be content with the simpler ending.

The importance of a playlet's ending is so well understood in vaudeville that the insistence upon a "great finish" to every playlet has sometimes seemed to be over-insistence, for, important as it is, it is no more important than a "great opening" and "great scenes." The ending is, of course, the final thing that quickens applause, and, coming last and being freshest in the mind of the audience, it is more likely to carry just a fair act to success than a fine act is likely to win with the handicap of a poor finish. But, discounting this to be a bit under the current valuation of "great finishes," we still may round out this discussion of the playlet's three important parts, with this temperate sentence:

> A well constructed playlet plot is one whose Beginning states the premises of its problem clearly and simply, whose Middle develops the problem logically and solves the entanglement in a "big" scene, and whose Ending rounds out the whole satisfyingly— with a surprise, if fitting.

But, temperate and helpful as this statement of a well constructed plot may be, there is something lacking in it. And that something lacking is the very highest test of plot—lightly touched on at various times, but which, although it enters into a playwright's calculations every step of the way, could not be logically considered in this treatise until the structure had been examined as a whole: I mean the formidable-sounding, but really very simple dramatic unities.

III. THE THREE DRAMATIC UNITIES

Now, but only for a moment, we must return to the straight line of investigation from which we swerved in considering the structural parts of a

---

[80] See Chapter XVIII, section III, par. 4.

playlet plot.

At the beginning of this chapter we saw that a simple narrative of events is made a plot by the addition of a crisis or entanglement, and its resolution or untying. Now, the point I wish to present with all the emphasis at my command, is that complication does not mean complexity.

1. Unity of Action

In other words, no matter how many events you place one after another—no matter how you pile incident upon incident—you will not have a plot unless you so *inter-relate* them that the removal of anyone event will destroy the whole story. Each event must depend on the one preceding it, and in turn form a basis for the one following, and each must depend upon all the others so vitally that if you take one away the whole collapses. [81]

(a) *Unity of Hero is not Unity of Action.* One of the great errors into which the novice is likely to fall, is to believe that because he makes every event which happens happen to the hero, he is observing the rule of unity. Nothing could be farther from the truth—nothing is so detrimental to successful plot construction. [82]

Aristotle tried to correct this evil, which he saw in the plays of the great Athenian poets, by saying: "The action is the first and most important thing, the characters only second;" and, "The action is not given unity by being made to concern only one person."

Remember, unity of action means unity of *story*.

(b) *Double-Action is Dangerous to Unity.* If you have a scene in which two minor characters come together for a reason vital to the plot, you must be extremely careful not to tell anything more than the facts that are vital. In long plays the use of what is called "double-action "—that is, giving to characters necessary to the plot an interest and a destiny separate from that of the chief characters—is, of course, recognized and productive of fine results. But, even in the five-act play, the use of double-action is dangerous. For instance: Shakespere developed Falstaff so humorously that today we sometimes carelessly think of "Henry IV" as a delightful comedy, when in reality it was designed as a serious drama—and is most serious, when Falstaff's lines are cut from the reading version to the right proportions for to-day's stage effect. If Shakespere nodded, it is a nod even the legitimate dramatist of today should take to heart, and the playlet writer—peculiarly restricted as to time—must engrave deeply in his memory.

The only way to secure unity of action is to concentrate upon your problem or theme; to realize that you are telling a *story*; to remember that each character, even your hero, is only a pawn to advance the story; and to cut away rigorously all non-essential events. If you will bear in mind that a playlet is only as good as its plot, that a plot is a *story* and that you must give to your story, as has been said, "A completeness—a kind of universal dovetailedness, a sort of general oneness," you

---

[81] See Aristotle, Poetics, Chapter VIII, and also Poe's criticism, The American Drama.
[82] See Freytag's Technique of the Drama, p. 36.

will have little difficulty in observing the one playlet rule that should never be broken—Unity of action.

2. Unity of Time

The second of the classical unities, unity of time, is peculiarly perplexing, if you study to "understand" and not merely to write. Briefly—for I must reiterate that our purpose is practice and not theory—the dramatists of every age since Aristotle have quarreled over the never-to-be-settled problem of what space of time a play should be permitted to represent. Those who take the stand that no play should be allowed to show an action that would require more than twenty-four hours for the occurrences in real life, base their premise on the imitative quality of the stage, rather than upon the selective quality of art. While those who contend that a play may disregard the classical unity of time, if only it preserves the unity of action, base their contention upon the fact that an audience is interested not in time at all—but in story. In other words, a play preserves the only unity worth preserving when it deals with the incidents that cause a crisis and ends by showing its effect, no matter whether the action takes story-years to occur or happens all in a story-hour.

If we were studying the long drama it might be worth our while to consider the various angles of this ancient dispute, but, fortunately, we have a practical and, therefore, better standard by which to state this unity in its application to the playlet. Let us approach the matter in this way:

Vaudeville is variety—it strives to compress into the space of about two hours and a half a great number of different acts which run the gamut of the entertainment forms, and therefore it cannot afford more than an average of twenty minutes to each. This time limit makes it difficult for a playlet to present effectively any story that does not occur in consecutive minutes. It has been found that even the lowering of the curtain for one second to denote the lapse of an hour or a year, has a tendency to distract the minds of the audience from the story and to weaken the singleness of effect without which a playlet is nothing.

On the other hand, this "rule" is not unbreakable: a master craftsman's genius is above all laws. In "The System" the first scene takes place in the evening; scene two, a little later the same evening; and scene three later that same night. The story is really continuous in time, but the story-time is not equal to the playing-time even though this playlet consumes nearly twice twenty minutes. But, you will note, the scenery changes help to keep the interest of the audience from flagging, and also stamp the lapses of time effectively.

A still greater violation of the "rule"—if it were stated as absolutely rigid—is to be found in Mr. Granville's later act, "The Yellow Streak," written in collaboration with James Madison. Here scene two takes place later in the evening of the first scene, and the third scene after a lapse of four months. But these two exceptions, out of many that might be cited, merely prove that dramatic genius can mold even the rigid time of the vaudeville stage to its needs.

Of course, there is the possibility of foreshortening time to meet the exigencies of vaudeville when the scene is not changed. For instance: a character telephones that he will be right over and solve the whole situation on which the punch of the playlet depends, and he enters five actual minutes later—although in real life it would take an hour to make the trip. This is an extreme instance, as time foreshortening goes, because it is one where the audience might grasp the disparity, and is given for its side-light of warning as well as for its suggestive value.

More simple foreshortenings of time are found in many playlets where the effect of an hour-or-more of events is compressed into the average twenty minutes. As an example of this perfectly safe use of shortening, note the quickness with which Harry returns to Miss Carey's apartment when he goes out to change into his regimentals. And as still safer foreshortenings, note the quickness with which Fred Saltus enters after Miss Carey goes to bed leaving Angela on the couch; and the quickness with which Angela falls in love with him—in fact, the entire compression inherent in the dramatic events which cannot be dissociated from time compression.

A safe attitude for a playlet writer to take, is that all of his action shall mimic time reality as closely as his dramatic moment and the time-allowance of presentation will permit. This is considered in all dramatic art to be the ideal.

A good way to obviate disparaging comparison is to avoid reference to time—either in the dialogue or by the movements of events.

To sum up the whole matter, a vaudeville playlet may be considered as preserving unity of time when its action occurs in continuous minutes of about the length the episode would take to occur in real life.

3. Unity of Place

The commercial element of vaudeville often makes it inadvisable for a playlet to show more than one scene—very often an otherwise acceptable playlet is refused production because the cost of supplying special scenes makes it a bad business venture. [83]

Yet it is permissible for a writer to give his playlet more than one place of happening—if he can make his story so compact and gripping that it does not lose in effect by the unavoidable few seconds' wait necessary to the changing of the scenery. But, even if his playlet is so big and dramatic that it admits of a change of scenes, he must conform it to the obvious vaudeville necessity of scenic alternation. [84]With this scenic "rule" the matter of unity of place in the playlet turns to the question of a playwright's art, which rules cannot limit.

This third and last unity of the playlet may, however, for all save the master-craftsman, be safely stated as follows:

Except in rare instances a playlet should deal with a story that requires but one set of scenery, thus conserving the necessities of commercial vaudeville, aiding the smooth running of a performance, and preserving the dramatic unity of place.

---

[83] See Chapter III.
[84] See Chapter I.

We may now condense the three dramatic unities into a statement peculiarly applicable to the playlet—which would seem as though specially designed to fulfill them all:

A playlet preserves the dramatic unities when it shows one action in one time and in one place.

And now it may be worth while once more to sum up what I have said about the elements of plot—of which the skeleton of every playlet must be made up:

A mere sequence of events is not a plot; to become a plot there must develop a crisis or entanglement due to a conflict of the characters' wills; the entanglement must be of such importance that when it is untangled the characters will be in a different relation to each other—changed in themselves by the crisis. A plot is divided into three parts: a Beginning, a Middle and an Ending. The Beginning must state the premises of the playlet's problem clearly and simply; the Middle must develop the problem logically and solve the entanglement in a "big" scene, and the Ending must round out the whole satisfyingly—with a surprise, if fitting. A plot, furthermore, must be so constructed that the removal of anyone of its component parts will be detrimental to the whole. It is told best when its action occurs in continuous time of about the length the episode would take to occur in real life and does not require the changing of scenery. Thus will a playlet be made to give the *singleness* of effect that is the height of playlet art.

CHAPTER XV

THE CHARACTERS IN THE PLAYLET

IN this chapter the single word "character" must, of necessity, do duty to express three different things. First, by "characters," as used in the title, I mean what the programs sometimes more clearly express by the words "persons of the play." Second, in the singular, it must connote what we all feel when we use the word in everyday life, as "he is a man of—good or bad—character." And third, and also in the singular, I would also have it connote, in the argot of the stage, "a character actor," meaning one who presents a distinct type—as, say, a German character, or a French character. It is because of the suggestive advantage of having one word to express these various things that the single term "characters" is used as the title of this chapter. But, that there may be no possible confusion, I shall segregate the different meanings sharply.

I. CHARACTERS VERSUS PLOT

In discussing how a playwright gets an idea, you will recall, we found that there are two chief ways of fashioning the playlet: First, a plot may be fitted with characters; second, characters may be fitted with a plot. In other words, the plot may be made most prominent, or the characters may be made to stand out above the story. You will also remember we found that the stage—the vaudeville quite as much as the legitimate—is "character-ridden," that is, an actor who has made a pronounced success in the delineation of one character type forever afterward wants another play or playlet "just like the last, but with a different plot," so that he can go right on playing the same old character. This we saw has in some cases resulted in the story being considered merely as a vehicle for a personality, often to the detriment of the playlet. Naturally, this leads us to inquire: is there not some just balance between characters and plot which should be preserved?

Were we considering merely dramatic theory, we would be perfectly right in saying that no play should be divisible into plot and characters, but that story and characters should be so closely twinned that one would be unthinkable without the other. As Brander Matthews says, "In every really important play the characters make the plot, and the story is what it is merely because the characters are what they are." An exceptionally fine vaudeville example—one only, it is agreeable to note, out of many that might be quoted from vaudeville's past and present—that has but two persons in the playlet is Will Cressy's "The Village Lawyer." One is a penniless old lawyer who has been saving for years to buy a clarionet. A woman comes in quest of a divorce. When he has listened to her story he asks twenty dollars advance fee. Then he persuades her to go back home—and hands the money back. There is a splendid climax. The old lawyer stands in the doorway of his shabby office looking out into the night. "Well," he sighs, "maybe I couldn't play the darned thing anyway!" If the lawyer had not been just what he was there would have been no playlet. But vital as the indissoluble union of plot and characters is in theory, we are not discussing theory; we are investigating practice, and practice from the beginner's standpoint, therefore let us approach the answer to our question in this way:

When you were a child clamoring for "a story" you did not care a snap of your fingers about anything except "Once upon a time there was a little boy—or a giant—or a dragon," who did something. You didn't care what the character was, but whatever it was, it had to do something, to be doing something all of the time. Even when you grew to youth and were on entertainment bent, you cared not so much what the characters in a story were, just so long as they kept on doing something—preferably "great" deeds, such as capturing a city or scuttling a ship or falling in love. It was only a little later that you came to find enjoyment in reading a book or seeing a play in which the chief interest came from some person who had admirable qualities or was an odd sort of person who talked in an odd sort of way. Was it George Cohan who said "a vaudeville audience is of the mental age of a nine-year-old child"?

Theoretically and, of course, practically too, when it is possible, the characters of a playlet should be as interesting as the plot. Each should vitally depend upon the other. But, if you must choose whether to sacrifice plot-interest or character-interest, save the interest of plot every time. As Aristotle says, "the action is the first and most important thing, the characters only secondary."

How a playwright begins to construct a play, whether he fits a plot with characters, or fits characters with a plot, does not matter. What matters is how he ends. If the story and the characters blend perfectly the result is an example of the highest art, but characters alone will never make a stage story—the playlet writer must end with plot. *Story* is for what the stage is made. Plot is the life blood of the playlet. To vivify cold dramatic incidents is the province of playlet characters.

II. THE PERSONS OF THE PLAYLET

While it is true that, no matter with what method he begins, a playwright may end by having a successful playlet, the clearer way to understanding is for us to suppose that you have your plot and are striving to fit it with live people—therefore I shall assume that such is the case. For if the reverse were the case and the characters were all ready to fit with a plot, the question would be primarily not of characters but of plot.

1. The Number of Persons

How many people shall I have in my playlet? ought to be one of the very first questions the writer asks, for enough has been said in the earlier chapters, it would seem, to establish the fact that vaudeville is first of all a commercial pursuit and after that an artistic profession. While there can be no hard and fast rule as to the number of persons there may be in a playlet, business economy dictates that there shall be no more than the action of the playlet positively demands. But before I say a short word about this general "rule," permit me to state another that comes fast upon its heels: A really big playlet—big in theme, in grip of action, and in artistic effect—may have even thrice the number of characters a "little" playlet may possess. Merit determines the number.

Let us find the reasons for these two general statements in this way:

In "The Lollard" there are four persons, while in "The System " there are thirteen speaking parts and a number of "supers." Would it then be correct to suppose that "The System" is a "bigger" playlet than "The Lollard"? It would not be safe to assume any such judgment, for the circuit that booked "The System" may have been in need of a playlet using a large number of persons to make what is known as a "flash," therefore the booking manager may have given orders that this playlet be built to make that flash, and the total return to the producer might not have been any greater proportionally than the return to the producer of the numerically smaller "The Lollard." Therefore of two playlets whose total effects are equal, the one having the lesser number of persons is the better producing gamble, and for this reason is more likely to be accepted when offered for sale.

If you will constantly bear in mind that you are telling a story of action and not of character, you will find very little difficulty in reducing the number of players from what you first supposed absolutely necessary. As just one suggestion: If your whole playlet hangs on an important message to be delivered, the property man, dressed as a messenger boy, may hand in the message without a word. I have chosen this one monotonously often-seen example because it is suggestive of the crux of the problem—the final force of a playlet is affected little by what the character says when he delivers a vital message. All that matters is the message itself. The one thing to remember in reducing the number of characters to the lowest possible number is—plot.

Four Persons the Average. While there are playlets ranging in number of characters from the two-person "The Village Lawyer," through "The Lollard's" four, to "The System's" thirteen speaking parts, and even more in rare instances, the average vaudeville playlet employs four people. But it is a fact of importance to note that a three-person playlet can be sold more easily—I am assuming an equal standard of merit—than a four-person playlet. And, by the same law of demand, a two-person playlet wins a quicker market than a three-person playlet. The reason for this average has its rise in the demands of the dramatic, and not merely in economy. The very nature of the playlet makes it the more difficult to achieve dramatic effect the more the number of characters is reduced. But while four persons are perfectly permissible in a playlet designed for vaudeville's commercial stage, the beginner would do well to make absolutely sure that he has reduced his characters to their lowest number before he markets his playlet, and, if possible, make a three-person or a two-person offering.

2. Selecting the Characters

There would seem to be little need, in this day of wide curiosity about all the forms of writing and those of playwriting in particular, to warn the beginner against straying far afield in search of characters whom he will not understand even when he finds them. Yet this is precisely the fault that makes failures of many otherwise good playlets. The whole art of selecting interesting characters may be summed up in one sentence—choose those that you know. The most interesting characters in the world are rubbing elbows with you every day.

Willard Mack—who developed into a successful legitimate playwright from vaudeville, and is best known, perhaps, for the expansion of his vaudeville act, "Kick in," into the long play of the same name—has this to say on the subject: "I say to the ambitious playwright, take the types you are familiar with. Why go to the Northwest, to New Orleans in the 40's, to the court of Louis XIV, for characters? The milkman who comes to your door in the morning, the motorman on the passing street car, the taxi driver, all have their human-interest stories. Anyone of them would make a drama. I never attempt to write anything that has not suggested itself from something in real life. I must know it has existed." [85]

Precisely as it is impossible to tell anyone how to grasp the dramatic and transplant it into a playlet, is it impossible to show how to seize on character and transplant it to the stage. Only remember that interesting characters are all about you, and you will have little difficulty—if you have, as the French say, the "flare."

III. FITTING CHARACTERS TO PLOT

It would seem that a playwright who has his plot all thought out would experience little difficulty in fitting the characters of a playlet into their waiting niches; it is easy, true enough—if his plot is perfectly dovetailed and motivated as to character. By this I mean, that in even a playlet in which plot rides the characters, driving them at its will to attain its end, logic must be used. And it certainly would not be logical to make your characters do anything which such persons would not do in real life. As there must be unity in plot, so must there be unity in character.

The persons in a playlet are not merely puppets, even if plot is made to predominate. They are—let us hope—live persons. I do not mean that you have transplanted living people to the stage, but that you have taken the elements of character that you require out of life and have combined these into a consistent whole to form characters necessary to your playlet. Therefore, you must be careful to make each character uniform throughout. You must not demand of any character anything you have not laid down in the premises of your problem—which presupposes that each character possesses certain definite and logical characteristics which make the plot what it is.

Bearing this single requirement firmly in mind, you must so motivate your plot that everything which occurs to a character rises out of that character's personality; you must make the crisis the outward evidence of his inner being and the change which comes through the climax the result of inner change. This was considered in the chapters on the dramatic and on plot construction and expressed when I said: It is the *meaning* hidden in the events that makes the dramatic. It is this inner meaning that lies in the soul of the character himself which marks the change in his own character and his own outward life.

---

[85] Willard Mack on the "Vaudeville Playlet," The New York Dramatic Mirror, March 3, 1915.

IV. CHARACTERIZATION

How a playwright delineates character in the persons of his playlet, is at once the easiest thing to explain and the most difficult for which to lay down helpful methods, for while the novelist and the short-story writer have three ways of telling their readers what manner of man it is in whom he asks interest, the dramatist has but two.

1. Methods of Characterization

First, a playwright may build up a characterization by having one character tell another what sort of a person the third is. Second, he may make the character show by his own speech and actions what he is. This latter is the dramatic way, and peculiarly the playlet way.

As the first method is perfectly plain in itself, I shall dismiss it with the suggestive warning that even this essentially undramatic method must partake of the dramatic to be most effective: to get the most out of one character's describing a second to a third, the reason for the disclosure must be bone-and-brawn a part of the action.

The two elements of the dramatic method are: First, the character may disclose his inner being by his own words, and second, by his actions.

The first is so intimately connected with the succeeding chapter on dialogue that I shall postpone its consideration until then and discuss here the disclosure of character through action.

When you meet a man whom you have never met before, you carry away with you a somewhat complete impression. Even though he has spoken but a word or two, his appearance first of all, the cut of his clothes, his human twinkle, the way he lights his cigar, the courteous way in which he gives precedence to another, or his rough way of "butting into" a conversation, all combine to give him a personality distinct from every other man's. What he does not disclose of himself by actions, you read into his personality yourself. "First impressions are the strongest," is a common saying—we make them strong by reading character on sight, by jumping at conclusions. Man does not need to have a whole life laid before him to form a judgment. Little things are what drive character impressions home.

It is this human trait of which the playwright makes use in the delineation of character. The playlet writer has even less time than the legitimate dramatist to stamp character. He must seize on the essentials, and with a few broad strokes make the character live as distinct from all other men.

For much of his characterization—aside from that absolutely inherent in the plot—the playlet writer depends upon the actor. By the use of costumes and of make-up, the age and station in life, even the business by which a character earns his daily bread, are made clear at a glance. And by the trick of a twitching mouth, a trembling hand, or a cunningly humble glance, the inner being is laid bare, with the help of a few vital words which are made to do duty to advance the story as well.

In a word, the playwright and the actor work in partnership, with broad strokes, relying upon the eager imagination of the audience to amplify the tiny sketch into a well-rounded, full personality. This is the method simply stated. It does not admit of the laying down of precepts.

2. The Choice of Names

In the old days of vaudeville the persons of a playlet were often named to fit their most prominent characteristic; for instance, a sneaky fellow would be named Sam Sly, and a pretty girl Madge Dimples. But with the change in fashion in the long play, the playlet has relegated this symbolical method of naming characters to burlesque and the lurid types of melodrama, and even there it is going out of fashion.

Today, names are carefully chosen to seem as life-like as do the characters themselves. Instead of trying to express characteristics by a name, the very opposite effect is sought, except when the character would in real life have a "monicker," or the naming of the character in the old way would serve to relate the act more closely to its form and awaken pleasing reminiscences. [86]The method today is to select a name that shall fit a character in a general way and yet be so unobtrusive that it will not be remarked.

Simple names are always the best. The shorter they are the better—usually nicknames, if true to life and the character, have a "homey" sort of sound that is worth securing. Bill, and Jack, and Madge, and Flo, or anyone of a hundred others, sound less formidable than William, and James, and Margaret, and Florence. Names that are long and "romantic" are usually amusing; merely listen to Algernon, Hortense, and Reginald Montmorency, and you have to smile—and not always with pleasure.

But for a name to be simple or short or unromantic does not solve the problem for all cases. A long "romantic" name might be the very best one you could choose for a certain character. [87]The name you should select depends on what effect you wish to secure. No one can tell you just what name to choose for a character you alone have in mind.

But do not make the mistake of pondering too long over the naming of your characters. It is not the name that counts, it is the character himself, and behind it all the action that has brought the character into being—your gripping plot.

And now, let us sum up this brief discussion of characters and characterization before we pass on to a consideration of dialogue. Because of time-restriction, a playlet must depend for interest upon plot rather than upon character. The average number of persons in a playlet is four. Interesting characters are to be found everywhere, and the playlet writer can delineate those he rubs elbows with better than those he does not know well and therefore cannot fully understand. The same unity demanded of a plot is required of a character—characters must be consistent. Characterization is achieved by the dramatic method of letting actions speak for themselves, is done in broad strokes growing out of the plot itself, and is conveyed in close partnership with the actor by working on the minds of the audience who take a meagre first impression and instantly build it up into a full portrait.

---

[86] See The System and My Old Kentucky Home, in the Appendix.
[87] See The Villain Still Pursued Her in the Appendix.

CHAPTER XVI

DIALOGUE IN THE PLAYLET

WE have now come to one of the least important elements of the playlet—yet a decorative element which wit and cleverness can make exceedingly valuable.

If it is true that scenery is the habitation in which the playlet moves, that its problem is the heart beating with life, that the dramatic is the soul which shines with meaning through the whole, that plot is the playlet's skeleton which is covered by the flesh of the characters—then the dialogue is, indeed, merely a playlet's clothes. Clothes do not make a man, but the world gives him a readier welcome who wears garments that fit well and are becoming. This is the whole secret of dialogue—speeches that fit well and are becoming.

1. What is Dialogue?

It has been said that "Romeo and Juliet" played in English in any country would be enjoyed by everyone, even though they could not understand a word of what was said. There is a story told about a Slav in Pennsylvania who could not speak one word of English, but who happened to come up from his work as a laborer in a coal mine just as the people were filing in to the performance of "The Two Orphans," and as he had nothing in particular to do, in he went—and nearly broke up the performance by the loudness of his sobbing. I shall never forget an experience of my own, when I took a good French friend to see David Warfield in "The Music Master"; this young chap could not understand more than a word here and there, but we were compelled to miss the last act because he cried so hard during the famous lost-daughter scene that he was ashamed to enter the theatre after the intermission.

Every great play is, in the last analysis, a pantomime. Words are unnecessary to tell a stage story that has its wellspring deep in the emotions of the human heart. Words can only embellish it. A great pantomimist—a Mlle. Dazie, who played Sir James M. Barrie's "The Pantaloon" in vaudeville without speaking a word; a Pavlowa, who dances her stories into the hearts of her audience; a Joe Jackson, who makes his audiences roar with laughter and keeps them convulsed throughout his entire act, with the aid of a dilapidated bicycle, a squeaky auto horn and a persistently annoying cuff—does not need words to tell a story.

The famous French playwright Scribe—perhaps the most ingenious craftsman the French stage has ever seen—used to say, "When my subject is good, when my scenario (plot) is very clear, very complete, I might have the play written by my servant; he would be sustained by the situation;—and the play would succeed." Plutarch tells us that Menander, the master of Greek comedy, was once asked about his new play, and he answered: "It is composed and ready; I have only the verses (dialogue) to write." [88]

If it is true that a great play, being in its final analysis a pantomime, is

---

[88] Reported in A Study of the Drama, by Brander Matthews.

effective without dialogue, and if some famous dramatists thought so little of dialogue that they considered their plays all written before they wrote the dialogue, then speech must be something that has little *comparative* value—something primarily employed to aid the idea behind it, to add emphasis to plot—not to exist for itself.

2. The Uses of Dialogue

Dialogue makes the dramatic story clear, advances it, reveals character, and wins laughter—all by five important means:

(a) *Dialogue Conveys Information of Basic Events at the Opening.* As we saw in the discussion of the structural elements of plot, there are of necessity some points in the basic incidents chosen for the story of a playlet that have their roots grounded in the past. Upon a clear understanding of these prior happenings which must be explained immediately upon the rise of the curtain, depends the effect of the entire sequence of events and, consequently, the final and total effect of the playlet. To "get this information over" the characters are made to tell of them as dramatically as possible. For instance:

Angela Maxwell knocks on Miss Carey's door the instant the curtain rises on "The Lollard," and as soon as Miss Carey opens the door Angela says: "Listen, you don't know me, but I've just left my husband." And the dialogue goes on to tell why she left Harry, clearly stating the events that the audience must know in order to grasp the meaning of those that follow.

At the very beginning of a playlet the dialogue must be especially clear, vividly informing and condensed. By "condensed," I meant the dialogue must be tense, and supported by swift action—it must without delay have done with the unavoidable explanations, and quickly get into the rising movement of events.

(b) *Dialogue Brings out the Incidents Clearly.* Never forgetting that action makes dialogue but that dialogue never makes action, let us take the admirable surprise ending of "The System," for an example:

The Inspector has left, after giving The Eel and Goldie their freedom and advising them to clear out and start life anew. The audience knows they are in hard straits financially. How are they going to secure the money to get away from town? Goldie expresses it concisely: "Well, we're broke again (tearfully). We can't go West now, so there's no use packing." This speech is like a sign-post that points out the condition the events have made them face. And then like a sign-post that points the other way, it adds emphasis to the flash of the surprise and the solution when The Eel, stealthily making sure no one will see him and no one can hear him, comes down to Goldie, sitting forlornly on the trunk, taps her on the shoulder and shows her Dugan's red wallet. Of course, the audience knows that the wallet spells the solution of all their problems, but The Eel clinches it by saying, "Go right ahead and pack."

Out of this we may draw one observation which is at least interesting, if not illuminating: When an audience accepts the premises of a playlet without question, it gives over many of its emotions and most of its reasoning power into the author's hands. Therefore the author must think for his audience and keenly suggest by dialogue that something is about to happen, show it as happening, and make it perfectly clear by dialogue that it has actually happened. This is the use to which dialogue is put most tellingly—bringing out the incidents in clear relief and at the very same time interpreting them cunningly.

(c) *Dialogue Reveals Character Humanly*. Character is tried, developed and changed not by dialogue, but by action; yet the first intimate suggestion of character is shown in dialogue; and its trials, development and change are brought into clear relief—just as events, of which character-change is the vital part, are made unmistakably clear—by the often illuminating word that fits precisely. As J. Berg Esenwein says, "Just as human interest is the heart of the narrative, so human speech is its most vivid expression. In everyday life we do not know a man until we have heard him speak. Then our first impressions are either confirmed, modified, or totally upset." [89]

It is by making all of his characters talk alike that the novice is betrayed, whereas in giving each character individuality of speech as well as of action the master dramatist is revealed. While it is permissible for two minor characters to possess a hazy likeness of speech, because they are so unimportant that the audience will not pay much attention to them, the playlet writer must give peculiar individuality to every word spoken by the chief characters. By this I do not mean that, merely to show that a character is different, a hero or heroine should be made to talk with a lisp or to use some catch-word—though this is sometimes done with admirable effect. What I mean is that the words given to the chief characters must possess an individuality rising from their inner differences; their speech should show them as not only different from each other, but also different from every other character in the playlet—in the whole world, if possible—and their words should be just the words they and no others would use in the circumstances.

If you will remember that you must give to the dialogue of your chief characters a unity as complete as you must give to plot and character as shown through action, you will evade many dialogue dangers. This will not only help you to give individuality to each character, but also save you from making a character use certain individual expressions at one time and then at another talk in the way some other character has spoken. Furthermore, strict observance of this rule should keep you from putting into the mouth of a grown man, who is supposed to be most manly, expressions only a "sissy" would use; or introducing a character as a wise man and permitting him to talk like a fool. As in life, so in dialogue—consistency is a test of worth.

Keep your own personality out of the dialogue. Remember that your characters and not you are doing the talking. You have laid down a problem in your playlet, and your audience expects it to fulfill its promise dramatically—that is, by a mimicry of life. So it does not care to listen to one man inhabiting four bodies and talking like a quartet of parrots. It wants to hear four different personalities talk with all the individuality that life bestows so lavishly—in life.

---

[89] Writing the Short-Slory, page 247.

You will find little difficulty in keeping your individuality out of dialogue if you will only remember that you cannot write intelligently of characters you do not know. Make use of the characters nearest you, submerge yourself in their individualities, and you will then be so interested in them that you will forget yourself and end by making the characters of your playlet show themselves in their dialogue as individual, enthrallingly entertaining, new, and—what is the final test of all dialogue—convincing.

(d) *Dialogue Wins Laughter.* There are three sources from which laughter rises out of dialogue. First, from the word that is a witticism, existing for its own sake. Second, from the word that is an intensely individual expression of character—the character-revealing phrase. Third, the word that is funny because it is spoken at the right instant in the action. All three have a place in the playlet, but the last, the dialogue that rises out of and illuminates a situation, is productive of the best results. This is but another way of saying what cannot be too often repeated, that the playlet is plot. [90]

Even in dialect, dialogue does not bother with anything much but plot-expression of character. Indicate the odd twist of a character's thoughts as clearly as you can, but never try to reproduce all his speech phonetically. If you do, you will end disastrously, for your manuscript will look like a scrambled alphabet which nobody can decipher. In writing dialect merely suggest the broken English here and there—follow the method so clearly shown in "The German Senator." Remember that the actor who will be engaged to play the part has studied the expression of that particular type all his life. His method of conveying what you intend is likely to be different from your method. Trust him—for you must.

(e) *Dialogue Advances the Action and Rounds Out the Plot.* Precisely in the way that incidents are brought out clearly by dialogue, dialogue advances the action and rounds out the plot at the curtain. Clear as I hope the method has been made, I wish to point out two dialogue peculiarities which come with the rise of emotion.

First, as the action quickens, there inevitably occurs a compression inherent in the dramatic that is felt by the dialogue. Joe Maxwell's epitome of vaudeville as he once expressed it to me in a most suggestive discussion of the two-a-day, illustrates this point better, perhaps, than a chapter would explain: "Vaudeville is meat," he said, "the meat of action, the meat of words." There is no *time* in vaudeville climaxes for one word that does not point out, or clinch home the action. Here action speaks louder than words. Furthermore, in the speed of bodily movement there is actually no time for words. If two men are grappling in a life and death struggle they can't stop for speech.

And second, as the playlet nears its ending there is no *need* for explanatory words—if the preceding action has been dramatic. Every new situation rises out of the old, the audience knows it all now, they even foresee the climax, and, in a well constructed playlet, they feel the coming-to-an-end thrill that is in the air. What need is there for dialogue? Only a need for the clearing, clinching kind, and for

---

[90] See Chapter V, in which humor was discussed in relation to the monologue.

The Finish Line. While the last-speech of a playlet is bone of the bone and blood of the blood of plot, the finish line is peculiarly a part of dialogue. It is here, in the last line, that the tragic has a strangely illuminating force and the comic must be given full play. Indeed, a comedy act that does not end in a "scream" is hardly worth anything. And, as comedy acts are most in demand in vaudeville, I shall relate this discussion solely to the comic ending. Here it is, then, in the last line of a comedy act, that the whole action is rounded neatly off with a full play of fancy—with emphasis on the use of wit.

Of course I do not mean that the last line may be permitted to stray away from the playlet and crack an unrelated joke. But the last line, being a completing line, may return to some incident earlier than the closing action. It may with full profit even go back to the introduction, as "The Lollard's" last line takes Miss Carey back to her interrupted sleep with, "Now, thank Gawd, I'll get a little sleep."

Or it may be merely a quaint line, like that which ended a very successful playlet which has stuck in my memory, but whose title I have forgotten. Here the sweethearts were brought together, they flew into each other's arms, they kissed. Naturally the curtain was on that kiss, but no—they drew apart and the girl rubbed her lips with the back of her hand. "Aw," said the boy, "what you rubbing it off for?" And the girl, half-crying, half-laughing, answered, "I ain't rubbing it off; I'm rubbing it *in!*"

Or the last line may be a character line, rounding back to the opening, perhaps, but having its mainspring in character, like the last line of "The Village Lawyer": "Well," he sighs—as he watches the money with which he could have satisfied his longing to buy a clarionet, disappear—"Maybe I couldn't play the darned thing anyway!" [91]

Example after example might be quoted to illustrate every possible variation, yet in the end we would come to the very same conclusions these four instances reveal. The finish line is the concluding thought of the action. It may round back to the opening plainly; bring out sharply the most prominent point developed; vividly present a pleasing side-light with a punch; illuminate a character point; take some completing element and twist it into a surprise— indeed, the finish line may present anything at all, so long as it thrills with human interest and laughter.

3. Fit and Becoming Dialogue

In playlet dialogue there is as much need of the dramatic spirit as in the playlet plot. Not what is said in real life, but what must be said to express the action concisely, is its aim. Playlet dialogue cannot take time to reproduce small talk. It must connote, not denote, even the big things. To omit is more important than to include. A whole life must be compressed into a single speech and entire stages of progression be epitomized in a single sentence. True enough, in really big scenes a character may rise to lofty expression; but of all playlet moments, here sane selection and compression are most vital. The wind of talk must be

---

[91] Chapter XV, section I.

made compressed air.

Conversation for conversation's sake is the one thing, above all others that stamps a playlet as in vain. I have seen producing manager after producing manager run through manuscripts to select for careful reading the ones with short speeches. Those weighty with long speeches were returned unread. Why? Because experience had taught them that a playlet filled with long speeches is likely to be filled with little else. They realize that conversation as an art died the day the first automobile did the mile in sixty flat. Speed is what the playlet needs, and talk slows the track. In the classic words of vaudeville, if you must talk, "hire a hall."

Where is it you hear more clever lines than anywhere else? In vaudeville. Where is it that slang hits the hardest? In vaudeville. On what stage do people talk more nearly like you and I talk? The vaudeville stage. For vaudeville is up-to-the-minute—vaudeville is the instant's dramatic review.

And it is this speech of the instant that playlet dialogue needs— the short, sharp, seemingly thoughtless but vividly pulsating words of everyday life. If today men talked in long speeches filled with grandiloquent periods, the playlet would mimic their length and tone, but men today do not speak that way and the playlet must mimic today's shortness and crispness. As Alexander Black says, "The language of the moment is the bridge; that carries us straight to the heart of the whole world, and all the past. Life or fancy that comes in the language of the moment comes to us *translated*. Fantastically, the language of the street is always close to the bones of art. It is always closer to the Bible and to all the big fellows than the language of the drawing rooms. Art is only the *expression* of ideas. Ideas, emotions, impulses, are more important than the *medium*, just as religion is more important than theology. There is just as much excuse for saying 'theology for its own sake' as for saying 'art for art's sake.' The joy of a new word should make us grateful for the fertility of the street out of which most of the really strong words come. The street doesn't make us fine, but it keeps us from being too sweet and thin. It loves the punch. And the punch clears the path." It is the punch in dialogue that the playlet demands.

Before we agree upon what is fit and becoming dialogue, I think it advisable to condense into a few words all that I have said on the subject. In its final analysis a playlet is a pantomime. Dialogue is primarily employed to add emphasis to the plot. It does this by conveying information of basic events at the opening; by bringing out the succeeding incidents clearly, by revealing character humanly; by winning laughter; by advancing the action; and by rounding out the plot in a finish line which thrills with human interest and, in the comedy playlet, with laughter. And now, what is fit and becoming dialogue? Fit dialogue is—what fits the plot exactly. Becoming dialogue is—what makes the plot *seem* even better. But dialogue cannot make plot better, it can only make it seem better—it can only dress it. Remember that.

CHAPTER XVII

"BUSINESS" IN THE PLAYLET

IN considering the "business" of the playlet, we have come to the place where it would seem that writing must be left behind and the function of the producer entered upon. For business is the detail of stage action and movement. But, while it is the peculiar function of the producer to invent and to incorporate into the playlet little bits of everyday movements of the characters to lend the effect of real life to the mimic picture, it is the province of the writer—in reducing his words to the lowest possible number, in an effort to secure that "economy of attention" which is the foundation of all art—to tell as much of his story as he can by actions that speak even louder than words. Every great playwright is as much a producer as he is a writer.

As we saw in Chapter VII, "business" includes every movement an actor makes while he is on the stage. Thus a facial expression may be called "business," *if it lends a peculiar significance to a line.* And a wild leap of a man on horseback through a window—this has actually been done in a vaudeville act—is also called business. In fact everything, from "mugging," [92] walking about, sitting down, picking up a handkerchief, taking off or putting on a coat, to the wordless scenes into which large parts of the story are condensed and made clear solely by situation—everything is called "business." But to differentiate the actor's part from the work of the playwright, I shall arbitrarily call every action which is as indivisible from acting as facial play, "pantomime"; while I shall employ the word "business" to express the use of movement by the playwright for the purpose of condensing large parts of the story and telling it wordlessly.

1. The Part Business Plays in the Dramatic [93]

Let us turn to that part of the third scene of "The System" where The Eel and Goldie—who have been given their liberty "with a string to it" by Inspector McCarthy in his anxiety to catch Officer Dugan red-handed—are "up against it" in their efforts to get away from town. They have talked it all over in Goldie's flat and The Eel has gone out to borrow the money from Isaacson, the "fence." Now when The Eel closes Goldie's door and runs downstairs, Goldie listens intently until the outer door slams, then begins to pack. She opens the trunk first, gets her jacket from the couch where she has thrown it, puts it in the trunk and then goes up into the bedroom and gets a skirt. She shakes the skirt as she comes down stage. Then a long, low whistle is heard—then the rapping of a policeman's club.

"Bulls!" she gasps. Looking up at the light burning, she turns it out and closes

---

[92] "Mugging," considered by some to be one of the lowest forms of comedy, is bidding for laughter by facial contortions unrelated to the action or the lines—making the scene subservient to the comical faces made by the actor.
[93] The impossibility of keeping separate the *designing* and the *writing* of business, will be seen as the chapter progresses, therefore I shall treat both freely in one.

the trunk at the same time. And she stands still until she sees the shadow of a man's hand cast by the moonlight on the wall. Then she gives a frightened exclamation and cowers on the sofa.

Here we have packed into little more than sixty seconds a revelation of the fear in which all crooks live, the unthinking faith and love Goldie bears The Eel, and a quiet moment which emphasizes the rush of the preceding events—a space also adding punch to the climax of incidents which follow hot upon its heels. When the long, low whistle sounds and the policeman's club raps out its alarm, the audience feels that the action is filled with tense meaning—The Eel has been caught. That hand on the wall is like a coming event casting its shadow before, and when Goldie gives her frightened exclamation and cowers on the couch, her visible fear—coming in contrast to her commonplace packing to get away—builds up the scene into a thrill that is capped by the meaningful window entrance of Dugan. "Ah!" says the audience, "here's the first time they've gotten together alone. It's the first time we've really seen that Dugan is behind it all. Something big is going to happen."

All of these revealing flashes, which illumine like searchlights, are told by movement. The only word that is spoken is Goldie's cry "Bulls!" The only other sounds are the whistle and the rapping of the club. But if Goldie had taken up the time with telling the audience how glad she was to pack and get away with The Eel to a new life, and if she had expressed her fear by bewailing the hardness of fate—the dramatic effect would have been lost. Do you see how words can kill and soundless movements vivify?

In "The Lollard," when Miss Carey wants to disillusionize Angela, she does not sit down and argue her out of her insane infatuation for Fred; nor does she tell Angela that Fred is a "lollard" and weakly unmask him by describing his "lollard" points. She cries "Fire! Fire! Fire!" Whereupon Fred dashes out on the stage and Angela and the audience with their own eyes behold Fred as a "lollard." Here the whole problem of the playlet is solved in a flash. Not one word of explanatory dialogue is needed.

In "Three of a Kind," a comedy playlet produced by Roland West, two crooks fleece a "sucker" and agree to leave the money in a middle room while they sleep in opposite rooms. They say they trust each other implicitly, but each finds a pretext to sit up and watch that money himself. The comedy rises from their movements around the room as they try to outmaneuver each other.

These three examples plainly show how movement, unexplained by dialogue, may be used to condense a middle action, a climax, and an opening. Now, if you will turn to the surprise ending of "The System"—which has been discussed before in its relation to dialogue—you will see how business may condense an ending. Indeed, the very essence of the surprise ending lies in this dramatic principle. Of course, how the condensation of story into movement is to be made in any given case depends upon the material, and the writer's purpose. But as a part of the problem let us see

2. How Pantomime Helps to Condense Story and Illumine Character

Consider the inimitable gesture the Latins use when they wish to express their helplessness. The shoulders shrug until the man seems folding into himself, his hands come together approaching his face and then he drops them despairingly to his side as if he would say: "But what can I do?" A gesture such as this reveals in a flash the depths of a human soul. Volumes could say no more.

This is what the actor may bring to your playlet, and what you, with the greatest caution, may sometimes—though rarely—indicate in your manuscript.

"Walk up stage," said David Belasco to an actor who was proving "difficult," "and when you turn your back, get some meaning into it. Make your back express—the whole play, if you can." Most certainly you would not write this in the directions for a playlet—the producer would laugh at it and the actor would be indignant. But you might with the greatest helpfulness direct that the character turn his back—and this is the point of the problem—if, by turning his back on some one, the character conveys, say, contempt for or fearlessness of an enemy's bravado. Every direction for acting in your playlet must be of such a kind that *anyone* can convey the meaning—because the emphasis is inherent in the situation. A stage direction ought not to depend for its value on the actor's ability. If this were not so, play writing would consist chiefly in engaging fine actors.

When an actor receives a part he studies it not only to learn the lines, but with the desire to familiarize himself with the character so thoroughly that he may not seem to be playing it. He hopes to make the audience feel that the character is alive. For this reason, it is not amiss to indicate characteristic actions once in a while. A good example of this is found in "The Lollard," where Angela says to Miss Carey: "But—excuse me—how do you know so many different kinds of men if you've never been married?"

"Boarders," says Miss Carey quickly. "To make ends meet, I've always had to have a male boarder since I was left an orphan." "She rises—turns her back to audience—gives a touch to her pigtail, during laugh on this line. This business always builds laugh," say the directions. It is such little touches that stamp a character as individual; and therefore they are just the little touches the playwright may add to his manuscript by way of suggestion to the actor. They may be very helpful, indeed, but they should be made with great care and discretion. For the actor, if he is a capable performer, is ready when rehearsal begins with many suggestions of a like nature. He will often suggest something that will not only exhibit character clearly, but will also condense story by eliminating needless words and movement.

For instance: F. F. Mackay was rehearsing to play the French count in the famous old play, "One of Our Girls." Mr. Bronson Howard had directed in his manuscript that the count, when struck across the face with a glove by an English officer, should become very violent and angry, in accordance with the popular notion of an excitable Frenchman's character. "But Mr. Mackay," says Daniel Frohman, "argued that the French count, having been shown in the play to be an expert duellist with both the rapier and the pistol, and having faced danger frequently, was not liable to lose control of himself. Mr. Howard readily saw the point. The result was one of the most striking situations in the American drama; for the Frenchman received the insult without the movement of a muscle. He stood rigid. Only the flash of the eye for an instant revealed his emotion. Then the audience saw his face grow red, and then pale. This was followed by the quiet announcement from the count that he would send his seconds to see the Englishman.

"This exhibition of facial emotion betrayed by the visible rush of blood to the actor's face was frequently noted at the time. It was a muscular trick, Mr. Mackay told me. He put on a tight collar for the scene and strained his neck against it until the blood came, and when he released the pressure, and the blood receded, the effect was reached. It was a splendid moment, and it is one of the many effects that have been studied out during the progress and development of a play during rehearsals."

It is for the great majority of such little touches, therefore, that the playwright must depend on the actor and the producer to add to his playlet. However, the playwright may help to the limit of his ability, by giving very short, very carefully thought out directions in his manuscript. But it is much better for the novice to disregard suggestions to the actor for character analysis and even to be sparing with his hints for facial expressions or slight movements—and to content himself with an effort to condense his story in the broader ways.

3. How Tediously Long Speeches may be Broken up by Movement

As the playlet is primarily action, and as the audience expects the playlet to keep moving all the time, it is a common practise to try to trick the audience into believing every speech is vibrant with emotional force, by keeping the actors moving about the stage. But the fact that a really vital speech may be killed by a movement which distracts the attention of the audience ought to be proof positive that needless movements about the stage are merely a confession of poverty in the playlet. Nevertheless, as a long explanatory speech seems sometimes unavoidable, I devote two or three short paragraphs to what has saved some playlets from absolute failure.

If you are unable to tell every bit of your story by dramatic means and therefore face a long speech that may seem tiresomely wordy, break it up with natural movements which lend a feeling of homely reality to the scene. For instance, don't let the character who is delivering that long speech tell it all uninterruptedly from the chair in which he is sitting. Let him rise after he has spoken two or three sentences and cross to the other character, or do something that will illustrate a point in his story, or have the one who is listening interrupt now and then. Inject motive into the interruptions if you can; but in any event, keep your characters moving.

But make the movements natural. To this end, study the movements of the men and women about you. Try to invent new ways of expressing the old things in movement. Strive not so much to be "different," as to be vividly interesting. You can make the movements of your characters about the stage as brilliant as dialogue.

Above all, make sure that you do not let your characters wander about the stage aimlessly. To make it a complete unity every little scene demands as careful thought as does the entire playlet. A playlet may be suggestively defined as a number of minute-long playlets moving vividly one after the other to make a vivid whole. Remember this, and you may be able to save a tiresome scene from ruining the entire effect of your playlet.

4. Why Business is More Productive of Comedy than Dialogue

As a playlet is nothing if it is not action, so a comedy playlet is nothing if its comedy does not develop from situations. By "action," as the word is used here, I mean that the story of the playlet is told by the movements of its characters. In real life, you know, comedy and tragedy do not come from what persons say they are going to do—but from what they actually do. Therefore, the merry jests that one character perpetrates upon another must be told not in words, but by showing the character actually perpetrating them on the victim. In a comedy playlet, the playwright must be a practical joker. Every funny happening in a playlet is a "scene that must be shown."

For instance, in "Billy's Tombstones," the football player who is in love with the girl, whom he has followed half around the world, is shown first as losing his "tombstones"—his false teeth, made necessary by the loss of his real ones in a famous college game; then he is shown in his wild efforts to pronounce his sweetheart's name without the dental help. Much of the comedy arises from his efforts to pronounce that loved name—and the climax comes when the lost tombstones are found and Billy proposes to her in perfect speech that lingers fondly on her name.

In farce—particularly in the old farces which depended on mistaken identity, a motive force considered hardly worthy of use today—the comedy arises very rarely from a witty saying in itself. The fun usually depends upon the humorous situations that develop. "The New Coachman"—one of those old farcical "screams"—contained an exceptionally fine example of this point and is pertinent to-day because it had no relation to mistaken identity in this humorous scene. Here the best fun of the comedy came from the use of a stepladder by the supposed coachman, who got all tangled up in it. After the first misstep with that stepladder, there was never any time for more than a word here and there. Of course, such a scene depends upon the actor almost entirely, and therefore cannot be indicated in the business by the playwright, but I use it for an example because it is a peculiarly brilliant instance of the fact that hearty laughter depends not on hearing, but on seeing.

But do not make the mistake of trying to patch together a comedy playlet from the bits of funny stage business you have seen in other acts. If you present such a manuscript to a producer you may be very sure it will be refused, for there are plenty of producers and performers in vaudeville who can supply such an act at a moment's notice from memory.

The sort of comedy expected from the playwright is comedy that develops from situation. It is in the invention of new situations and new business to fit these situations that the playlet writer finds his reward in production and profit.

5. Entrances, Exits and the Stage-Cross

Among the many definitions of drama—frequently misleading, but equally often helpful—there is one which holds the whole art of play writing lies in getting the characters on the stage naturally and effectively and getting them off again—naturally and effectively. But, even the most daring of definition makers has not yet told us how this is to be accomplished in all cases. The fact is, no one can tell us, because a method that would be natural and effective in a given playlet, would very likely be most unnatural and ineffective in another. All that can be said is that the same dramatic sense with which you have constructed the story of your playlet will carry you forward in the inevitable entrances and exits. How these moments are to be effective, lies in the very nature of the story you are telling. This is boldly begging the question, but it is all that may with honest helpfulness be said.

However, regarding the stage-cross, and allied movements of the actors, there are two suggestions that may be helpful. The first is founded on the old theory that a scene ought to be "dressed" all the time—that is, if one character moves across the stage, the other ought to move a little up stage to give him room to cross and should then move down on the opposite side, to keep the scene dressed or "balanced." But no hard and fast rule can be given, even for the stage-cross. If it seems the easy and natural thing for the characters to do this, all well and good. But you should feel no compulsion about it and really should give to the matter but little thought.

The second is based on the common-sense understanding at which you yourself will arrive if you will take the trouble to notice how the slightest movement made by one of two persons to whom you are telling a story distracts the other's attention. Briefly, never indicate business for a character during the moments when short and vitally important speeches are conveying information to the audience.

Both of these minor suggestions may be summed up in this sentence with which I shall dismiss the subject: The box sets in which the playlet is played in vaudeville are usually not very deep and are so arranged that every part of the scene is in plain view from practically every seat in the house, therefore you may forget that your story is being played in a mimic room and may make your characters move as if the room were real. If you will only keep in mind you should have little trouble.

6. How "Business" is Indicated in Manuscript

In the old days before the boxed set, the manuscript of a play bristled with such cryptic signs as R. U. E., and L. F. E., meaning, when reduced to everyday English, "right upper entrance," "left first entrance," and the like. But as the old "entrances" of the stage have been lost with the introduction of the box set, which closely mimics a real room—being, indeed, a room with the fourth wall removed—the modern stage directions are much simpler. "Right door," "centre door," "left door," are the natural directions to be found in a playlet manuscript today.

It is a good general rule to avoid in your stage directions expressions which show you are dealing with a stage scene and not a scene of real life. In the first place, if you attempt to be technical, you are very likely to be over-technical and confusing. In the second place, you will be more likely to produce a life-like playlet if you are not forever groping among strange terms, which make you conscious all the time that you are dealing with unreality. Therefore choose the simplest directions, expressed in the fewest possible words, to indicate the effects you have carefully thought out: Never forget that reality and simplicity go hand in hand.

And now it may be of advantage to sum up what has been said about stage business in this chapter. We have seen how business may be used to condense the story of a playlet; how business is often—though not always—the very heart of the dramatic; how pantomime may be skillfully used to condense salient parts of the playlet story and illumine character; how business may be employed to break up a clumsy but necessarily long speech—thus sometimes saving a playlet from the failure of the tedious;—and why business is more productive of comedy than is dialogue. We have concluded that the playlet writer must not ape what has already been done, but can win success only in the measure he succeeds in bringing to his playlet new business which makes his new situations all the more vivid and vital. Finally, we have seen that entrances and exits must be natural and effective, and that all stage business should be conceived and thought of and indicated in the manuscript as simple expressions of reality.

With this chapter, the six elements of a successful playlet have been discussed from the angle of exposition. In the next chapter I shall make use of all this expository material and shall endeavor to show how playlets are actually written.

CHAPTER XVIII

WRITING THE PLAYLET

WHILE it is plain that no two writers ever have, nor ever will, go about writing a playlet in precisely the same way, and impossible as it is to lay down rules which may be followed with precision to inevitable success, I shall present some suggestions, following the logical order of composition.

First, however, I must point out that you should study the vaudeville stage of *this week*, not of last year or even of last month, before you even entertain a germ idea for a playlet. You should be sure before you begin even to think out your playlet, that its problem is in full accord with the very best, and that it will fit into vaudeville's momentary design with a completeness that will win for it an eager welcome.

You should inquire of yourself first, "Is this a comedy or a serious playlet I am about to write?" And if the latter, "*Should* I write a serious playlet?"

One of vaudeville's keenest observers, Sime Silverman, editor of Variety, said when we were discussing this point: "Nobody ought to write a tragic or even a serious playlet who can write anything else. There are two or three reasons why. First, vaudeville likes laughter, and while it may be made to like tears, a teary playlet must be exceedingly well done to win. Second, the serious playlet must be so well done and so well advertised that usually a big name is necessary to carry it to success; and the 'name' demands so much money that it is sometimes impossible to engage an adequate supporting cast. Third, the market for tragic and serious playlets is so small that there is only opportunity for the playlet master; of course, there sometimes comes an unknown with a great success, like 'War Brides,' [94] but only rarely. Therefore, I would advise the new writer to write comedy."

Miss Nellie Revell, whom B. F. Keith once called "The Big Sister of Vaudeville," and who was Vaudeville Editor of the New York Morning Telegraph before becoming General Press Representative of the Orpheum Circuit, summed up her years of experience as a critic in these words:

"The new writer should first try his hand at a comedy playlet. Then after he has made a success of comedy, or if he is sure he can't write anything but sobby playlets, let him try to make an audience weep. Vaudeville, like any other really human thing, would rather laugh than cry, yet if you make vaudeville cry finely, it will still love you. But a serious playlet must be mighty well done to get over—therein lies a stumbling block sometimes. A few great artists can make vaudeville sob finely—but only a few. Comedy, good comedy, always gets by.

"How many comedy playlets are there to one serious playlet in vaudeville? I should say about ten to one. That ought to convince anybody that comedy is the thing to write for vaudeville."

There have been many hybrid playlets which have combined tragedy and

---

[94] Written by Miss Marion Craig Wentworth, and played by Olga Nazimova.

comedy to give some particular star an opportunity to show versatility in acting. [95] But some of these playlets have been merely vehicles for a personality, and therefore cannot be considered in this discussion.

On the other hand, there have been some serious playlets which have had comedy twists, or a light turn, which brought the curtain down amid laughter that was perfectly logical and in good taste. An example of the surprise ending that lightens the gloom is found in "The Bomb," finely played by Wilton Lackaye, in which the Italian who so movingly confesses to the outrage is merely a detective in disguise, trapping the real bomb thrower—and suddenly he unmasks. If a serious playlet can be made to end with a light touch that is fitting, it will have a better chance in vaudeville. But this is one of the most difficult and dangerous effects to attempt. The hazard is so great that success may come but once in many efforts. [96]

Since comedy should be the new writer's aim, the following discussion, while conceived with the broad view to illustrate the writing of the playlet in general, brings into particular prominence the writing of comedy.

I. WHEN TO BEGIN

When should you begin to write your playlet? Assuming that you already have a germ idea, the next step is to express your theme in a single short sentence, and consider it as your playlet problem, which must be proved logically, clearly and conclusively. To do this you must dovetail your incidents into a playlet plot; but how far should you think out your playlet before beginning to set it down on paper?

1. The Use of the Scenario

Nearly all the playlet writers with whom I have talked during a period of more than five years have with surprising unanimity declared in favor of beginning with the scenario, the summary of the dramatic action. But they disagree as to the completeness with which the scenario should be drawn up.

Some merely sketch the main outlines of the plot and leave to the moment of actual writing the details that often make it a success. Others write out a long scenario, boiling it down to the essence for the stage version. Still other playlet writers carry their scenarios just far enough to make sure that they will not have to think about the details of plot when they set about writing the dialogue—they see that there is an effective reason for the entrance of each character and a clear motive for exit. But, however they disagree as to the completeness the scenario should show, they all agree that the plot should be firmly fixed in its general outlines before pen is set to paper.

It may be of suggestive value as well as of interest to point out that in olden times the scenario was the only part of the play the playwright wrote. The groundwork of the plot was fixed beyond change, and then the actors were

---

[95] See Chapter XII, section II, topic 2.
[96] See Chapter XIV, section II, topic 3.

permitted to do as they pleased within these limits. Even today, in the construction of hurried entertainments for club nights at the various actors' clubhouses, often only the scenario or general framework of the act is typewritten and handed to the performers who are to take part. All that this tells them is that on some given cue they are to enter and work opposite so-and-so, and are, in turn, to give an agreed-upon cue to bring on such-and-such a performer. In a word, the invaluable part of any dramatic entertainment is the scenario.

One valuable aid to the making of a clear and effective scenario is the use of a diagram of the set in which the act is to be played. Reference to Chapter IV, "The Scenery Commonly Found in Vaudeville Theatres," will place in your hands a wide—if not an exhaustive— range of variations of the commonly found box sets. Within the walls of any one of these diagrams you may carefully mark the exact location of chairs, tables and any other properties your action demands. Then, knowing the precise room in which your characters must work, you can plot the details of their movements exactly from entrances to exits and give to your playlet action a clearness and preciseness it might not otherwise possess.

2. The Scenario not an Unalterable Outline

But there is one point I feel the necessity of emphasizing, whose application each one must determine for himself: While you ought to consider your scenario as directive and as laying down the line that should be followed, you ought not to permit your playlet to become irrevocably fixed merely because you have written your scenario. It is often the sign of a dramatic mind, and of a healthy problem too, that the playlet changes and develops as the theme is carefully considered. To produce the very best work, a scenario must be thought of as clay to be molded, rather than as iron that must be scrapped and melted again to be recast.

II. POINTS TO BRING OUT PROMINENTLY

This section is so arranged that the elements of writing discussed in the preceding chapters are summarized, and the vital elements which could not be considered before are all given their proper places in a step-by-step scheme of composition. The whole forms a condensed standard for review to refresh your memory before writing, and by which to test your playlet after it is written.

Every playlet must have a beginning, a middle and an ending. The beginning must state the premises of the problem clearly and simply; the middle must develop the problem logically and solve the entanglement in a "big" scene, and the ending must round out the whole satisfyingly—with a surprise, if fitting.

1. Points the Beginning Must Emphasize

Because the total effect of a playlet is complete oneness, there lie in the "big" scene and in the ending certain results of which the beginning must be the beginning or immediate cause. Such causes are what you must show clearly.

(a) *The Causes before the Curtain Rose.* If the causes lie far back in events that occurred before the curtain rose, you must have those events carefully and clearly stated. But while you convey this necessary exposition as dramatically as possible, be sure to make the involved dramatic elements subservient to clearness.

(b) *The Causes that Occur after the Curtain Rises.* If the causes do not lie in the past, but occur after the curtain rises, you must show them as clearly occurring right then and there. They must be as plain as dawn, or the rest of the playlet will be shrouded in the darkness of perplexing doubts.

(c) *The Character Motive from which the Complication Rises.* If the causes lie in character, you must show the motive of the person of the playlet from whose peculiar character the complication rises like a spring from its source. You must expose the point of character plainly.

But in striving to make your premises clear do not make the mistake of being prolix—or you will be tedious. Define character sharply. Tell in quick, searching dialogue the facts that must be told and let your opening scenes on which the following events depend, come with a snap and a perfectly adequate but nevertheless, have-done-with-it feeling.

2. Points that Must Be Brought out in the Middle

In every scene of your playlet you must prepare the minds of your audience to accept gladly what follows—and to look forward to it eagerly. You must not only plainly show what the causes of every action *are*, but you must also make the audience feel what they *imply*. Thus you will create the illusion which is the chief charm of the theatre—a feeling of superiority to the mimic characters which the gods must experience as they look down upon us. This is the inalienable right of an audience.

(a) *The Scenes that Make Suspense.* But while foreshadowing plainly, you must not forestall your effect. One of the most important elements of playlet writing is to let your audience guess *what* is going to happen—but keep them tensely interested in *how* it is going to happen. This is what creates the playlet's enthralling power—suspense.

It is so important to secure suspense in a playlet that an experienced writer who feels that he has not created it out of the body of his material, will go back to the beginning and insert some point that will pique the curiosity of the audience, leaving it unexplained until the end. He keeps the audience guessing, but he satisfies their curiosity finely in the finish—this is the obligation such a suspense element carries with it.

(b) *The Points that Balance the Preparation with the Result.* Nothing could be more disastrous than to promise with weighty preparation some event stupendously big with meaning and then to offer a weak little result. And it would be nearly as unfortunate to foreshadow a weak little fulfillment and then to present a tremendous result. Therefore, you must so order your events that you balance the preparation with the result, to the shade of a dramatic hair.

But take care to avoid a too obvious preparation. If you disclose too plainly what you are aiming at your end is defeated in advance, because your audience is bound to lapse into a cynically smiling does-this-fellow-take-us-for-babies? attitude.

The art of the dramatic is the art that conceals art. The middle of your playlet must conceal just enough to keep the stream of suspense flowing eagerly toward the end, which is dimly seen to be inevitably approaching.

(c) *The One Event that Makes the Climax Really Big.* From the first speech, through every speech, and in every action, your playlet has moved toward this one event, and now you must bring it out so prominently that everything else sinks into insignificance. This event is: *The change in the relations of the characters.*

This is the planned-for result of all that has gone before. Bear firmly in mind that you have built up a suspense which this change must *crown*. Keep foremost the fact that what you have hidden before you must now disclose. Lay your cards on the table face up—all except one. This last card takes the final trick, completing the hand you have laid down, and everyone watches with breathless interest while you play:

3. The Single Point of the Finish

If you can make this final event a surprise, all the better. But if you cannot change the whole result in one dramatic disclosure, you must be content to lay down your last card, not as a point in itself surprising, but nevertheless dramatically.

The Finish must be Complete—and Completely Satisfy. You have sprung your climax; you have disclosed what it is that changes the relations of your characters; now you must show that those relations *have* been changed. And at the same time you bring forward the last strand of plot that is loose and weave it into the now complete design. You must account for everything here in the finish, and do it with speed.

III. PUTTING PUNCH INTO THE IDEA

Now let us say that you have expanded the first draft of your plastic scenario into a nearly perfect manuscript. But as you read it over, you are not content. You feel that it lacks "punch." What is "punch," and how are you going to add it when it is lacking?

Willard Mack says: "'Punch' is the most abused word I know. The dramatic punch is continually confused with the theatrical trick. Critics said the third act of 'Kick In'[97]—in which the detective is overpowered in a hand-to-hand fight after a hypodermic has been jabbed into his wrist—had a punch. It didn't. What it really had was a theatric trick. But the human punch was in the second act, when the little frightened girl of the slums comes to see her wounded lover—who is really dead. If the needle should suddenly be lost in playing the third act the scene would be destroyed. But the other moment would have its appeal regardless of theatrical detail."

Punch comes only from a certain strong human appeal in the story. Punch is the thing that makes the pulse beat a little quicker, because the heart has been touched. Punch is the precise moment of the dramatic. It is the second in which the revelation flashes upon the audience.

---

[97] Developed into a long play from the vaudeville act of the same name.

While whatever punch you may be able to add must lie in the heart of your material—which no one but yourself can know—there are three or four ways by which you may go about finding a mislaid punch.

If you have turned the logical order of writing about and let your playlet drag you instead of your driving it, you may find help in asking yourself whether you should keep your secret from the audience.

1. Have You Kept Your Audience in Ignorance Too Long?

While it is possible to write a most enthralling novel of mystery or a detective short-story which suddenly, at the very last moment, may disclose the trick by which it has all been built up, such a thing is not successfully possible in a playlet. You must not conceal the identity of anyone of your characters from the audience. Conceal his identity from every other character and you may construct a fine playlet, but don't conceal his motive from the audience.

The very nature of the drama—depending as it does on giving to the spectator the pleasure of feeling omniscient—precludes the possibility of "unheralded surprise." For instance, if you have a character whom the audience has never seen before and of whom they know nothing suddenly spring up from behind a sofa where he has overheard two other characters conspiring—the audience may think he is a stage-hand. How would they know he was connected with the other characters in the playlet if you neglected to tell them beforehand? They could not know. The sudden appearance of the unknown man from behind the sofa would have much the effect of a disturbance in the rear of the theatre, distracting attention from the characters on the stage and the plot of the playlet.

If your plot calls for an eavesdropper behind a sofa—though I hope you will never resort to so ancient a device—you must first let the audience know who he is and why he wants to eavesdrop; and second you must show him going behind that sofa. The audience must be given the god-like pleasure of watching the other two characters approach the sofa and sit down on it, in ignorance that there is an enemy behind it into whose hands they are delivering themselves.

This is only a simple instance, but it points out how far the ramifications to which this problem of not keeping a secret from the audience may extend. Moreover, it should suggest that it is possible that your playlet lacks the required punch—because you have kept something secret that you ought to have disclosed. Therefore, go through your playlet carefully and try to discover just what you have not treated with dramatic frankness.

On the other hand, of course, if you decide you must keep a secret—some big mystery of plot—you must be sure that it is worth keeping. If you build up a series of mysterious incidents, the solution must be adequate to the suspense. But, I have treated this angle of secret-keeping in "preparation versus result," so I shall now direct your attention to the other side of the problem of dramatic frankness—which may be the cause of the lack of punch:

2. Have You been too Frank at the Beginning?

Go back through the early moments of your playlet and see if you have not given the whole thing away at the very beginning. If you have, you have, as we saw, killed your suspense, which is the road on which punch lies in wait. The way to remedy this defect is to condense the preparation and so express it in action and by dialogue that you leave opportunity for a revealing flash.

In going over your manuscript you must strive to attain the correct balance between the two. The whole art lies in knowing just what to disclose and it when to disclose it—and what not and when not to disclose.

3. Have You Been Too "Talky"?

Remember that vaudeville has no time for "fine speeches." Cut even the lines you have put in for the purpose of disclosing character, and—save in rare instances—depend chiefly on character revelation through *action*.

4. Have You Lost Your Singleness of Effect by Mixing Playlet Genres?

One of the most common reasons why playlets lack the effect of vital oneness is to be found in the fault of mixing the kinds: for example, making the first half a comedy and the second half a tragedy. It is as if a song began with one air and suddenly switched to a totally different melody. If your playlet is a comedy, make it a comedy throughout; it if is a deeply human story, let it end as it began; [98]if you are writing a straight drama or a melodrama, keep your playlet straight drama or melodrama all the way through. Go over your playlet with the eye of a relentless critic and make sure that you have not mixed your genres, which only in the rarest cases can be done effectively.

5. Are You Sure Your Action Is All Vital?

Finally, if every other investigation has failed to develop the needed punch, go over your playlet again to see if it is possible that you have erred in the first principle of the art. If you have permitted even one tiny scene to creep in that does not hold a vital meaning to the single point of your climax, you have lost by so much the possibility of the punch. Remember, here, that a great playlet can be played without a single word being spoken and still be vividly clear to everyone. Realizing this, chop every second of action that is not vital.

6. The Punch Secured.

But long before you have exhausted these suggestions you will have developed your punch. Your punch has risen out of your material— if you possess the sense of the dramatic. If the punch has not developed—with a series of minor punches that all contribute to the main design of the "heart wallop"— there is something wrong with your material.

But even a realization of this ought not to discourage you, for there are instances every day of well-known playwrights who have chosen the wrong material. We all have seen these plays. You must do as they do—cast your playlet aside and begin anew with new material. The man who keeps at it is the only one who wins—but he must keep at it with the right stuff.

---

[98] See Chapter XIV, section II, topic 3.

IV. SELECTING A PROPER TITLE

When you have trimmed your playlet by cutting off *all* the trimmings, your thoughts naturally turn to a title. More than likely you have selected your title long before you have written "curtain"—it is possible a title sprang into your mind out of the germ idea. But even then, you ought now to select the *proper* title.

1. What is a Proper Title?

A proper title is one that both names a playlet and concisely suggests more than it tells. For instance, "The System" suggests a problem vital to all big cities—because the word "system" was on everybody's tongue at the time. "The Lollard" piques curiosity—what is a "lollard," you are inclined to want to know; it also carries a suggestion of whimsicality. "The Villain Still Pursued Her," tells as plainly as a whole paragraph could that the playlet is a travesty, making fun of the old blood-and-thunder melodrama. "In and Out" is a short, snappy, curiosity-piquing name; it is a title that hangs out a sign like a question mark. "Kick In" is of the same class, but with the added touch of slang. "War Brides" is another luring title, and one that attracts on frankly dramatic and "problem" grounds. "Youth" is a title that suggests much more than it tells—it connotes almost anything. "Blackmail" has the punch of drama and suggests "atmosphere" as well. But these are enough to establish the fact that a good title is one which suggests more than it tells. A good title frankly advertises the wares within, yet wakens eager curiosity to see what those wares are.

2. What is an Improper Title?

An improper title, first, is one that does not precisely fit a playlet as a name; or second, that tells too much. For instance, "Sweets to the Sweet" is the title of a playlet whose only reason for being so named is because the young man brings the girl a box of candy—it does not name the playlet at all precisely, its connotation is misleading. Do not choose a title just because it is pretty. Make your title really express the personality of your playlet. But more important still, do not let your title tell too much. If "The Bomb" were called "The Trap," much of the effect of the surprise would be discounted, and the unmasking of the detective who confesses to throwing the bomb to trap the real criminal would come as something expected. In a word, be most careful not to select a title that "gives it all away."

3. Other Title Considerations

A short title seems to be the playlet fashion today; but tomorrow the two- or three-word title may grow to a four- or five-word name. Yet it will never be amiss to make a title short.

This same law of good use points to a similar variation in the context of even the short title—I mean that every little while there develops a fad for certain words. There may at any time spring up a wide use of words like "girl," or "fun," or color words, like "red " or "purple" or "blond." But your close study of the vaudeville of the moment will show you when these fad-words may be used advantageously in a title.

You need never worry over-long about a title for your playlet if you put the emphasis in your own mind upon the fact that your title is an advertisement.

V. MAKING THE PLAYLET A HIT

But when you have a playlet manuscript that is full of laughter and vibrant with dramatic thrills, and even after you have sold it to a manager who has produced it, your work as a playlet writer is not done. You still must cut and polish it until it is a flawless gem that flashes from the stage. As Edgar Allan Woolf expressed it to me in one of our conversations:

"The work of the author of a one-act comedy is not over until, after several weeks of playing, his playlet has been so reshaped and altered by him that not a single dull spot remains. Individual lines must be condensed so that they are as short as they possibly can be made. The elimination of every unnecessary word or phrase is essential. Where a line that develops the plot can be altered so that it will still serve its purpose, and also score a laugh on its own account, it must be so changed. Where lines cannot be changed, bits of comedy business may perhaps be inserted to keep the audience from lapsing into listlessness. For it is a deplorable fact that a vaudeville audience that is not laughing outright at a comedy becomes listless. Vaudeville managers never book a playlet that makes an audience smile—for while the humor that brings a smile may be more brilliant than the comedy that gets a laugh, it must always be remembered that vaudeville audiences come to laugh and not to smile. Some of the biggest laughs in every one of my many acts I put in after the acts had been playing some weeks. And I attribute whatever success they have had later in the best vaudeville theatres to the improvements I have made during their 'breaking in' periods."

To sum up: While no two writers ever have written and never will write a playlet in precisely the same way, the wise beginner chooses for his first playlet a comedy theme. Your germ idea you express in a single short sentence which you consider as the problem of your playlet, to be solved logically, clearly and conclusively. Instinct for the dramatic leads you to lift out from life's flowing stream of events the separate incidents you require and to dovetail them into a plot which tells the story simply by means of characters and dialogue skillfully blended into an indivisible whole, flashing with revealing meaning and ending with complete satisfaction.

After you have thought out your playlet, you set down so much of it as you feel is necessary in the form of a scenario. But you do not consider this scenario as unchangeable. Rather you judge the value of the idea by the freedom with which it grows in effectiveness. And while this process is going on, you carefully select the basic points in the beginning of the story that must be brought out prominently.

Then you develop the story by making the points that foreshadow your "big" scene stand out so as to weave the enthralling power of suspense. You let your audience guess *what* is going to happen, but keep them tensely interested in *how* it is going to happen. And you prepare your audience by a carefully preserved balance between the promise and the performance for the one big point of the climax which changes the relations of the characters to each other.

After you have shown the change as happening, you punch home the fact that it has happened, and withhold your completing card until the finish. In your finish you play the final card and account for the last loose strand of the plot, with a speed that does not detract from your effect of complete satisfaction.

In seeking to "punch up" your playlet, you go over every word, every bit of characterization, every moment of action, and eliminate single words, whole speeches, entire scenes, to cut down the playlet to the meat, seeking for lost punches particularly in the faults of keeping secrets that should be instantly disclosed, and in the too frank disclosures of secrets that ought to be kept in the beginning. And out of this re-writing there rises into view the "heart wallop" which first attracted you.

Finally, when your playlet is finished, you decide on a proper title. Remembering that a title is an advertisement, you choose a short name that both *names* and *lures*. And then you prepare the manuscript for its market—which is discussed in a later chapter.

But when you have written your playlet and have sold it to a manager who has produced it, your work is not yet done. You watch it in rehearsal, and during the "breaking in" weeks you cut it here, change it there, make a plot-line do double duty as a laugh-line in this spot, take away a needless word from another—until your playlet flashes a flawless gem from the stage. The final effect in the medium of expression for which you write it is UNITY. Every part—acting, dialogue, action—blends in a perfect whole. Not even one word may be taken away without disturbing the total effect of its vital oneness.

CHAPTER XIX

THE ELEMENTS OF A SUCCESSFUL ONE-ACT MUSICAL COMEDY

If you were asked, "What is a one-act musical comedy?" you might answer: "Let's see, a one-act musical comedy is—is—. Well, all I remember is a lot of pretty girls who changed their clothes every few minutes, two lovers who sang about the moon, a funny couple and a whole lot of music."

Hazy? Not at all. This is really a clear and reasonably correct definition of the average one-act musical colnedy, for this type of act is usually about fifty per cent. girl, twenty per cent. costumes and scenery, twenty-five per cent. music, and usually, but not always, five per cent. comedy. A musical comedy, therefore, is not music and comedy—it is girls and music. That is why the trade name of this, one of the most pleasing of vaudeville acts, is—a girl-act."

It was the girl-act, perhaps more than any other one style of act, that helped to build vaudeville up to its present high standing. On nearly every bill of the years that are past there was a girl-act. It is a form of entertainment that pleases young and old, and coming in the middle or toward the end of a varied program, it lends a touch of romance and melody without which many vaudeville bills would seem incomplete.

A girl-act is a picture, too. Moreover, it holds a touch of bigness, due to the number of its people, their changing costumes, and the length of time the act holds the stage. With its tuneful haste, its swiftly moving events, its rapid dialogue, its succession of characters, and its ever-changing, colorful pictures, the one-act musical comedy is not so much written as put together.

1. The Musical Elements

Technically known as a girl-act, and booked by managers who wish a "flash"—a big effect—the one-act musical comedy naturally puts its best foot foremost as soon as the curtain rises. And, equally of course, it builds up its effects into a concluding best-foot.

The best-foot of a musical comedy is the ensemble number, in which all the characters—save the principals, sometimes—join in a rousing song. The ensemble *is* musical comedy, and one-act musical comedy is—let this exaggeration clinch the truth—the ensemble. [99]

Between the opening and the closing ensembles there is usually one other ensemble number, and sometimes two. And between these three or four ensembles there are usually one or two single numbers—solos by a man or a woman—and a duet, or a trio, or a quartet. These form the musical element of

---

[99] Of course, I am discussing the usual musical comedy—the flash of a bill—in pointing out so forcefully the value of the ensemble. There have been some fine one-act musical comedies in which the ensemble was not used at all. Indeed, the musical comedy in one act without any ensemble offers most promising possibilities.

the one-act musical comedy.

2. Scenery and Costumes—The Picture-Elements

While the one-act musical comedy may be played in one set of scenery only, it very often happens that there are two or three different scenes. The act may open in One, as did Joe Hart's "If We Said What We Thought," and then go into Full Stage; or it may open in Full Stage, go into One for a little musical number, and then go back into a different full-stage scene for its finish. It may even be divided into three big scenes—each played in a different set—with two interesting numbers in One, if time permits, or the act be planned to make its appeal by spectacular effects.

Very often, as in Lasky's "A Night on a Houseboat," a big set-piece or a trick scene is used to give an effect of difference, although the entire act is played without dropping a curtain.

To sum up the idea behind the use of musical comedy scenery: it is designed to present an effect of bigness—to make the audience feel they are viewing a "production."

The same thought is behind the continual costume changes which are an integral part of the one-act musical comedy effect. For each ensemble number the girls' costumes are changed. If there are three ensembles there are three costumes, and four changes if there are four ensembles. Needless to say, it sometimes keeps the girls hustling every minute the act is in progress, changing from one costume to another, and taking that one off to don a third or a fourth.

The result in spectacular effect is as though a scene were changed every time an ensemble number is sung. Furthermore, the lights are so contrived as to add to this effect of difference, and the combination of different colors playing over different costumes, moving about in different sets, forms an ever-changing picture delightfully pleasing and big.

Now, as the musical comedy depends for its appeal upon musical volume, numbers of people, sometimes shifting scenery, a kaleidoscopic effect of pretty girls in ever changing costumes and dancing about to catchy music, it does not have to lean upon a fascinating plot or brilliant dialogue, in order to succeed. But of course, as we shall see, a good story and funny dialogue make a good musical comedy better.

3. The Element of Plot

If your memory and my recollection of numerous musical comedies of both the one-act and the longer production of the legitimate stage are to be trusted, a plot is something not vital to the success of a musical comedy. Indeed, it is actually true that many a musical comedy has failed because the emphasis was placed on plot rather than on a skeleton of a story which showed the larger elements to the best advantage. Therefore I present the plot element of the average one-act musical comedy thus:

Whereas the opening and the finish of the playlet are two of its most difficult parts to write, in the musical comedy the beginning and the finish are ready-made to the writer's hand. However anxious he may be to introduce a novel twist of plot at the end, the writer is debarred from doing so, because he must finish with an ensemble number where the appeal is made by numbers of people, costumes, pretty girls and music. At the beginning, however, the writer may be as unconventional as he pleases—providing he does not take too long to bring on his first ensemble, and so disappoint his audience, who are waiting for the music and the girls. Therefore the writer must be content to "tag on" his plot to an opening nearly always— if not always—indicated, and to round his plot out into an almost invariably specified ending.

Between the opening and the closing ensembles the writer has to figure on at least one, and maybe more, ensembles, and a solo and a duet, or a trio and a quartet, or other combinations of these musical elements. These demands restrict his plot still further. He must indeed make his plot so slight that it will lead out from and blend into the overshadowing stage effects. Necessarily, his plot must first serve the demands of scenery and musical numbers— then and only then may his plot be whatever he can make it.

The one important rule for the making of a musical comedy plot is this: *The plot of a one-act musical comedy should be considered as made up of story and comedy elements so spaced that the time necessary for setting scenery and changing costumes is neither too long nor too short.*

More than one dress rehearsal on the night before opening has been wisely devoted to the precise rehearsing of musical numbers and costume changes only. The dialogue was never even hastily spoken. The entire effort was directed to making the entrances and exits of the chorus and principals on time. "For," the producer cannily reasons, "if they slip up on the dialogue they can fake it—but the slightest wait on a musical number will seem like a mortal wound."

If you recall any of Jesse L. Lasky's famous musical acts, "A Night at the Country Club," "At the Waldorf," "The Love Waltz," "The Song Shop" (these come readily to mind, but for the life of me I cannot recall even one incident of any of their plots), you will realize how important is the correct timing of musical numbers. You will also understand how unimportant to a successful vaudeville musical comedy is its plot.

4. Story Told by Situations, Not by Dialogue

As there is no time for studied character analysis and plot exposition, and little time for dialogue, the story of a musical comedy must be told by broad strokes. When you read "A Persian Garden," selected for full reproduction in the Appendix because it is one of the best examples of a well-balanced musical comedy plot ever seen in vaudeville, you will understand why so careful a constructionist as Edgar Allan Woolf begins his act with the following broad stroke:

The opening chorus has been sung, and instantly an old man's voice is heard off stage. Then all the chorus girls run up and say, "Oh, here comes the old Sheik now."

Again, when Paul wishes to be alone with Rose, Mr. Woolf makes Paul turn to Phil and say, "What did I tell you to do?" Then Phil seizes Mrs. Schuyler and runs her off the stage into the house.

Mr. Woolf's skill built this very broad stroke up into a comedy exit good for a laugh, but you and I have seen other exits where the comedy was lacking and the mechanics stood out even more boldly.

So we see that the same time-restriction which makes a musical comedy plot a skeleton, also makes the exits and entrances and the dialogue and every happening structurally a skeleton so loosely jointed that it would rattle horribly— were it not for the beautiful covering of the larger effects of costumes, scenery and music. Therefore the overshadowing necessity for speed makes admissible in the musical comedy broad strokes that would not be tolerated anywhere else.

It is by willingly granting this necessary license that the audience is permitted to enjoy many single musical numbers and delightful ensembles within the time-limits vaudeville can afford for anyone act. So we see why it is—to return to the bald expository statement with which this division begins—that the writer must consider his story and his comedy scenes only as time-fillers to make the waits between musical numbers pleasantly interesting and laughter-worthwhile.

5. The Comedy Element

Plainly recognizing the quickness with which one character must be brought on the stage and taken off again, and thoroughly appreciating that whatever is done between the musical numbers must be speedily dismissed, let us now see what forms of comedy are possible.

Obviously the comedy cannot depend upon delicate shades. It must be the sort of comedy that is physical rather than mental. Slap-stick comedy would seem to be the surest to succeed.

But while this is true, there is no need to depend entirely on the slap-stick brand of humor. For instance, while we find in "A Persian Garden" one whole comedy scene built on the killing of mosquitoes on Phil's face—certainly the slap-stick brand, even though a hand delivers the slap—we also have the comedy of character in Mrs. Schuyler's speeches.

Comedy rising directly out of and dependent upon plot, however, is not the sort of comedy that usually gives the best results, because plot is nearly always subservient to the musical and picture making elements. But the comedy element of plot may be made to run throughout and can be used with good effect, if it is the kind that is easily dismissed and brought back. This is why so many musical comedies have made use of plots hinged on mistaken identity, Kings and Princesses in masquerade, and wives and husbands anxiously avoiding each other and forever meeting unexpectedly.

Still, plot-comedy may be depended upon for at least one big scene, if the idea is big enough. For instance, the internationally successful "The Naked Truth" possessed a plot that was big enough to carry the musical comedy on plot-interest alone, if that were necessary. Indeed, it might have been used as a good farce without music. The whole act hung on a magic statue in whose presence nothing but the truth could be told, on pain of parting from one's clothes. And the comedy scenes that developed out of it carried a series of twists and turns of real plot-interest that made the musical numbers all the more delightful and the whole act a notable success. The musical element of this delightful vaudeville form makes certain other humorous acts fit into the musical comedy structure. For instance, if the comedy character is left alone on the stage, he can with perfect propriety deliver a short monologue. Or he may do anything else that will win laughter and applause.

And the two-act, even more perfectly than the monologue, fits into the musical comedy. No matter what the two-act is, if it is short and humorous, it may be used for one of the ornamental time-gap stoppers. A quarrel scene may be just what is needed to fill out and advance the plot. But more often, the flirtation two-act is the form that best suits, for the nature of the musical comedy seems best expressed by love and its romantic moments. Indeed, the flirtation two-act is often a little musical comedy in itself, minus a background of girls. As an example, take Louis Weslyn's very successful two-act, "After the Shower." [100] You can easily imagine all the other girls in the camping party appearing, to act as the chorus. Then suppply a talkative chaperon, and you have only to add her comical husband to produce a fine musical comedy offering.

So we see once more that the one-act musical comedy is the result of assembling, rather than of writing. There is no need of adding even one instruction paragraph here.

Before we take up the one or two hints on writing that would seem to present themselves in helpful guise, you should read Edgar Allan Woolf's "A Persian Garden." Turn to the Appendix and this act will show you clearly how the writer welds these different vaudeville forms into one perfect whole.

---

[100] See the Appendix.

CHAPTER XX

PUTTING TOGETHER THE ONE-ACT MUSICAL COMEDY WITH HINTS ON MAKING THE BURLESQUE TAB

UNLESS you have a definite order to write a one-act musical comedy, it would seem, from the comparatively small part the writer has in the final effect, that the novice had better not write the musical comedy at all. Although this would appear to be clear from the discussion of the elements in the preceding chapter, I want to make it even more emphatic by saying that more than once I have written a musical comedy act for the "small time" in a few hours—and have then spent weeks dovetailing it to fit the musical numbers introduced and whipping the whole act into the aspect of a "production."

But there is one time when even the amateur may write a musical comedy—when he has a great idea. But I do not mean the average musical comedy idea—I mean such an idea as that which made "The Naked Truth" so successful. And in the hope that you may possess such an idea, I offer a few hints that may prove helpful in casting your idea into smooth musical comedy form.

As I have already discussed plot in the chapters devoted to the playlet, and have taken up the structure of the monologue and the two-act in the chapters on those forms, there is now no need for considering "writing" at all save for a single hint. Yet even this one suggestion deals less with the formal "writing" element than with the "feel" of the material. It is stated rather humorously by Thomas J. Gray, who has written many successful one-act musical comedies, varying in style from "Gus Edwards' School Boys and Girls" to "The Vaudeville Revue of 1915"—a musical travesty on prevailing ideas—and the books of a few long musical successes, from comedy scenes in "Watch your Step" to "Ned Wayburn's Town Topics," that "Musical comedy, from a vaudeville standpoint, and a 'Broadway' or two-dollar standpoint, are two different things. A writer has to treat them in entirely different ways, as a doctor would two different patients suffering from the same ailment. In vaudeville an author has to remember that nearly everyone in the audience has some one particular favorite on the bill—you have to write something funny enough to: please the admirers of the acrobat, the magician, the dancer, the dramatic artist, the rag-time singer and the moving pictures. But in 'Broadway' musical comedy it is easier to please the audiences because they usually know what the show is about before they buy their tickets, and they know what to expect. That's why you can tell 'vaudeville stuff' in a 'Broadway' show—it's the lines the audience laugh at.

"To put it in a different way, let me say that while in two-dollar musical comedy you can get by with 'smart lines' and snickers, in vaudeville musical comedy you have to go deeper than the lip-laughter. You must waken the laughter that lies deep down and rises in appreciative roars. It is in ability to create situations that will produce this type of laughter that the one-act musical comedy writer's success lies."

1. An Average One-Act Musical Comedy Recipe

While it is not absolutely necessary to open a musical comedy with an ensemble number, many fine acts do so open. And the ensemble finish seems to be the rule. Therefore let us assume that you wish to form your musical comedy on this usual style. As your act should run anywhere from thirty to fifty minutes, and as your opening number will consume scarcely two minutes, and your closing ensemble perhaps three, you have—on a thirty-five minute basis— thirty minutes in which to bring in your third ensemble, your other musical numbers and your dialogue.

The third ensemble—probably a chorus number, with the tenor or the ingenue, or both, working in front of the chorus—will consume anywhere from five to seven minutes. Then your solo will take about three minutes. And if you have a duet or a trio, count four minutes more. So you have about eighteen minutes for your plot and comedy—including specialties.

While these time hints are obviously not exact, they are suggestive of the fact that you should time everything which enters into your act. And having timed your musical elements by some such rough standard as this—or, better still, by slowly reading your lyrics as though you were singing—you should set down for your own guidance a schedule that will look something like this:

Opening ensemble	2	minutes

Dialogue
    Introducing Plot,
    First Comedy Scenes
	4	"

Solo	3	"
Dialogue Comedy and Specialties	5	"
Ensemble number	5	"

Dialogue
    Specialties, Comedy.
    Plot climax—perhaps
    a "big" love scene,
    leading into
	7	"

Duet	4	"

Dialogue
    Plot Solution—the
    final arrangement
    of characters
	2	"

Closing ensemble	3	"
	35	"

Of course this imaginary schedule is not the only schedule that can be used; also bear firmly in mind that you may make any arrangement of your elements that you desire, within the musical comedy form. Let me repeat what I am never tired of saying, that a rigid adherence to any existing form of vaudeville act is as likely to be disastrous as a too wild desire to be original. Be as unconventional as you can be within the necessary conventional limits. This is the way to success.

You have your big idea, and you have the safe, conventional ensemble opening, or a semi-ensemble novelty opening. Also you have a solo number for the tenor or the ingenue, with the chorus working behind them. Finally you have your ensemble ending. Now, within these boundaries, arrange your solo and duet—or dispense with them, as you feel best fits your plot and your comedy. Develop your story by comedy situations—don't depend upon lines. Place your big scene in the last big dialogue space—the seven minutes of the foregoing schedule—and then bring your act to an end with a great big musical finish.

2. Timing the Costume Changes

Although the schedule given allows plenty of time for costume changes, you must not consider your schedule as a ready-made formula. Read it and learn the lesson it points out—then cast it aside. Test every minute of your act by the test of time. Be especially careful to give your chorus and your principal characters time to make costume changes.

In gauging the minutes these changes will take, time yourself in making actual changes of clothing. Remember that you must allow one minute to get to the dressing room and return to the stage. But do not make the mistake of supposing that the first test you make in changing your own clothes will be the actual time it will take experienced dressers to change. You yourself can cut down your time record by practice—and your clothes are not equipped with time-saving fasteners. Furthermore, it often happens that the most complicated dress is worn in the first scene and a very quick change is prepared for by under-dressing—that is, wearing some of the garments of the next change under the pretentious over-garments of the preceding scene. These are merely stripped off and the person is ready dressed to go back on the stage in half a minute.

But precise exactness in costume changes need not worry you very much. If you have been reasonably exact, the producer—upon whom the costume changes and the costumes themselves depend—will add a minute of dialogue here or take away a minute there, to make the act run as it should.

3. The Production Song

Certain songs lend themselves more readily to effective staging, and these are called "production songs." For instance: "Alexander's Ragtime Band" could be—and often was—put on with a real band. The principal character could sing the first verse and the chorus alone. Then the chorus girls could come out in regimentals, each one "playing" some instrument—the music faked by the orchestra or produced by "zobos"—and when they were all on the stage, the chorus could be played again with rousing effect. During the second verse, sung as a solo, the girls could act out the lines. Then with the repetitioin of the chorus, they could produce funny characteristic effects on the instruments. And then they could all exit—waiting for the audience to bring them back for the novelties the audience would expect to be introduced in an encore.

This is often the way a "popular song" is "plugged" in cabarets, musical comedies, burlesque, and in vaudeville. It is made so attractive that it is repeated again and again—and so drummed into the ears of the audience that they go out whistling it. Ned Wayburn demonstrated this in his vaudeville act "Staging an Act." He took a commonplace melody and built it up into a production—then the audience liked it. George Cohan did precisely the same thing in his "Hello, Broadway"; taking a silly lyric and a melody, he told the audience he was going to make 'em like it; and he did—by "producing it."

But not every "popular song" lends itself to production treatment. For instance, how would you go about producing "When it Strikes Home"? How would you stage "When I Lost You"? Or—to show you that serious songs are not the only ones that may not be producible— how would you put on "Oh, How that German Could Love"? Of course you could bring the chorus on in couples and have them sing such a sentimental song to each other—but that would not, in the fullest sense, be producing it.

Just as not every "popular song" can be produced, so not every production song can be made popular. You have never whistled that song produced in "Staging an Act," nor have you ever whistled Cohan's song from "Hello, Broadway." If they ever had any names I have forgotten them, but the audience liked them immensely at the time.

As many production songs are good only for stage purposes, and therefore are not a source of much financial profit to their writers, there is no need for me to describe their special differences and the way to go about writing them. Furthermore, their elements are precisely the same as those of any other song—with the exception that each chorus is fitted with different catch lines in the place of the regular punch lines, and there may be any number of different verses. [101]Now having your "big" idea, and having built it up with your musical elements carefully spaced to allow for costume changes, perhaps having made your comedy rise out of the monologue and the two-act to good plot advantage, and having developed your story to its climax in the last part of your act, you assemble all your people, join the loose plot ends and bring your musical comedy to a close with a rousing ensemble finish.

HINTS ON MAKING THE BURLESQUE TAB

The word "tab" is vaudeville's way of saying "tabloid," or condensed version. While vaudeville is in itself a series of tabloid entertainments, "tab" is used to identify the form of a musical comedy act which may run longer than the average one-act musical comedy. Although a tabloid is almost invariably in one act, it is hardly ever in only one scene. There are usually several different sets used, and the uninterrupted forty-five minutes, or even more than an hour, are designed to

---

[101] See Chapter XXII.

give a greater effect of bigness to the production.

But the greatest difference between the one-act musical comedy and the burlesque tab does not lie in playing-time, nor bigness of effect. While a one-act musical comedy is usually intended to be made up of carefully joined and new humorous situations, the burlesque tab—you will recall the definition of burlesque—depends upon older and more crude humor.

James Madison, whose "My Old Kentucky Home" [102] has been chosen as showing clearly the elements peculiar to the burlesque tab, describes the difference in this way:

"Burlesque does not depend for success upon smoothly joined plot, musical numbers or pictorial effects. Neither does it depend upon lines. Making its appeal particularly to those who like their humor of the elemental kind, the burlesque tab often uses slap-stick comedy methods. Frankly acknowledging this, vaudeville burlesque nevertheless makes a clean appeal. It does not countenance either word or gesture that could offend. Since its purpose is to raise uproarious laughter, it does not take time to smooth the changes from one comedy bit to the next, but one bit follows another swiftly, with the frankly avowed purpose to amuse, and to amuse for the moment only. Finally, the burlesque tab comes to an end swiftly: it has made use of a plot merely for the purpose of stringing on comedy bits, and having come toward the close, it boldly states that fact, as it were, by a swift rearrangement of characters—and then ends."

While the burlesque tab nearly always opens with an ensemble number, and almost invariably ends with an ensemble, there may be more solos, duets, trios, quartets and ensembles than are used by the musical comedy—if the act is designed to run for a longer time. But as its appeal is made by humor rather than by musical or pictorial effect, the burlesque tab places the emphasis on the humor. It does this by giving more time to comedy and by making its comedy more elemental, more uproarious.

In a burlesque tab, the comedy bits are never barred by age—providing they are sure-fire—and therefore they are sometimes reminiscent. [103] The effort to give them freshness and newness is to relate the happenings to different characters, and to introduce the bits in novel ways.

Therefore, it would seem obvious that the writing of the burlesque tab is not "writing" at all. It is stage managing. And as the comedy bits are in many cases parts of the history of the stage—written down in the memories of actor and producer—the novice had better not devote his thoughts to writing burlesque. However, if he can produce bits of new business that will be sure-fire, he may find the burlesque tab for him the most profitable of all opportunities the vaudeville stage has to offer. That, however, is a rare condition for the beginner.

---

[102] See the Appendix
[103] Mr. Madison informed me that the "statuary bit" in "My Old Kentucky Home" is one of the oldest "bits" in the show business. It is even older than Weber and Field's first use of it a generation ago.

CHAPTER XXI

THE MUSICAL ELEMENTS OF THE POPULAR SONG

THE easiest thing in the world is to write a song; the most difficult, to write a song that will be popular. I do not mean a "popular" song, but a song everybody will whistle—for few songs written for the populace really become songs of the people. The difference between poverty and opulence in the business of song-writing is—whistling.

What is the difference, then, between the man who can "write songs" and the one who can write songs everybody will whistle? Wherein lies the magic? Here is the difference, unexplained it is true, but at least clearly stated:

There are hundreds of men and women all over the land who can rhyme with facility. Anyone of them can take almost any idea you suggest off hand, and on the instant sing you a song that plays up that idea. These persons are the modern incarnations of the old time minstrels who wandered over the land and sang extemporaneous ditties in praise of their host for their dinners. But, remarkable as the gift is, many of these modern minstrels cannot for the life of them put into their songs that something which makes their hearers whistle it long after they leave. The whistle maker is the one who can rhyme with perhaps no more ease than these others, but into his song he is able to instil the magic—sometimes.

But what is this magic that makes of song-writing a mystery that even the genius cannot unerringly solve each time he tries? Not for one moment would I have you believe that I can solve the mystery for you. If I could, I should not be writing this chapter—I should be writing a song that could not fail of the greatest sale in history. Still, with the kind assistance of the gentlemen in the profession—as the prestidigitator used to say in the old town hall when he began his entertainment—I may be able to lift the outer veils of the unknown, and you may be able I to face the problem with clearer-seeing eyes.

I called for help first from Irving Berlin, without doubt the most successful popular song writer this country has ever known; then the assistance of phenomenally successful writers of such diverse genius as Charles K. Harris, L. Wolfe Gilbert, Ballard MacDonald, Joe McCarthy, Stanley Murphy, and Anatol Friedland, was asked and freely given. It is from their observations, as well as from my own, that the following elements of the art of whistle-making have been gathered.

Although we are interested only in the lyrics of the popular song, we must first consider the music, for the lyric writer is very often required to write words to music that has already been written. Therefore he must know the musical elements of his problem.

I. Music and Words are Inseparable

Think of any popular song-hit, and while you are recollecting just "how it goes," stand back from yourself and watch your mental processes. The words of the title first pop into your mind, do they not? Then do not you find yourself whistling that part of the music fitted to those words? Conversely, if the music comes into your mind first, the words seem to sing themselves. Now see if the bars of music you remember and whistle first are not the notes fitted to the title.

If these observations are correct, we have not only proof of the inseparable quality of the words and the music of a popular song, but also evidence to which you can personally testify regarding the foundations of lyric-writing.

But first let us hear what Berlin has to say about the inseparable quality of words and music: "The song writer who writes both words and music, has the advantage over the lyric writer who must fit his words to somebody else's music and the composer who must make his music fit someone else's words. Latitude—the mother of novelty—is denied them, and in consequence both lyrics and melody suffer. Since I write both words and music, I can compose them together and make them fit. I sacrifice one for the other. If I have a melody I want to use, I plug away at the lyrics until I make them fit the best parts of my music, and vice versa. "For instance: 'In My Harem' first came to me from the humorous possibility that the Greeks, who at that time were fighting with the Turks, might be the cause of a lot of harems running loose in Turkey. I tried to fit that phrase to a melody, but I couldn't. At last I got a melody; something that sounded catchy; a simple 'dum-te-de-dum.' I had it,

> In my harem,
> In my harem.

"With 'Ragtime Violin' I had the phrase and no music. I got a few bars to fit, then the melody made a six-syllable and then a five-syllable passage necessary. I had it:

> Fiddle up! Fiddle up!
> On your violin.

"The lyric of a song must sing the music and the music sing the words."

Charles K. Harris, who wrote the great popular success, "After the Ball," so far back in the early days of the popular song that some consider this song the foundation of the present business, has followed it up with innumerable successes. Mr. Harris has this to, say on the same point:

"I believe it is impossible to collaborate with anyone in writing a popular song. I don't believe one man can write the words and another the music. A man can't put his heart in another's lyrics or music. To set a musical note for each word of a song is not all—the note must fit the word." But, while Mr. Harris's words should be considered as the expression of an authority, there is also considerable evidence that points the other way. Just to mention a few of the many partnerships which have resulted in numerous successes, there are Williams and Van Alstyne, who followed "Under the Shade of the Old Apple Tree" with a series of hits; Ballard MacDonald and Harry Carroll, who made "On the Trail of the Lonesome Pine" merely the first of a remarkably successful brotherhood;

Harry Von Tilzer with his ever varying collaborators, and L. Wolfe Gilbert, who wrote "Robert E. Lee," "Hitchy Koo," and other hits, with Louis Muir, and then collaborated with Anatol Friedland and others in producing still other successes. These few examples out of many which might be quoted, show that two persons can collaborate in writing song-hits, but, in the main, as Mr. Berlin and Mr. Harris say, there are decided advantages when words and music can be done together by one writer.

What is absolutely essential to the writing of songs which will make the nation whistle, may be stated in this principle:

The words and music of a song must fit each other so perfectly that the thought of one is inseparable from the other.

And now before we turn to the essential elements of the words, to which I shall devote the next chapter, permit me to name a few of the elements of popular music that may be helpful to many modern minstrels to know. In fact, these are all the suggestions on the writing of popular music that I have been able to glean from many years of curious inquiry. I believe they represent practically, if not quite, all the hints that can be given on this subject. [104]

2. One Octave is the Popular Song Range

The popular song is introduced to the public by vaudeville performers, cabaret singers, and demonstrators, whose voices have not a wide range. Even some of the most successful vaudeville stars have not extraordinary voices. Usually the vaudeville performer cannot compass a range of much more than an octave. The cabaret singer who has command of more than seven notes is rare, and the demonstrator in the department store and the five-and ten-cent store usually has a voice little better than the person who purchases. Therefore the composer of a song is restricted to the range of one octave. Sometimes, it is true, a song is written in "one-one," or even "one-two" (one or two notes more than an octave), but even such "rangey" songs make use of these notes only in the verses and confine the chorus to a single octave. But in the end, the necessity for the composer's writing his song within one octave to make an effective offering for his introducing singers, works out to his advantage. The average voice of an octave range is that possessed by those who buy popular songs to sing at home.

Now here is a helpful hint and another bit of evidence from the music angle, to emphasize the necessity for the perfect fitting of words and music. Let me state it as Berlin did, in an article written for the Green Book Magazine:

3. Melodies Should Go Up on Open Vowels

"Melodies should go up on open vowels in the lyrics—A, I or O. E is half open and U is closed. Going up on a closed vowel makes enunciation difficult."

---

[104] Because of the obvious impossibility of adequately discussing syncopation and kindred purely technical elements, ragtime has not been particularly pointed out. The elements here given are those that apply to ragtime as well as to nearly every other sort of popular song.

Experience is the only thing warranted to convince beyond doubt, so test this rule on your own piano. Then take down the most popular songs you have in your collection and measure them by it.

4. Put "Punch" in Music Wherever Possible

As we shall see later, another definition of the popular song-hit might be, "A song with a punch in the lyrics and a punch in the music." Berlin expressed the application to the problem of melody by the following:

"In the 'International Rag,' for example, I got my punch by means of my melody. I used the triplet, the freak, from out of my bag of tricks:

> Raggedy melody,
> Full of originality.

5. Punch is Sometimes Secured by Trick of Repetition

Anatol Friedland, who composed the music of "My Persian Rose," and L. Wolfe Gilbert's "My Little Dream Girl," in discussing this question, said:

"Ten notes may be the secret of a popular song success. If I can make my listeners remember ten notes of a song that's all I ask. Whenever they hear these ten notes played they'll say, 'That's. . .,' and straightway they'll begin to whistle it. This is the music punch, and it depends on merit alone. Now here's one angle of the musical punch trick:

"To make a punch more punchy still, we repeat it at least once, and sometimes oftener, in a song. You may start your chorus with it, repeat it in the middle, or repeat it at the end. Rarely is it repeated in the verse. High-brow composers call it the theme. For the popular song composer, it's the punch. Clever repetition that makes the strain return with delightful satisfaction, is one of the tricks of the trade—as well as of the art of popular music."

6. A Musical Theme Might be Practically the Entire Song

If what Friedland says is so, and you may turn to your well-thumbed pile of music for confirmation, the theme or the punch of popular music may prove the entire song. I mean, that in its final sales analysis, the magic bars are what count. To carry this logical examination still further, it is possible for a popular song to be little more than theme. As a musical theme is the underlying melody out of which the variations are formed, it is possible to repeat the theme so often that the entire song is little more than clever repetitions.

One of the most common methods is to underlay a melody with what E. M. Wickes, [105]one of the keenest popular song critics of today, calls the "internal vamp." This is the keeping of a melody so closely within its possible octave that the variations play around a very few notes. Try on your piano this combination—D, E flat, and E natural, or F natural, with varying tempos, and

---

[105] Mr. Wickes has been contributing to The Writer's Monthly a series of valuable papers under the general caption, "Helps for Song Writers."

you will recognize many beginnings of different famous songs they represent. Either the verse of these songs starts off with this combination, or the chorus takes these notes for its beginning. "Sweet Adeline" and "On the Banks of the Wabash" are but two of the many famous songs built on this foundation. Of course, there are other combinations. These few combinations taken together might be considered as the popular idea of "easy music."

And now it is through the consideration of the importance of the variations of the theme that we may come to an understanding of what, for the want of a better phrase, I shall call unexpected punches.

7. Punches not Suggested by the Theme

The impossibility of adequately pointing out by words the specific examples of what I mean in certain songs makes it necessary for me to direct you back to your own piano. Run over a group of your favorites and see how many musical punches you can find that are not due directly to the theme. Pick out the catchy variations in a dozen songs—you may chance on one or two where the biggest punch is not in the theme. Of course you may trace it all back to the theme, but nevertheless it still stands out a distinct punch in the variation. If you can add this punch to your theme-punch, your song success is assured.

8. Use of Themes or Punches of Other Songs

When Sol P. Levy, the composer of "Memories," the "Dolly Dip Dances," and a score of better-class melodies, shared my office, one of our sources of amusement was seeking the original themes from which the popular songs were made. As Mr. Levy was arranging songs for nearly all the big publishers, we had plenty of material with which to play our favorite indoor sport. It was a rare song, indeed, whose musical parent we could not ferret out. Nearly all the successful popular songs frankly owned themes that were favorites of other days—some were favorites long "before the war."

Berlin's use of "Way down upon the Swanee River"—"played in ragtime"—for a musical punch in "Alexander's Ragtime Band," was not the first free use of a theme of an old favorite for a punch, but it was one of the first honestly frank uses. The way he took Mendelssohn's "Spring Song" and worked it into as daring a "rag" as he could achieve, is perhaps the most delightfully impudent, "here-see-what-I-can-do," spontaneously and honestly successful "lift" ever perpetrated. Berlin has "ragged" some of the most perfect themes of grand opera with wonderful success, but not always so openly. And other composers have done the same thing.

The usual method is to take some theme that is filled with memories and make it over into a theme that is just enough like the familiar theme to be haunting. This is the one secret or trick of the popular song trade that has been productive of more money than perhaps any other.

This lifting of themes is not plagiarism in the strict sense in which a solemn court of art-independence would judge it. Of course it is well within that federal law which makes the copyrightable part of any piece of music as wide open as a barn door, for you know you can with "legal honesty" steal the heart of any song, if you are "clever" enough, and want it. The average popular song writer who makes free use of another composer's melody, doubtless would defend his act with the argument that he is not writing "serious music," only melodies for the passing hour and therefore that he ought to be permitted the artistic license of weaving into his songs themes that are a part of the melodic life of the day. [106]But, although some song writers contend for the right of free use, they are usually the first to cry "stop thief" when another composer does the same thing to them. However, dismissing the ethics of this matter, right here there lies a warning, not of art or of law, but for your own success.

Never lift a theme of another popular song. Never use a lifted theme of any song—unless you can improve on it. And even then never try to hide a theme in your melody as your own—follow Mr. Berlin's method, if you can, and weave it frankly into your music.

Now, to sum up all that has been said on the music of the popular song: While it is an advantage for one man to write both the words and music of a song, it is not absolutely essential; what is essential is that the words and music fit each other so perfectly that the thought of one is inseparable from the other. One octave is the range in which popular music should be written. Melodies should go up on open vowels in the lyrics. A "punch" should be put in the music wherever possible. Punch is sometimes secured by the trick of repetition in the chorus, as well as at the beginning and end. The theme may be and usually is the punch, but in the variations there may be punches not suggested by the theme. Themes, semi-classical, or even operatic, or punches of old favorites may be used—but not those of other popular songs—and then it is best to use them frankly.

To state all this in one concise sentence permit me to hazard the following:

The music-magic of the popular song lies in a catchy theme stated at, or close to, the very beginning, led into clever variations that round back at least once and maybe twice into the original theme, and finishing with the theme—which was a punch of intrinsic merit, made stronger by a repetition that makes it positively haunting.

---

[106] An interesting article discussing the harm such tactics have done the popular song business is to be found over the signature of Will Rossiter in the New York Star for March 1, 1913.

CHAPTER XXII

THE ELEMENTS OF A SUCCESSFUL LYRIC

ONE question about song-writing is often asked but will never be settled: Which is more important, the music or the words? Among the publishers with whom I have discussed this question is Louis Bernstein, of Shapiro, Bernstein & Co. He summed up what all the other publishers and song-writers I have known have said:

"A great melody may carry a poor lyric to success, and a great lyric may carry a poor melody; but for a song to become widely popular you must have both a great melody and a great lyric."

This is but another way of stating the fact noted in the preceding chapter, that the words and music of a popular song-hit are indivisible. And yet Mr. Bernstein gives an authoritative reply to the question with which this chapter opens.

Charles K. Harris put it in another way. Referring particularly to the ballad—and to the particular style of ballad that has made him famous—he said:

"The way to the whistling lips is always through the heart. Reach the heart through your lyrics, and the lips will whistle the emotion via the melody. When the heart has not been touched by the lyric, the lips will prove rebellious. They may, indeed, whistle the melody once, even twice, but it takes more than that to make a song truly popular. A catchy tune is not sufficient in itself. It goes far, it is true, but it will not go the entire distance of popularity, or even two-thirds of the distance, unless it is accompanied by a catchy lyric."

You may read into this a leaning toward the lyric, if you like. And it might be better if you did, for you would then realize that your part of a popular song must be as "great" as you can make it. But whatever may be your opinion, it does not alter the fact that both Mr. Harris and Mr. Bernstein have pointed out—catchy words are needed as much as catchy melody. And permit me to say very humbly that personally I have no leaning toward the musical one of the twins: my reason for discussing first the musical elements, is that a lyric writer often is called on to fit words to music, and because an understanding of the musical elements forms a fine foundation for an easy, and therefore a quick, dissection of the popular song—that is all.

I. WHAT A POPULAR SONG LYRIC IS

In its original meaning, a lyric is verse designed to be sung to the accompaniment of music. Nowadays lyrical poetry is verse in which the poet's personal emotions are strongly shown. Popular song-lyrics especially are not only designed to be sung, but are verses that show a great deal of emotion—any kind of emotion. But remember this point: Whatever and how great soever may be the emotion striving for expression, the words designed to convey it do not become lyrics until the emotion is *shown*, and shown in a sort of verse which we shall presently examine. If you *convey* emotion, your words may be worth thousands of dollars. If you fail to convey it, they will be only a sad joke.

As illustrations of this vital point, and to serve as examples for the examination of the elements of the popular lyric, read the words of the following famous songs; and while you are reading them you will see vividly how music completes the lyric. Stripped of its music, a popular song-lyric is often about as attractive as an ancient actress after she has taken off all the make-up that in the setting of the stage made her look like a girl. Words with music become magically one, the moving expression of the emotion of their day.

IMPORTANT NOTE

All the popular song lyrics quoted in this volume are copyright property and are used by special permission of the publishers, in each instance personally granted to the author of this book. Many of the lyrics have never before been printed without their music. Warning:—Republication in any form by anyone whosoever will meet with civil and criminal prosecution by the publishers under the copyright law.

ALEXANDER'S RAGTIME BAND

Words and Music by IRVING BERLIN

Oh, ma honey, oh, ma honey,
Better hurry and let's meander,
Ain't you goin', ain't you goin,'
To the leader man, ragged meter man,
Oh, ma honey, oh, ma honey,
Let me take you to Alexander's grand stand, brass band,
Ain't you comin' along?

CHORUS
Come on and hear, come on and hear
Alexander's ragtime band,
Come on and hear, come on and hear,
It's the best band in the land,
They can play a bugle call like you never heard before,
So natural that you want to go to war;
That's just the bestest band what am, honey lamb,
Come on along, come on along,
Let me take you by the hand,
Up to the man, up to the man, who's the leader of the band,
And if you care to hear the Swanee River played in ragtime,
Come on and hear, come on and hear Alexander's ragtime Band.

Oh, ma honey, oh, ma honey,
There's a fiddle with notes that screeches,
Like a chicken, like a chicken,

And the clarinet is a colored pet,
Come and listen, come and listen,
To a classical band what's peaches, come now, somehow,
Better hurry along.

THE TRAIL OF THE LONESOME PINE

Words by   Music by
BALLARD MACDONALD   HARRY CARROLL

On a mountain in Virginia stands a lonesome pine,
Just below is the cabin home, of a little girl of mine,
Her name is June,
And very very soon,
She'll belong to me,
For I know she's waiting there for me,
'Neath that old pine tree.
REFRAIN

In the Blue Ridge mountains of Virginia,
On the trail of the lonesome pine,
In the pale moonshine our hearts entwine,
Where she carved her name and I carved mine,
Oh, June, like the mountains I'm blue,
Like the pine, I am lonesome for you,
In the Blue Ridge mountains of Virginia,
On the trail of the lonesome pine.
I can hear the tinkling water-fall far among the hills,
Bluebirds sing each so merrily, to his mate rapture thrills,
They seem to say, Your June is lonesome too.
Longing fills her eyes,
She is waiting for you patiently,
Where the pine tree sighs.

WHEN THE BELL IN THE LIGHTHOUSE RINGS DING DONG

Lyric by   Music by
ARTHUR J. LAMB   ALFRED SOLMAN

Just a glance in your eyes, my bonnie Kate,
  Then over the sea go I,
While the sea-gulls circle around the ship,
  And the billowy waves roll high.
And over the sea and away, my Kate,
  Afar to the distant West;
But ever and ever a thought I'll have,
  For the lassie who loves me best.

REFRAIN
When the bell in the lighthouse rings ding, dong,
When it clangs with its warning loud and long,
  Then a sailor will think of his sweetheart so true,
  And long for the day he'll come back to you;
And his love will be told in the bell's brave song
When the bell in the lighthouse rings ding, dong,
  Ding! Dong! Ding! Dong!
When the bell in the lighthouse rings
  Ding! Dong! Ding! Dong!

For a day is to come, my bonnie Kate,
  When joy in our hearts shall reign
And we'll laugh to think of the dangers past,
  When you rest in my arms again.
For back to your heart I will sail, my Kate,
  With love that is staunch and true;
In storm or in calm there's a star of hope,
  That's always to shine for you.

SWEET ITALIAN LOVE

Words by   Music by
IRVING BERLIN   TED SNYDER

Everyone talk-a how they make-a da love
Call-a da sweet name like-a da dove,
It makes me sick when they start in to speak-a
Bout the moon way up above.
What's-a da use to have-a big-a da moon?
What's the use to call-a da dove
If he no like-a she, and she no like-a he,
The moon can't make them love. But,

CHORUS
Sweet Italian love,
Nice Italian love,
You don't need the moon-a-light your love to tell her,
In da house or on da roof or in da cellar,
Dat's Italian love,
Sweet Italian love;
When you kiss-a your pet,
And it's-a like-a spagette,
Dat's Italian love.
Ev'ryone say they like da moon-a da light,

There's one-a man up in da moon all-a right,
But he no tell-a that some other nice feller
Was-a kiss your gal last night.
Maybe you give your gal da wedding-a ring,
Maybe you marry, like-a me
Maybe you love your wife, maybe for all your life,
But dat's only maybe. But,

CHORUS
Sweet Italian love,
Nice Italian love,
When you squeeze your gal and she no say, "Please stop-a!"
When you got dat twenty kids what call you "Papa!"
Dat's Italian love,
Sweet Italian love;
When you kiss one-a time,
And it's-a feel like-a mine,
Dat's Italian love!

OH HOW THAT GERMAN COULD LOVE
Words by　　　　Music by
IRVING BERLIN　　　TED SNYDER

Once I got stuck on a sweet little German,
　And oh what a German was she,
The best what was walking, well, what's the use talking,
　Was just made to order for me.
So lovely and witty; more yet, she was pretty,
　You don't know until you have tried.
She had such a figure, it couldn't be bigger,
　And there was some one yet beside.

CHORUS
Oh how that German could love,
　With a feeling that came from the heart,
She called me her honey, her angel, her money,
　She pushed every word out so smart.
She spoke like a speaker, and oh what a speech,
　Like no other speaker could speak;
Ach my, what a German when she kissed her Herman,
　It stayed on my cheek for a week.

This girl I could squeeze, and it never would hurt,
　For that lady knew how to squeeze;
Her loving was killing, more yet, she was willing,
　You never would have to say please.

I just couldn't stop her, for dinner and supper,
  Some dishes and hugs was the food;
When she wasn't nice it was more better twice;
  When she's bad she was better than good.

Sometimes we'd love for a week at a time,
  And it only would seem like a day;
How well I remember, one night in December,
  I felt like the middle of May.
I'll bet all I'm worth, that when she came on earth,
  All the angels went out on parade;
No other one turned up, I think that they burned up
  The pattern from which she was made.

WHEN IT STRIKES HOME

Words and Music by CHARLES K. HARRIS

You sit at home and calmly read your paper,
Which tells of thousands fighting day by day,
Of homeless babes and girls who've lost their sweet-hearts,
But to your mind it all seems far away.

REFRAIN
When it strikes home, gone is the laughter,
  When it strikes home your heart's forlorn,
When it strikes home the tears fall faster,
  For those dear ones who've passed and gone.
And when you hear of brave boys dying,
  You may not care, they're not your own;
But just suppose you lost your loved ones,
  That is the time when it strikes home.
Out on the street, a newsboy crying "Extra,"
  Another ship has gone down, they say;
'Tis then you kiss your wife and little daughter,
  Give heartfelt thanks that they are safe today.

MY LITTLE DREAM GIRL

Words by   Music by
L. WOLFE GILBERT   ANATOL FRIEDLAND

The night time, the night time is calling me,
It's dream-time, sweet dream-time, for you and me.
I'm longing, I'm longing to close my eyes,

For there a sweet vision lies.
REFRAIN

My little dream girl,
You pretty dream girl,
Sometimes I seem, girl, to own your heart.
Each night you haunt me,
By day you taunt me,
I want you, I want you, I need you so.
Don't let me waken,
Learn I'm mistaken,
Find my faith shaken, in you, sweetheart.
I'd sigh for,
I'd cry for, sweet dreams forever,
My little dream girl, good-night.

While shadows are creeping through darkest night,
In dream-land, sweet dream-land, there's your love-light.
It's beaming, it's gleaming, and all for me,
Your vision I long to see.

MEMORIES

Lyric by   Music by
BRETT PAGE   SOL. P. LEVY

Oh, those happy days, when first we met, before you
  said good-bye,
You soon forgot, I can't forget, no matter how I try,
Those happy hours like incense burn,
   They're all that's left for me,
You took my heart and in return
   You gave a memory.

Oh, memories, dear memories, of days I can't forget,
Dear memories, sweet memories, my eyes with tears grow wet,
  For like a rose that loves the sun,
  And left to die when day is done,
  I gave my all, the heart you won,
Sweetheart, I can't forget.

In all my dreams I dream of you, your arms enfold
  me, dear.
Your tender voice makes dreams seem true, your
  lips to mine are near.
But when I turn your kiss to take,

You turn away from me,
In bitter sadness I awake,
　Awake to memory.

Oh, memories, dear memories, a face I can't forget,
Oh, memories, sweet memories, a voice that haunts me yet,
　For like a rose that loves the sun,
　And left to die when day is done,
　I gave my all, the heart you won,
Sweetheart, I can't forget.

PUT ON YOUR OLD GREY BONNET

Words by　　　　　Music by
STANLEY MURPHY　　PERCY WENRIGHT

On the old farm-house veranda
There sat Silas and Miranda,
　Thinking of the days gone by.
Said he "Dearie, don't be weary,
You were always bright and cheery,
　But a tear, dear, dims your eye."
Said she, "They're tears of gladness,
Silas, they're not tears of sadness,
　It is fifty years today since we were wed."
Then the old man's dim eyes brightened,
And his stern old heart it lightened,
　As he turned to her and said:

CHORUS

"Put on your old grey bonnet with the blue ribbons
on it,
While I hitch old Dobbin to the shay,
And through the fields of clover, we'll drive up to Dover,
On our Golden Wedding Day."
It was in the same old bonnet,
With the same blue ribbon on it,
　In the old shay by his side,
That he drove her up to Dover,
Thro' the same old fields of clover,
　To become his happy bride.
The birds were sweetly singing
And the same old bells were ringing,
　As they passed the quaint old church where they were wed.
And that night when stars were gleaming,

The old couple lay a-dreaming,
　Dreaming of the words he said:

THERE'S A LITTLE SPARK OF LOVE STILL BURNING

Words by　　　　Music by
JOE MCCARTHY　　FRED FISCHER

There was a fire burning in my heart,
Burning for years and for years,
Your love and kisses gave that flame a start,
I put it out with my tears;
You don't remember, I can't forget,
That old affection lives with me yet,
I keep on longing, to my regret,
I know I can't forget.

CHORUS
There's a little spark of love still burning,
And yearning down in my heart for you,
There's a longing there for your returning,
I want you, I do!
So come, come, to my heart again,
Come, come, set that love aflame,
For there's a little spark of love still burning,
And yearning for you.
I left you laughing when I said good-bye,
Laughing, but nobody knew
How much relief I found when I could cry,
I cried my heart out for you;
I've loved you more than you ever know,
Though years have passed I've wanted you so,
Bring back the old love, let new love grow,
Come back and whisper low:

WHEN I LOST YOU
By IRVING BERLIN

The roses each one, met with the sun,
Sweetheart, when I met you.
The sunshine had fled, the roses were dead,
Sweetheart, when I lost you.

CHORUS
I lost the sunshine and roses,
I lost the heavens of blue,
　I lost the beautiful rainbow,
I lost the morning dew;

> I lost the angel who gave me
> Summer the whole winter through,
> I lost the gladness that turned into sadness,
> When I lost you.
>
> The birds ceased their song, right turned to wrong,
> Sweetheart, when I lost you.
> A day turned to years, the world seem'd in tears,
> Sweetheart, when I lost you.

II. QUALITIES OF THE POPULAR SONG LYRIC

Having read these eleven lyrics of varying emotions, note the rather obvious fact that

1. Most Popular Songs Have Two Verses and One Chorus

I am not now speaking of the "production song," which may have a dozen verses, and as many different catch-lines in the chorus to stamp the one chorus as many different choruses, but only of the popular song. And furthermore, while two different choruses are sometimes used in popular songs, the common practice is to use but one chorus.

Now let us see the reason for a peculiarity that must have struck you in reading these lyrics.

2. A Regular Metre is Rare

Metre is the arrangement of emphatic and unemphatic syllables in verse on a measured plan, and is attained by the use of short syllables of speech varied in different rotations by long syllables. The metrical character of English poetry depends upon *the recurrence of similarly accented syllables at short and more or less regular intervals.* Let us take this as the definition of what I mean by metre in the few sentences in which I shall use the word.

Among recognized poets there has always been a rather strict adherence to regularity of form. Indeed, at times in the history of literature, poetry, to be considered poetry, had to confine itself to an absolutely rigid form. In such periods it has been as though the poet were presented with a box, whose depth and breadth and height could not be altered, and were then ordered to fill it full of beautiful thoughts expressed in beautiful words, and to fill it exactly, or be punished by having his work considered bad.

In ages past this rigidity of rule used to apply to the song-poet also, although the minstrel has always been permitted more latitude than other poets. To-day, however, the poet of the popular song may write in any measure his fancy dictates, and he may make his metre as regular or as irregular as he wishes. He may do anything he wants, in a song. Certainly, his language need not be either exact or "literary." Practically all that is demanded is that his lyrics convey emotion. The song-poet's license permits a world of metrical and literary sinning. I am not either apologizing for or praising this condition—I am simply stating a proved fact.

3. Irregularity of Metre May Even Be a Virtue

Even without "scanning" the lyrics of the eleven songs you have just read their irregularity of metre is plain. It is so plain that some of the irregularities rise up and smite your ears. This is why some popular songs seem so "impossible" without their music. And the reason why they seem so pleasing with their music is that the music takes the place of regularity with delightful satisfaction. The very irregularity is what often gives the composer his opportunity to contribute melodious punches, for the words of a popular song are a series of catchy phrases. In some cases irregularity in a song may be the crowning virtue that spells success.

4. Regularity and Precision of Rhymes Are Not Necessary

There is no need to point to specific examples of the lack of regularity in the recurrence of rhymes in most of the lyric specimens here printed, or in other famous songs. Nor is there any necessity to instance the obvious lack of precise rhyming. Neither of these poetic qualities has ever been a virtue of the average popular song-poet.

So far as the vital necessities of the popular song go, rhymes may occur regularly or irregularly, with fine effect in either instance, and the rhymes may be precise or not. To rhyme *moon* with *June* is not unforgivable. The success of a popular song depends on entirely different bases. Nevertheless, a finely turned bit of rhyming harmony may strike the ear and stand out from its fellows like a lovely symphony of fancy. If you have given any attention to this point of rhyming you can recall many instances of just what I mean.

5. Strive for Regular and Precise Rhyming—If Fitting

If you can be regular and if you can be precise in the use of rhymes in your song-poem, be regular and be precise. Don't be irregular and slovenly just because others have been and succeeded. You will not succeed if you build your lyrics on the faults and not on the virtues of others. The song-poem that gleams like a flawless gem will have a wider and more lasting success—all other things being equal.

On the other hand, it is absolutely fatal to strive for regularity and precision, and thereby lose expression. If you have to choose, choose irregularity and faulty rhymes. This is an important bit of advice, for a song-poem is not criticized for its regularity and precision—it is either taken to heart and loved in spite of its defects, or is forgotten as valueless. As Winifred Black wrote of her child, "I love her not for her virtues, but oh, for the endearing little faults that make her what she is."

6. Hints On Lyric Measures

Reference to the lyrics already instanced will show you that they are written in various measures. And while it is foreign to my purpose to discuss such purely technical points of poetry, [107]permit me to direct your attention to a few points of song measure.

An individual poetic measure is attained by the use of metre in a certain distinct way. Because the normal combinations of the emphatic and the unemphatic syllables of the English language are but five, there are only five different poetic measures. Let us now see how an investigation of the bafflingly unexact measures of our examples will yield—even though their irregular natures will not permit of precise poetic instances—the few helpful hints we require.

(a) *The first measure*—called by students of poetry the trochaic measure—is founded on the use of a long or emphatic syllable followed by a short or unemphatic syllable, It has a light, tripping movement, therefore it is peculiarly fitted for the expression of lively subjects. One of our examples shows this rather clearly:

    ʽ   ʽ   ʽ   ʽ   ʽ

There's a | little | spark of | love still | burning

Yet this is not a measure that is commonly found in the popular song. Other combinations seem to fit popular song needs quite as well, if not better.

(b) *The second measure*—called the iambic measure—is the reverse of the first. That is, the short or unemphatic syllable precedes the long or emphatic syllable. "Alexander's Ragtime Band " uses this measure at the beginning of the chorus.

    ʽ   ʽ   ʽ   ʽ

Come on | and hear | come on | and hear

The first verse of Mr. Harris's song shows this measure even more clearly:

    ʽ   ʽ   ʽ   ʽ   ʽ

You sit | at home | and calm | ly read | your pa | per

This second measure, being less sustained in syllabic force, is more easily kept up than the first measure. It is therefore in common use.

(c) *The third measure*—called the dactylic measure—is formed of a combination of three syllables. Its characteristic is an emphatic syllable followed by two unemphatic syllables, as:

    ʽ   ʽ

The | old oak en | buck et

    ʽ   ʽ

The | iron bound | buck et

(d) *The fourth measure*—called by the frighteningly long name of amphibrachic measure—is formed by a short or unemphatic syllable followed by a long or emphatic syllable, which is followed again by another short or unemphatic syllable.

    ʽ   ʽ   ʽ

I won der | who's kiss ing | her now

---

[107] The Art of Versification, by J. Berg Esenwein and Mary Eleanor Roberts—one of the volumes in "The Writer's Library"—covers this subject with a thoroughness it would be useless for me to attempt. Therefore if you wish to take this subject up more in detail, I refer you to this excellent book.

(e) *The fifth measure*—called anapestic measure—is made up of two short or unemphatic followed by a long or emphatic syllable.

When the bell | in the light | house rings ding | dong

All these three-syllabic measures have a quicker movement than the two-syllabic, owing to the greater number of unaccented, unemphatic syllables. They lend themselves to a rushing impetuosity of expression which is the notable characteristic of the popular song. But they are not always regular, even in high-grade poetry. Therefore in the popular song we may look for, and certainly be sure to find, all sorts of variations from the regular forms here given. Indeed, regularity, as has been clearly pointed out, is the exception and not the rule; for few single lines, and, in a still more marked degree, almost no songs, adhere to one measure throughout. Precisely as "apt alliteration's artful aid" may be used or not used as may suit his purpose best, so the song-writer makes regularity of measure subservient to the effect he desires.

However, I give these examples not with a view to the encouragement of either regularity or irregularity. My purpose is to show you what combinations are possible, and to say, as the jockey whispers in the eager ear of the racehorse he has held back so long, "Go to it!" Break every rule you want to—only break a record. As Mr. Berlin said, "I've broken every rule of versification and of music, and the result has often been an original twist. In popular songs a comparative ignorance of music is an advantage. Further, since my vocabulary is somewhat limited through lack of education, it follows that my lyrics are simple."

This is only Berlin's modest way of saying that not one in ten successful song-writers know anything about the art of music, and that very few are well enough educated to err on the side of involved language and write other than simple lyrics. He drew the application as to himself alone, although his native genius makes it less true of him than of many another less gifted. The big point of this observation lies in his emphasis on the fact that

7. Simple Lyrics and Simple Music Are Necessary

Perhaps in Mr. Berlin's statement rests the explanation of the curious fact that nearly all the successful popular song-writers are men who had few educational advantages in youth. Most of them are self-made men who owe their knowledge of English and the art of writing to their own efforts. Conversely, it may also explain why many well-educated persons strive for success in song writing in vain. They seem to find it difficult to acquire the chief lyric virtue—simplicity.

Not only must the words of a popular song be "easy," but the *idea* of the lyric must be simple. You cannot express a complex idea in the popular song-form, which is made up of phrases that sometimes seem short and abrupt. And, even if you could overcome this technical difficulty, you would not find an audience that could grasp your complex idea. Remember that a majority of the purchasers of popular songs buy them at the five- and ten-cent store. To sell songs to this audience, you must make your music easy to sing, your words easy to say and your idea simple and plain.

8. Rhythm the Secret of Successful Songs

Being barred from other than the simplest of ways, by his own limitations, his introducers and his market, the song-writer has to depend upon a purely inherent quality in his song for appeal. This appeal is complex in its way, being composed of the lure of music, rhyme and emotion, but when analyzed all the parts are found to have one element in common. This element to which all parts contribute is *rhythm*.

Now by rhythm I do not mean rhyme, nor metre, nor regularity. It has nothing necessarily to do with poetic measures nor with precision of rhymes. Let me attempt to convey what I mean by saying that the rhythm of a song is, as Irving Berlin said, *the swing*. To the swing of a song everything in it contributes. Perhaps it will be clearer when I say that rhythm is compounded of the exactness with which the words clothe the idea and with which the music clothes the words, and the fineness with which both words and music fit the emotion. Rhythm is singleness of effect. Yet rhythm is more—it is singleness of effect plus a sort of hypnotic fascination.

And here we must rest as nearly content as we can, for the final effect of any work of art does not admit of dissection. I have shown you some of the elements which contribute to making a popular song popular, and in the next chapter we shall see still others which are best discussed in the direct application of the writing, but even the most careful exposition must halt at the heart of the mystery of art. The soul of a song defies analysis.

9. Where the "Punch" in the Lyric is Placed

Just as it is necessary for a popular song to have a punch somewhere in its music, so it must come somewhere in its lyric. Just what a lyrical punch is may be seen in the chorus of "The Trail of the Lonesome Pine."

> In the Blue Ridge Mountains of Virginia,
> On the trail of the lonesome pine,
> In the pale moonshine our hearts entwine,
> Where she carved her name and I carved mine,
> *Oh, June, like the mountains I'm blue,*
> *Like the pine, I am lonesome for you!*
> In the Blue Ridge mountains of Virginia,
> On the trail of the lonesome pine.

The underlined words are plainly the punch lines of this famous song—the most attractive lines of the whole lyric. Note where they are placed—in the chorus, and next to the last lines. Read the chorus of "My Little Dream Girl" and you will find a similar example of punch lines:

> *I'd sigh for,*
> *I'd cry for, sweet dreams forever,*

> My little dream girl, good night.

These, also, are placed next to the last lines of the chorus.
The punch lines of "When it Strikes Home," are found in

> And when you hear of brave boys dying,
> You may not care, they're not your own,
> *But just suppose you lost your loved one*
> *That is the time when it strikes home.*

Here the punch is placed at the very end of the chorus.

Now test every song on your piano by this laboratory method. You will find that while there may be punch lines at the end of the verses there are nearly always punch lines at the end of the chorus. There must be a reason for this similarity in all these popular songs. And the reason is this: The emphatic parts of a sentence are the beginning and end. The emphatic part of a paragraph is the end. If you have a number of paragraphs, the last must be the most emphatic. This is a common rule of composition founded on the law of attention—we remember best what is said last. The same thing is true of songs. And songwriters are compelled by vaudeville performers to put a punch near the end of their choruses because the performer must reap applause. Thus commerce keeps the song-writer true to the laws of good art. Therefore remember:

The most attractive lines of a popular song must be the last lines, or next to the last lines, of the chorus.

This holds true whether the song is a "sob" ballad or a humorous number. And—strictly adhering to this rule—put a punch, if you can, at the end of each verse. But whether you put a punch at the end of a verse or not, always put a punch close to the end of your chorus.

10. Contrast an Element of the "Punch"

One of the easiest ways of securing the vitally necessary punch lies in contrast. Particularly is this true in humorous songs—it is the quick twist that wins the laughter. But in all songs contrast may form a large part of the punch element.

The ways of securing a contrast are too many to permit of discussion here, but I name a few:

You may get contrast by switching the application as Harris did in:

> You may not care, they're not your own,
> But just suppose you lost your loved one.

Or you may get contrast by changing your metre and using a contrasting measure. While you may do this in the middle of the chorus, it is nearly always done *throughout* the chorus. I mean that the measure of the chorus is usually different from the measure used in the verse.

And of course when you change the measure of your lyric, the movement of the music changes too. It is in the resulting contrasting melody that lies much of the charm of the popular song.

But, whatever means you use, be sure you have a contrast somewhere in your lyric—a contrast either of subject matter, poetic measure or musical sounds.

11. Love the Greatest Single Element

If you will review all the great song successes of this year and of all the years that are past, you will come to the conclusion that without love there could be no popular song. Of course there have been songs that have not had the element of love concealed anywhere in their lyrics, but they are the exceptions.

If your song is not founded on love, it is well to add this element, for when you remember that the song's reason for being is emotion, and that the most moving emotion in the world is love, it would seem to be a grave mistake to write any song that did not offer this easy bid for favor. If you have not love in your lyrics make haste to remedy the defect.

The ballad is perhaps the one form by which the greatest number of successful song-writers have climbed to fame. It is also one of the easiest types to write. It should seem worth while, then, for the newcomer to make a ballad one of his earliest bids for fame.

12. The Title

The title of a song is the advertising line, and therefore it must be the most attractive in your song. It is the whole song summed up in one line. It may be a single word or a half-dozen words. It is not the punch line always. It is often the very first line of the chorus, but it is usually the last line.

There is little need for constructive thought in choosing a title. All that is necessary is to select the best advertising line already written. You have only to take the most prominent line and write it at the top of your lyrics. Study the titles of the songs in this chapter and you will see how easy it is to select your title after you have written your song.

To sum up: a great lyric is as necessary to the success of a popular song as a great melody, but not more necessary. A lyric is a verse that conveys a great deal of emotion. Most popular songs have two verses and one chorus. A regular metre is rare; irregularity may even be a virtue. The regular occurrence of rhymes and precise rhymes are not necessary—but it is better to strive after regularity and precision. There are five lyrical measures common to all poetry, but you may break every rule if you only break a record. Rhythm—the swing—is the secret of successful songs. Every lyric must have one or more punch lines—which may occur at the end of each verse, but must be found in the last lines of the chorus. Contrast—either of idea, poetic measure or music—is one sure way of securing the punch. Love is the greatest single element that makes for success in a song idea. The one-word standard of popular-song writing is *simplicity*—music easy to sing, words easy to say, the idea simple and plain.

CHAPTER XXIII

WRITING THE POPULAR SONG

IN the preceding chapters we saw how the elements of a popular song are nearly identical in music and in lyrics, no matter how the styles of songs may differ. In this chapter we shall see how these elements may be combined—irrespective of styles—into a song that the boy on the street will whistle, and the hand organs grind out until you nearly go mad with the repetition of its rhythm.

Not only because it will be interesting, but because such an insight will help to a clear understanding of methods I shall ask you to glance into a popular song publisher's professional department.

I. A POPULAR SONG IN THE MAKING

A very large room—an entire floor, usually—is divided into a reception room, where vaudeville and cabaret performers are waiting their turns to rehearse, and half-a-dozen little rooms, each containing a piano. As the walls of these rooms are never very thick, and often are mere partitions running only two-thirds of the way to the ceiling, the discord of conflicting songs is sometimes appalling. Every once in a while some performer comes to the manager of the department and insists on being rehearsed by the writers of the latest song-hit themselves. And as often as not the performer is informed that the writers are out. In reality, perhaps, they are working on a new song in a back room. Being especially privileged, let us go into that back room and watch them at work.

All there is in the room is a piano and a few chairs. One of the chairs has a broad arm, or there may be a tiny table or a desk. With this slender equipment two persons are working as though the salvation of the world depended on their efforts. One of them is at the piano and the other is frowning over a piece of paper covered with pencil marks.

Perhaps the composer had the original idea—a theme for a melody. Perhaps the lyric writer had one line—an idea for a song. It does not matter at all which had the idea originally, both are obsessed by it now.

"Play the chorus over, will you?" growls the writer. Obediently the composer pounds away, with the soft pedal on, and the writer sings his words so that the composer can hear them. There comes a line that doesn't fit. "No good!" they say together.

"Can't you change that bar?" inquires the writer.

"I'll try," says the composer. "Gimme the sheet."

They prop it up on the piano and sing it together.

"Shut up!" says the composer. And the writer keeps still until the other has pounded the offending bar to fit.

Or perhaps the writer gets a new line that fits the music. "How's this?" he cries with the intonation Columbus must have used when he discovered the new world.

"Punk!" comments the composer. "You can't rhyme 'man' with 'grand' and get away with it these days."

"Oh, all right," grumbles the harassed song-poet, and changes both lines to a better rhyme. "I don't like that part," he gets back at the composer, "it sounds like 'Waiting at the Church.'"

"How's this, then?" inquires the composer, changing two notes.

"Fine," says the lyric writer, for the new variation has a hauntingly familiar sound, too elusive to label—is amazingly catchy.

For hours, perhaps, they go on in this way—changing a note here, a whole bar there, revising the lyric every few lines, substituting a better rhyme for a bad one, and building the whole song into a close-knit unity.

At last the song is in pretty good shape. As yet there is no second verse, but the "Boss" is called in and the boys sing him the new song. "Change 'dream' to 'vision'—it sounds better," he says; or he may have a dozen suggestions—perhaps he gives the song a new punch line. He does his part in building it up, and then the arranger is called in.

With a pad of manuscript music paper, and a flying pencil, he jots down the melody nearly as fast as the composer can pound it out on tne piano. "Get a 'lead-sheet' ready as quick as you can, commands the Boss. "We'll try it out tonight."

"Right!" grunts the arranger, and rushes away to give the melody a touch here and there. As often as not, he comes back to tell the composer how little that worthy knows about music and to demand that a note be changed or a whole bar recast to make it easier to play, but at last he appears with a "lead-sheet"—a mere suggestion of the song to be played, with all the discretion the pianist commands—and the composer, the lyric writer and the "Boss" go across the street to some cabaret and try out the new song.

Here, before an audience, they can tell how much of a song they really have. They may have something that is a "winner," and they may see that their first judgment was wrong—they may have only the first idea of a hit.

But let us suppose that the song is a "knock 'em off their seats" kind, that we may get down to the moral of this little narrative of actual happenings. The "pluggers" are called in and bidden to memorize the song. They spend the afternoon singing it over and over again—and then they go out at night and sing it in a dozen different places all over the city. On their reports and on what the "Boss" sees himself as he visits place after place, the decision is made to publish immediately or to work the song over again. It is the final test before an audience that determines the fate of any song. The new song may never be sung again, or tomorrow the whole city may be whistling it.

And now permit me to indicate a point that lies in the past of the song we have seen in process of manufacture: From somewhere the composer gets an idea for a melody—from somewhere the lyric writer gets an idea for a lyric.

But we must put the music of a song to one side and devote our attention to the lyric.

II. POINTS ON SONG BUILDING

1. Sources of Ideas for Song Lyrics

As a popular song becomes popular because it fits into the life of the day and is the individual expression of the spirit of the moment, Charles K. Harris was doubtless right when he said:

"The biggest secret of success, according to my own system, is the following out in songs of ideas current in the national brain at the moment. My biggest song successes have always reflected the favorite emotion—if I may use the word—of the people of the day. How do I gauge this? Through the drama! The drama moves in irregular cycles, and changes in character according to the specific tastes of the public. The yearly mood of the nation is reflected by the drama and the theatrical entertainment of the year. At least, I figure it out this way, and compose my songs accordingly.

"Here are just two instances of my old successes built on this plan: When 'The Old Homestead' and 'In Old Kentucky' were playing to crowded houses, I wrote 'Midst the Green Fields of Virginia' and 'In the Hills of Old Carolina,' and won. Then when Gillette's war plays, 'Held by the Enemy' and 'Secret Service' caught the national eye, I caught the national ear with 'Just Break the News to Mother.' But these are examples enough to show you how the system works."

Irving Berlin said, "You can get a song idea from anywhere. I have studied the times and produced such songs as 'In My Harem' when the Greeks were fleeing from the Turks and the harem was a humorous topic in the daily newspapers. And I have got ideas from chance remarks of my friends. For instance:

"I wrote 'My Wife's Gone to the Country' from the remark made to me by a friend when I asked him what time he was going home. 'I don't have to go home,' he said, 'my wife's gone to the country.' It struck me as a great idea for a title for a song, but I needed a note of jubilation, so I added 'Hooray, Hooray!' The song almost wrote itself. I had the chorus done in a few minutes, then I dug into the verse, and it was finished in a few hours."

L. Wolfe Gilbert wrote "Robert E. Lee" from the "picture lines" in one of his older songs, "Mammy's Shuffling Dance" and a good old-fashioned argument that he and I had about the famous old Mississippi steamboat. That night when I came back to the office we shared, Gilbert read me his lyric. From the first the original novelty of the song was apparent, and in a few days the country was whistling the levee dance of 'Daddy' and 'Mammy,' and 'Ephram' and 'Sammy,' as they waited for the Robert E. Lee. Had Gilbert ever seen a levee? No—but out of his genius grew a song that sold into the millions.

"Most of our songs come from imagination," said Joe McCarthy. "A song-writer's mind is ever alert for something new. What might pass as a casual remark to an outsider, might be a great idea to a writer. For instance, a very dear young lady friend might have said, 'You made me love you—I didn't want to do it.' Of course no young lady friend said that to me—I just imagined it. And then I went right on and imagined what that young lady would have said if she had followed that line of thought to a climax."

"It's the chance remark that counts a lot to the lyric writer," said Ballard MacDonald. "You might say something that you would forget the next minute—while I might seize that phrase and work over it until I had made it a lyric."

But, however the original idea comes—whether it creeps up in a chance remark of a friend, or the national mood of the moment is carefully appraised and expressed, or seized "out of the air," let us suppose you have an idea, and are ready to write your song. The very first thing you do, nine chances out of ten, is to follow the usual method of song-writers:

2. Write Your Chorus First

The popular song is only as good as its chorus. For whistling purposes there might just as well be no verses at all. But of course you must have a first verse to set your scene and lead up to your chorus, and a second verse to finish your effect and give you the opportunity to pound your chorus home. Therefore you begin to write your chorus around your big idea.

This idea is expressed in one line—your title, your catchy line, your "idea line," if you like—and if you will turn to the verses of the songs reproduced in these chapters you will be able to determine about what percentage of times the idea line is used to introduce the chorus. But do not rest content with this examination; carry your investigation to all the songs on your piano. Establish for yourself, by this laboratory method, how often the idea line is used as a chorus introduction.

Whether your idea line is used to introduce your chorus or not, it is usually wise to end your chorus with it. Most choruses—but not all, as "Put on your Old Grey Bonnet," would suggest—end with the idea line, on the theory that the emphatic spots in any form of writing are at the beginning and the end—and of these the more emphatic is the end. Therefore, you must now concentrate your chorus to bring in that idea line as the very last line.

3. Make the Chorus Convey Emotion

As we saw in the previous chapter, a lyric is a set of verses that conveys emotion. The purpose of the first verse is to lead up to the emotion—which the chorus expresses. While, as I shall demonstrate later, a story may be proper to the verses, a story is rarely told in the chorus. I mean, of course, a story conveyed by pure narrative, for emotion may convey a story by sheer lyrical effect. Narrative is what you must strive to forget in a chorus—in your chorus you *must* convey emotion *swiftly*—that is, with a punch.

While it is impossible for anyone to tell you how to convey emotion, one can point out one of the inherent qualities of emotional speech.

4. Convey Emotion by Broad Strokes

When a man rushes through the corridors of a doomed liner he does not stop to say, "The ship has struck an iceberg—or has been torpedoed—and is sinking, you'd better get dressed quickly and get on deck and jump into the boats." He hasn't time. He cries, "The ship's sinking! To the boats!"

This is precisely the way the song-writer conveys his effect. He not only cuts out the "thes" and the "ands" and the "ofs" and "its" and "perhapses"—he shaves his very thoughts down—as the lyrics printed in these chapters so plainly show—until even logic of construction seems engulfed by the flood of emotion. Pare down your sentences until you convey the dramatic meaning of your deep emotion, not by a logical sequence of sentences, but by revealing flashes.

5. Put Your Punch in Clear Words Near the End

And now you must centre all your thoughts on your punch lines. Punch lines, as we saw, are sometimes the entire point of a song—they are what makes a "popular" lyric get over the footlights when a performer sings the song and they are the big factor—together with the music punches—that make a song popular. However lyrical you have been in the beginning of your chorus, you must now summon all your lyrical ability to your aid to write these, the fate-deciding lines.

But note that emotion, however condensed the words may be that express it, must not be so condensed that it is incoherent. You must make your punch lines as clear in words as though you were drawing a diagram to explain a problem in geometry. The effect you must secure is that of revealing clearness.

Be very careful not to anticipate your punch lines. For instance, if Mr. Gilbert had used "All day I sigh, all night I cry," before "I'd sigh for, I'd cry for, sweet dreams forever" in his "My Little Dream Girl," the whole effect would have been lost. As your punch lines must be the most attractive lines, keep them new and fresh, by excluding from the rest of your song anything like them.

If you can put your punch in the very last lines, fine. If you wish to put your punch lines just before the last two lines—in the third and fourth lines from the last—well and good. But it is never wise to put your punch so far from the end that your audience will forget it before you finish and expect something more. It is a good rule to write your punch lines and then end your song.

Having constructed your chorus from a beginning that uses or does not use your idea line, and having by broad strokes that convey emotion developed it into your punch lines, you end your chorus, usually, but not invariably, with your idea line—your title line.

Now you are ready to write your first verse.

6. Make the First Verse the Introduction of the Chorus

If you have characters in your song, introduce them instantly. If you are drawing a picture of a scene, locate it in your first line. If your song is written in the first person—the "you and I" kind—you must still establish your location and your "you and I" characters at once. If you keep in mind all the time you are writing that your first verse is merely an introduction, you will not be likely to drag it out.

(a) *Write in impersonal mood*—that is, make your song such that it does not matter whether a man or a woman sings it. Thus you will not restrict the wide use of your song. Anyone and everyone can sing it on the stage. Furthermore, it will be apt to sell more readily.

(b) *"Tell a complete story"* is a rule that is sometimes laid down for popular song-writers. But it depends entirely upon what kind of song you are writing whether it is necessary to tell a story or not. "A story is not necessary," Berlin says, and an examination of the lyrics in the preceding chapter, and all the lyrics on your piano, will bear him out in this assertion.

All you need remember is that your song must express emotion in a catchy way. If you can do this best by telling a story, compress your narrative into your verses, making your chorus entirely emotional.

(c) *"Make your verses short"* seems to be the law of the popular song today. In other years it was the custom to write long verses and short choruses. Today the reverse seems to be the fashion. But whether you decide on a short verse or a long verse—and reference to the latest songs will show you what is best for you to write—you must use as few words as possible to begin your story and—with all the information necessary to carry over the points of your chorus—to lead it up to the joining lines.

7. Make Your Second Verse Round Out the Story

You have introduced your chorus in your first verse, and the chorus has conveyed the emotion to which the first verse gave the setting. Now in your second verse round out the story so that the repetition of the chorus may complete the total effect of your song.

More than upon either the first verse or the chorus, unity of effect depends upon the second verse. In it you must keep to the key of emotion expressed in the chorus and to the general trend of feeling of the first verse. If your first verse tells a love-story of two characters, it is sometimes well to change the relations of the characters in the second verse and make the repetition of the chorus come as an answer. But, whatever you make of your second verse, you must not give it a different story. Don't attempt to do more than round out your first-verse story to a satisfying conclusion, of which the chorus is the completing end.

And now we have come to

8. The Punch Lines in the Verses

Toward the end of each verse it is customary to place punch lines which are strong enough pictorially to sum up the contents of the verse and round it out into the chorus. In humorous songs, these punch lines are often used as the very last lines, and the first line of the chorus is depended on to develop the snicker into a laugh, which is made to grow into a roar with the punch lines of the chorus. In other words, there are in every song three places where punch lines must be used. The most important is toward the end of the chorus, and the other places are toward the end of the verses.

9. Don'ts for Verse Last-Lines

Don't end your lines with words that are hard to enunciate—there are dozens of them, of which are "met," and most of the dental sounds. Experience alone can teach you what to avoid. But it may be said that precisely the same reason that dictates the use of open vowels on rising notes, dictates that open sounds are safest with which to end lines, because the last notes of a song are often rising notes. This applies with emphatic force, also, to your chorus. Never use such unrhetorical and laugh-provoking lines as the grotesquely familiar "and then to him I did say."

Don't always feel that it is necessary to tell the audience "here is the chorus." Imagination is common to all, and the chorus is predicted by the turn of thought and the "coming to it" feeling of the melody.

III. ASSEMBLING THE SONG

Having gone over your verses and made sure that you have punch lines that rise out of the narrative effect into revealing flashes, and are completed and punched home by the punch lines of the chorus, and having made sure that your lyrics as a whole are the best you can write, you must give thought to the music.

1. The "One Finger Composer's" Aid

If you are the sort of modern minstrel who has tunes buzzing in his head, it is likely that you will have composed a melody to fit your lyrics. The chances are that you know only enough about music to play the piano rather indifferently. Or, you may be an accomplished pianist without possessing a knowledge of harmony sufficient to admit of your setting down your melody in the form of a good piano score. But even if you are only able to play the piano with one finger, you need not despair. There are dozens of well-known popular song composers who are little better off. You may do precisely what they do—you can call to your aid an arranger. This is the first moral I shall draw from the true story with which this chapter begins.

As the composer played over his melody for the arranger to take down in musical notes, you may sing, whistle or play your melody on the piano with one finger, for the arranger to take down your song. All you need give him is the bare outline of your melody. At best it will be but a forecasting shadow of what he will make out of it. From it he will make you a "lead-sheet," the first record of your melody. Then, if you desire, he will arrange your melody into a piano part, precisely identical in form with any copy of a song you have seen. With this piano version—into which the words have been carefully written in their proper places—you may seek your publisher.

For taking down the melody and making an "ink lead-sheet," the arranger will charge you from one to two dollars. For a piano copy he will charge you anywhere from three to ten dollars—the average price is about five dollars.

2. Be Sure Your Words and Music Fit Exactly

Here we may draw the second moral from the little scene we witnessed in the song publisher's room—this is the big lesson of that scene. In a word, successful song-writers consider a song not as a lyric and a melody, but as a composite of both. A successful song is a perfect fusing of both. The melody writer is not averse to having his melody changed, if by changing it a better song can be made. And the successful lyric writer is only too glad to change his words, if a hit can be produced. With the one end in view, they go over their song time after time and change lyrics and melody with ruthless hands until a whistle-making unity rises clear and haunting.

This is what you must now do with your song. You must bend all your energies to making it a perfect blend of words and music—a unity so compressed and so compactly lyrical that to take one little note or one little word away would ruin the total effect.

This is why

3. Purchasing Music for a Song is Seldom Advisable

If you are invited to purchase music for a new song, it is the part of wisdom to refuse—because only in very rare instances has a successful song been the result of such a method. The reason is perfectly plain, when you consider that the composer who offers you a melody for a cash price is interested only in the small lump sum he receives. You are his market. He does not care anything about the market the music must make for itself, first with a publisher and then with the public.

Therefore, no matter how willing a composer may appear to change his melody to fit your song, scan his proposition with a cynical eye. On the surface he will make the music fit, but he would be wasting his time if he worked over your lyric and his music to the extent that a composer who is paid by the ultimate success of a song would have to labor.

It is very much better to take your chances with even an inferior melody maker who is as much interested as you are in a final success. And when you have found a composer, do not quibble about changing your words to fit his music. And don't fear to ask him to change his melody, wherever constant work on the song proves that a change is necessary. It is only by ceaselessly working over both words and melody that a song is turned into a national whistle.

IV. SEEKING A PUBLISHER [108]

You have written your lyrics, and you have fashioned your melody, or you have found a composer who is anxious to make his melody fit your lyrics so perfectly that they have been fused into a unity so complete that it seems all you have to do to start everybody whistling it is to find a publisher. And so you set about the task.

1. Private Publication Seldom Profitable

While it is perfectly true that there have been many songs that have paid handsome profits from private publication, it is more nearly exact to believe that private publication never pays. Printers and song publishers who make a business

---

[108] The matter under this section would seem to be an integral part of the following Chapter, "Manuscripts and Markets," but it is included in this chapter because some of the points require a discussion too expansive for the general treatment employed in describing the handling of other stage material.

of this private trade will often lure the novice by citing the many famous songs "published by their writers." Whenever you see such an advertisement, or whenever such an argument is used in a sales talk, dig right down to the facts of the case. Nine chances out of ten, you will find that the writers are successful popular song publishers—it is their business to write for their own market. Furthermore—and this is the crux of the matter—they have a carefully maintained sales force and an intricate outlet for all their product, which would take years for a "private publisher" to build up. Really, you cannot expect to make any money by private publication, even at the low cost of song-printing these days—unless you are willing to devote all your energies to pushing your song. And even then, the song must be exceptional to win against the better organized competition.

2. Avoid the "Song Poem" Advertiser

It is never my desire to condemn a class even though a majority of that class may be worthy of reproach. Therefore, instead of inveighing against the "song-poem" fakir with sounding periods of denunciation, permit me to state the facts in this way:

The advertisers for song-poems may be divided into two classes. In the first class are publishers who publish songs privately for individuals who have enough money to indulge a desire to see their songs in print. The writer may not intend his song for public sale. He wishes to have it printed so that he may give copies to his friends and thus satisfy his pride by their plaudits. It is to these song-writers that the honest "private publisher" offers a convenient and often cheap opportunity. His dealings are perfectly honest and fair, because he simply acts as a printer, and not as a publisher, for he does not offer to do more than he can perform.

The second class of song-poem advertisers lure writers by all sorts of glowing promises. They tell you how such and such a song made thousands of dollars for its writer. They offer to furnish music to fit your lyrics. They will supply lyrics to fit your music. They will print your song and push it to success. They will do anything at all—for a fee! And I have heard the most pitiful tales imaginable of high hopes at the beginning and bitter disappointment at the end, from poor people who could ill afford the money lost.

These "publishers" are not fair—they are not honest. They make their living from broken promises, and pocket the change with a grin over their own cleverness. Why these men cannot perform what they promise is perfectly plain in the light of all that has been said about the popular song. It does not need repetition here. If you wish to publish your song privately for distribution among your friends, seek the best and cheapest song printer you can find. But if you hope to make your fortune through publication for which you must pay—in which the publisher has nothing to lose and everything to win—take care! At least consider the proposition as a long shot with the odds against you—then choose the fairest publisher you can find.

3. How to Seek a Market for Your Song

But let us hope that you are the sort of song-writer who is anxious to test his ability against the best. You do not care to have your song published unless it wins publication on its merits—and unless you can be reasonably sure of making some money out of it. You aspire to have your song bear the imprint of one of the publishers whose song-hits are well known. To find the names and addresses of such publishers you have only to turn over the music on your piano. There is no need to print individual names here.

But a few words of direction as to the way you should approach your market may be helpful. I quote here the composite opinion of all the well-known song publishers with whom I have talked:

"To find a great song in the manuscripts that come through the mail—is a dream. It is rare that the mail brings one worthy of publication. If I were a song-writer I should not submit my song through the mails. Of course, if I were far from the big markets I should be compelled to. But if I were anywhere near the market I should go right to the publisher and demonstrate the song to him.

"You see, I must be convinced that a song is a winner before I'll gamble my money on its publication. And the only way I can be easily convinced is to be compelled to listen to the song. Naturally, being a song publisher, I think I know a hit when I hear it—I may 'kid' myself into believing I can pick winners, but I can be made to see the possibilities by actual demonstration, where I might 'pass a song up' in manuscript."

Therefore, it would seem wise to offer a song through the mails only when a personal visit and demonstration are impossible. You need not copyright your song, if you send it to a reputable publisher. All you need do is to submit it with a short letter, offering it on the usual royalty basis, and *enclose stamps for return*, if it is not available. From two to four weeks is the usual time required for consideration.

If you are near a song publisher, the very best thing you can do is to fortify yourself with unassailable faith in your song and then make the publisher listen to you. If you have a song that shows any promise at all, the chances are that you will come out of the door an hour later with a contract.

CHAPTER XXIV

MANUSCRIPTS AND MARKETS

IT is in the hope of directing you to your market that this chapter is designed. But there is no form of writing for which it is more difficult to point out a sure market than for vaudeville material. Even the legitimate stage—with its notorious shifting of plans to meet every veering wind—is not more fickle than the vaudeville stage. The reason for this is, of course, to be found in the fact that the stage must mirror the mind of the nation, and the national mind is ever changing. But once let the public learn to love what you have given them, and they will not jilt your offering in a day. The great advantage the writer of vaudeville material today has over every one of his predecessors, lies in the fact that the modern methods of handling the vaudeville business lend him security in the profits of his success.

1. Preparing the Manuscript

(a) *The acceptable manuscript forms into which all vaudeville material may be cast* may be learned by consulting the examples of the different vaudeville acts given in the appendix to this volume. A moment's examination of them will show you that there is no difference between the manuscript *ways* of presenting the different acts. All are made up of the names of characters, business and dialogue. Therefore they may all be discussed at the same time.

(b) *Have your manuscript typewritten.* This suggestion has the force of law. While it would seem self-evident that a manuscript written out in long hand has a mussy appearance, however neat the writing may be, the many hand-written manuscripts I have tried to read suggest the necessity for pointing out this fact. You surely handicap your manuscript by offering it in long hand to a busy producer.

(c) *The two recognized methods for the typing of stage manuscripts.* First, the entire manuscript is typed in black, blue or purple. Then, after the manuscript is complete, the name of the character above each speech is underlined in red ink, and every bit of business throughout the manuscript is also underlined in red. This method is illustrated below.

-36-

ACT II)
    GRAVES. Yes. (Turns To Dictionary) That's All. (Ellen, Though Curious, Continues Reading In An Undertone To Her Father, Marlin And John. Graves Opens The Dictionary, Starts At Sight Of The Note, Snatches It Up With Trembling Fingers, And Reads It. His Fury Rises. After A Pause, Crumpling The Note, He Turns To Burton And Speaks With An Effort)
GRAVES. Burton!
    (Startled By His Tone, The Others Turn And Regard Graves Curiously)
BURTON. Yes, sir.

GRAVES. Where's Sam?
BURTON. He went out, sir—
GRAVES. Went out?
BURTON. Y-yes, sir. About a quarter of an hour ago.
GRAVES. Where to?
BURTON. He didn't say, sir.
(GRAVES Turns Away Helplessly. Burton Listens And Then Exits C. Graves Walks Up And Down, Wringing His Hands)
MEAD. Anything wrong?
GRAVES (LAMELY) No, no. Don't mind me. Marlin's proposition's all right—
(PAUSE. SUSAN ENTERS R AND IS TROUBLED AT SIGHT OF GRAVES'S EMOTION)
SUSAN (APPROACHING HIM) Father—!
GRAVES (UNABLE LONGER TO RESTRAIN HIMSELF) Hell's fire!
MEAD. Christopher!

Second, a typewriter using two colors is employed. The name of the character above each speech is typed in red, and red is used to type the bits of business. The speeches alone are typed in black, blue or purple as the case may be. The following example illustrates this method.

-32-

ACT I)

BOOTH

Heavens! It reads like a fairy tale, doesn't it?

HENRY

I don't know; does it?

BOOTH

Yes; and many thanks. I'll do my best not to let you regret it.—Only, in the old fairy tale, you know, it always ended with the—the young man's marrying the—the rich old geezer's daughter!

HENRY

(CHUCKLING)
And I'm the rich old geezer, eh? Well, I mightn't 'a' been half as rich this minute if it wasn't for you!—Heigho!
(SIZES UP BOOTH)

Now, I suppose my cantankerous daughter wouldn't have you, Piercy; not if I said anything to her about it. But if she would—and you was willin'—
(HELEN AND BOOTH EXCHANGE ELOQUENT GLANCES)
—why, you're just about the feller I'd want her to have.
(Helen Dances A Little Skirt Dance Of Delight Between The Door L And The Screen. Then She Darts Into The Adjoining Room, Being Observed Only By Booth)

BOOTH

(WITH SPONTANEITY)
Say, Boss, put her there again!
(ANOTHER HANDSHAKE)
Do you know, you and I are getting to be better friends

Either of these methods serves the same purpose equally well. The aim is to separate the names and business from the dialogue, so that the difference may be plain at a glance. The use of either of these ways of typing a manuscript is desirable, but not absolutely necessary.

(d) *Use a "record ribbon"* in typewriting manuscript, because a "copying ribbon" smudges easily and will soil the hands of the reader. Observation of this mechanical point is a big help in keeping a manuscript clean—and respecting the temper of your judge.

(e) *Neatness* is a prime requisite in any manuscript offered for sale. Be sure that the finished copy is free from erasures and penciled after-thoughts. "Do all your after-thinking beforehand," or have a clean, new copy made.

(f) *Re-copy a soiled manuscript* as soon as it shows evidence of handling. Keep your "silent salesman" fresh in appearance.

(g) *Bind your manuscript in a flexible cover* to give it a neat appearance and make it handy to read.

(h) *Type your name and address in full* on the outside of the cover, and on the first white page. Thus you stamp the manuscript as *your* act, and it always bears your address in case of loss.

(i) *Have your act copyrighted* is a bit of advice that would seem needless, but many performers and producers refuse to read an act unless it is copyrighted. The copyright—while it is not as good proof in court as a public performance—is nevertheless a record that on such and such a date the author deposited in the Library of Congress a certain manuscript. This record can be produced as incontrovertible evidence of fact. The view of the performer and the producer is that he wishes to protect the author as much as possible—but himself more. He desires to place beyond all possibility any charge of plagiarism. Therefore, copyright the final version of your act and typewrite on the cover the date of copyright and the serial number.

(j) *How to copyright the manuscript of a vaudeville act.* Write to the Register of Copyrights, Library of Congress, Washington, D.C., asking him to send you the blank form prescribed by law to copyright an unpublished dramatic composition.

Do not send stamps, as it is unnecessary. In addition to the blank you will receive printed instructions for filling it out, and full information covering the copyright process. The fee is one dollar, which includes a certificate of copyright entry. This covers copyright in the United States only; if you desire to copyright in a foreign country, consult a lawyer.

(k) *The preparation of a scene plot* should not be a difficult task if you will remember that you need merely draw a straight-line diagram—such as are shown in the chapter on "The Vaudeville Stage and its Dimensions"—so as to make your word-description perfectly clear. On this diagram it is customary to mark the position of chairs, tables, telephones and other properties incidental to the action of the story. But a diagram is not absolutely necessary. Written descriptions will be adequate, if they are carefully and concisely worded.

(l) *The preparation of property plots and light plots* has been mentioned in the chapter on "The Vaudeville Stage and Its Dimensions," therefore they require a word here. They are merely a list of the properties required and directions for any changes of lighting that may occur in the act. For a first presentation of a manuscript, it is quite unnecessary for you to bother about the technical plots (arrangement plans) of the stage. If your manuscript is acceptable, you may be quite sure that the producer will supply these plots himself.

(m) *Do not offer "parts" with your manuscript.* A "part" consists of the speeches and business indicated for one character, written out in full, with the cues given by the other characters—the whole bound so as to form a handy copy for the actor to study. For instance, there would be four "parts" in a four-people playlet manuscript—therefore you would be offering a producer five manuscripts in all, and the bulk of your material might deter a busy man from reading it carefully. If your manuscript progresses in its sale to the point where parts are desired, the producer will take care of this detail for you. And until you have made a sale, it is a waste of money to have parts made.

2. The Stage Door the Vaudeville Market-Place

Unlike nearly every other specialized business, there is a market in each city of the country for vaudeville material. This market is the stage door of the vaudeville theatre. While it would be unlikely that a dramatist would find a market for a long play at the "legitimate" stage door—although this has happened—there are peculiar reasons why the stage door may be your market-place. A large percentage of vaudeville performers are the owners of their own acts. They buy the material, produce it themselves, and play in it themselves. And they are ever on the lookout for new material.

Not only is there a market at the stage door, but that market changes continually. Without fear of exaggeration it may be said that with the weekly and sometimes semi-weekly changes of the bill in each house, there will in time flow past the stage door nearly all the acts which later appear in vaudeville.

Offering a manuscript at the stage door, however, should not be done without preparation. As you would not rush up to a business man on the street or spring at him when he emerges from his office door, you certainly would not care to give a vaudeville performer the impression that you were lying in wait for him.

(a) *The personal introduction* is a distinct advantage in any business, therefore it would be an advantage for you to secure, if possible, a personal introduction to the performer. However, you must be as discriminating in choosing the person to make that introduction as you would were you selecting an endorser at a bank. A stage-hand or an usher is likely to do you more harm than good. The "mash notes" they may have carried "back stage" would discount their value for you. The manager of the theatre, however, might arrange an introduction that would be of value. At least he can find out for you if the performer is in the market at the time.

(b) *The preliminary letter is never amiss*, therefore it would seem advisable to write to the performer for whom you feel sure you have an act that will fit. Make the letter short. Simply ask him if he is in the market for material, state that you have an act that you would like him to read, and close by requesting an appointment at his convenience.

Do not take up his time by telling him what a fine act you have. He does not know you, and if you praise it too highly he may be inclined to believe that you do not have anything worth while. But do not under-rate your material, either, in the hope of engaging his attention by modesty. Leave it for him to find out if you have an act, first, that is worth while, and second, that fits him.

If you do not hear from the performer, you may be sure that he is not interested in your act. He may be out for the first few weeks in a brand new act, and not in the market at all. So if you do not hear from him, wait until another act comes along and you see someone for whom your act is "just made."

(c) *Should you receive a favorable reply* to your request for an appointment, you may be reasonably sure that your prospective purchaser at least needs a new act. In meeting your appointment, be on time, and have someone with you. A woman, of course, would have a chaperon, precisely as she would if she were meeting any other stranger. And a man might care to have someone to engage the attention of the performer's companion and leave him an uninterrupted opportunity to talk business.

(d) *Ask for an immediate reading* of your manuscript, or at least request it read the next day, when you can be present while he is reading it. Do not leave a manuscript to be returned to you by mail. Vaudeville performers are as honest as any other class of men, but they are busy people and the thing that is put off is forgotten. They are in one town today and miles away tomorrow, and they may leave the manuscript on the bureau of their hotel room intending to mail it at the last minute—and rush away and forget it. Therefore you should ask for an immediate reading. It will take a performer only a few minutes to decide if he cares to consider your act. He knows of what he is in need—and usually is prepared to tell you.

(e) *Do not ask for specific criticism*, for of all people in the world vaudeville performers are the most good-hearted. They would rather please you than hurt you. They will evade the point nine times out of ten; so save them and yourself needless embarrassment. And thus you may also avoid a false valuation of your manuscript.

(f) *If the performer cannot use the act himself*, and if the act possesses merit, the chances are that he will suggest some other performer who might want it. If he does not suggest someone himself, ask him. Vaudeville performers know what other performers want, because they are continually discussing plans for "next season." You may thus pick up some valuable information, even if you do not dispose of the particular manuscript you have for sale.

3. Producing Your Act Yourself

While you are likely at many turns of the sales road to have offered you an opportunity to produce your own act, this method of finding a market is rarely advisable. You would not start a little magazine to get your short-story into print; your story could not possess that much value even if it were a marvel—how much less so if you were unable to find someone willing to buy it!

But there is a still more important reason why you should not rush into producing your act yourself. Producing is a specialized business, requiring wide experience and exact knowledge. Besides, it is one of the most expensive pastimes in the world. Without a most comprehensive experience and peculiar abilities, failure is sure. Do not attempt private production even if you are offered the services of a performer or a producer in whom you have absolute faith. Remember, if they thought your act was really worth while they would be anxious to reap the profits for themselves.

4. Selling an Act to a Producer

While any performer who owns his act is a producer in the sense that he "produces" his act, there are men who make a business of buying manuscripts, engaging people, and producing many acts in which they do not themselves play. Producers who may own a dozen acts of all different kinds would seem to offer to the writer for vaudeville an ideal market. How, then, is the writer to get in touch with them?

(a) *Selling through a Play broker* is a method that is precisely the same as though you consigned a bill of goods to a commission agent, and paid him for disposing of it. The play broker reads your manuscript and engages to try to dispose of it for you, or returns it as not likely to fit in with the particular line of business of which he makes a specialty. If your act is really good and yet the broker is able to make some suggestions that will improve it, he is likely to offer such suggestions, purely in the hope of earning a commission, and in this way he may prove of distinct value as a critic. In any event, if he accepts a manuscript to sell for you, he will offer it in the quarters he thinks most likely to produce it and will attend to all the business incidental to the making of the contract.

For this service the broker charges a ten per cent commission. This commission is paid either on the price of outright sale, or on the royalty account. If the act is sold on royalty, he will collect the customary advance and also the weekly payments. After deducting his commission, he will remit the balance to you.

On the last page of this chapter you will find a partial list of well-known play brokers. Although I do not know of any who deal exclusively in vaudeville material, any one of the agents who handles long plays is glad to handle an exceptionally fine playlet.

(b) *Seeking a personal interview with a producer* is usually productive of one result: The office-boy says, "Leave your manuscript, and he'll read it and let you know." Anxious as he is to secure good material, a man who is busily engaged in producing vaudeville acts has little time to spend on granting personal interviews. And there is another reason—he fears you will try to read your act to him. A personal reading by the author is either a most distressing affair, because the average writer cannot read stage material as it should be read, or else it is very dangerous to the listener's judgment. Many a producer has been tricked into producing an act whose merits a masterly reader has brought out so finely that its fatal faults were forgotten. And so the producer prefers to read a manuscript himself. Alone in his office he can concentrate on the act in hand, and give to it the benefit of his best judgment.

(c) *Offering a manuscript by mail* is perfectly safe. There has never come to my knowledge one clearly proved instance of where a producer has "stolen an idea."

(d) *Send your manuscript by registered mail and demand a return receipt.* Thus you will save losses in the mail and hold a check against the loss of your manuscript in the producer's office. And when you send your manuscript by mail, invariably enclose stamps to pay the return to you by registered delivery. Better still, enclose a self-addressed envelope with enough postage affixed to insure both return and registry.

(e) *Three weeks for consideration* is about the usual time the average producer requires to read a manuscript at his leisure. In times when a producer is actively engaged in putting on an act, he may not have an hour in the week he can call his own. Therefore have patience, and if you do not receive a reply from him in three weeks, write again and courteously remind him that you would like to have his decision at his earliest convenience. Impatient letters can only harm your chance.

5. Hints on Prices for Various Acts

What money can be made by writing vaudeville material? This is certainly the most interesting question the writer for vaudeville can ask. Like the prices of diamonds, the prices of vaudeville acts depend on quality. Every individual act, and each kind of act, commands its own special price. There are two big questions involved in the pricing of every vaudeville manuscript. First, of what value is the act itself? Second, what can the performer or the producer afford to pay or be made to pay for the act?

The first question cannot be answered for even a class of acts. The value of each individual act determines its own price. And even here there enters the element inherent in all stage material— a doubt of value until performance before an audience proves the worth of the act. For this reason, it is customary for the purchaser of a vaudeville act to require that it first make good, before he pays for it. "Try and then buy," is the average vaudevillian's motto. If you are a good business man you will secure an advance against royalty of just as much as you can make the producer "give up." Precisely as in every other business, the price of service depends upon the individual's ability to "make a deal."

The answer to the second question likewise depends upon the vaudeville writer's individual ability as a business man. No hints can be given you other than those that you may glean from a consideration of average and record prices in the following paragraphs.

(a) *The monologue* is usually sold outright. The performer nearly always will tell you—with no small degree of truth—that the monologist makes the monologue, not the monologue the monologist. Many a monologue has sold for five dollars, and the purchaser been "stung" at that price. But very rarely is a monologue bought outright in manuscript—that is, before a try-out. A monologue must prove itself "there," before a monologist will pay any more than a small advance for the exclusive privilege of trying it out.

If the monologue proves itself, an outright offer will be made by the performer. While there are no "regular rates," from two hundred and fifty dollars to seven hundred dollars may be considered as suggestive of the market value of the average successful monologue.

In addition to this, the monologist usually retains the author to write new points and gags for him each week that he works. This, of course, increases the return from a monologue, and insures the writer a small weekly income.

In very rare cases monologues are so good and, therefore, so valuable that authors can retain the ownership and rent them out for a weekly royalty. In such a case, of course, the author engages himself to keep the material up to the minute without extra compensation. But such monologues are so rare they can be counted on the fingers of one hand. There is little doubt that "The German Senator" is one of the most valuable monologue properties—if it does not stand in a class by itself—that has ever been written. For many years it has returned to Aaron Hoffman a royalty of $100 a week, thirty and forty weeks in the year. This may be considered the record price for a monologue.

(b) *The vaudeville two-act* varies in price as greatly as the monologue. Like the monologue, it is usually sold outright. The performers use precisely the same argument about the two-act that is used about the monologue. It is maintained that the material itself is not to be compared with the importance of its presentation. When a two-act has been tried out and found "there," the performers or the producer will offer a price for it.

The same rule, that vaudeville material is worth only as much as it will bring, applies to the two-act. From two hundred and fifty dollars to whatever you can get, may be considered suggestive of two-act prices. Although more two-acts have sold outright for less than three hundred dollars than have sold above five hundred dollars, a successful two-act may be made to yield a far greater return if a royalty arrangement is secured.

Whether it is a two-act, or any other vaudeville act, the royalty asking price is ten per cent of the weekly salary. This rate is difficult to enforce, and while five per cent is nearer the average, the producer would rather pay a definite fixed figure each week, than a percentage that must be reckoned on what may be a varying salary. Usually a compromise of a flat amount per playing week is made when a royalty is agreed on.

(c) *The playlet* varies in returns amazingly. While one small-time producer pays no advance royalty and a flat weekly royalty of from ten dollars to fifteen dollars a week—making his stand on the fact that he gives a longer playing season than his average competitor—many a big-time producer pays a good round advance and as high as $100 a week royalty.

Edgar Allan Woolf has said: "The desire for the one-act comedy is so great that even an unknown writer can secure an advance royalty as great as is paid to the author of a three-act play, if he has written a playlet which seems to possess novelty of story and cleverness of dialogue."

George V. Hobart is reported to have had a variously-quoted number of playlets playing at the same time, each one of which returned him a weekly royalty of $100 a week. And half a dozen other one-act playwrights might be named who have had nearly equal success.

On the other hand, Porter Emerson Brown is quoted as saying: "The work of writing a playlet is nearly as great as writing a three-act play, and the returns cannot be compared."

One of the collaborators on a famous big-time success received forty dollars a week for three seasons as his share. Another playlet writer was paid one hundred dollars a week for one act, and only twenty dollars a week for another. And a third was content with a ten-dollars-a-week royalty on one act, at the same time that another act of his was bringing him in fifty dollars a week.

These examples I have cited to demonstrate that the return from the playlet is a most variable quantity. The small-time pays less than the big-time, and each individual act on both small- and big-time pays a different royalty.

When a playlet—either comedy or straight dramatic—is accepted for production, it is customary, although not an invariable rule, that an advance royalty be paid "down." When the act proves successful, one or more of three propositions may be offered the writer: outright sale at a price previously agreed upon; outright sale to be paid in weekly royalties until an agreed upon figure is reached, when ownership passes from the author to the producer; the more customary weekly royalty. As I have said before, what price you receive for your act finally depends upon your keenness in driving a bargain.

In nearly every case, outright sale has its advantage in the fact that the author need not then worry about collecting his royalty. Of course, when a recognized producer puts out the act there need be no concern about the royalty, so in such instances a royalty is preferable. But in some cases, as when the performer is making long jumps and has a hard time making railroad connections, a weekly royalty has its disadvantages in causing worry to the author.

(d) *The one-act musical comedy* is usually bought outright—after the act "gets over." While many a "book" is contracted for in advance at a small figure, to be doubled or trebled on success, it is also true that royalties are paid. In this case, the custom is to divide the royalty equally between the writer of the book and lyrics, and the composer of the music. When a third person writes the verses of the songs and ensemble numbers, the royalty is usually split three ways. It would be misleading to quote any figures on the musical comedy, for the reason that circumstances vary so greatly with each that there are no standards.

(e) *The burlesque tab* pays about the same rates as the one-act musical comedy, its kindred form.

(f) *The popular song*, unlike the other material treated in this volume, has a well established royalty price: one cent a copy is the standard. Of this, half a cent goes to the writer of the lyric, and half a cent to the composer of the music.

As a popular song, to be considered successful, must sell anywhere from half a million to a million copies, it is easy to estimate the song-writer's return. If the same man writes both the words and the music he will receive from five to ten thousand dollars—or twenty-five hundred to five thousand dollars if he divides with another—for being able to make the nation whistle. Of course, many song-writers have two successful songs selling in a year— therefore you may double the figures above to estimate some successful song-writers' incomes. But it may safely be said that the song-writer who has an income of twelve thousand dollars a year is doing very well indeed! There are many more professional song-writers who work year after year for the salary of the average business man in every other line of endeavor. Don't count your royalty-chickens too soon.

6. Important Lists of Addresses
SOME OF THE MORE PROMINENT PLAY BROKERS

AMERICAN PLAY COMPANY, 33 W. 42d St., New York
MARY ASQUITH, 145 W. 45th St, New York
ALICE KAUSER, 1402 Broadway, New York
DARCY AND WOLFORD, 114 W. 39th St., New York
KIRKPATRICK, LTD., 101 Park Ave., New York
MODERN PLAY CO., Columbus Circle, New York
LAURA D. WILK, 1476 Broadway, New York
GEORGE W. WINNIETT, 1402 Broadway, New York
PAUL SCOTT, 1402 Broadway, New York
SANGER AND JORDAN, 1430 Broadway, New York
MRS. M. A. LEMBECK, 220 W. 42nd St., New York
A LIST OF WELL KNOWN VAUDEVILLE PRODUCERS

The producers given here offer a market which varies so widely in each instance that no attempt has been made to list their needs. Some are interested in other lines of the amusement business as well; and their activities elsewhere must be taken into consideration as determining factors in their special market needs. No division of these producers into big-time and small-time producers is made, because such a distinction would be likely to be misleading rather than helpful.

ARTHUR HOPKINS, 1493 Broadway, New York
JOSEPH HART, 1520 Broadway, New York

JESSE L. LASKY, 120 W. 41St St., New York
PLAYLET PRODUCING COMPANY, 1564 Broadway, New York
B. A. ROLFE, 1493 Broadway, New York
JOE MAXWELL, INC., 360 W. 125th St., New York
ROLAND WEST PRODUCING COMPANY, 260 W. 42d St., New York
HARRY RAPF, 1564 Broadway, New York
PAT CASEY, 1499 Broadway, New York
BILLIE BURKE, 1495 Broadway, New York
JOE PAIGE SMITH, 1493 Broadway, New York
ALF. T. WILTON, 1564 Broadway, New York
JOHN C. PEEBLES, 1564 Broadway, New York
JAMES PLUNKETT, 1564 Broadway, New York
C. M. BLANCHARD, 1579 Broadway, New York
LEWIS AND GORDON, Columbia Theatre Building, 7th Ave. at 47th St., New York
MAX HART, 1564 Broadway, New York
JAMES J. ARMSTRONG, Columbia Theatre Building, 7th Ave. at 47th St., New York
WILLIAM A. BRADY, The Playhouse, 137 W. 48th St., New York
BART McHUGH, Land Title Building, Philadelphia
MENLO E. MOORE, 22 W. Monroe St., Chicago
MINNIE PALMER, 35 Dearborn St., Chicago

THE LARGER CIRCUITS AND BOOKING OFFICES

The following vaudeville circuits, while they may not maintain regular producing departments, produce acts every now and then.

THE UNITED BOOKING OFFICES OF AMERICA, 1564 Broadway, New York. This organization books the B. F. Keith Theatres and allied small- and big-time houses
ORPHEUM CIRUIT COMPANY, 1564 Broadway, New York
LOEW'S THEATRICAL ENTERPRISES, 1493 Broadway, New York
POLI'S CIRCUIT, 1493 Broadway, New York
THE WESTERN VAUDEVILLE MANAGERS' ASSOCIATION, Majestic Theatre Building, Chicago
GUS SUN CIRCUIT, New Sun Theatre Building, Springfield, Ohio
BERT LEVEY CIRCUIT, Alcazar Theatre Building, San Francisco
PANTAGE'S CIRCUIT, Seattle
SULLIVAN AND CONSIDINE, Seattle

To these markets nearly every booking agent and manager in the vaudeville business might be added. Each one has a list of acts he handles that need new material from time to time. And often the agent or manager will add to his list of clients by producing an exceptionally fine act himself.

The reason such a list is not given here is that it would require a small volume merely for the names and addresses. Consultation of "The Clipper Red Book"—a handy directory of theatrical agents, sold at ten cents—will supply this information. A knowledge of the special kinds of acts handled by each agent or manager, and the producers previously given as well, may be gathered by a careful reading of the various theatrical specialized journals. This knowledge can only be acquired a bit here and a little there through persistent attention to the notices of new acts and announcements of plans.

PUBLISHERS OF VAUDEVILLE MATERIAL
SAMUEL FRENCH, 28 W. 38th St., New York
T. S. DENNISON, Chicago

PROMINENT THEATRICAL PAPERS
VARIETY, 1536 Broadway, New York
THE DRAMATIC MIRROR, 1493 Broadway, New York
THE NEW YORK MORNING TELEGRAPH, 50th St. & 8th Ave., New York
THE NEW YORK STAR, 1499 Broadway, New York
THE CLIPPER, 47 W. 28th St., New York
THE BILLBOARD, 1465 Broadway, New York
THE DRAMATIC NEWS, 17 W. 42d St., New York
THE NEW YORK REVIEW, 121 W. 39th St., New York
THE THEATRE MAGAZINE, 8 W. 38th St., New York
THE GREEN BOOK MAGAZINE, North American Building, Chicago.

CHAPTER XXV

HOW A VAUDEVILLE ACT IS BOOKED

WHILE an understanding of how a vaudeville act is transformed from a manuscript into a commercial success may not be necessary to the writing of a good act, such a knowledge is absolutely necessary to the writer who hopes to make money by his work. For this reason I shall devote this final chapter to a brief discussion of the subject.

Permit me, therefore, to take the manuscript of an act, assuming for my purpose that it represents a monologue or a two-act, a playlet or a musical comedy, and trace its commercial career from the author's hands, into a producer's, through a booking office, to success. Anyone of the famous examples printed in this volume could be so taken and its history told, but no one would combine in its experience all the points that should be given. So I shall ask you to imagine that the act whose commercial story I am about to tell represents in itself every kind of act to be seen in vaudeville. I shall call this act by the name of "Success."

When Mr. Author, the writer of "Success," received a letter from Mr. Producer accepting the act and requesting him to call at his office to discuss terms, Mr. Author was delighted and hurried there as fast as he could go.

The office boy ushered him into Mr. Producer's private office, and before the caller could get his breath Mr. Producer had made him an offer. He accepted the offer without haggling over the terms, which seemed to Mr. Author very satisfactory. To tell the truth, he would have accepted almost anything, so eager was he to get his first act on the stage, so it was lucky for him that the terms were really fair.

He had hardly folded up the contract and stowed it, with the advance royalty check, in his bosom pocket, before Mr. Producer plunged into business. He pressed a button for the office boy and told him to tell Mr. Scenic Artist to come in. Now Mr. Scenic Artist was the representative of a great scenic studio, and he sketched a design for a special set in a jiffy; then he thought of another, and then of a third. And Mr. Producer and he were so interested in combining all their good ideas into one admirable set that Mr. Author was startled when they shoved a sketch under his nose and asked for suggestions. He made two that were pertinent to the atmosphere he had imagined for his room, and when they were incorporated in the sketch, Mr. Producer O. K'd it and Mr. Scenic Artist bowed himself out, promising to have a model ready the next day.

Mr. Producer then rang for Miss Secretary, and told her to have Mr. Star, Miss Leading Lady and other performers in the office next morning at eleven o'clock, gave her a list of the characters he wished to cast, and handed her the manuscript with an order to get out parts, and to have them out that night. He turned to Mr. Author with a request for the incidental music for the act. Mr. Author told him he had none. Then Mr. Producer reached for the telephone, with the remark that the music could wait, and called up the United Booking Offices of America.

After a few minutes wait, Mr. Producer got the special Mr. Booking Manager for whom he had inquired, told him he had an act for which he wanted a break-in week, and as he hesitated and named a date three weeks later, Mr. Author was sure the act had been booked. Mr. Author marveled that the act should be contracted to appear when it was not even yet out of manuscript form, but when he mentioned this with a smile, Mr. Producer wanted to know how he ever would get "time" for an act if he didn't engage it ahead. He explained that he had a regular arrangement with Mr. House Manager to play new acts in his house at a small "break-in" salary. It was an arrangement convenient to him and gave Mr. House Manager fine acts at small cost.

After this, Mr. Producer rose from his desk and Mr. Author went out, promising to be on hand that evening at eight to go over the manuscript and make some changes that Mr. Producer promised to prove were necessary to the success of the act. And as he passed through the outer office, Mr. Author heard Miss Secretary explain over the telephone that Mr. Producer wished a hall at eleven o'clock two days later to rehearse a new act.

Promptly at eight o'clock that night Mr. Author presented himself at the office again, and found Mr. Producer busily engaged in reading the manuscript. A tiny paper model of the mimic room in which the act was to be played stood upon the desk. When he stooped he saw that the walls were roughly colored after the sketch they had discussed and that the whole scene bore an amazing likeness to the place of his imagination. Mr. Producer explained that he had had the model rushed through to make it possible for them to "get down to brass tacks" at once. The act needed so many little changes that they would have to get busy to have it ready for the morning.

When Mr. Producer began discussing various points about the act, Mr. Author could not for the life of him imagine what all these changes could be. But when Mr. Producer pointed out the first, Mr. Author wondered how he ever had imagined that the heroine could do the little thing he had made her do—it was physically impossible. Point after point Mr. Producer questioned, and point after point they changed, but there was only the one glaring error. A motive was added here, a bit of business was changed there, and as they worked they both grew so excited that they forget the time, forgot everything but that act. And when the manuscript at last dropped from their exhausted hands, it looked as if an army had invaded it.

Mr. Author glanced at the pile of nicely bound parts and sighed. All that work would have to be done over! "Only another one of my mistakes," smiled Mr. Producer as he scribbled an order to Miss Secretary, attached it to the manuscript, together with these now useless parts, and laid them on her desk, as he and Mr. Author went out into the cool night air. "See you tomorrow at eleven," said Mr. Producer as they parted. And Mr. Author looking at his watch wondered why he should take the trouble to go home at all.

At eleven Mr. Author found the little outer office crowded with actors and actresses. Miss Secretary was busily directing the typing of the new manuscript and parts. Mr. Producer was late. After Mr. Author had waited an hour in the private office, Miss Secretary came in and said he should wait no longer, because Mr. Producer had been called out of town to straighten out some trouble which had developed in one of his acts and had just telephoned that he would not be in until late that afternoon. Rehearsal would be as scheduled next morning, Miss Secretary explained. The performers would be on hand, and she hoped to goodness they would have some idea of their parts by then. Mr. Author wanted to know how the cast could be engaged when Mr. Producer was away, and Miss Secretary told him that Mr. Producer knew the capabilities of everyone who had called and had even directed her to engage the ones he named.

The following morning Mr. Author saw his characters for the first time in the flesh—and was disappointed. Also, the rehearsal was a sad awakening; it wasn't anything like he had imagined it would be. They all sat around on chairs and Mr. Producer told them what the act was all about. Then he suggested that they go through it once, at any rate. Chairs were placed to mark the footlights, chairs were used to indicate the doors and window, and chairs were made to do duty as a table, a piano and everything else.

Finally they got started and limped through the lines, reading their parts. Then Mr. Producer began to show them how he wanted it done, and before he had finished he had played every part in the act. They went through the act once more with a myriad of interruptions from Mr. Producer, who insisted on getting things right the very first time, and then he knocked off, calling it a day's work.

The next morning Mr. Author was on hand early with some suggestions: one Mr. Producer adopted, the others he explained into forgetfulness—and rehearsing began in earnest. They worked all morning on the first quarter of the act and went back at it late that afternoon. Miss Leading Lady unconsciously added one line and it was so good that it was kept in the act. Then Mr. Star did something that made them all laugh, and they put that in. Of course some pretty lines in the dialogue had to come out to make room, but they came out, and Mr. Author never regretted their loss. And the next day it was the same, and the day after that, and the seventh day, and the eighth day.

Then came a day when Mr. Author saw the act taking shape and form, and when he spoke to Mr. Producer about it, Mr. Producer said he thought that after all the act might whip around into something pretty good.

A few days later when Mr. Author arrived at the rehearsal hall, there were three strange men facing the company, who were going through the act for the first time without interruptions from Mr. Producer. Mr. Author wondered who they were, and watched their faces with interest to see how they liked his act. After a while he came to consider as great compliments the ghosts of smiles flickering across their jury-like faces. And when it was all over the performers gathered in one corner, and Mr. Producer came over to him, and the three men whispered among themselves. Mr. Producer explained that they were booking managers, and then Mr. Author sensed the psychological reason for the unconscious drawing together of the different clans.

His heart beat rather violently when the three men came across the room, and he felt a great wave of gladness sweep over him when the tallest of the three pulled out a little black book and said, "Mr. Producer, I'll pencil it in one of my houses for next week at this figure," and he showed Mr. Producer what he had written.

"And I'll take you for the second break-in, as we agreed when you 'phoned," said the shortest man. "And I'll take the third at that."

Then it was that Mr. Author felt a great admiration for Mr. Producer, because Mr. Producer dared assert his personality. Mr. Producer objected to the figure, talking of the "name" of Mr. Star.

"That's every penny he's worth," came the adamant answer.

Then Mr. Producer mentioned transportation costs, and the cost of hauling scenery, as additional arguments.

"Why didn't you say special set at first?" said the smallest man; "I'll give you this advance." Then all four looked, and they all agreed.

Then Mr. Author was introduced, quite casually. "Guess your act'll get by," conceded one of the jury generously, as they all left.

"So you're going to open a week earlier?" gasped Mr. Author to Mr. Producer, when they were alone in the interval between the exit of the three and the entrance upon the scene of the performers, who came swiftly across the room to learn their fate. "And you've booked three weeks more!"

"Well," said Mr. Producer, "you know the boys only pencilled those weeks in—pencil marks can be rubbed out."

The next day as they were on their way to the train to go up to the town where the act was to open, Mr. Producer suddenly remembered that he had forgotten to send Miss Secretary up to the Booking Offices for his contract. He wanted that contract particularly, for he had a feud of long standing with the manager of that particular house. So up he rushed to get that contract, with Mr. Author tagging at his heels.

It was the first time Mr. Author had seen even the waiting room of a booking office—it amazed him by its busy air. A score or more performers crowded its every inch of space. They were thickest around a little grilled window, behind which stood a boy who seemed to know them all. Some he dismissed with a "Come in tomorrow." Others he talked with at length, and took their cards. When he had a handful he disappeared from the window.

But Mr. Producer was calling Mr. Author. Mr. Producer stood holding open the inner door. So in Mr. Author went—to another surprise. Here there was no crush of people—here there was no rush, and little noise. Stenographers stood about, seemingly idle, and at a dozen little desks sat a dozen men quietly bending over rather odd-looking books, or talking with the few men who came in.

One of these men Mr. Author recognized as Mr. Booking Manager, for whom they were to play the second week. He was about to speak to him, when up came a bustling little man who said, "Do you want Miss Headliner for the week of the thirtieth? I can give her to you."

"Nope, all filled. Give you the week of the twenty-third."

"All right."

Mr. Booking Agent made a note in his little book, and Mr. Booking Manager bent over his desk and wrote Miss Headliner's name in his big book—and a business transaction was consummated.

Then Mr. Booking Agent hustled over to another desk and repeated his offer of the week of the thirtieth.

"Sorry, give you the week of the twenty-third," said this man.

"Just filled it," said Mr. Booking Agent. "Can't you give me the thirtieth? Who's got the thirtieth open?"

The man at the next desk heard him. "Who for? Miss Headliner? All right, I'll take her."

Just then Mr. Producer came out of a little room and Mr. Author followed him in a wild dash to catch the train. In the smoker he asked Mr. Producer to explain what he had seen in the Booking Offices. And Mr. Producer said: "Each one of those men you saw up there is in charge of the shows of one, or maybe three or four vaudeville theatres in different cities. It is their duty to make up the shows that appear in each of their houses. For instance, Mr. Booking Manager, whose house we are playing this week, books the shows in four other houses.

"The man you heard ask him if he would take Miss Headliner for the thirtieth, is Miss Headliner's business representative. His name is Mr. Booking Agent. Besides Miss Headliner, he is the representative for maybe fifty other acts. For this service he receives a commission of five per cent of Miss Headliner's salary and five per cent on the salaries of all the acts for whom he gets work. It is his business to keep Miss Headliner booked, and he is paid by her and his other clients for keeping them working.

"Mr. Booking Manager, on the other hand, is not paid a commission. He receives a flat salary for the work that he does for his houses. You remember you met him yesterday, when he penciled 'Success' in for the house we are on our way to play. Well, that is also a part of his business. For some of his houses that like to make a big showing at little expense, he must dig up new big acts like ours, which are breaking-in.

"Now, the price I get for this act for the breaking-in weeks, is mighty low. But this is customary. That is the reason why the performers have to be content with half salaries, and you with half-royalty. But this price does not affect the future price I will receive. It is marked on the books as the 'show price.' That means that it is recorded in the book-keeping department by the cashier as the price for which I am showing this act to the managers. When the act has made good, a price is set on the act, and that is the standard price for the other houses that book through these offices. The book-keeper watches the prices like a hawk, and if I tried to 'sneak a raise over,' he would catch it, and both yours truly and Mr. Booking Manager would be called up on the carpet by the head of the Offices. The only increase that is permitted is when a new season rolls around, or two or three booking managers agree to an increase and consult the office head about boosting the salary on the books."

That night Mr. Author rather expected to see a dress rehearsal of the act; he was disappointed. But the next morning there was a full dress rehearsal, played in the brand new special set which had come up with them and that now shone like a pretty picture in the dingy theatre.

It rather amazed Mr. Author to note that the emphasis of this rehearsal was not put on the speeches, but upon the entrances and exits, and the precise use and disposal of the various properties employed. A glimmering of the reason came to him when Mr. Star promised to murder anyone who moved a book that he used in his "big" scene. "Unless it is here—right here—I'll never be able to reach it and get back for the next bit without running."

And so the rehearsal went on, with no effort to improve the lines, but only to blend the physical movements of everyone of the performers to make a perfect whole and to heighten the natural effect of even the most natural action. Then the dress rehearsal came to an end, and the entire party went out to see the town.

That night, after the performance, they worked again on the act, because Mr. Producer had been seized by an idea. And when they had gone through the act time and again to incorporate that idea, they all went wearily to bed, praying for success next day.

At ten o'clock in the morning Mr. Author was at the theatre. He found that other acts had preceded him. The stage was littered with trunks and scenery, trapeze bars, animal cages and the what-not of a vaudeville show. Each performer as he came in was greeted by the doorman with the gift of a brass check, on which there was stamped a number. This number told the performer in what order he was entitled to rehearse. Vaudeville is a democracy—first come, first rehearsed.

The stage hands were busy rolling in trunks which express-men had dumped on the sidewalk, the electrician was busy mentally rehearsing light effects according to the formula on a printed light plot which was being explained to him by a performer. "Props" was busy trying to satisfy everyone with what he had on hand, or good-naturedly sending out for what had not been clearly specified on the property plot. The spot-light man in the gallery out front was busy getting his lamp ready for the matinee, and consulting his light plot. And the stage-manager was quite the busiest one of them all, shoving his scenery here and there to make room for the newly arrived sets, directing the flying of the hanging stuff, and settling questions with the directness of a czar.

Suddenly through the caverny house sounded the noise of the orchestra tuning up. The leader appeared and greeted the performers he knew like long lost brothers and sisters, and then Brass Check Number One dropped into his hand, and the Monday morning rehearsal began. Then it was that Mr. Author learned that it is not the acts, which are rehearsed on Monday morning, it is the vaudeville orchestra, and the light men and "Props."

This was borne in forcibly when Mr. Producer arrived with the performers and "Success" went into rehearsal. Although the entire staff of the theatre had been rehearsed the night before at the final dress rehearsal, Mr. Producer wished to change some lights, to instruct "Props" more clearly, and to jack up the orchestra into perfection. Therefore they all went through the act once more. Then the scrub-women appeared and demanded the centre of the stage with great swishes of watery cloths. The curtain came down to hide the stage from the front of the house, and the first early comers of the audience filtered in.

Mr. Author has never been able to recall just how "Success" played that first performance. He has dim memories of a throbbing heart, fears that lines would be forgotten or the whole "big" scene fall to pieces; and finally of a vast relief when the curtain came down, amid—applause. The curtain went up and came down a number of times, but Mr. Author was too busy pinching himself to make sure that he wasn't dreaming, to count how many curtains the act took.

It seemed to him like a tremendous hit, but Mr. Producer was in a rage. There were scores of points that had not "got over," half a dozen of his finest effects had been ruined, and he was bound those points should "get over," and those effects shine out clear and big.

Looking back on that week, Mr. Author recalls it as a nightmare of changes. They cut out speeches, and changed speeches, and took out bits of business, and added new bits—they changed everything in the act, and some of the changes they changed back again, until by Saturday the act was hardly to be recognized. And then they played two more performances to crowded houses that applauded like madmen; and Mr. Producer smiled for the first time.

Then they moved to the next theatre, and the first performance showed even Mr. Author that all the work had been wise. Now he was even more anxious than Mr. Producer to make the many changes by which this week was marked. And by the end of the week "Success" looked like—success.

They were preparing for a week of great things in the next town, when Wednesday night a cancellation notice came for that precious week. Something had gone wrong, and the pencilled date had to be rubbed out. Of course, by all the laws of the legislatures that week should never have been rubbed out, because there was a contract fully binding on both the theatre and Mr. Producer. But the week was rubbed out of sight, nevertheless, and Mr. Producer—knowing vaudeville necessities and also knowing that only the most dire necessity made Mr. Booking Manager "do this thing to him"—forgave it all with a smile and was quite ready to get back to town when Monday morning rolled around.

But Monday morning there occurred a "disappointment" at another theatre in a town only a few miles away. The act that was to have played that date was wrecked, or had overslept itself. Anyway, the resident house manager telephoned to the Booking Offices that he was shy one act. Now it happened that the act that "disappointed," was of the same general character as "Success." The Booking Manager knew this, and remembered that "Success" was within a few miles and with an open week that ought to have been filled. Therefore, just as Mr. Producer and Mr. Author were leaving the hotel to join the other members of "Success" at the railroad station, Mr. Producer was called to the telephone—long distance.

In less time than it takes to recount it, the resident manager who was suffering from a disappointment, and Mr. Producer, suffering from the lack of a playing week, were both cured of their maladies at the same time. And so, instead of going back to town, "Success" rushed to the next city and played its week.

Now, in this last week of breaking-in, Mr. Author realized one fact that stands out rather prominently in his memory; it is a simple little fact, yet it sums up the entire problem of the show business. Perhaps the rush of events had made it impossible before for the truth to strike home as keenly as it did when there suddenly came to him a tiny little bit of business which made a very long speech unnecessary. He explained it to Mr. Producer, and Mr. Producer seized on it instantly and put it into the act. That night the act went better than it had ever gone before. This little bit of condensation, this illuminating flash which was responsible for it, "punched up" the big scene into a life it had never had before. Then it was that there also flashed upon Mr. Author's mind this truth:

A dramatic entertainment is not written on paper. It is written with characters of flesh and blood. Strive as hard as man may, he can never fully foretell how an ink-written act will play. There is an inexplicable something which playing before an audience develops. Both the audience and the actors on the stage are affected. A play—the monologue and every musical form as well—is one thing in manuscript, another thing in rehearsal, and quite a different thing before an audience. Playing before an audience alone shows what a play truly is. Therefore, a play can only be made—after it is produced. Even in the fourth week of playing—the first week of metropolitan playing—Mr. Author and Mr. Producer made many changes in "Success" that were responsible for the long popularity it enjoyed. Mr. Author had learned his lesson well. He approached his next work with clearer eyes.

APPENDIX

NINE FAMOUS VAUDEVILLE ACTS COMPLETE

"THE GERMAN SENATOR," A Monologue, by Aaron Hoffman.
"THE ART OF FLIRTATION," A Two-Act, by Aaron Hoffman.
"AFTER THE SHOWER," A Flirtation Two-Act, by Louis Weslyn.
"THE VILLAIN STILL PURSUED HER," A Travesty Playlet, by Arthur Denvir.
"THE LOLLARD," A Comedy Playlet, by Edgar Allan Woolf.
"BLACKMAIL," A Tragic Playlet, by Richard Harding Davis.
"THE SYSTEM," A Melodramatic Playlet, by Taylor Granville.
"A PERSIAN GARDEN," A One-Act Musical Comedy, by Edgar Allan Woolf.
"My OLD KENTUCKY HOME," A One-Act Burlesque, by James Madison.

A WORD ABOUT THE ACTS

The nine acts which are given, complete, in the following pages are representative of the very best in vaudeville. Naturally, they do not show every possible vaudeville variation—a series of volumes would be required for that—but, taken together, they represent all the forms of the talking vaudeville act that are commonly seen.

THE MONOLOGUE
The German Senator

This monologue by Aaron Hoffman has been chosen as perhaps the best example of the pure monologue ever written. Originally used by Cliff Gordon—continually being changed to keep it up-to-the-minute—it has, since his death, been presented by numerous successors of the first "German Senator." It is doubtful if any other dramatic work—or any other writing—of equal length, and certainly no monologue, has returned to its author so much money as "The German Senator" has earned.

THE TWO-ACTS
The Art of Flirtation

For more years than perhaps any other vaudeville two-act, this exceptionally fine example of two-act form has been used by various famous German comedians. It may be considered to stand in much the same relation to the two-act that "The German Senator" does to the monologue. Its author, also Mr. Aaron Hoffman, holds a unique position among vaudeville and musical comedy writers.

After the Shower

This delightful little example of lover's nonsense was played for more than four years by Lola Merrill and Frank Otto. It has been instanced as one of the daintiest and finest flirtation-couple-acts that the two-a-day has seen. Mr. Louis Weslyn has written perhaps more successful acts of this particular style than any other author.

THE PLAYLETS
The Villain Still Pursued Her
This travesty, one of the most successful on record, was used for years to star Mrs. Frank Sheridan. Written by Mr. Arthur Denvir, whose specialty is travesties, it undoubtedly became the inspiration for the many similar acts that created the travesty-vogue of 1912-15.

The Lollard
Edgar Allan Woolf, who wrote this delightful satirical comedy, is perhaps the most successful writer of playlets in this country. For many years he has turned out success after success for famous legitimate stars, while still other performers have become vaudeville stars in his acts. Mr. Woolf himself chose "The Lollard" as representative of his best comedies. The star role, Angela Maxwell, was created in this country by Miss Regina Cornelli, and in England by Miss Hilda Trevelyan.

Blackmail
Richard Harding Davis needs no introduction. This remarkable little tragedy was produced for the Orpheum Circuit by Mr. Charles Feleky, who declares it to be "the best tragic playlet I have produced." From so eminent a vaudeville producer, this is, indeed, high praise. The character of Richard Fallon was created by Mr. Walter Hampden.

The System
Without doubt, this act is the best of the many big productions with which Mr. Taylor Granville has supplied The United Booking Offices of America, during his many years as a producing star. Mr. Junie McCree, who collaborated with Mr. Granville, was once president of "The White Rats," the vaudeville actors' union, and is now a successful vaudeville writer. Mr. Edward Clark, the third collaborator, has written many successful vaudeville acts.

"The System" is said to have been characterized by Mr. George M. Cohan as the best one-act melodrama he ever saw. Its extraordinary popularity in this country and in England is but added proof of the tenseness of its scenes and its great ending.

THE ONE-ACT MUSICAL COMEDY
A Persian Garden
Played by Louis Simons season after season, this real comedy set to music is without question Mr. Edgar Allan Woolf's best effort in this field. Unlike the usual musical comedy, this act possesses dialogue interest as well as pleasing brilliancy. It has won its many years of success not because of scenery, costumes

and the chorus, but by the sterling worth apparent in the manuscript divorced from them.

THE BURLESQUE TAB
    My Old Kentucky Home
    Perhaps the most characteristic of the burlesque acts in vaudeville, this "Tab" has been played in various guises in the two-a-day and in burlesque for many seasons. It is the work of a writer who justly prides himself on his intimate knowledge of the burlesque form, and who possesses the most complete library of burlesque manuscripts in America. To the thousands of readers of "Madison's Budget," James Madison requires no introduction.
    Permission to publish these acts has, in each instance, been personally granted to the author of this volume. This kind permission covers publication in this book only. Republication of these acts in whole or in part, in any form whatsoever, is expressly prohibited.
    Stage presentation of any of the acts is likewise forbidden. A *Special Warning* has been inserted in the introductory page of every act, at the request of each author. The reason for such repetition is to be found in the commercial value of successful vaudeville material, and in the fact that the general public has never precisely understood the reservations permitted to the author of a dramatic work under the copyright law. Infringements of any sort are subject to severe penalties under United States law and will be rigidly prosecuted.
    To the writers of these acts the author of this volume wishes to express his deep appreciation for the permissions that enable him to print as illustrations of his text some of the finest acts that vaudeville has ever seen.
    The German Senator
    A Monologue
    By Aaron Hoffman
    Author of "The Politicians," "The Belle of Avenue A,"
    "The Newly-weds and their Baby", "Let George Do It,"
    "School Days," Etc., Etc.

THE GERMAN SENATOR
    My dear friends and falling citizens:
    My heart fills up with vaccination to be disabled to come out here before such an intelligence massage of people and have the chance to undress such a large conglomerated aggravation.
    I do not come before you like other political speakers, with false pride in one hand and the Star Strangled Banana in the other.
    I come before you as a true, sterilized citizen, a man who is for the public and against the people, and I want to tell you, my 'steemed friends, when I look back on the early hysterics of our country, and think how our forefathers strangled to make this country voss iss is it; when you think of the lives that was loosed and the blood that was shredded, we got to feel a feeling of patriotic symptoms—we got to feel a patriotic symp—symps—you got to feel the patri—you can't help it,

you got to feel it.

I tell you, our hearts must fill up with indigestion when we look out to see the Statue of Liberty, the way she stands, all alone, dressed up in nothing, with a light in her hand, showing her freedom.

And what a fine place they picked out for Liberty to stand.

With Coney Island on one side and Blackwell's Island on the other.

And when she stands there now, looking on the country the way it is and what she has to stand for, I tell you tears and tears must drop from her eyes. Well, to prove it—look at the ocean she filled up.

And no wonder she's crying. Read the nuisance papers. See what is going on.

Look what the country owes.

According to the last report of the Secretary of the Pleasury, the United States owes five billion dollars.

Nobody knows what we owe it for;

And nobody ever sees what we have got for it; [109]

First read the monologue including this point, then read it skipping the point—thus you will see, first, what a complete "point" is; second, what "blending" means; and third, how a monologist may shorten or lengthen his routine by leaving out or including a point. [end footnote]

And if you go to Washington, the Capsule of the United States, and ask them, THEY don't even know THEMSELVES.

Then they say, what keeps the country broke is the Pay-no-more Canal.

It cost the Government nine thousand dollars an hour to dig the canal. THINK OF THAT!

Nine thousand dollars an hour for digging, and the worst of it is, they ain't digging.

Up to date, it has cost a hundred and seventy million dollars to dig a hole—they've been at it for over nine years—and the only hole they've dug is in the United States Treasury.

Every six months, the Chief Engineer, he comes up with a report;

He says: "Mr. Congress, the canal is getting better every day, a million dollars MORE please."

He gets the money, goes out, buys a couple of shovels, then sends back a telegram: HOORAY—The digging is very good, the two oceans will soon be one.

Can you beat that?

Before they started the canal it didn't cost us nothing, and we had two oceans.

And by the time they get through, it'll cost us three hundred million and we'll only have one.

And now that the canal is nearly finished, it looks like it was going to get us into trouble.

Japan is against it on one side and England don't like it on the other.

---

[109] Here begins the "Panama Canal point," referred to in Chapter V. It continues until the "End of Panama Canal Point" footnote below.

And that's why we've got to have a navy. [110]
Of course, we've got a navy.
But everybody is kicking about it.
Why should they kick?
All we appropriated for the navy last year was four million dollars.
And there's eighty million people in this country.
And that figures a nickel apiece.
And what the hell kind of a navy do you expect for a nickel?

Still they are crying that the country is in destitution circumstances. That is inconsis—inconsis—you can't deny it.

Our country has got a superabum, a superabum—a superabum—we've got a lot of money.

There's money lying in the treasury that never was touched. And the first fellow that will touch it will get six months.

The whole trouble is the trusts.

Look what the cold storage trust have done with the eggs. Sixty cents a dozen—for the good ones. And the good ones are rotten.

Then they say the reason prices are going up is because wages are getting higher.

But why should they raise the price of eggs?
The chickens ain't getting any more wages.
And if meat goes up any higher, it will be worth more than money.
Then there won't be any money.
Instead of carrying money in your pocket, you'll carry meat around.
A sirloin steak will be worth a thousand dollar bill.

When you go down to the bank to make a deposit, instead of giving the cashier a thousand dollar bill, you'll slip him a sirloin steak.

If you ask him for change, he'll give you a hunk of bologny.
If they keep on, we won't be able to live at all.
Statistics prove that the average wages of the workingman is one dollar a day.

Out of that, he's got to spend fifty cents a day for food; fifty-five cents for rent; ten cents for car fare.

And at the end of a hard day's work—he owes himself fifteen cents.
Yet the rich people say that the poor people are getting prosperous.

They say, look at our streets. You see nothing but automobiles. You don't see half the poor people now that you used to.

Certainly you don't.

Half of them have already been run over and the other half is afraid to come out.

Why, between the automobiles and the trusts the poor man hasn't got a chance to live.

And if only the gas trust gets a little stronger, the price of gas will go up so high a poor man won't even be able to commit suicide.

---

[110] End of "Panama Canal point." See footnote above, also Chapter V.

They'll have him both ways. He can't live and he can't die.

And that's why I am with the socialists.

They say, "Down with the trusts! Do away with money. Make everything equal."

Imagine a fellow going into a jewelry store and saying:

"Give me a diamond ring, here's a lemon."

But the socialists have got some good ideas for the working people. And my heart and soul is with the labor class of people. I am for labor unions.

But what help are the labor unions to the working man?

Look at it in the right light.

A man pays twenty-five dollars to join a union. He gets a job in a shop for two dollars a day, works two weeks, the union gets out on a strike and he owes himself a dollar.

The unions are crying the days are too long.

They want the days shorter. They want the days should be eight hours long.

But think of the fellows out in the North Pole where the days are six months long. That's the place for the poor man to live.

When the landlord comes around and says, "Rent," all you have to do is to tell him to come around the day after tomorrow.

Then Andrew Carnigger, he comes out and tells us you should save money and put it in the bank.

What's the use of putting your money in the bank?

It's easy enough to put it in, but it aint so easy to get it out. When you want to take your money out, you got to give the cashier sixty days notice.

And did you ever figure out how far a cashier can go in sixty days?

Then they say, as the world goes on, we are improving.

It's ridiculum.

We were better off years ago than we are now.

Look at Adam in the Garden of Eat-ing.

Life to him was a pleasure;

There was a fellow that had nothing to worry about.

Anything he wanted he could get.

But the darn fool had to get lonesome.

And that's the guy that started all our troubles.

We would be all right today, if it wasn't for Adam and Evil.

Then they say that Adam fell for an apple.

It just shows how men have improved.

No man would fall for an apple today.

It would have to be a peach.

And I tell you, it's no wonder that women feel stuck up. They say they can do more than men can do.

That's very true, when you go back to the first woman, Eve.

She was only one little woman, all by herself, and she put the whole human race on the bum.

Could a man do that?

And yet she was only a rib out of Adam's side.

It just goes to show you what a cheap proposition woman was.

Nowadays, when you want to marry a woman, you got to buy a diamond ring, take her to the theatres, buy her taxicheaters, and what's left of your wages you got to spend on candy and tango trots and turkey teas. There's where Adam had it on all of us.

All Eve cost him was one bone.

It all goes to show you how much better off man was in those days than today, and while John D. Rottenfeller, the great Philosopede, he comes out and says, nobody has a right to be poor; he says, anybody can live on eighteen dollars a week.

He don't have to tell us that.

Let him tell us how to get the eighteen.

And still that great statesment, William Chinning Bryan, he comes out and says, we are living in a great country. He says we are living in a country of excitement intelligence and education.

That's very true.

Look at our public school system.

A child can go to school for nothing, and when he grows up to be a man and he is thoroughly educated, he can go into the public school and be a teacher and get fifty dollars a month.

And the janitor gets ninety-five.

That shows you how education is coming to the front. Wouldn't it better, instead of sending a child to school, to learn him to clean out a cellar?

And what's the cause of all the trouble?

The House of Representatives.

We send them to Washington to look out for the people and the only time they look out for the people is when they look out the window and see them coming.

Then they get $7,500 a year. They spend $10,000 a year, and at the end of the year they have $100,000 saved.

No wonder they are careless with our money.

That's all they got to do. Sit around Washington and touch the treasury.

Every couple of days a fellow comes into Congress and says:

"Good morning, Congress, let me have $4,000,000."

That's all they do, is make touches for millions.

You never heard of those suckers making a touch for a quarter, or a half a dollar.

To show you what they do with our money, look at our Weather Bureau Department.

We pay a fellow $10,000 a year. For what?

To tell us when it's going to rain.

And he don't know himself.

But he don't want to know.

He knows that if he ever guesses it right, he is going to lose his job. But believe me, it's a soft job.

Nothing to do.

He gets up in the morning, eats a nice breakfast, smokes a good fat cigar; then he looks out of the window and says, "Fine weather to-day."

Then he takes his umbrella and goes out for a walk. I tell you, my dear friends, the way the country stands now, the country stands on the brink of a preci—the country stands on the brink of a precip—and if somebody shoves it, it is going over.

And the cause of all the trouble in the country is the crooked politics.

And that's why the women suffering gents have gotten together and are fighting for their rights.

And you can't blame them.

Now I see where one married woman has hit on a great idea.

She says there's only one protection for the wives.

And that's a wives' union.

Imagine a union for wives.

A couple gets married.

And as soon as they get settled, along comes the walking delegate and orders a strike.

Then imagine thousands and thousands of wives walking up and down the streets on strike, and scabs taking their places.

The Art of Flirtation

A Two-Act for Two Men

by Aaron Hoffman

Author of "Toblitz, or The End of the World,"

"The New Leader," "The Son of Solomon,"

"The Speaker of the House," Etc., Etc.

THE ART OF FLIRTATION

STRAIGHT: Say, whenever we go out together, you always got a kick coming. What's the matter with you?

COMEDIAN: Nothing is the matter with me.

STRAIGHT: With you always everything is the matter.

COMEDIAN: What's the trouble?

STRAIGHT: The trouble is you don't know nothing.

COMEDIAN: Yes, I do.

STRAIGHT: You know! If I only knew one-half of what you don't know, I would know twice as much as the smartest man in the world.

COMEDIAN: What you got against me?

STRAIGHT: You ain't a gentlemen.

COMEDIAN: What is a gentlemen?

STRAIGHT: A gentlemen is a man who knows how to act senseless vit people no matter vat happens.

COMEDIAN: I am a gentlemen, I always act senseless.

STRAIGHT: You are a gentlemen! Look at you. How can a man be a gentlemen with such a face like that. There are two kinds of men—gentlemen and rummies. I am a gentlemen, you are a rummy.

COMEDIAN: I am a rummy? I know how to act vit people. Ven you met your friends down the street, vat did you say to them?

STRAIGHT: I said come on and have a drink. I spoke like a gentlemen.

COMEDIAN: And ve all vent to have a drink.

STRAIGHT: Ve did.

COMEDIAN: Didn't I pay for it?

STRAIGHT: Sure—that shows you are a rummy.

COMEDIAN: No, that shows I was a gentlemen.

STRAIGHT: Dat's right. In a saloon you are a gentlemen.

COMEDIAN: Sure I am. I act just a bartender.

STRAIGHT: But the trouble with you is you don't know how to mingle.

COMEDIAN: Oh, I can mingle.

STRAIGHT: You don't know the first thing about mingling. As a mingler you are a flivver. Among men you are all right, but as soon as I take you out to some parties and dinners and you see some women around, your brains get loose.

COMEDIAN: Why—what do I do?

STRAIGHT: It makes no resemblance what you do or what you say. No matter how you do it—no matter how you say it, the women get insulted. You ain't got the least consumtion how to be disagreeable to the ladies.

COMEDIAN: Oh, I know how to be disagreeable to a lady. You ought to hear me talk to my wife.

STRAIGHT: To your wife? Any man can be disagreeable to his wife. But tink of other women—the trouble with you is, you have no, as the French people say, you have no *savoir faire*.

COMEDIAN: No what?

STRAIGHT: I say that you ain't got no, what the French people call, *savoir faire*.

COMEDIAN: What's dot?

STRAIGHT: *Savoir faire*.

COMEDIAN: Oh, I can salve for fair.

STRAIGHT: You can salve for fair; yes, but you ain't got no *savoir faire*. You are not a mingler. You have no vit, no humor. You ain't got no *esprit*.

COMEDIAN: Vere do you get all dose words?

STRAIGHT: I get them because I am a gentlemen.

COMEDIAN: Then I'm glad I am a rummy.

STRAIGHT: Sure you're a rummy. If you wasn't a rummy, you'd have *esprit*.

COMEDIAN: Oh, I had a spree lots of times.

STRAIGHT: Not a spree. I mean *esprit*. I mean you ain't got no refinement—like me. I got polish.

COMEDIAN: You're a shine.

STRAIGHT: No, I ain't a shine. I am a lady killer.

COMEDIAN: One look at you is enough to kill any lady.

STRAIGHT: I am a Beau Brummel. Ven I am with the ladies, I talk to dem vit soft words; I whisper sweet nothings, but you, you rummy you, you don't know how to make the ladies feel unhappy.

COMEDIAN: How do you make them unhappy?

STRAIGHT: You got to be disagreeable to them.

COMEDIAN: And vat do you do to be disagreeable to ladies?

STRAIGHT: The only vay to be disagreeable to a lady, you got to flirt vit her.

COMEDIAN: Flirt. Vat does that mean flirt?

STRAIGHT: Flirting is a thing that begins in nothing. You say something, you talk like everything and you mean nothing, and it liable to end up in anything. A flirtation is a clan-destination meeting with a lady.

COMEDIAN: Vat kind of a meeting is dot?

STRAIGHT: Don't you know? Ven you flirt, you meet a pretty woman in a shady spot.

COMEDIAN: Oh, you meet a shady woman in a pretty spot.

STRAIGHT: Not a shady woman. A pretty woman in a shady spot.

COMEDIAN: How do you know so much about flirting?

STRAIGHT: Now you come to it. I got here a book on the art of flirtation. Here it is. (biz. shows book.)

COMEDIAN: What is the name of that book?

STRAIGHT: The art of flirtation. How to make a lady fall in love with you for ten cents.

COMEDIAN: A lady fell in love with me once and it cost me Five Hundred Dollars.

STRAIGHT: That's because you didn't have this book. This book tells you how to make love. This book is full of the finest kind of love.

COMEDIAN: For ten cents.

STRAIGHT: Yes, for ten cents.

COMEDIAN: Oh, it's ten cents love.

STRAIGHT: No, it ain't ten-cent love. It's fine love (opens book). See—here is the destructions. Right on the first page you learn something. See—how to flirt with a handkerchief.

COMEDIAN: Who wants to flirt with a handkerchief? I want to flirt with a woman.

STRAIGHT: Listen to what the book says. To a flirter all things have got a language. According to this book, flirters can speak with the eye, with the fan, with the cane, with the umbrella, with the handkerchief, with anything. This book tells you how to do it.

COMEDIAN: For ten cents.

STRAIGHT: Shut up. Now when you see a pretty woman coming along who wants to flirt with you, what is the first thing a man should do?

COMEDIAN: Run the other way.

STRAIGHT: No, no. This is the handkerchief flirtation. As soon as a pretty woman makes eyes at you, you put your hands in your pockets.

COMEDIAN: And hold on to your money.

STRAIGHT: No, you take out your handkerchief. (biz.)

COMEDIAN: Suppose you ain't got a handkerchief?

STRAIGHT: Every flirter must have a handkerchief. It says it in the book. Now you shake the handkerchief three times like this (biz.). Do you know what that means?

COMEDIAN: (Biz. of shaking head.)

STRAIGHT: That means you want her to give you—

COMEDIAN: Ten cents.

STRAIGHT: No. Dat means you want her to give you a smile. So you shake the handkerchief three times like this (biz.), then you draw it across you mouth like this (biz.). What does that mean?

COMEDIAN: That means you just had a glass of beer.

STRAIGHT: No, dat means "I would like to speak with you."

COMEDIAN: And does she answer?

STRAIGHT: She got to, it says it in the book.

COMEDIAN: Does she answer you with a handkerchief?

STRAIGHT: Yes, or she might umbrella.

COMEDIAN: Over the head.

STRAIGHT: Sure. If she answers you with de umbrella over the head, that means something. Ven she holds the umbrella over her head, she means that she is a married woman.

COMEDIAN: Den you quit flirting.

STRAIGHT: No, den you commence. If she shakes it dis way (biz.), dat means—

COMEDIAN: Her husband is coming.

STRAIGHT: No. Dat means "You look good to me." Den you hold your handkerchief by the corner like dis (biz.).

COMEDIAN: Vat does that mean?

STRAIGHT: Meet me on the corner.

COMEDIAN: Och, dat's fine (takes handkerchief). Den if you hold it dis way, dat means (biz.) "Are you on the square?"

STRAIGHT: You are learning already. You will soon be a flirter. Now I vill show you how you flirt according to the book. You are a man flirter, and I am a beautiful female.

COMEDIAN: You are what?

STRAIGHT: A female. A female.

COMEDIAN: Vat's dat, a female?

STRAIGHT: A female. Don't you know what fee means? Fee, that means money. Male, that means man. Female. That means "Get money from a man." That's a female. I am a beautiful woman and just to teach you how to flirt, I am going to take a walk thro' the park.

COMEDIAN: I thought you were a gentlemen.

STRAIGHT: No. No. Just for an instance I am a lady. I will walk past in a reckless way, and I will make eyes at you.

COMEDIAN: If you do, I will smash my nose in your face.

STRAIGHT: No. No. When I make eyes at you, you must wave your handkerchief at me three times. Den you reproach me vit all the disrespect in the world and den you take off your hat and you say something. Vat do you say?

COMEDIAN: Ten cents.

STRAIGHT: No. No. You say something pleasant. You speak of the weather, for instance. You say "Good-evening, Madam, nice day."

COMEDIAN: Suppose it ain't a nice day?

STRAIGHT: No matter what kind of a day it is, you speak about it. Now I'm the lady and I am coming. Get ready.

(STRAIGHT does burlesque walk around COMEDIAN. . . . STRAIGHT stops and drops handkerchief.)

COMEDIAN: Say—you dropped something.

STRAIGHT: I know it. I know it. Flirt. Flirt.

(COMEDIAN biz. of pulling out red handkerchief.)

COMEDIAN: I am flirting. I am flirting.

STRAIGHT: What are you trying to do, flag a train? Why don't you pick up my handkerchief?

COMEDIAN: I don't need any, I got one.

STRAIGHT: (Picks up handkerchief and turns.) Oh, you rummy you. Why don't you reproach me and say something about the weather?

COMEDIAN: All right, you do it again.

STRAIGHT: Now don't be bashful! Don't be bashful! Here I come (biz. of walk).

COMEDIAN: (pose with hat.) Good evening. Are you a flirter?

STRAIGHT: Oh you fool (gives COMEDIAN a push).

COMEDIAN: Oh, what a mean lady dat is.

STRAIGHT: You musn't ask her if she's a flirter. You must say something. De way it says in the book. You must speak of something. If you can't speak of anything else, speak of the weather.

COMEDIAN: All right, I'll do it again this time.

STRAIGHT: This is the last time I'll be a lady for you. Here I come (biz.).

COMEDIAN: Good evening, Mrs. Lady. Sloppy weather we're having.

STRAIGHT: Sloppy weather! It's no use; I can't teach you how to be a flirter, you got to learn it from the book. Listen. Here is what it says. "After you made the acquaintanceship of de lady, you should call at her house in the evening. As you open the gate you look up at the vindow and she will wave a handkerchief like this (biz.). That means, somebody is vaiting for you."

COMEDIAN: The bulldog.

STRAIGHT: No. The flirtess. "You valk quickly to the door."

COMEDIAN: The bulldog after you.

STRAIGHT: Dere is no bulldog in this. You don't flirt vith a bulldog.

COMEDIAN: But suppose the bulldog flirts with you?

STRAIGHT: Shut up. "She meets you at the door. You have your handkerchief on your arm" (biz.)

COMEDIAN: And the dog on my leg.

STRAIGHT: No, the handkerchief is on your arm. Dat means "Can I come in?"

COMEDIAN: And den what do you do?
STRAIGHT: If she says "Yes," you go in the parlor, you sit on the sofa, side by side, you take her hand.
COMEDIAN: And she takes your vatch.
STRAIGHT: No. You take her hand, den you say: "Whose goo-goo luvin' baby is oosum?"
COMEDIAN: Does it say that in the book?
STRAIGHT: Sure.
COMEDIAN: Let me see it. (COMEDIAN tears out page.) Den vat do you do?
STRAIGHT: You put her vaist around your arms—
COMEDIAN: And den?
STRAIGHT: Den you squeeze it—
COMEDIAN: And den?
STRAIGHT: She'll press her head upon your manly shoulder—
COMEDIAN: And den—
STRAIGHT: She looks up into your eyes—
COMEDIAN: And den?
STRAIGHT: You put the other arm around her—
COMEDIAN: And den?
STRAIGHT: You hold her tight—
COMEDIAN: And den?
STRAIGHT: You turn down the gas—
COMEDIAN: And den?
STRAIGHT: She sighs—
COMEDIAN: And den?
STRAIGHT: You sigh—
COMEDIAN: And den?
STRAIGHT: Dat's the end of the book.
COMEDIAN: Is dat all?
STRAIGHT: Sure. What do you want for ten cents?
COMEDIAN: But vat do you do after you turn down the gas?
STRAIGHT: Do you expect the book to tell you everything?

AFTER THE SHOWER

CHARACTERS
    THE FELLOW
    THE GIRL

SCENE: A pretty country lane in One, (Special drop) supposed to be near Lake George. Rustic bench on R. of stage. When the orchestra begins the music for the act, the girl enters, dressed in a fashionable tailor-made gown, and carrying parasol. She comes on laughing, from L., and glancing back over her shoulder at THE FELLOW, who follows after her, a few paces behind. THE GIRL wears only one glove, and THE FELLOW is holding out the other one to her as he makes his entrance. He is dressed in a natty light summer suit and wears a neat straw hat.

    THE GIRL: (As she comes on with a little run.) I don't see why on earth you insist upon following me.

    THE FELLOW: (Lifting his hat.) I never knew why I was *on earth* until I met you. (Waving glove at her.) Say, this is your glove—you *know* it's your glove.

    THE GIRL: (Laughingly.) It must belong to somebody else.

    THE FELLOW: No, it doesn't. I saw you drop it. Besides, you are wearing only one glove, and this one matches it.

    THE GIRL: (Stopping on right of stage near rustic bench and turning to face him, holding out her hand.) You are right. It *is* my glove. I'll take it, please.

    THE FELLOW: (Stopping to gaze at her admiringly.) No, on second thought, I'll *keep* it. (He folds it up tenderly, and places it in the upper left-hand pocket of his coat.) I'll keep it right here, too,—near my heart.

    THE GIRL: Oh, what nonsense! You've never seen me but three times in your life.

    THE FELLOW: (Coming nearer her.) Yes—that's true. And you look better every time I see you. Say, you do look awfully nice this morning. Nobody would think, from your appearance, that you belonged to a camping party here on the shore of Lake George. I guess that thunder storm last night didn't bother you a little bit. Why, you look as if you were out for a stroll on Fifth Avenue.

    THE GIRL: (Aside.) Little does he know that I got caught in that shower and am now wearing my chum, Genevieve's, gown. (To him.) What a jollier you are! You look pretty natty yourself this morning, it seems to me.

    THE FELLOW: (Aside.) This suit of clothes I got from Tommy Higgins has made a hit with her. I guess I'll just let her think they belong to me, and won't tell her that I got soaked in the rain last night. (To her, lifting his hat again.) I'm tickled nearly to death to have you say such complimentary things to me. It makes me glad I came on this camping trip.

    THE GIRL: You belong to the camping party flying the flag of the skull and cross-bones, don't you?

    THE FELLOW: Yes—all the boys are young doctors, except me.

    THE GIRL: And what are you?

THE FELLOW: I'm the patient.

THE GIRL: Are you sick?

THE FELLOW: Love-sick.

THE GIRL: (Turning up her nose.) How ridiculous! What brought you to Lake George?

THE FELLOW: You.

THE GIRL: I! Oh, you are too absurd for anything. Give me my glove, please, and let me go.

THE FELLOW: (Coming still nearer.) Don't be rash. There's no place to go. All of your camping party have gone on a boating trip except yourself. You're surely not going back there and hang around the camp all alone?

THE GIRL: (In surprise.) How did YOU know that the rest of my party had gone away for the day?

THE FELLOW: I saw 'em start. Why didn't you go with 'em?

THE GIRL: I had nothing to wear but this tailor-made gown, and a girl can't go boating in a dress like this. I only intended to stay two days when I came up here from New York to join the camp, and was not prepared with enough clothes. I've sent home for clothes and am expecting them to arrive at the camp this morning— *that's* why I didn't go boating, since you are impertinent enough to ask. (She gives him an indignant look.)

THE FELLOW: I beg your pardon. Won't you sit down?

THE GIRL: No, I will not. (Still looking quite indignant, she sits down immediately on bench. He sits down beside her.)

THE FELLOW: Neither will I. (He looks at her out of the corners of his eyes, and she turns her face away, nervously tapping the stage with one foot.)

THE GIRL: You seem to know all that has been going on at our camp. I believe you have been spying on us.

THE FELLOW: Not at all. I know one of the girls in your camp.

THE GIRL: (Sarcastically.) Oh, you do! (She tosses her head.) So you have been following me up in order to send some message to another girl. Who is she?

THE FELLOW: Genevieve Patterson.

THE GIRL: (Aside.) I'll *never* let him know now that I have on Genevieve's clothes.

THE FELLOW: But you're mistaken. I've already sent the message. It was about *you*.

THE GIRL: About *me*? What about me?

THE FELLOW: I wanted Genevieve to introduce us. Say—you haven't told me your name yet.

THE GIRL: I don't intend to. I think you are very forward.

THE FELLOW: Shall I tell you *my* name?

THE GIRL: By no means.

THE FELLOW: You're not interested?

THE GIRL: Not a bit.

(There is a pause. She keeps her head turned away. He looks upward and all around, somewhat embarrassed.)

THE FELLOW: (Finally breaking the silence.) Are there any bugs in your camp?

THE GIRL: (Facing him angrily.) Sir!

THE FELLOW: I mean gnats, mosquitoes—things like that.

THE GIRL: Yes. I was badly bitten last night by a mosquito.

THE FELLOW: (Very much interested.) Where did he get you?

THE GIRL: (Laughing.) Well, you are so fresh that I can't be mad at you. You're *too* funny. Since you want to know so much, he *got me* on the knee. I wasn't far-seeing enough to bring mosquito netting. It's a bad bite.

THE FELLOW: Is it possible?

THE GIRL: Don't you believe it?

THE FELLOW: Well, I'm not far-seeing enough to know for sure. (With a sly glance at her knees.)

THE GIRL: How silly of you! But say—I know a joke on you. I saw you fall in the lake yesterday.

THE FELLOW: (Nodding his head.) While I was fishing?

THE GIRL: Yes; it was so amusing. I don't know when I've enjoyed such a hearty joke. How did you come to fall in?

THE FELLOW: I *didn't* come to fall in. I came to fish.

THE GIRL: I also saw that man with the camera over in your camp. What was he dojng?

THE FELLOW: Oh, he was a moving picture man from New York. He was taking moving pictures of our cheese.

THE GIRL: Preposterous! Have you caught any fish since you came?

THE FELLOW: Only a dog-fish, with a litter of puppies.

THE GIRL: (With wide-open eyes.) How interesting! What did you do with them?

THE FELLOW: We made frankfurter sausages out of the little ones, and we are using the big one to guard the camp.

THE GIRL: To guard the camp?

THE FELLOW: Yes—it's a watch-dog fish.

THE GIRL: Well, I've heard of sea-dogs, but I never knew before that—

THE FELLOW: Oh, yes—quite common. I suppose, of course, you heard the cat-fish having a concert last night.

THE GIRL: No—surely you are joking.

THE FELLOW: No, indeed—they were all tom-cats.

THE GIRL: Who ever heard of such a thing?

THE FELLOW: Well, you've heard of tom-cods, haven't you?

THE GIRL: Yes, of course, but—

THE FELLOW: Well, why not tom-cats then? Say, you must be sure to come over to our camp and see the collection in our private aquarium. We have two compartments, and keep the little daughter fish on one side, and—

THE GIRL: The daughter fish!

THE FELLOW: (Nodding his head.) Yes, and the son-fish on the other. (THE GIRL springs to her feet, angrily.)

THE GIRL: You are simply guying me. I shan't listen to you another moment. Give me my glove, sir, I demand it.

THE FELLOW: (Also jumping to his feet and grasping her by the arm.) Oh, please don't get mad. We were getting along so nicely, too.

THE GIRL: (Sneeringly.) "WE" were getting along so nicely. You mean YOU were. I wasn't.

THE FELLOW: Yes, you were doing FINE. You were listening to me, and I can get along all right with anybody that will listen to me. Besides—ah-ah—fraulein—mam'selle—you know, I don't know your name—besides I—I—I like you. I—I think you're the sweetest girl I've ever seen.

THE GIRL: (Turning her head away, and releasing her arm from his grasp.) Oh, pshaw! You've said that to a hundred girls.

THE FELLOW: No—believe me, I have not. YOU'VE made a mighty big hit with me. I'm hard hit this time. I—

THE GIRL: (Laughing in spite of herself.) Oh, you foolish boy. How can you expect me to believe you? I'll bet anything that your coat pockets are filled with love letters from other girls this very minute.

THE FELLOW: You are wrong. You are unjust. Clementina, you are—

THE GIRL: (Indignant again.) Clementina! How *dare* you address me by such a ridiculous—

THE FELLOW: Oh, pardon me. I thought Clementina was quite poetic. Besides, I've got to call you something. You do me a terrible injustice. On my word of honor—as a—as a *fisherman*—I haven't a love letter in my coat pocket—or anywhere else. I am young, innocent, virtuous and—

THE GIRL: (Bursting into laughter again.) And utterly foolish, I should judge. You are afraid to let me search your pockets.

THE FELLOW: Afraid? Who's afraid? Me afraid! Well, I'd be tickled to death to have you search my pockets. I *dare* you to search my pockets. I dare you—understand? (He faces her and throws up his hands over his head.)

THE GIRL: You dare me, do you? Well, I just *won't* take a dare. I'll do it.

THE FELLOW: Go ahead and do it. I repeat, I *dare* you! If you doubt my word, prove to your satisfaction that I never lie. I *dare* you!

THE GIRL: (Leaning her parasol against bench, and stepping up to him in very business-like manner.) Very well, then. I accept your challenge. You can't bluff me out. I believe that ALL men lie when they talk to women, and I am under the impression that you are no exception. Keep your hands up in the air—promise?

THE FELLOW: I promise.

THE GIRL: This is the first time I've ever held up anybody, but here goes. (She searches his right-hand pocket.) I don't suppose you've ever been robbed before?

THE FELLOW: Oh, yes—I was once surrounded by a band of robbers.

THE GIRL: (Still searching.) Indeed! On a public highway?

THE FELLOW: (Still holding up his hands.) No, in a New York hotel cafe. They were the waiters.

THE GIRL: (Taking her hand out of right-hand pocket.) Well, there's nothing in that one but a box of matches. How about this one? (She thrusts her hand into the lower left-hand pocket, and pulls out a letter, written on dainty writing paper.) Ah! this is what I expected to find. Perfumed note paper. (She looks at it critically.) Yes, this is the one—no need to search further.

THE FELLOW: What the devil!—(His hands drop to his sides, and he opens his eyes in amazement.)

THE GIRL: (Turning on him angrily.) Sir—such language!

THE FELLOW: Oh, I beg your pardon—but—but—(He points to letter.) I—I—that letter isn't mine. I can't understand how it got into my pocket. I—(Suddenly a look of enlightenment comes into his face. Aside, he says.) By thunder!—I had forgotten all about it. This suit of clothes belongs to Tommy Higgins. Oh, what a mess I've made of it. She'll never believe me *now* if I tell her I am wearing another fellow's suit. (To her, excitedly.) Say—listen to me, honestly that letter was not written to me, Tommy Higgins, you see—

THE GIRL: (Waving him aside.) No excuses. You probably thought you didn't have it with you. Falsehoods are always found out, you see. I was right. You are like all the rest of the men—a born liar—only with this difference—you are a *bigger* liar than the average. You are really in a class all by yourself. (With the letter held out before her, she scans it eagerly.)

Oh, this is immense!—this is delicious!

THE FELLOW: (Making a grab for the letter.) Give that to me, please.

THE GIRL: Not on your life. It may not be proper to read other people's letters, but the present circumstances are unusual. I shall certainly read it—and read it aloud. I want to make you swallow every word and see how they agree with you. Listen to I this, you barbaric Ananias. (She reads aloud.) "My beloved Affinity—Come back to town next Saturday without fail. Just slip away from the other boys at the camp. Tell them that an important business matter demands your presence in the city. I am crazy to see you. Life without you is very stupid. Come to me, my dearest, without delay.

Always your own,

Clementina."

THE FELLOW: (Collapsing in a heap on the bench.) CLEMENTINA!!

THE GIRL: (Folding up the letter and looking at him in utter scorn.) So *that's* where you got the name! So you were thinking of the writer of this letter when you addressed ME by the name of Clementina a while ago. Simply outrageous! (She stamps her feet.)

THE FELLOW: (With a groan.) Oh, Lord! I just happened to say "Clementina" because I thought it was a pretty name. Won't you believe me? I don't know who this Clementina is. I never saw the writer of that letter in all my life. That letter was meant for Tommy Higgins. This suit of clothes—

THE GIRL: (Interrupting.) Don't even attempt to make ridiculous explanations. Don't make yourself more of a liar than you have already proved. I won't listen to another word from you. I didn't want to listen to you in the first place. Here is your affinity's letter, sir. (She hands it to him. He takes it and stuffs it angrily into the coat pocket.) Now, let me have my parasol, please, and my glove. (She reaches for the parasol, but he catches it up and holds it behind his back, as he rises from the bench.)

THE FELLOW: You shall not go away until you hear what I want to say. Tommy Higgins—

THE GIRL: Oh, bother Tommy Higgins!

THE FELLOW: Yes. That's what I say—only stronger. But listen, please—

THE GIRL: Don't discuss the matter further. My parasol and glove; sir! (She is facing him angrily.)

THE FELLOW: Oh, come now. Don't be so hard on a fellow. I tell you that letter wasn't written to me. What if I should search your pockets and find a letter that belonged to somebody else? How would you feel about it?

THE GIRL: You would never find anything in MY pockets that I am ashamed of—that is, if I HAD any pockets. But I have no pockets.

THE FELLOW: (Pointing with one hand at the right side of her jacket.) I beg your pardon. It seems that you know how to tell 'em, too. What's that, if it isn't a pocket?

THE GIRL: (In embarrassment.) Oh—yes—so it is. (Aside.) I had forgotten that I was wearing Genevieve's suit.

THE FELLOW: Well, turn about is fair play, isn't it? I'm going to search *your* pocket now.

THE GIRL: You mean to insinuate that I have anything in my pocket of a compromising nature? How dare you!

THE FELLOW: You won't believe ME! Why should *I* believe you? For all I know, you may be a far different kind of girl than I took you to be.

THE GIRL: (Very angry.) You are insulting, sir. But since I stooped so low as to search your pockets, I will give you the satisfaction of searching mine—and then that will be an end of our acquaintance. You can then go your way—and I'll go my way.

THE FELLOW: We'll see about that. Hold up your hands.

THE GIRL: (Darting furious glances at him and holding her hands over her head.) Very well, sir. Hurry up, please, and have it over with. (THE FELLOW very deliberately goes to bench, leans the parasol up against it, just as THE GIRL had done before, and imitating the business-like way in which she had gone through his pockets, he comes up to her and pushes up his coat sleeves, as if preparing for a serious piece of business.)

THE FELLOW: (Still mimicing her manner.) I don't suppose you've ever been held up before?

THE GIRL: (Icily.) No—you are the first burglar I have ever met.

THE FELLOW: Promise to hold your hands up until I have finished?

THE GIRL: (Scornfully.) Of course, I'm a girl of my word.

THE FELLOW: All right then. (He deliberately kisses her squarely on the lips, while her hands are held up over her head. She gives a cry and starts to drop her hands and push him away, but he catches her arms and gently holds them up over her head again.) No, no, I'm not through yet.

THE GIRL: You are a brute. You are not worthy to associate with a respectable girl. (THE FELLOW thrusts his hands into the pocket of her jacket and puns out a box of cigarettes and a letter. He holds them up before her horrified eyes.)

THE FELLOW: Well. I'll be—(He starts to say "damned," but stops just in time. THE GIRL'S arms drop limply to her sides, and with eyes staring in complete bewilderment she staggers to the bench and collapses down upon it.)

THE GIRL: Good heavens!

THE FELLOW: (Blinking his eyes at the articles which he holds before him.) What innocent playthings! A box of Pall Malls and a letter—no doubt, an affinity letter. (He shakes his head, soberly.) Well, well! And you just said I wasn't fit to associate with you.

THE GIRL: (Her breast heaving in great agitation.) Oh, this is a terrible mistake! What could Genevieve have been doing with those things?

THE FELLOW: (Turning on her, quickly.) Genevieve?

THE GIRL: Yes, Genevieve.

THE FELLOW: Genevieve Patterson.

THE GIRL: Yes, Genevieve Patterson—the girl you know—my best friend. Oh, *can't* you understand? Those things don't belong to me. They are—(She stops abruptly, bites her lips, clasps her hands. Then says, aside.) Oh, what am I doing? I mustn't allow Genevieve's reputation to be ruined. I might as well take the blame and brave it out myself. This situation is frightful. (She turns to him again.) I can't explain, but don't—oh, please don't think that I—that I—(She stops, looking as if she is about to cry.)

THE FELLOW: (Again looking at the articles and shaking his head.) And you always looked like such a nice girl, too. Cigarettes—and— (He opens up the letter.)

THE GIRL: (Suddenly springing to her feet.) You must not read that letter. It does not belong to me. You have no right to read that letter.

THE FELLOW: But you read the letter that didn't belong to me.

THE GIRL: It *did* belong to you.

THE FELLOW: It didn't!

THE GIRL: DID!

THE FELLOW: Didn't!

THE GIRL: (Running forward and trying to grab the letter, which he holds out of her reach.) I *forbid* you to read that letter. I swear to you, it is not mine.

THE FELLOW: (Still holding it out of her reach and looking it over.) By George! You are right—it is NOT yours. It is MINE!

THE GIRL: YOURS?

THE FELLOW: Yes, mine. It's the very message I sent to Genevieve Patterson yesterday—the letter in which I asked for an introduction to you. (He hands it to her.) Here—read it yourself, if you don't believe me this time. (THE GIRL wonderingly takes the letter and reads it to herself, her lips moving and her eyes wide open in surprise.)

THE GIRL: (As she finishes she looks sweetly up at him.) Then you are

NOT such a liar after all. You *did* tell me the truth.

THE FELLOW: Nothing but the truth.

THE GIRL: But what about that other letter?

THE FELLOW: (Taking her by the shoulder and speaking quickly.) Now, you've *got* to listen. That other letter was written to Tommy Higgins. I was caught in the shower last night, and had to borrow this suit of clothes from Tommy.

THE GIRL: (A glad smile gradually coming over her face.) O-h-h!

THE FELLOW: But how did you come to have my letter written to Genevieve?

THE GIRL: Oh, *don't* you understand? (She looks at him beseechingly.)

THE FELLOW: (The truth suddenly striking him.) Oh-h-h-! I see! You got caught in the shower, too. You borrowed that tailor-made suit from Genevieve.

THE GIRL: Can you doubt it?

THE FELLOW: But the cigarettes?

THE GIRL: I can't account for them. I only know—

THE FELLOW: Never mind. I don't care. (He stuffs the cigarettes into his own pocket and grasps both of her hands in his own.) Tell me—you don't think I'm the biggest liar in the world, do you?

THE GIRL: (Archly.) No—not quite.

THE FELLOW: (Slipping his arm around her.) And if you were married—to—to a fellow like me, you'd make him an awfully good wife, wouldn't you?

THE GIRL: (Laughing.). No—I'd try to make HIM a good husband. (He bends over and is just about to kiss her when a MAN'S VOICE is heard off stage to the Right.)

MAN'S VOICE: (Off stage.) Hey, there, Miss—your trunk has come. (THE FELLOW and THE GIRL spring apart, guiltily.)

THE FELLOW: (Bitterly.) Just when I had it all cinched. (THE GIRL runs to the bench, picks up her parasol, still laughing.)

THE GIRL: It's the wagon from the railroad station, with my clothes from town. Good-bye. (She starts off, Right.)

THE FELLOW: But you're coming back again?

THE GIRL: Well—maybe—perhaps—If you're good. (She exits laughing.)

THE FELLOW: She's got me going. My head's in a muddle, and I feel like a sailor full of horn-pipes. And that reminds me of Tommy Higgins' latest song. It goes like this: (Here is introduced comic song. At finish THE GIRL comes running on from Right, dressed in a pretty summer dress, and carrying another pretty silk parasol. THE FELLOW takes his hat off and holding it high over his head, exclaims:) Here comes the rainbow after the shower!

THE GIRL: I must explain to you—I saw Genevieve—the cigarettes belong to her brother, Jack.

THE FELLOW: And I've just found out what belongs to me.

THE GIRL: What?

THE FELLOW: You! (He takes her parasol, opens it, and holds it in front of them for an instant so that their faces are hidden from audience. This is music cue for the Conversation Number which brings the sketch to a finish.)

THE VILLAIN STILL PURSUED HER

CHARACTERS
    GLADYS DRESSUITCASE . . . . . A Deserted Wife
    ALPHONSO DRESSUITCASE . . . . Her Dying Che-ild
    MOE REISS DRESSUITCASE. . . . Her Fugitive Husband
    BIRDIE BEDSLATZ . . . . Her Doll-faced Rival
    ALGERNON O'FLAHERTY . . . . . The Villain Who Pursued Her

SCENE OF PROLOGUE
    STREET IN ONE. . . LIGHTS OUT
    Music: "Mendelssohn's Spring Song," Played in discords. Spot Light on L. I.

PROLOGUE
    Enter GLADYS wearing linen duster and dragging a big rope to which is attached a case of beer with about eight empty bottles in it. She stops C.
    GLADYS: (Tearfully.) At last I am almost home. Eleven miles walk from the sweat shop here, and that's some hoofing it, believe me. (Sways.) Oh, I am faint (Looks over shoulder at beer case.), faint for the want of my Coca-Cola. (Enter ALGERNON R. I—wears slouch hat, heavy moustache, red shirt and high boots. She is facing L.) Oh, I have a hunch I'm being shadowed—flagged by a track-walker! But I mustn't think of that. (Starts to drag case L.) I must get home to my dying child. He needs me—he needs me. (Exits L. I.)
    ALGERNON: (Goes L. C. and looks after her.) It is Gladys—found at last! (Enter BIRDIE L. I. She is in bright red with white plumes and is a beautiful, radiant adventuress.)
    BIRDIE: Did you get a good look at her?
    ALGERNON: Yes—it's Gladys and she's down and out—(Both together:) Curse her!
    ALGERNON: Now I can begin pursuing her again.
    BIRDIE: Yes, and I can gloat over her misery—and gloating's the best thing I do.
    ALGERNON: Come (fiercely!) We are wasting time.
    BIRDIE: She'll never know me with this dark hair and no make-up on.
    ALGERNON: (At L. I—still more fiercely.) Can that junk! Come! (Exits L. I.)
    BIRDIE: (Going to L. I.) He has me in his power. I must follow him. Curse him! (Exits after ALGERNON. Enter MOE REISS in bum evening-clothes and opera hat. Carries cane.)
    MOE REISS: (Reading from back of envelope.) Down this street and turn into the alley full of ash cans! I'm on the right track at last. Once more I shall see my wife and my little boy! Of course, she'll be sore because I ran away and deserted her, leaving her no alimony except the dying che-ild. But I must produce a real wife and child from somewhere or I'll lose the $9.75 my uncle left me. (Goes L. musingly.) Why do I love money so? Ay, that's the question. (Looking

up at gallery.) And what's the answer? (Points off L. with cane—dramatically.) We shall see—we shall see. (Dashes off L.)

The lights go out, and the Drop in One takes all the time that the clock strikes sixteen or seventeen to go up, so it is timed very slowly.

FULL STAGE SCENE
THE WRETCHED HOME OF GLADYS

A Mott Street Garret—everything of the poorest description. Old table down stage R., with chair on either side and waste paper basket in front. Cot bed down stage L. Old cupboard up stage C. Small stand at head of cot.

PHONSIE lies in cot, head up stage, covered up. He should weigh over two hundred pounds. He wears Buster Brown wig and nightie that buttons up the back. GLADYS is seated at table d. s. R., sewing on a tiny handkerchief. She is magnificently dressed and wears all the jewelry she can carry. Pile of handkerchiefs at back of table within reach and a waste basket in front of table where she can throw handkerchiefs when used.

As curtain rises, the clock off stage slowly strikes for the sixteenth or seventeenth time.

GLADYS: Five o'clock and my sewing still unfinished. Oh, it must be done to-night. There's the rent—six dollars. To-day is Friday—bargain day—I wonder if the landlord would take four ninety-eight.

(Business. PHONSIE snores.) And my child needs more medicine. The dog biscuits haven't helped him a bit, and his stomach is too weak to digest the skin foods. (Wood crash off stage.) How restless he is, poor little tot!!!! Fatherless and deserted, sick and emaciated—eight years have I passed in this wretched place, hopeless, hapless, hipless. At times the struggle seems more than I can bear, but I must be brave for my child, my little one. (Buries face in hands.) (Business. Sews.)

PHONSIE: (Business.) Mommer! Mommer! Are you there? (Blows pea blower at her.)

GLADYS: (Hand to cheek where he hit her.) Yes, dolling, mommer is here.

PHONSIE: Say, mommer, am I dying? (Loud and toughly.)

GLADYS: (Sadly.) I am afraid *not*, my treasure.

PHONSIE: Why not, mommer?

GLADYS: You are too great a pest to die, sweetheart.

PHONSIE: But the good always die young, don't they, mommer?

GLADYS: (Still sewing.) But you were not speaking about the good—you were speaking of yourself, my precious.

PHONSIE: Ain't I good, mommer, don't you think?

GLADYS: (Business.) Oh, I don't dare to think!!!! (Moves up stage.)

PHONSIE: Don't think if it hurts you, mommer.

GLADYS: (At dresser.) But come, it is time for your medicine. (Shows enormous pill.)

PHONSIE: (Scared.) What is that, mommer?

GLADYS: Just a horse pill, baby. (Puts it in his mouth.) There, that will help cure mother's little man. (At table.)

PHONSIE: Gee! That tasted fierce. (Business. Knock.) Some one is knocking, mommer.

GLADYS: They're always knocking mommer. (At door.)

VOICE: Have yez th' rint?

GLADYS: I haven't.

VOICE: Much obliged.

GLADYS: You're welcome.

PHONSIE: Who was that, mommer?

GLADYS: That was only the landlord for the rent. Alas, I cannot raise it.

PHONSIE: Then if you can't raise the rent, raise me, mommer. Can't I have the spot-light to die with?

GLADYS: Why certainly you shall have one. Mr. Electrician, will you kindly give my dying child a spot-light? (Business.) There, dearest, there's your spot-light.

PHONSIE: (Laughs.) Oh, that's fine. Mommer, can I have visions?

GLADYS: Why surely, dear, you can have all the visions you want. (Shoves opium pipe in his mouth and lights it.) Now tell mommer what you see, baby!

PHONSIE: Oh, mommer, I see awful things. I can see the Gerry society pinching me. And oh, mommer, I can see New York,[111] and there ain't a gambling house in the town.

GLADYS: He's blind!!!! My child's gone blind!!!! (PHONSIE snores.) He sleeps at last, my child, my little dying child!!!! (Enter ALGERNON and BIRDIE.)

GLADYS: (Discovers ALGERNON.) You!!!! (ALGERNON turns to Orchestra and conducts Chord with cane.) (GLADYS Left, ALGERNON C., BIRDIE R.)

ALGERNON: (Chord.) Yes, Gladys Dressuitcase, once more we meet!!!!!

GLADYS: And the lady with the Brooklyn[112] gown!! Ah, you will start, but I know you in spite of your disguise, Birdie Bedslatz.

BIRDIE: Disguise! What disguise?

GLADYS: Woman, you cannot deceive me. You've been to the dry-dock and had your face scraped.

BIRDIE: So, you still want war?

GLADYS: No, I want justice!!!! (ALGERNON conducts Chord.) You have tracked me like sleuthhounds. You have hunted me down after all these years. You have robbed me of home, husband, honor and friends. What then is left me? (L.)

BIRDIE: (Menacingly.) There is always the river.

GLADYS: What, you dare suggest that, you with your past!

BIRDIE: How dare you mention that to me! I am now writing Sunday stories for the New York "American."[113] (Crosses to left and sits.)

GLADYS: (Stunned.) Sophie Lyons, now I see it all.

---

[111] Substitute name of any big city.
[112] Substitute name of the local gag town.
[113] Substitute name of the local sensational newspaper.

ALGERNON: (Center.) I have here a mortgage.

GLADYS: A mortgage!!!! What is it on?

ALGERNON: I don't know. What difference does that make? It is a mortgage. That's all that's necessary.

GLADYS: Can it be a mortgage on the old farm?

ALGERNON: (Moves over to R.) Certainly, on the old farm!!!! The dear old homestead in New Hampshire. (Takes paper from pocket. Crosses over to GLADYS.) I have also the paper that always goes with the mortgage. Sign this paper and the mortgage shall be yours, refuse—and—do you mind my coming closer so that I can hiss this in your ear?

GLADYS: Not at all, come right over.

ALGERNON: (Close to GLADYS.) Refuse (Hiss), I say, and you and your child shall be thrown into the streets to starve. (Hiss.)

GLADYS: (Crosses R.) Oh, I must have time to drink—I mean think. But this is infamous. The landlord will—

ALGERNON: I am the landlord. Now will you sign the papers?

GLADYS: No, a thousand times no!!!!! (Chord.) (ALGERNON conducts Chord.) No!!!!

BIRDIE: (Hand to ear.) Good gracious, don't scream so, where do you think you are?

ALGERNON: You won't sign?

GLADYS: No, do your worst, throw me into the street with my child. He is sick, dying!!!!

ALGERNON: What's the matter with him? (Goes to bed.) (PHONSIE is heaving and whistling.) Great heavens, he has the heaves. (Goes R.)

BIRDIE: What are you doing for him?

GLADYS: Trying the hot air treatment.

BIRDIE: I should think you would be expert at that.

GLADYS: The doctor says he has grey matter in his brain.

BIRDIE: (Comes down L.) I am sorry, very sorry.

ALGERNON: Sorry! Bah, this is a cheap play for sympathy! (To GLADYS:) Will you sign the papers?

GLADYS: Never, I defy you: (To BIRDIE.) As for you, beautiful fiend that you are, you came between me and my husband; you stole him from me with your dog-faced beauty; I mean doll-faced. But I can see your finish, I can see you taking poison in about fifteen minutes.

BIRDIE: (Over to ALGERNON.) Put me wise, is this true?

ALGERNON: No, 'tis false, false as hell!!!!! (Points up.)

GLADYS: It's true, as true as heaven. (Points down.) I swear it.

ALGERNON: (Crosses up to GLADYS.) Why, curse you, I'll—

GLADYS: (With pistol.) Stand back!!!!! I'm a desperate woman!!!!!

ALGERNON: (Center.) Foiled, curse the luck, foiled by a mere slip of a girl.

BIRDIE: What's to be done?

ALGERNON: (Yells.) Silence!!!! (Business.) Once aboard the lugger the girl must and shall be mine!!!!

BIRDIE: But how do you propose to *lug her* there? (ALGERNON moves up to door.)

GLADYS: Oh, I see it all. You have brought this she-devil here to work off her bad gags on me. Man, have you no heart?

ALGERNON: (Comes down C.) Of course I have a heart. I have also eyes, ears, nose, tongue and—

BIRDIE: Brains, calves' brains—breaded.

ALGERNON: That will be about all from you. Go, leave us!

BIRDIE: Alone?

ALGERNON: Alone!

GLADYS: Alone!

PHONSIE: (In sepulchral tone.) Oh, Gee!

BIRDIE: But it's hardly decent. You need a tamer.

ALGERNON: Go! (Crosses to R.) Go, I say, before it is too late.

BIRDIE: Oh, there's no hurry. Every place is open.

ALGERNON: Don't sass me, Birdie Bedslatz, but clear out, scat!!!!

BIRDIE: Ain't he the awful scamp? (Starts to door.)

GLADYS: (Clinging to her.) No, you cannot, must not go. Don't leave me alone with that piano mover.

BIRDIE: I must go. I have poison to buy. (At door.) Ah, Algernon O'Flaherty, if there was more men in the world like you, there'd be less women like me—I just love to say that. Ta—ta. (PHONSIE blows pea-shooter at her as she Exits. She screams and grabs cheek.)

ALGERNON: (To GLADYS back.) So, proud beauty, at last we are alone!

GLADYS: Inhuman monster!!! What new villainy do you propose?

ALGERNON: None, it's all old stuff. Listen, Gladys. When I see you again, all the old love revives and I grow mad, mad.

GLADYS: You dare to speak of love to me? Why, from the first moment I saw you, I despised you. And now I tell you to your face that I hate and loathe you, for the vile, contemptible wretch that you are.

ALGERNON: (Center.) Be careful, girl! I can give you wealth, money, jewels—jewels fit for a king's ransom.

GLADYS: (Runs into his arms.) Oh, you can—Where are they?

ALGERNON: They are in hock for the moment, but see, here are the tickets. I shall get them out, anon.

GLADYS: Dastardly wretch!!!!! With your pawn tickets to try and cop out a poor sewing girl. (Up at door.) There is the door, go! (Points other way.)

ALGERNON: (Up to her.) Why curse you, I'll—

GLADYS: Strike, you coward! (Chord.) (ALGERNON conducts Chord.)

ALGERNON: Coward!!!! (He conducts same Chord an Octave higher.)

GLADYS: Yes, coward. . . . Now go, and never cross this threshold again!!

ALGERNON: (Going up stage.) So, I'm fired with the threshold gag? Very well, I go, but I shall return. . . . I shall return! (Exits.)

PHONSIE: (Blows pea-blower after him.) Who was that big stiff, mommer, the instalment man?

GLADYS: No, darling, he is the floor-walker in a slaughter house.

PHONSIE: Mommer, when do I eat?

GLADYS: Alas, we cannot buy food, we are penniless.

PHONSIE: If you would only put your jewels in soak, mommer.

GLADYS: What, hock me sparks? Never! I may starve, yes, but I'll starve like a lady in all my finery!

PHONSIE: Mommer, I want to eat.

GLADYS: What shall I do? My child hungry, dying, without even the price of a shave! Oh, my heart is like my brother on the railroad, breaking—breaking—breaking—(Weeps.)

PHONSIE: Ah, don't cry, mommer. You'll have the whole place damp. You keep on sewing and I'll keep on dying.

GLADYS: Very well. (Drying eyes.) But first I'll go out and get a can of beer. Thank goodness, we always have beer money.

PHONSIE: Oh yes, mommer, do rush the growler. Me coppers is toastin'. And don't forget your misery cape and the music that goes with you, will you, mommer?

GLADYS: I'll get those.

PHONSIE: And you'd better take some handkerchiefs. You may want to cry. But don't cry in the beer, mommer, it makes it flat.

GLADYS: Thank you, baby, I do love to weep. Oh, if we only had a blizzard, I'd take you out in your nightie. But wait, sweetheart, wait till it goes below zero. Then you shall go out with mommer, bare-footed.

PHONSIE: Don't stand chewing the rag with the bartender, will you, mommer?

GLADYS: Only till he puts a second head on the beer. (Exit R.)

PHONSIE: Gee, it's fierce to be a stage child and dying. I wonder where my popper is? I want my popper—I want my popper. (Bawls.)

MOE REISS: (Enters.) Why, what is the matter, my little man?

PHONSIE: Oh, I'm so lonely, I want my popper.

MOE REISS: And where is your popper?

PHONSIE: Mommer says he is in Philadelphia. (Sniffles.)

MOE REISS: (Lifts hat reverently.) Dead, and his child doesn't know. And where is your mama?

PHONSIE: Oh, she's went out to chase the can.

MOE REISS: And what is your name, my little man?

PHONSIE: Alphonso. Ain't that practically the limit?

MOE REISS: Alphonso? I once had a little boy named Alphonso, who might have been about your age.

PHONSIE: And what prevented him?

MOE REISS: (Sighs.) Alas, I lost him!

PHONSIE: That was awful careless of you. You oughtn't to have took him out without his chain. (Sniffs.)

MOE REISS: What's the matter with your nose?

PHONSIE: I have the glanders—and the heaves. I get all the horse diseases.

Father was a race track tout.

MOE REISS: A race track tout? What is your last name?

PHONSIE: Dressuitcase, Alphonso Dressuitcase.

MOE REISS: Dressuitcase? And have you heavy shingle marks on your person, great blue welts?

PHONSIE: You bet I have, and my popper put them there, too.

MOE REISS: Why, it's my boy, Phonsie, my little Phonsie. Don't you know me? It's popper. (Slams him in face hard with open hand.)

PHONSIE: Well, your style is familiar, but you don't need to show off!

GLADYS: (Enters. Carrying Growler carefully.) Moe! Moe! My husband! (Buries face in can.)

MOE REISS: Gladys! Gladys! My wife! (Takes can from GLADYS.)

PHONSIE: (Comes between them.) Here, I want to have my fever reduced. (Back to bed.)

GLADYS: Where have you been all these years, Moe?

MOE REISS: Just bumming around, just bumming around. When I deserted you and copped out Birdie Bedslatz, I went from bad to worse, from Jersey City to Hoboken. [114]When my senses returned, I was insane.

GLADYS: My poor husband, how you must have suffered!

MOE REISS: At heart, I was always true to you and our little boy, and I want to come back home.

GLADYS: But tell me, Moe, how are you fixed? (Tries to feel his vest pocket.)

MOE REISS: Fine, I am running a swell gambling joint.

GLADYS: Splendid! Now, Phonsie shall have proper nourishment.

MOE REISS: He shall have all the food he can eat. (Up to bed.)

GLADYS: Yes, and all the beer he can drink.

MOE REISS: Great heavens, I could never pay for that.

GLADYS: Ah, then he will have to cut out his souse. Dear little chap; he loved to get tanked up. Oh look at him, Moe, he is the living image of you. I think if he lives, he will be a great bull fighter. (PHONSIE has finished the beer, and is sucking at a nipple on large bottle marked "Pure Rye.")

MOE REISS: Then he does take after me—dear little chap. (Hits him.)

GLADYS: Indeed he does. But is it safe for you to come here, Moe?

MOE REISS: Not with Whitman [115]on my trail. You know, Gladys, in the eyes of the world, I am guilty.

GLADYS: Then the world lies. (Chord. ALGERNON comes on from R. I and conducts and then Exits.) I still trust you, my husband, though the police want you for stealing moth balls. (Crash off.) What's that? (Runs to door.) Oh, it's the health department. They have come with the garbage wagon to arrest you. Quick, in there. (Points to door R.)

MOE REISS: No, let them come. I am here to see my wife and here I shall remain.

---

[114] Local.
[115] Local District Attorney.

GLADYS: But for our child's sake. See, he holds up his little hands and pleads for you to go. (PHONSIE in pugilistic attitude.)

PHONSIE: Say, pop, if you don't get a wiggle on and duck in there, there'll be something doing. (Business.)

MOE REISS: My boy, I can refuse you nothing. (Exits.)

GLADYS: (At door C.) They are sneaking up, on rubbers! (To PHONSIE.) Lie down, Fido. (Guarding door R. Enter ALGERNON and BIRDIE, Door C.)

ALGERNON: There's some hellish mystery here!

BIRDIE: You can search me.

ALGERNON: (Sees GLADYS.) Aha! Now will you sign those papers?

GLADYS: Never. (Bus.) I'll sign nothing. (Down R.)

ALGERNON: (Takes carrot from his hip pocket.) You won't? There, curse you, take that. (Hits her in neck with carrot.)

GLADYS: In the neck! In the neck, where I always get it!

ALGERNON: (Center.) Quick, Birdie, seize the child and run.

BIRDIE: (Left, looks scornfully at PHONSIE.) You've got your nerve. He weighs a ton!!

PHONSIE: Oh! She's going to kidnap me!! Assistance!!

ALGERNON: Silence!! Enough!! (To GLADYS.) I have just come from the Society for the Prevention of Cruelty to Animals.

GLADYS: Well?

ALGERNON: I have reported to them that your child has the heaves.

GLADYS: Well?

ALGERNON: The Society is sending a horse ambulance to take him to the dump.

GLADYS: Dump? To the dump?!!! No, no, it's a cruel, hideous jest! Take away my little dying boy? It would kill him, you understand, it would kill him!!

PHONSIE: (Toughly.) Sure, it would kill me!! (Bites off big chew of Tobacco.)

ALGERNON: Nevertheless, in five minutes the horse ambulance will be here.

GLADYS: Oh no! no! no! What if my child should die?

ALGERNON: Then they will make glue out of his carcass.

GLADYS: Glue. Aw! (Shakes snow on herself from box hanging over the table L.)

PHONSIE: I don't want to be no glue, mommer, I'd be all stuck up.

GLADYS: (Goes C. to PHONSIE.) Why this fiendish plot? What have I done that you thus pursue me?

ALGERNON: (R. C.) You repulsed my hellish caresses.

GLADYS: Oh, I will do anything to save my child. I'll try to love you. . . . I will love! See? (Business.) (Into his arms.) I love you now!

MOE REISS: (Enter, center.) What's this? My wife in that man's arms? Oh! (Crosses L.)

GLADYS: (At right, to MOE REISS.) Oh, Moe, I can explain. (Grabs his throat and shakes him.)

MOE REISS: (To GLADYS.) Explain!!! How? I go away and desert you for eight years. (Turns from her and goes L.) In that short absence you forget your husband. (Turns to her.) I return to find you in his arms, before my very nose. (Smashes PHONSIE in face.) (Business.) (He sees BIRDIE.) You, Birdie!

BIRDIE: Yes, I, little Birdie—Birdie on the spot.

MOE REISS: Ah, you she-fiend, you lady demon! (Kisses her.)

GLADYS: (Screams.) No, no! (Runs to him.) It's all a plot! A hideous plot to part us! This man has complained to the S. P. C. A. that our little Phonsie has the heaves. They are sending a horse ambulance to take him to the dump! They'll make *glue* out of his carcass! (To ALGERNON.) You see what you have done! (Beats him on back.) Tell my husband, you devil, tell him the truth!!!

ALGERNON: (To MOE REISS) (C.) Well, if you must know the truth, your wife loves me and was forcing her caresses upon me when you entered.

MOE REISS: It's true then, it's true?

PHONSIE: (Sits up.) No, popper, it's false, and I can prove it.

ALGERNON: The child is delirious from the heaves!

PHONSIE: I'll heave you out of here in a minute. Listen, popper, mommer's done the best she could. It ain't easy to nurse a dying child who is liable to croak at any moment. But she's done that, popper, she's often went without her dill pickle so I could have my spavin cure. She thought I might get well and strong and maybe get a job as a safe mover. But I've been so busy dying I couldn't go to work. (Shakes fist at ALGERNON.) Don't believe that man, popper; I'm dying, cross my heart if I ain't dying, so I couldn't tell a lie. (Back to bed.)

MOE REISS: Oh, my boy! My boy! (heart-brokenly.) (Hits PHONSIE.)

GLADYS: Dh, Moe Reiss, don't you believe him?

ALGERNON: (Left of C.) Of course not, he saw you with your arms around my neck.

MOE REISS: Yes, I saw it, I seen it.

BIRDIE: I can swear to it, if necessary.

PHONSIE: I can swear too, popper, want to hear me?

MOE REISS: No, I have heard enough. Now I intend to act. (Throws off coat, L.)

ALGERNON: What do you mean?

MOE REISS: I mean that either you or I will never leave this place alive. For I tell you plainly, as sure as there is a poker game above us, I mean to kill you!

ALGERNON: (Throws off coat and hat.) Well, if it's a roughhouse you're looking for, I'm right there with the goods. (Struggle.)

PHONSIE: Give him an upper cut, popper, soak him!!!

BIRDIE: Knife him, Algernon, knife him! (Has out her hat pin.) (During struggle, PHONSIE shoots three times.) (As they struggle to window, ALGERNON turns back, and PHONSIE sees [after third shot] his vest is a target and fires three times. Bell on each shot.) Curse you, you've got me. Here are your three cigars. (Falls dead, C.)

MOE REISS: (Kneels and feels heart.) Dead!!! Who could have done this?

PHONSIE: Father, I cannot tell a lie, I done it with my little hatchet. (Shows big gun and a picture of George Washington. All the others lift American flags and wave them.) (PHONSIE L. waving flag, MOE and GLADYS C. BIRDIE dead in chair R.)

THE LOLLARD

CHARACTERS
   ANGELA MAXWELL
       HARRY MAXWELL
  FRED SALTUS
     MISS CAREY

SCENE: The apartment of Miss Carey, a hardworking modiste about 45 years of age, rather sharp in manner, very prudish and a hater of men.

TIME: About 2 A.M.

When the curtain rises, the stage is dark. First, "feminine snores" are heard, then a sharp ringing of bell. Then MISS CAREY from her bed in next room (curtained off, but partly visible) calls out:

MISS CAREY: Who is it?

VOICE: (Off stage.) It's me. Open!

MISS CAREY: (Poking her night-capped head out of curtains.) Well, who are you?

VOICE: (Off stage.) You don't know me. But that's all right. Please let me in—hurry! Hurry!

MISS CAREY: (Rising and getting into a kimono.) Well—whoever you are—what do you mean by waking me at two in the morning? I'll report this to the janitor. (She turns up light and opens door. ANGELA MAXWELL rushes in—in fluffy peignoir—her hair in pretty disorder—her hands full of wearing apparel, etc., as if she just snatched same up in haste. An opera coat, a pair of slippers, etc.)

ANGELA: (Rushing in—closing door after her and silencing MISS CAREY by the mysterious way she seizes her by the wrist.) Listen, you don't know me, but I've just left my husband.

MISS CAREY: (Sharply.) Well, that's no reason why I should leave my bed.

ANGELA: (Reassuringly.) You can go right back again, dear—in fact, I'll go with you and we'll talk it over there.

MISS CAREY: I don't wish to talk it over anywhere, and—

ANGELA: Well, surely, you don't think it was wrong of me to leave Harry—now do you?

MISS CAREY: I never blame any woman for leaving any man.

ANGELA: See, I knew it. After I fired the Wedgewood vase at him—and just for doing it he was brute enough to call me "Vixen,"— I snatched up as much as I could that was worth taking, and left him *forever*. (Suddenly, as she sees dress on model.) Oh, what a lovely little frock. (Back to other tone.) Yes, forever; and it was only when I stood out in the cold hall that I realized it would have been better to have left him forever when I was all dressed in the morning. (Beginning to shiver and weep.) Take my advice, dear, if you ever leave your husband, never do it on a *cold night*.

MISS CAREY: (Sharply.) I'm not married.

ANGELA: (Weeping copiously and shivering.) Well, then, you needn't bother, dear, about the weather, 'cause you never will be married.

MISS CAREY: No, I never will—catch me selling my freedom to any selfish brute of a man.

ANGELA: (As before.) See, I knew it. I said to myself, that little lady on the second floor who makes dresses with a long, thin nose—

MISS CAREY: (Outraged.) Makes dresses with a long, thin nose?

ANGELA: Yes—she's the only one in the whole apartment house I can go to—she's the only one won't give Harry right.

MISS CAREY: No man is ever right.

ANGELA: I'm commencing to believe all men are brutes.

MISS CAREY: Of course they are. (Commencing to thaw.) Have a cup of tea. (She goes to table to prepare tea things.)

ANGELA: Thanks—I brought my own tea with me. (Takes a little paper bag of tea out of one of the slippers and crosses to MISS CAREY.) If I had struck him with the vase, I could understand his calling me "Vixen" (Beginning to weep again.)—but I only flung it at him, 'cause I cracked it by accident in the morning, and I didn't want him to find it out. He was always calling me "butter-fingers." (Sits at opposite side of table.)

MISS CAREY: Oh, he was always calling you names.

ANGELA: No, that's all he ever called me—"Butter-fingers." (Cries again.)

MISS CAREY: (Pouring tea.) Oh, he's the kind that just loves to stay home and nag.

ANGELA: I'd like to catch any husband I ever get, nag.

MISS CAREY: Oh, a pouter—I know that kind.

ANGELA: Oh, no. Why, every time I insulted him he kissed me—the brute. (After a second's pause.) But—excuse me—how do you know so many kinds of men if you've never been married?

MISS CAREY: (Quickly.) Boarders—to make ends meet, I've always had to have a male boarder since I was left an orphan. (She rises—turns her back to audience—gives a touch to her pigtail, during the laugh to this line. This business always builds laugh.)

ANGELA: (Absent-mindedly.) Well, I've heard that male boarders are very nice.

MISS CAREY: I've never had a nice one yet, but I've named nearly all the style male brutes there are. What kind of a brute have you? (She sips tea.)

ANGELA: Why, I don't know—I've often wondered—you might call Harry a "lollard."

MISS CAREY: A lollard?

ANGELA: Yes, I invented the word, and believe me, a woman suffers with a lollard. (At this, MISS CAREY lets her spoon fall in cup.)

MISS CAREY: I should think she would. How did a sweet young thing like you ever meet such a type of a vertebrate?

ANGELA: At a military ball, and oh Mrs.—

MISS CAREY: *Miss* Carey.

ANGELA: Miss Carey—he was the handsomest specimen. His hair looked so spick—his shoulders were so big and broad—his teeth so white—and his skin, well, Miss Carey, if you'd seen him, I'll bet you'd have just gone crazy to kiss him yourself. (MISS CAREY, who is drinking tea, nearly chokes on this—coughing on the tea which goes down the wrong way.)

MISS CAREY: (After the business.) How did he lose his looks?

ANGELA: By becoming a lollard. Listen! (They pull chairs in front of table together, teacups in hand.) It happened on the honeymoon— on the train—as we sat hand in hand, when all at once, the wind through the window, started to blow his hair the wrong way, and oh, Miss Carey, what do you think I discovered?

MISS CAREY: He had been branded on the head as a criminal.

ANGELA: Oh nothing so pleasant as that—but the hair that I thought grew so lovely and plentifully, had been coaxed by a wet brush from the back over the front, and from the east over to the west. (Indicates by imitating action on her own head.)

MISS CAREY: Oh, a lollard is a disappointment of the hair.

ANGELA: No, Miss Carey, no. Listen. I said, "Oh, Harry, your hair which I thought grew so evenly and plentifully all over your head really only grows in patches." He only answered, "Yes, and now that we're married, Angela, I don't have to fool you by brushing it fancy anymore." In despair, I moaned "Yes, Harry—fool me—go on love, fool me and brush it fancy."

MISS CAREY; (Rising and crossing R.) That was your first mistake. No woman should ever call any man "love."

ANGELA: Oh, I didn't know what I said—I was so busy the whole journey pulling his hair from the back to the front and the east to the west (Same business of illustrating.)—and then, oh Miss Carey, what do you think was the next thing I discovered?

MISS CAREY: (In horror.) His *teeth* only grew in patches.

ANGELA: No, but I had fallen in love with a pair of tailor's shoulder-pads—yes—when he took off his coat that night, he shrunk so, I screamed (Pause—as laugh comes here.)—thinking I was in a room with a strange man—but all he muttered was "Angie, I can loll about in easy things now, I'm married"—and that's how gradually his refined feet began to look like canal-boats—his skin only looked kissable the days he shaved—twice a week—his teeth became tobacco stained—and to-night—to-night, Miss Carey, he stopped wearing hemstitched pajamas and took to wearing canton flannel night shirts. (In depth of woe after the big laugh this gets.) Miss Carey, have you ever seen a man in a canton flannel night shirt?

MISS CAREY: (After an expression of horror.) I told you I am not married.

ANGELA: (Innocently.) Oh, excuse me, I was thinking of your boarders. (MISS CAREY screams "what" and shows herself insulted beyond words.) Is it any wonder my love for him has grown cold? Men expect a woman to primp up for them—we must always look our best to hold their love—but once they wheedle us into signing our names to the marriage contract—they think (Suddenly, seeing dress again.)—Oh Miss Carey, what do you charge for a frock like that?

MISS CAREY: I have no night rates for gowns, Mrs.—

ANGELA: Just call me Angie—'cause I probably will live with you now. (Slips her arm through MISS CAREY'S, laying her head on the older woman's shoulder.)

MISS CAREY: (Disengaging her.) We'll talk that over in the morning— if you want, you may sleep upon that couch—I'll put out the light. (She does so.) I'm going to bed—I must get a little rest. (She gives a sharp turn and goes to her room. Blue light floods stage. Through the half open curtain she is seen having trouble with her bed covers—getting them too high up, then too far down, etc. Big laughs on this business.)

ANGELA: (Taking down hair.) Miss Carey, you said you were an orphan— I'm an orphan, too. (There is no answer.) I can't tell you how I appreciate your insisting on my staying—let me make your breakfast in the morning, Miss Carey. (No answer.) Harry might at least try to find me. Aren't men brutes, Miss Carey?

MISS CAREY: (Loudly from within.) They certainly are.

ANGELA: (Lets peignoir slip off her shoulders, is in pretty silk pajamas.) In the morning, I must think how I can earn my own living. (She lies down as snores come from next room.) Miss Carey, are you asleep? (Snore.) Oh dear, she's asleep before I am—she might have waited. (A key is heard in the door—Angela sits up in alarm—as key turns, she screams.) Oh Miss Carey, wake up—someone's at the door—wake up. (Miss Carey jumps up and out of bed.)

MISS CAREY: Good Lord—what is it now? (Puts up light—the door opens, and immaculately dressed, handsome young man in evening clothes, white gloves, etc., enters—FRED SALTUS.)

ANGELA: Burglars! (She runs behind curtain of MISS CAREY'S room.)

MISS CAREY: You simpleton. I told you I had a male boarder. This is it, Mr. Saltus.

FRED: Oh, Miss Carey, pardon me—I'd have come in by the back door, but I didn't know you were entertaining company.

MISS CAREY: I'm not entertaining anyone—I'm trying to get a little rest before it's time for me to get up—and young lady, if you'll come out of my room and let me in, I'll beg of you not to disturb me again. (She shoves ANGELA out in her pajamas, unintentionally knocking her into MR. SALTUS, and goes back to bed.) (Ad. lib. talk.)

ANGELA: (Embarrassed and rushing behind the frock on the dressmaker's figure.) I've made her awfully cross—but I thought it must be a burglar—'cause, you see, I never knew boarders were allowed out so late at night.

FRED: (Recognizing her.) What are you doing here?

ANGELA: (Forced to confess.) I've left my husband. (He gives a whistle of surprise.) You know he's the man on the floor below—you may have seen me with him—once in a great while.

FRED: I've seen you often (Delighted.)—and so you've left him, eh?

ANGELA: Yes—and I'm really quite upset about it—naturally he's the first husband I've ever left—and you can imagine how a woman feels if *you've* left *your* husband—that is your wife. (All in one breath.) Are you married?

FRED: No indeed—not a chance.

ANGELA: (Quickly fishes her opera cloak off couch—slips it over her and goes to couch.) Then come here and sit down. (He does so.) I should think the girls would all be crazy about you.

FRED: Oh—they are—are you boarding here too now?

ANGELA: Yes, but Miss Carey doesn't know it yet.

FRED: Tell me, have you ever noticed me coming in or going out of the building?

ANGELA: Oh yes, indeed—I used to point you out to Harry and show him how you always looked so immaculate and dapper—just as he used to look before we were married. (Starting to weep.)

FRED: Oh, you'll go back to your home to-morrow.

ANGELA: No—I'll never enter it again—never again—except for lunch.

FRED: Then you're planning a divorce?

ANGELA: (As it dawns on her—with a smile.) I suppose it would be well to get something like that.

FRED: Is he in love with another woman?

ANGELA: (Indignantly.) My Harry—I guess not. (His hand is stretched toward her—in anger she slaps it.)

FRED: Then you'll never get it (Making love to her.) unless you fall in love with another man and let your husband get the divorce.

ANGELA: (Innocently.) I think I'd like that better—I'll tell Miss Carey (She approaches curtain—a snore makes her change her mind.)—I'll tell her later.

FRED: I'm awfully glad I'm a fellow boarder here. (He advances to her—as he is about to put his arm about her—suddenly a pounding on door and a gruff voice without:) Open—open!

ANGELA: (In terror.) Oh, it's my husband—it's Harry.

FRED: Don't talk, or he'll hear you.

ANGELA: I'll hide—and you open, or he'll break down the door.

FRED: I'll have nothing to do with this mixup.

HARRY: (Loudly, without.) Open, or I'll bang—down—the—door.

ANGELA: If you don't open, he'll do it—he's a regular "door-banger."

FRED: Well, I'll not.

ANGELA: Then I'll get Miss Carey. (Up to curtains again.) Miss Carey—Miss Carey—get up.

MISS CAREY: (Sticking her head out of curtains.) My Gawd, what is it now?

ANGELA: (After struggle as to how to explain.) My husband is here to see us.

MISS CAREY: Confound your husband.

HARRY: (Outside.) I want my wife.

ANGELA: (Pleading.) Oh, Miss Carey, the poor man wants his wife— tell him I'm not here.

MISS CAREY: (Jumping up—to FRED.) You go to your room, Mr. Saltus—I'll bet you were afraid to open the door. (FRED goes to his room.) And you go into my bed—if he sees you, I'll never get any sleep.

ANGELA: Don't hurt my Harry's feelings, Miss Carey—he's awfully sensitive. (She goes behind curtains.)

MISS CAREY: No, I won't hurt his feelings—(Opening door fiercely for HARRY.) What do you want?

HARRY: (Pushing her aside as he rushes in.) My wife—she's in here.

MISS CAREY: (Following him down.) She's not here—and you get out—what do you mean by waking me up at this hour?

HARRY: I've waked up everybody else in the building—why should *you* sleep?

MISS CAREY: I've never seen you before, but now that I have, I don't wonder your wife left you.

HARRY: Madam, you look like a woman who could sympathize with a man.

MISS CAREY: With a man? Never—now get out.

HARRY: (Making a tour of the room—she following.) Not till I've searched your place—my wife must be here.

MISS CAREY: I don't know your wife—and I don't want to.

HARRY: Why, madam—I'm crazy about her—suppose I'm the only man in the world who would be, but she's my doll.

MISS CAREY: Well, you've lost your doll—good night.

HARRY: Oh, I'll get her back again—but a change has seemed to come over her of late, and to-night she broke out in a fury and hit me violently over the head with a Wedgewood vase.

ANGELA: (Rushing out—ready to slap him again.) Oh Harry, I did not—it never touched you.

MISS CAREY: (Throwing up her hands.) Now I'll never get to sleep.

HARRY: (Turning on MISS CAREY.) Oh, I understand it all—it's you who've come between us—you designing, deceitful homebreaker.

MISS CAREY: You leave my apartment—you impertinent man.

HARRY: Not without my wife.

ANGELA: Then you'll stay forever—'cause I'm not going with you. (She sits right of little table.)

MISS CAREY: See here—you argue this out between you—but I'm going to bed—but don't you argue above a whisper or I'll ring for the police—the idea of you two galavanting about my apartments. (Going behind curtains.)

(A funny scene ensues between husband and wife—they start their argument in whispered pantomime—she shakes her finger at him—he shakes back at her—it finally grows slightly louder and louder until they are yelling at each other.)

ANGELA: (Screaming.) If you say the vase hit you—you're a wicked—

HARRY: I don't care anything about the vase—you're coming downstairs with me. (He pulls her off chair and swings her R.)

ANGELA: (Falling on couch.) I'm not.

HARRY: (Grabbing her again.) You are.

ANGELA: I'm not. (He tries to pull her to door—she bites his finger, and breaking away, runs up to curtains again.) Miss Carey, Miss Carey, wake up, he bit me. (MISS CAREY dashes out in fury, ANGELA hangs to her.) Oh, Miss Carey, you're the only one I have in all the world to keep me from this monster. Oh, Miss Carey, pity me, make believe you're my mother.

MISS CAREY: I told you I'm not married.

ANGELA: Well, think how you'd feel if you were and I were your own little girl and a wicked man was ill-treating me, etc. (She finally touches the mother vein in MISS CAREY.)

MISS CAREY: (Affected.) Go into my room, dear. (She leads her up to bed behind curtains. After Angela disappears behind curtains, MISS CAREY turns—facing HARRY.) I'll settle with this viper. (Coming down.) Aren't you ashamed of yourself?

HARRY: Why should I'be ashamed?

MISS CAREY: (Resolutely.) Because you're a lollard.

HARRY: I'm what?

MISS CAREY: You're one of those vile creatures whose hair grows from east to west. (Dramatically.) Where are your refined feet now?)

HARRY: (Thinking she's mad.) What on earth are you talking about?

MISS CAREY: The man she fell in love with and married was spick and span—his shoulders were big and broad—his teeth were white—and his skin—well, if he were standing before me now, I'd be just crazy to kiss him myself.

HARRY: I was all that you say when I married her—that's how I won her.

MISS CAREY: And now you're *not* all that I say—that's how you *lost* her. You can't blame a little woman if she thinks she's getting a man of gold and she finds she's got a gold brick.

HARRY: Why, I'm not different now than I was then—only before I was married I was like all men, I did everything to appear at my best— to fool her.

MISS CAREY: Fool her now—we women love to be fooled. We want to be proud of our husbands. Most of us get gold bricks, but we don't want anyone else to know it.

HARRY: By George, there may be something in all this. How did you come to know it?

MISS CAREY: I'm an old maid, and old maids know more about men than anyone—that's why they stay old maids. What were you wearing the first time you met?

HARRY: (Reminiscently.) A suit of regimentals.

MISS CAREY: (Hurrying up to door.) Quick, go downstairs and put 'em on and come up as quick as you can.

HARRY: (Looks at himself in glass near door.) By George—you're right. Oh, Miss Carey, I am a lollard. (He runs off.)

MISS CAREY: You're a lollard, all right. Now young woman—get your things together and get ready to go—young woman, do you hear me? (She goes up to curtains, and opens them—there lies ANGELA cozily huddled in a heap, fast asleep.) Well, if the little fluff hasn't fallen asleep. Here—wake up—the idea.

ANGELA: (In her sleep.) Harry, be gentle with Miss Carey—she can't help it. (MISS CAREY shakes her so she jumps up.) Oh Miss Carey— hello.

MISS CAREY: Now get your things together—your husband is coming for you in a minute.

ANGELA: (A la Ibsen.) I shall never return to Harry again— I've left him for life.

MISS CAREY: You'll not stay here all that time.

ANGELA: (As she comes down, dreamily.) No, I intend to marry another—and oh, Miss Carey, his hair is so spick—his shoulders so broad—his teeth are so white.

MISS CAREY: Good Lord, woman, now you're commencing with another. Who is it?

ANGELA: Surely you must have foreseen my danger—I'm in love with your boarder.

MISS CAREY: Why, you must be crazy—girl—I won't let you enter into such a madness.

ANGELA: (In horror.) Oh Miss Carey, don't tell me you're in love with him yourself. (MISS CAREY sinks in chair.) But you'll not get him.

MISS CAREY: Why, my dear, I wouldn't have him for a birth-day present and neither will you. (After an ad lib. argument.) We'll see. (She calls off in next room.) Fire! Fire!! Fire!!!

(ANGELA gets scared and starts to run one way as FRED runs in—in canton flannels without toupee, etc., etc. ANGELA flops. After audience has seen FRED'S condition, he realizes presence of ladies and rushes back to door—sticking his head out.)

FRED: Where? Where's the fire?

MISS CAREY: Go back to your bed, Mr. Saltus. (With a look at ANGELA.) There was a fire.

ANGELA: (Disgusted.) But Miss Carey—has—put—it—out.

(On word "out" she gestures him out of room and out of her life. FRED closes door as he withdraws head.)

ANGELA: Oh Miss Carey, what an awful lollard *that* is. (There is a ring at bell.) (Music commences sweet melody.)

MISS CAREY: (Knowing it is HARRY.) Open the door and see who it is.

(ANGELA opens the door—HARRY stands there in regimentals—handsome, young and dapper. ANGELA falls back in admiration.)

HARRY: Angela.

ANGELA: Oh, Harry darling!

MISS CAREY: He does look good!

ANGELA: (As she picks up her belongings.) I'm going home with you.

MISS CAREY: (As ANGELA goes up to HARRY.) Don't forget your tea dress. (Hands her the little bag.)

ANGELA: I'm so tired, Harry—take me home. (He lifts his tired little wife up in his arms and as he goes out, she mutters:) You're not such a bad lollard after all.

MISS CAREY: (Going to put out light.) Now, thank Gawd, I'll get a little sleep.

BLACKMAIL

CHARACTERS
RICHARD FALLON, a millionaire mine owner.
"LOU" MOHUN, a crook.
KELLY, a Pinkerton detective.
MRS. HOWARD:

SCENE
The scene shows the interior of the sitting room of a suite in a New York hotel of the class of the Hotel Astor or Claridge. In the back wall a door opens into what is the bedroom of the suite. The hinges of this door are on the right, the door knob on the left. On the wall on either side of the door is hung a framed copy of a picture by Gibson or Christy. In the left wall, half way down, is a door leading to the hall. Higher up against the wall is a writing desk on which are writing materials and a hand telephone. Above this pinned to the wall is a blueprint map. In front of the desk is a gilt chair without arms. Above and to the right of the gilt chair is a Morris chair facing the audience. In the seat of the chair is a valise; over the back hangs a man's coat.

In the right wall are two windows with practical blinds. Below them against the wall, stretches a leather sofa. On it is a suitcase, beside it on the floor a pair of men's boots. Below the sofa and slightly to the left stands a table, sufficiently heavy to bear the weight of a man leaning against it. On this table are magazines, a man's sombrero, a box of safety matches, a pitcher of ice water and a glass, and hanging over the edge of the table, in view of the audience, are two blue prints held down by pieces of ore. The light that comes through the two windows is of a sunny day in August.

WHEN THE CURTAIN RISES
RICHARD FALLON is discovered at table arranging the specimens of ore upon the blue prints. He is a young man of thirty-five, his face is deeply tanned, his manner is rough and breezy. He is without a coat, and his trousers are held up by a belt. He is smoking a cigar.

FALLON crosses to Morris chair, opens valise, turns over papers, clothing, fails to find that for which he is looking and closes the valise. He recrosses to suit case which is at lower end of the sofa. He breaks it open and searches through more papers, shirts, coats. Takes out another blue print, tightly rolled. Unrolls it, studies it, and apparently satisfied, with his left hand, places it on table.

In attempting to close the suit case the half nearer the audience slips over the foot of the sofa, and there falls from it to the floor, a heavy "bull dog" revolver. FALLON stares at it, puzzled, as though trying to recall when he placed it in his suit case. Picks it up. Looks at it. Throws it carelessly into suit case and shuts it. His manner shows he attaches no importance to the revolver. He now surveys the blue prints and the specimens of ore, as might a hostess, who is expecting guests, survey her dinner table. He crosses to hand telephone.

FALLON: (To 'phone.) Give me the room clerk, please. Hello? This is Mr. Fallon. I'm expecting two gentlemen at five o'clock. Send them right up. And, not now, but when they come, send me up a box of your best cigars and some rye and seltzer. Thank you. (Starts to leave telephone, but is recalled.) What? A lady? I don't know any. I don't know a soul in New York! What's her name? What—Mrs. Tom Howard? For heaven's sake! Tell her I'll be there in one second! What? Why certainly! Tell her to come right up. (He rises, muttering joyfully.) Well, well, well!

(Takes his coat from chair and puts it on. Lifts valise from chair and places it behind writing desk. Kicks boots under sofa. Places cigar on edge of table in view of audience. Looks about for mirror and finding none, brushes his hair with his hands, and arranges his tie. Goes to door L. and opens it, expectantly.)

MRS. HOWARD enters. She is a young woman of thirty. Her face is sweet, sad, innocent. She is dressed in white—well, but simply. Nothing about her suggests anything of the fast, or adventuress type.

Well, Helen! This is fine! God bless you, this is the best thing that's come my way since I left Alaska. And I never saw you looking better.

MRS. HOWARD: (Taking his hand.) And, it's good to see you, Dick. (She staggers and sways slightly as though about to faint.) Can I sit down? (She moves to Morris chair and sits back in it.)

FALLON: (In alarm.) What is it? Are you ill?

MRS. HOWARD: No, I'm—I'm so glad to find you—I was afraid! I was afraid I wouldn't find you, and I *had* to see you. (Leaning forward, in great distress.) I'm in trouble, Dick—terrible trouble.

FALLON: (Joyfully.) And you've come to me to help you?

MRS. HOWARD: Yes.

FALLON: That's fine! That's bully. I thought, maybe, you'd just come to talk over old times. (Eagerly.) And that would have been fine, too, understand—but if you've come to me because you're in trouble, then I know you're still my good friend, my dear old pal. (Briskly.) Now, listen, you say you're in trouble. Well, you knew me when I was down and out in San Francisco, living on free lunches and chop suey. Now, look at me, Helen, I'm a bloated capitalist. I'm a millionaire.

MRS. HOWARD: (Nervously.) I know, Dick, and I'm so glad! That's how I knew you were here, I read about you this morning in the papers.

FALLON: And half they said is true, too. See those blue prints? Each one of them means a gold mine, and at five, I'm to unload them on some of the biggest swells in Wall Street. (Gently.) Now, all that that means is this: I don't know what your trouble is, but, if money can cure it, you *haven't got any trouble*.

MRS. HOWARD: Dick, you're just as generous and kind. You haven't changed in any way.

FALLON: I haven't changed toward you. How's that husband of yours? (Jokingly.) I'd ought to shot that fellow.

MRS. HOWARD: (In distress.) That's why I came, Dick. Oh, Dick—

FALLON: (Anxiously, incredulously.) Don't tell me there's any trouble between you and Tom? Why, old Tom he just worships you. He loves you like—

MRS. HOWARD: That's it. And I want to *keep* his love.

FALLON: (Laughingly.) Keep his love? Is that all you've got to worry about? (Throughout the following scene, Mrs. Howard speaks in a fateful voice, like a woman beaten and hopeless.)

MRS. HOWARD: Dick, did you ever guess why I didn't marry you?

FALLON: No, I knew. You didn't marry me because you didn't love me, and you *did* love Tom.

MRS. HOWARD: No, I didn't know Tom then. And I thought I loved you, until I met Tom. But I didn't marry you, because it wouldn't have been honest—because, three years before I met you, I had lived with a man—as his wife.

FALLON: Helen! (His tone is one of amazement, but not of reproach. In his astonishment, he picks the cigar from the table, puffs at it standing and partly seated on the table.)

MRS. HOWARD: (In the same dead level, hopeless voice.) I was seventeen years old. I was a waiter girl at one of Fred Harvey's restaurants on the Santa Fe. I was married to this man before a magistrate. (Fallon lifts his head.) Three months later, when he'd grown tired of me, he told me the magistrate who had married us was not a magistrate but a friend of his, a man named Louis Mohun, and he brought this man to live with us. I should have left him then, that was where I did wrong. That was all I did that was wrong. But, I couldn't leave him, I couldn't, because I was going to be a mother—and in spite of what he had done—I begged him to marry me.

FALLON: And—he wouldn't?

MRS. HOWARD: Maybe he would—but—he was killed.

FALLON: (Eagerly.) You?

MRS. HOWARD. (In horror.) God, no!

FALLON: It's a pity. That's what you should have done.

MRS. HOWARD: He was a gambler, one night he cheated—the man he cheated, shot him. Then—my baby—died! After two years I came to San Francisco and met you and Tom. Then you went to Klondike and I married Tom.

FALLON: And, you told Tom?

MRS. HOWARD: (Lowering her face.)

FALLON: Helen!

MRS. HOWARP: I know, but I was afraid. I loved him so, and I was afraid.

FALLON: But Tom would have understood. Why, you thought you were married.

MRS. HOWARD: I was afraid. I loved him too much. I was too happy, and I was afraid I'd lose him. (FALLON shakes his head.) But, we were leaving San Francisco forever—to live in the East—where I thought no one knew me.

FALLON: Well?

MRS. HOWARD: Well, one man knew me. Mohun, the man who played the magistrate. He came East, too. Three years ago he saw me one night with Tom in a theatre. He followed us and found out where I lived. The next morning he came to see me, and threatened to tell! And, I was terrified, I lost my head and gave him money. (Slowly.) And I have been giving him money ever since.

FALLON: Helen! You! Fall for blackmail? Why, that isn't you. You're no coward! You should have told the swine to go to Hell, and as soon as Tom came home, you should have told him the whole story.

MRS. HOWARD: (Fiercely.) My story, yes! But not a story Mohun threatens to tell! In a week he had it all backed up with letters, telegrams, God knows what he didn't make me out to be—a vile, degraded creature.

FALLON: And who'd have believed it?

MRS. HOWARD: Everybody! He proved it! And my children. He threatened to stop my children on the way to school and explain to them what kind of a woman their mother was. So, I paid and paid and paid. I robbed Tom, I robbed the children. I cheated them of food, and clothes, I've seen Tom look almost ashamed of us. And when I'd taken all I'd dared from Tom, I pretended I wanted to be more independent, and I learned typewriting, and needlework and decorating, and I worked at night, and when Tom was at the office—to earn money—to give to Mohun. And each time he said it was the last, and each time he came back demanding more. God knows what he does with it, he throws it away—on drink, on women, opium.

FALLON: Dope fiend, too, hey?

MRS. HOWARD: He's that, too; he's everything that's vile; inhuman, pitiless, degenerate. Sometimes, I wonder why God lets him live. (Her voice drops to a whisper.) Sometimes, I almost pray to God to let him die. (FALLON who already has determined to kill MOHUN, receives this speech with indifference, and continues grimly to puff on his cigar.) He's killed my happiness, he's killing me. In keeping him alive, I've grown ill and old. I see the children growing away from me, I see Tom drawing away from me. And now, after all my struggles, after all my torture, Tom must be told. Mohun is in some *new* trouble. He must have a thousand dollars! I can no more give him a thousand dollars than I can give him New York City. But, if I don't, he'll *tell! What* am I to do?

FALLON: (Unmoved.) When did you see this—this *thing* last?

MRS. HOWARD: This morning. He'd read about you in the papers. He knows I knew you in San Francisco. He said you'd "struck it rich," and that you'd give me the money. (Rises, and comes to him.) But, get this straight, Dick. I didn't come here for money. I don't want money. I won't take money. I came to you because you are my best friend, and Tom's best friend, and because I need a *man's brain*, a man's advice.

FALLON: (Contemptuously.) Advice! Hell! Am I the sort of man that gives girls—*advice?* (With rough tenderness.) Now, you go home to Tom, and tell him I'm coming to dinner. (Impressively.) And leave this *leech* to me. And, *don't* worry. This thing never happened, it's just a bad dream, a nightmare. Just throw it from your shoulders like a miner drops his pack. It's never coming back into your life again.

MRS. HOWARD: (Earnestly.) No! I won't *let* you pay that man! He'd hound you, as he's hounded me!

FALLON: (Indignantly.) Pay him? Me? I haven't got enough *money* to pay him!

MRS. HOWARD: What!

FALLON: *No man* on earth has money enough to pay blackmail. Helen, this is what I think of a blackmailer: The *lowest* thing that crawls, is a man that sends a woman into the streets to earn money for him. Here, in New York, you call them "cadets." Now, there's only one thing on earth lower than a cadet, and that's the blackmailer, the man who gets money from a woman—by threatening her good name—who uses her past as a *club*—who drags out some unhappy act of hers for which she's repented, in tears, on her knees, which the world has forgotten, which God has forgiven. And, for that *past* sin, that's forgotten and forgiven, this blackguard crucifies her. And the woman—to protect her husband and her children, as you have done—to protect her own good name, that she's worked for and won, starves herself to feed that *leech*. And, you ask me, if *I'm* going to feed him, too! Not me! Helen, down in lower California, there are black bats, the Mexican calls "Vampire" bats. They come at night and fasten on the sides of the horses and drink their blood. And, in the morning when you come to saddle up, you'll find the horses too weak to walk, and hanging to their flanks these vampires, swollen and bloated and drunk with blood. Now, I've just as much sympathy for Mr. Mohun, as I have for those vampires, and, I'm going to treat him just as I treat them! Where is he?

MRS. HOWARD: Downstairs. In the cafe.

FALLON: Here, in this hotel?

MRS. HOWARD: Yes.

FALLON: (Half to himself.) Good!

MRS. HOWARD: He said he'd wait until I telephoned him that you would pay. If you won't, he's going straight to Tom.

FALLON: He is, is he? Helen, I hate to have you speak to him again, but, unless he hears your voice, he won't come upstairs. (Motions towards telephone.) Tell him I'll see him in ten minutes. Tell him I've agreed to make it all right.

MRS. HOWARD: But, *how*, Dick, *how?*

FALLON: Don't you worry about that. I'm going to send him away. Out of the country. He won't trouble you any more.

MRS. HOWARD: But he won't go. He's promised *me* to go many times—

FALLON: Yes, but he's not dealing with a woman, now, he's dealing with a man, with boots on. Do as I tell you.

(MRS. HOWARD sits at writing desk and takes receiver off telephone. FALLON leans against table right, puffing quickly on his cigar, and glancing impatiently at the valise that holds his revolver.)

MRS. HOWARD: Give me the cafe, please. Is this the cafe? I want to speak to a Mr. Mohun, he is waiting to be called up—oh, thank you. (To FALLON.) He's coming. (To 'phone.) I have seen that man and he says he'll take up that debt, and pay it. Yes, now, at *once*. You're to wait for ten minutes, until he can get the money, and then, he'll telephone you to come up. I don't know, I'll ask. (To Fallon.) He says it must be in *cash*.

FALLON: (Sarcastically.) Why, certainly! That'll be all right. (MRS. HOWARD Places her hand over the mouth piece.)

MRS. HOWARD: I'll not *let* you pay him!

FALLON: I'm not going to! I'm going to *give* him just what's coming to him. Tell him, it'll be all right.

MRS. HOWARD: (To 'phone.) He says to tell you, it'll be all right. The room is 210 on the third floor. In ten minutes, yes. (She rises.)

FALLON: Now, then, you go back to Tom and get dinner ready. Don't forget I'm coming to *dinner*. And the children must come to dinner, *too*. We'll have a happy, good old-time reunion.

MRS. HOWARD: (With hand on door knob of door left.) Dick, how can I thank you?

FALLON: Don't let me catch you trying.

MRS. HOWARD: God bless you, Dick. (With a sudden hope.) And you really believe you can make him *go*?

FALLON: Don't worry! I'm sure of it.

MRS. HOWARD: And, you think he won't come back?

FALLON: (After a pause, gravely.) I *know* he won't come back.

MRS. HOWARD: God bless you, Dick!

FALLON: See you at dinner.

(MRS. HOWARD exits. FALLON stands considering, and chewing on his cigar. Then, he crosses room briskly and lowers the blind at each window. Opens valise and examines revolver. Places the revolver in his left hip pocket. Then, in a matter-of-course manner from his right hand pocket, he draws his automatic pistol. This, as though assured he would find loaded, he examines in a quick, perfunctory way, and replaces. He crosses left to desk, and taking from it a cheque book, writes out a cheque, which he tears from the book, and holds in his right hand. With left hand he removes the receiver from the telephone.)

Give me Murray Hill 2828. Hello, is this the Corn and Grain Bank? I want to speak to the cashier. Hello, is that the cashier? This is Richard Fallon, of San Francisco, speaking from the Hotel Wisteria. I opened an account with you day before yesterday, for two hundred thousand dollars. Yes, this is Mr. Fallon speaking. I made out a cheque yesterday payable to Louis Mohun (Glances at cheque.), dated August 4th, for two thousand dollars. I want to know if he's cashed it in yet? He hasn't, hey? Good! (He continues to look at cheque, to impress upon audience, that the cheque they have just seen him write, is the one which he is speaking about.) Well, I want to stop payment on that cheque. Yes, yes. I made it out under *pressure*, and I've decided not to stand for it. Yes, *sort* of a hold up! I guess that's why he was afraid to cash it. You'll attend to that, will you? Thank you. Good-bye. (He takes an envelope from desk, places cheque in it and puts envelope in his breast pocket. Again takes off receiver.) Hello, give me the cashier, please. Am I speaking to the cashier of the hotel? This is Mr. Fallon in room 210. Is your hotel detective in the lobby? He is? Good! What—what sort of a man is he, is he a man I can rely on? A Pinkerton, hey? That's good enough! Well, I wish you'd give him a thousand dollars for me in hundreds. Ten hundred-dollar bills, and before you send them up, I wish you'd mark them and take their numbers. What? No, there's no trouble. I just want to see that the right bills go to the right people, that's all. Thank you.

(He crosses to door centre, and taking key from the bedroom side, places it in keyhole on side of door in view of the audience. He turns the key several times. He takes the revolver from his left hip pocket and holding it in his right hand, rehearses shooting under his left arm through his coat which he holds from him by the fingers of his left hand. Shifting revolver to his left hand, he takes the automatic from his right hip pocket, and goes through the motions of firing with both guns in opposite directions. His pantomine must show he intends making use of both guns at the same time, using one apparently upon himself, and the other, in earnest, upon another person. He replaces the revolvers in his pockets. There is a knock at the door.)

Come in.

(KELLY enters. In his hand he carries an envelope. He is an elderly man with grey hair, neatly dressed and carrying a straw hat. He has an air of authority. His manner to FALLON is respectful.)

KELLY: Afternoon, Mr. Fallon. I am Kelly, the house detective.

FALLON: Yes, I know. I've seen you in the lobby.

KELLY: Mr. Parmelee said I was to give you this. (Gives envelope to FALLON. FALLON takes out ten yellow-back bills.) There ought to be a thousand dollars there in hundreds.

FALLON: That's right. Now, will you just sit over there, and as I read the numbers, you write them down.

KELLY: Mr. Parmelee made a note of the numbers, Mr. Fallon.

FALLON: I know. I want you to identify them too.

KELLY: I can do that. I saw him mark them.

FALLON: Good. And if you saw these bills in the next five minutes you'd be able to swear they're the same bills you gave me?

KELLY: Sure. (Starts towards door.)

FALLON: Wait a minute. Sit down, Kelly. (KELLY seats himself in Morris chair, holding his hat between his knees.) Kelly, this hotel engages you from the Pinkertons to stay around the place, and—protect the guests?

KELLY: Yes, sir.

FALLON: Well, there's a man downstairs thinks he has a claim on this money. Now, I'd like you to wait in that bedroom and listen to what he says with a view to putting him in jail.

KELLY: Blackmail, Mr. Fallon?

FALLON: Yes, blackmail.

KELLY: (Eagerly.) And you're not going to stand for it?

FALLON: I am not!

KELLY: (Earnestly.) Good! That's the only way to treat those dogs. Never *give up*, never *give up*!

FALLON: No, but yesterday, I *had* to give up. He put a gun at my head.

KELLY: (Excitedly.) Where? Not in this hotel?

FALLON: Yes, in this room. I gave him a cheque for two thousand dollars. That made him think I was *easy*, and he telephoned this morning that he's coming back for another thousand, and he wants it in *cash*. That's why I marked those bills.

KELLY: Why, we got him *now*! He's as good as *dead*.

FALLON: (Startled.) What?

KELLY: I say, we've got him nailed now.

FALLON: Oh, yes. (Pause.) He hasn't turned in the cheque yet—I've just called up the bank to find out. I guess he means to hold *that* over my head, hey?

KELLY: More likely he's *afraid* of it. (Eagerly.) We may *get* that back, too. We may find it *on him*.

FALLON: What? Yes, as *you* say, we may find it on him.

KELLY: (Eagerly.) And as soon as he gets those bills in his clothes, you give me the high sign (Fiercely.)—and we'll *nail* him!

FALLON: Yes, we'll nail him. And, if he puts his gun in my face *today*, he won't catch me empty-handed the second time. (Draws automatic from his pocket.) I'm *ready* for him, today!

KELLY: (Greatly concerned.) Here, none of *that* stuff, Mr. Fallon. A gentleman like you can't take *that* chance.

FALLON: Chance? Kelly, I haven't *always* lived in a swell hotel. The man that gets the drop on *me—when* I've got a gun—has got to be damned quick.

KELLY: That's just what I mean! I'm not thinking of him, I'm thinking of *you*. Give me that gun.

FALLON: Certainly not.

KELLY: You don't want to go to jail for a rat like that.

FALLON: I don't mean to go to jail, and, I don't mean to die, either. For the last six years I've been living on melted ice and bacon. Now, I'm worth seven million dollars. I'm thirty-five years old and my life is in front of me. And, I don't mean to waste one hour of it in a jail, and I don't mean to let any blackmailer take it away from me.

KELLY: You don't want no judge to take it away from you, either! You're not in the Klondike.

FALLON: I guess, I've got a right to *defend* myself, *anywhere*.

KELLY: Yes, but you'll get excited and—

FALLON: (Quietly.) I? Excited? I never get excited. The last time I was excited was when I was seven years old, and the circus came to town.

KELLY: Don't mix up in this. What am *I* here for?

FALLON: You won't be here. How can you help me in that room, when a fellow's pumping lead into my stomach in this one?

KELLY: He won't pump no lead.

FALLON: (Carelessly.) I hope not. But, if he does, he's got to do it awful quick. (Motions towards centre door.) Now, you go in there and shut the door, and I'll talk out here. And you tell me if you can hear what I say? (KELLY goes into bedroom and closes door. FALLON walks to door R. with his back turned towards KELLY.) Have you got the door shut tight?

KELLY: (From bedroom.) Yes.

FALLON: (Speaks in a loud tone, to an imaginary person.) No, not another penny. If I pay you, will you promise not to take the story to the newspapers? I give you this thousand dollars—(Turns towards centre door. KELLY opens door.) Could you hear me?

KELLY: Yes, I could hear *you*, but *he* won't talk that loud. You put him in that chair (Points to Morris chair.)—so that he'll sit facing me, and you stand over there (Points at safe.)—so then he'll have to speak up.

FALLON: I see. Are you all ready?

KELLY: Yes. (KELLY closes door. FALLON goes to desk. Lifts both guns from his pocket an inch or two, and then takes receiver from telephone. To 'phone.) Give me the cafe, please. Is this the cafe? There's a Mr. Mohun down there waiting to hear from Mr. Fallon—yes. All right. Tell him to come up. (KELLY opens door.)

KELLY: Hist. Listen, this guy knows what he's up against; he knows it might land him in Sing Sing and he'll be leery of this door being shut. So, if he insists on looking in here, you speak up loud, and say, "That's my bedroom. It's empty." Say it quick enough to give me time to get out into the hall.

FALLON: I see.

KELLY: Then, when he's had his look around, you slam the door shut again, and I'll come back into the bedroom. Have you got it?

FALLON: I understand. (In loud voice.) That's my bedroom. It's empty.

KELLY: That's the office for me to sneak into the hall. (In bedroom, he disappears right.)

FALLON: (At open door, rehearsing.) You see, the room is empty. (Closes the door with a bang. Pause, then he calls.) Are you there now, Kelly?

KELLY: Yes, I'm here.

(FALLON stands looking at the key in the door. For an instant his hand falters over it as though he would risk turning it. Then, he shakes his head, and walks to table right. There is a low knock at door left.)

FALLON: Come in.

(MOHUN enters door left. He is lean, keen faced, watchful. He is a head taller than FALLON. His manner always has an undercurrent of insolence.)

MOHUN: Afternoon. Am I speaking to Mr. Fallon?

FALLON: Yes. Lou Mohun?

MOHUN: Yes. (MOHUN stands warily at the door. Glances cautiously around the room. Bends over quite openly to look under the sofa. For some seconds his eyes rest with a smile on bedroom door. He speaks slowly, unemotionally.) A mutual friend of ours said you wanted to see me.

FALLON: (Sharply.) We've no mutual friend. No one's in this but you and me. You want to get that straight!

MOHUN: (Easily.) All right. That's all right. Well, what do you want to see me about?

(FALLON speaks in a loud voice. In the speeches that follow, it must be apparent that his loud tone and excited manner is assumed, and is intended only to convince KELLY.)

FALLON: I understand, you think you have a claim on me for a thousand dollars. And, I'm going to give it to you. But, first, I want a plain talk with you. (Sharply.) Are you listening to me?

MOHUN: No, not yet. Before there's any plain talking, I want to know where that door leads to.

FALLON: What door? That? (In a louder voice.) That's my bedroom. It's empty. Is that what you want? Think I got someone in there? Do you want to look for yourself? (Opens door.) Go on in, and look. (MOHUN takes a step forward, and peers past FALLON into bedroom.) Go on, search it. Look under the bed.

MOHUN: I guess that's all right.

FALLON: Don't you *want* to look?

MOHUN: (Falling back to door left.) Not now. No need to, if you're willing to let me. (Impatiently.) Go on. What is it you want with me? (FALLON closes door with a slam. Comes down to table.)

FALLON: What do I want? I want you to understand that this is the last time you come to me for money.

MOHUN: (Indifferently.) That's all right.

FALLON: No, its not all right. (Takes out bills.) Before I give you this, you've got to promise me to keep silent. I'll stand for no more blackmail.

MOHUN: Don't talk so loud. I'm not deaf. Look here, Mr. Fallon, I didn't come here to be shouted at, I came here to get the money you promised me.

FALLON: Well, here it is. (Gives him bills. MOHUN sticks them in his right-hand vest pocket.) No, you listen to me. (As soon as he obtains the money, MOHUN'S manner changes. He is amused, and insolent.)

MOHUN: No, not a bit like it. Now that I've got *this*, you'll have to listen to me. (Moves deliberately to Morris chair and seats himself) Mr. Fallon, I don't like your tone.

FALLON: (Slowly.) You—don't—like my tone? I don't think I understand you.

MOHUN: You talk like you had a whip over me. You don't seem to see that I got you dead to rights.

FALLON: (In pretended alarm.) Have you?

MOHUN: Have I? I got a mortgage on you for life. You got in wrong when you gave me that money. Don't you see that? Mr. Fallon, I've been taking out information about you. Some 'Frisco lads tell me you used to be pretty sweet on a certain party, but she chucked you and married the other fellow. But the first day you come back a millionaire she visits your rooms—and you give her a thousand dollars! Why? She can't tell. You can't tell. But *I* can tell. I can tell her *husband*. He's only got to ask the hotel clerk and the cashier and the bell hops, and when I've told my story *as I'll tell it*—he's liable to shoot you. (There is a pause during which FALLON stares at MOHUN incredulously.) Let it sink in, Mr. Fallon.

FALLON: (Quietly.) I am—letting it sink in.

MOHUN: Now, a thousand dollars is all well enough from a lady that has to scrape to find it, but a thousand dollars from a millionaire like you is a joke. And unless you want me to go to the husband, you'll come across with fifty thousand dollars, and until I get it, I'm not going to leave this room.

FALLON: (Solemnly.) Then, I don't believe you are going to leave this room.

MOHUN: (Impudently.) Oh, I'll go when I'm ready.

FALLON: (Going up close to centre door.) Let me understand you. You are going to this husband with a lie that will wreck his faith in his wife, that will wreck his faith in his best friend, unless I give you a thousand dollars?

MOHUN: No! Fifty thousand dollars!

FALLON: Fifty thousand. It's the same thing. But, you'd keep quiet for ten dollars, wouldn't you, if that was all I had?

MOHUN: (Grinning at him.) If that was all you had.

FALLON: (In a whisper, slowly, impressively.) Then, Mr. Mohun (He raises his right arm.), may—God—have mercy—on your soul. (In loud, excited tones and purposely, so that MOHUN can see him, he turns his face towards the centre door.) I won't pay that fifty thousand. I won't stand for blackmail, you're robbing—(MOHUN leaps to his feet, and points at centre door.)

MOHUN: (Fiercely.) Here. What are you doing? You're trying to trap me? There *is* someone in that room. (FALLON laughs mockingly at MOHUN, but speaks for KELLY to hear.)

FALLON: Don't go near that room. (With his left hand he quickly turns the key in the door.) Don't lock that door! Don't lock that door! Kelly, he's locked the door. (He draws the revolver from his left pocket. KELLY is heard shaking the handle of the door, and beating upon the panel. FALLON speaks in a whisper.) I told you, you'd never leave this room, Mr. Mohun. (In a loud, excited tone.) Drop that gun. Drop that gun. Don't point that gun at me! (Still smiling mockingly at MOHUN, FALLON shoots twice through his own coat on the left side, throws the gun at MOHUN'S feet, and drawing his automatic pistol, shoves it against MOHUN'S stomach and fires. MOHUN falls back into the Morris chair dead.) (Shouts loudly.) Break in the door. Break in the door. (From his pocket he takes the envelope containing the cheque, and sticks it into the inside pocket of MOHUN'S coat. Then turns to table, right, as KELLY bursts open the door and sees MOHUN.)

KELLY: My God, Mr. Fallon. I *told* you to give me that gun!

FALLON: Have I hurt him?

KELLY: (Bending over body.) Hurt him? You've killed him! (FALLON with his face turned from KELLY, smiles. He speaks with pretended emotion.) Killed him? Here, you're an officer. (Throws gun on table.) I give myself up. (KELLY runs to hand telephone. FALLON picks up his cigar from the table and a box of matches. Starts to light cigar, but seeing KELLY at 'phone hesitates and listens eagerly.)

KELLY: (To 'phone.) Send the hotel doctor here. Quick! Mr. Fallon's wounded. (To FALLON.) Are you badly hurt? (FALLON places his left hand on his left hip under the coat and removes it showing the fingers covered with blood.)

FALLON: Only scratched.

KELLY: (To 'phone.) Some crank tried to shoot him up. Mr. Fallon fired back and killed him. (Pause.) *No!* Mr. Fallon killed *him*! (Pause.) Of course, in self-defense, you fool, *of course*, in self-defense! (KELLY slams back the receiver, and rising quickly, turns to the right and stands with hands on his hips, and back to audience, gazing down at MOHUN. He does not once look at FALLON.)

FALLON: (On hearing the words "in self-defense" sighs, smiles and striking the match, lights the cigar as

THE CURTAIN FALLS.

THE SYSTEM

CHARACTERS
    BILLY BRADLEY . . . . . . Alias "The Eel."
    DAN MCCARTHY . . . . . . Inspector of Police.
    TIM DUGAN . . . . Lieutenant of Police.
    JAMES O'MARA. . . . . . . Desk Lieutenant.
    OFFICER FLYNN . . . . . . Patrolman.
    BOBBY PERKINS . . . . . . A Police Reporter.
    HAROLD BROOKTHORNE . . . A Cub Reporter.
    MR. INBAD . . . . A Souse.
    JIM, TOM . . . . Central Office Men.
    MRS. DEMMING WORTHINGTON. A Noted Horsewoman.
    JANITRESS . . . . At 327 East Broadway.
    GOLDIE MARSHALL . . . . . The Eel's "Gal."
    Policemen, Citizens, Morbid Crowds, Etc.

SCENE I
    POLICE STATION, NEW YORK CITY. EVENING
    Door C. Door L. 2nd E. leading below to cells. Windows in flat R. and L. showing two green lights in front of Station. Street backing, showing the other side of Street. Bench at L. window, chair at R. window. Small platform R. 2, with desk, railing, etc. Chairs on Platform.
    AT RISE: (O'Mara at desk speaking through telephone. PERKINS in chair R., writing. FLYNN searching INBAD, who is intoxicated.)
    O'MARA: (Speaking through 'phone.) All right! Good-bye! (Puts 'phone down.) Take him down, that fellow is a champion souse.
    INBAD: (As FLYNN is jerking him off L.) Thatsh what I am, and I'll defend my title against all comers. (Exit INBAD followed by FLYNN.)
    PERKINS: (Coming R. to O'MARA.) That Worthington robbery will make a corking story, if it's true. (Starts for door C.)
    O'MARA: Well, why don't you wait till the pinch comes off and then get the story for sure?
    PERKINS: Your word's good enough.
    O'MARA: But I haven't given you me word. I don't know whether they've nailed him yet or not.
    PERKINS: (Coming back to desk railing R.) (Disappointed.) Oh, I thought you said they'd got him.
    O'MARA: That's the way you reporters twist everything. I said "Dugan was after him," that's all.
    PERKINS: Well, that's as good as got him; anything Dugan sets out to get, comes pretty near materializing. (Starts C., stops on meeting BROOKY, who enters door C.) Hello! Brooky! Just in time. Here's a chance for you to distinguish yourself in your new capacity.
    BROOKY: (Coming C.) Got a story?

PERKINS: A pippin! Listen to this. (Reads from notes.) "Police fishing. Make a big haul! Throw out the dragnet and once more capture the Eel." A very slippery article.

BROOKY: I don't understand.

PERKINS: Oh, can't you understand, the Eel is the nickname, the alias of one of the slickest crooks in the country, Billy Bradley.

BROOKY: Billy Bradley? Oh yes, I've heard of him.

PERKINS: Well, that's the Eel.

BROOKY: Oh I see; well, what about him?

PERKINS: He's been taken, or at least is going to be.

BROOKY: What's he done?

PERKINS: (Looking at BROOKY surprised.) You're up on that Worthington robbery, aren't you?

BROOKY: What robbery is that?

PERKINS: (Disgusted.) Don't tell me you don't know that burglars entered Mrs. Demming Worthington's house last night, and made off with a five thousand dollar necklace?

BROOKY: I hadn't heard of it.

PERKINS: Good heavens, man! hasn't your paper got it?

BROOKY: (Going L.) I don't know. I never read our paper. (Perkins follows BROOKY in disgust.)

O'MARA: (Smiling.) Well, I don't know but what you're just as well off. (Enter INSPECTOR door C., O'MARA comes from behind desk and stands above it for INSPECTOR to cross him.)

PERKINS: Good evenin', Inspector.

INSPECTOR: (Glancing about room, without stopping, goes straight to stool behind desk.) How are you, boys! (INSPECTOR salutes O'MARA as he passes him, O'MARA returns the salute, then goes to upper end of desk, where he stands.)

BROOKY: How do you do, sir.

INSPECTOR: (Back of desk.) Well, O'Mara. They've got the Eel.

O'MARA: They have?

INSPECTOR: Dugan is on his way up with him now.

PERKINS: I guess it will go pretty hard with him, won't it Inspector?

INSPECTOR: If he is guilty.

PERKINS: Well, he is, isn't he?

INSPECTOR: I believe every man innocent until proven guilty.

BROOKY: Bravo, Inspector! Those are my sentiments.

INSPECTOR: I've sent for Mrs. Worthington. When we get her, Goldie, the Eel and Dugan together, we shall be able to get a clearer view on the matter. Bring up Goldie. (O'MARA exits door L.)

PERKINS: (Coming R. C.) Inspector, has this girl Goldie Marshall ever been up before?

INSPECTOR: Well, she's been arrested a number of times, on shop-lifting charges, but we've never been able to prove anything on her.

PERKINS: Perhaps she's square after all.

INSPECTOR: Not at all unlikely; as I said before, I believe a person innocent until proven guilty.

BROOKY: (Crossing R. to railing of desk.) And as I said before—Bravo, old chap. (The INSPECTOR looks at BROOKY sternly and he retires up stage R. confusedly, bumping into chair, sits in it.)

PERKINS: (Crossing R. to railing.) Inspector?

INSPECTOR: Well?

PERKINS: I suppose many a person has been railroaded through the System?

INSPECTOR: (Rising angrily.) System! How dare you! What do you mean?

PERKINS: I—I—beg your pardon, Inspector, I—

BROOKY: (Rising from chair and coming down L. of PERKINS.) I say, don't make a bally ass of yourself.

INSPECTOR: Don't ever let me hear you say that again. (Voices of O'MARA and GOLDIE are heard off L.) (Enter GOLDIE, followed by O'MARA. Door L.)

GOLDIE: (Jerking away from O'MARA.) Well, don't yank my arm off. (Looking around room.) I know the way. (Starts R.)

O'MARA: (Following GOLDIE, catches her by the back of neck as she reaches C.) Don't give me any back talk or I'll yank your neck off.

INSPECTOR: O'Mara! let go your hold. Don't forget you're dealing with a woman. (O'MARA releases hold.)

GOLDIE: (Mockingly courteous.) Thanks, Inspector! What'll I send you for Christmas, a bunch of sweet forget-me-nots or a barrel of pickles?

INSPECTOR: Goldie, don't be so incorrigible.

GOLDIE: Gee! but you're an educated guy.

INSPECTOR: Have a seat. (O'MARA jumps for chair with mock politeness.)

GOLDIE: (To reporters.) He's polite, too. (Crosses to chair.)

INSPECTOR: Well, Goldie!

GOLDIE: (Sitting.) Well, Inspector!

INSPECTOR: Do you intend to stay here to-night or are you going to get bail?

GOLDIE: Where would I get bail?

INSPECTOR: I thought perhaps some gentleman friend of yours—

GOLDIE: (Rising angrily.) I ain't got no gentlemen friends. What do you think I am, a Moll? (Sits.)

INSPECTOR: Don't make any grand stand play now, Goldie!

GOLDIE: Well, if you mean that I'm a bad girl, you'd better not say it (Rising, crosses to desk and pounds angrily on railing.), 'cause I ain't, see?

INSPECTOR: Well, you don't deny that you and the Eel are sweethearts?

GOLDIE: Was, yes. Gee, we was goin' to get married, until in a jealous huff he tried to kill me and was shipped for two years for assault and battery, but it wasn't none of my doin's.

INSPECTOR: Didn't you prefer charges against him?

GOLDIE: I did not. Do you think I'd squeal on a pal? If it wasn't for Dugan, they'd turn the Eel loose. (Sits.)

INSPECTOR: Why Dugan?

GOLDIE: Didn't he shove him in?

INSPECTOR: He was simply acting in his official duty.

GOLDIE: Official duty, my eye.

INSPECTOR: What other motive could Mr. Dugan possibly have had?

GOLDIE: (With a sneer.) Maybe you don't know. Well, I'll tell you. He thought by shovin' the Eel out of the way, he could get me.

INSPECTOR: And did he?

GOLDIE: Not so as you could notice it. I ain't no fall guy for nobody.

INSPECTOR: Now that the Eel's been sprung, are you going back to him?

GOLDIE: (Almost in tears.) Oh gee! I wish I could, but there's nothing doin', he's sore on me.

INSPECTOR: When did you last see him?

GOLDIE: Just before he went up, two years ago.

INSPECTOR: How about this Worthington robbery, wasn't he in on it?

GOLDIE: (Hastily.) No, he wasn't.

INSPECTOR: (Quickly.) Who was?

GOLDIE: (After a slight pause as though to confess.) Well, I'll tell you. There was three of us, me, Jesse James, and Christopher Columbus. (Looks first at INSPECTOR then to PERKINS.) Ah, put it down on your little yellow paper.

INSPECTOR: (Angrily.) Answers like that'll get you nothing here.

GOLDIE: See, you won't believe me when I tell you.

INSPECTOR: Silence, I say! (To O'MARA.) Take her down. (GOLDIE rises from chair leisurely and strolls impudently L. as she comes to BROOKY.) Oh, poo! poo!

INSPECTOR: (Stopping GOLDIE at door L.) And you'll stay down unless you have a confession to make.

GOLDIE: (At door L.) Say, Inspector, if you're waitin' for a confession from me, you'll wait until pigs fly kites. (Exit door L. GOLDIE followed by O'MARA.) (PERKINS and BROOKY look off after them.)

BROOKY: What a little terror!

PERKINS: Looks mighty like her work, doesn't it, Inspector?

INSPECTOR: No! The job has all the ear marks of the Eel, but she undoubtedly is his accomplice. (Enter MRS. WORTHINGTON door C., she looks around uncomfortably and as she comes down C., BROOKY and PERKINS on seeing her, remove their hats. INSPECTOR rises and indicates chair R. C.) Ah! Mrs. Worthington! (Indicating Reporters.) Have you any objection to talking for publication?

MRS. WORTHINGTON: (Looking toward Reports.) No, not at all. (PERKINS has note paper and takes down as she talks.)

INSPECTOR: Will you kindly be seated? And we shall proceed? (MRS. W. sits.) Now in the first place, how long had this girl, Goldie Marshall, been in your employ?

MRS. WORTHINGTON: Just one week.

INSPECTOR: (Half aside.) That's about the time the Eel was sprung. (To Mrs. W.) Had you missed anything else up to the time of this robbery?

MRS. WORTHINGTON: No, nothing.

INSPECTOR: Who else was in the house at the time, besides yourself and the maid?

MRS. WORTHINGTON: Only my guests who were at dinner with me. Mr. Appleby and his wife.

INSPECTOR: The horseowner?

MRS. WORTHINGTON: Yes, and a Miss Hazelton from Pittsburgh.

INSPECTOR: Would you suspect them?

MRS. WORTHINGTON: Well, hardly.

INSPECTOR: Anyone else?

MRS. WORTHINGTON: Yes, Mr. Dugan.

INSPECTOR: What Dugan?

MRS. WORTHINGTON: Why, your Mr. Dugan here.

INSPECTOR: Oh, Tim Dugan.

MRS. WORTHINGTON: Yes, we're great friends, and he frequently dines at my house. (Low murmur begins in the distance and grows louder. MRS. W. rises in fear and appeals to the INSPECTOR, who comes from behind the desk and—)

INSPECTOR: Don't be alarmed, Mrs. Worthington, just step behind the desk. (MRS. WORTHINGTON steps back of desk and sits in chair below stool. INSPECTOR replaces the chair in which MRS. W. has been sitting in front of the window R. C. then returns to back of desk where he stands. The REPORTERS at first sound show excitement, PERKINS goes to door C. and looks off R. B.)

PERKINS: (At door C.) It's Dugan and he's got the Eel. (Goes down L. C.) (DUGAN is seen out of window R. bringing the EEL along, who is hand-cuffed. They are followed by a noisy crowd. DUGAN throws the EEL down, C., then chases the crowd away from door C.)

EEL: (Looks around smiling until he sees INSPECTOR.) Hello, Inspector! Gee! it's real oil for the wicks of my lamps to see you again.

DUGAN: (Coming down C.) Yes, he's tickled to death to see you, ain't you, Billy?

EEL: (Angrily.) The Eel to you, Copper; Billy to my pals.

INSPECTOR: Well, Billy!

EEL: That's right, Inspector, you're my pal. (Movement from INSPECTOR.) Oh, I ain't forgot when you was just a plain Bull and saved me from doin' my first bit on a phoney charge. They tried to railroad me, you remember, and Dugan here was runnin' the engine.

INSPECTOR: Oh, you've got Dugan wrong, Billy, he bears you no malice.

EEL: No, it's a mistake, he just loves me. Say, he thinks so much of me, that if he saw me drowning, he'd bring me a glass of water.

DUGAN: You know why you were brought here?

EEL: Sure, so's you could railroad me again.

INSPECTOR: Nonsense, Dugan has nothing against you personally.

EEL: Oh yes he has; when he was new on the force, I beat him up good. He was only a harness cop then, and one night he thought he made me coppin' a super from a lush, which you know ain't my graft. He started to fan me with a sap, so I just clubbed my smoke wagon, and before I got through with him, I made him a pick-up for the ambulance, and he ain't never forgot it.

INSPECTOR: What do you know about this Worthington robbery? (EEL looks around suspiciously.) Before you answer, Billy, I warn you to be careful, everything you say will be used against you.

EEL: Yes, and everything I don't say will be used, too. I know the system.

DUGAN: (Crossing R. to EEL. REPORTERS follow.) Well, what have you got to say?

EEL: (Taking time, looks around.) You don't think I'm goin' to address this Mass Meeting here. (BROOKY looks L. to see if there is anyone else there.)

INSPECTOR: You're not afraid to talk in front of a couple of newspaper reporters, are you?

EEL: (Grinning at INSPECTOR to gain time.) Roosevelt gets a dollar a word, where do I come in? (Resignedly.) All right, flag the pencil pushers and I'll gab my nob. (DUGAN turns L. to tell the REPORTERS to go. BROOKY says he don't understand. PERKINS pulls him off door C., remonstrating, going R.) (The INSPECTOR signs to DUGAN that they will now grill the EEL.)

INSPECTOR: This lady I suppose you know.

EEL: (Looks at MRS. WORTHINGTON.) I never lamped her before in my life.

DUGAN: That is Mrs. Worthington, the lady you robbed.

EEL: (Banteringly to MRS. WORTHINGTON to gain time.) Is it? How do you do, pleased to meet you. Gee! but you must be an awful mark to be robbed. (INSPECTOR raps on desk.) What was it I stole from you, Mrs. Worthington?

DUGAN: Nix on that bull. You know what you stole.

EEL: Yes, and I suppose you know what I stole before I stole it.

DUGAN: With dips like you, I always look far ahead.

EEL: Get out! you couldn't look far enough ahead to see the ashes on your cigar. Why, if it wasn't for your stool pigeons—

DUGAN: That's enough out of you.

EEL: Oh, go chase yourself. (DUGAN smashes at EEL, who ducks around back of him.)

INSPECTOR: Dugan!!! (When Dugan locates the EEL, he goes after him again. MRS. WORTHINGTON screams.)

INSPECTOR: None of that, Dugan! Remember, he had no marks on him when you brought him in. (DUGAN crosses L. in front of EEL and looks off door L. in subdued rage.) A little more civility out of you, Bradley.

EEL: All right, Inspector. (To MRS. W.) I beg your pardon, lady.

INSPECTOR: You have been brought here as a suspect in a five thousand dollar jewelry theft which happened at the home of Mrs. Worthington last night. (EEL makes no move.) Circumstances point strongly in your direction. Your former sweetheart, Goldie Marshall, was serving as maid to Mrs. Worthington at the time of the robbery.

EEL: And you think I planted her there as a stall.

DUGAN: Goldie spilled that much, and we didn't, have to third degree her.

EEL: So Goldie declared me in on this?

INSPECTOR: She couldn't help it, we knew it was a two-man's job.

EEL: She snitched me into a frame-up.

DUGAN: Same as she did two years ago.

EEL: Why say, Inspector, I ain't seen Goldie since I was sprung from the Pen.

DUGAN: Is that so? I got it straight that the first place you mozied to was Goldie's flat on East Broadway. You were trailed.

EEL: Sure I was, by one of you pathfinders at the Central Office. Oh, I've played tag with you before; Dugan, whatever you say, is.

INSPECTOR: Then you admit—

EEL: I don't admit nothin'.

INSPECTOR: Be careful what you say. Have you retained counsel?

EEL: A mouthpiece! What for?

INSPECTOR: You've got to be represented. Have you any money?

EEL: Sure! I left the hotel of Zebra clothed with a pocket full of smiles and a wad of joy. (INSPECTOR whispers for O'MARA to bring up GOLDIE. O'MARA exits door L.)

INSPECTOR: Well, the state will furnish you with an attorney.

EEL: What, one of them record shysters? Eighty years old and never won a case. No, thanks, Inspector. I'll plead my own case; then I got at least a chance to beat this rap.

DUGAN: You'd have a swell time pleading your own case.

EEL: Yes, and believe me I'll spring a sensation when I open up. I'll show up some of this rotten graft. I'll bust "The System " to smithereens. Dugan, I won't be railroaded—(EEL crosses in rage L. to Dugan.)

INSPECTOR: Bradley! hold your tongue, you've said enough.

EEL: I ain't said half what I'm going to say—

INSPECTOR: (Fiercely.) Not another word out of you. Do you understand?

EEL: (Coming down.) All right, Inspector. I don't want to get anybody that's right, in bad, but I've got something up my sleeve. (DUGAN laughs and goes up stage.) (GOLDIE enters door L. brought in by O'MARA. She is startled at seeing EEL, then pleadingly:)

GOLDIE: Billy! (EEL turns and is about to go to GOLDIE but stops.)

EEL: You snitched again! You snitched again! (Running L. to GOLDIE with arms up as though to hit her with hand-cuffs. GOLDIE snatches his upraised arms.)

GOLDIE: Oh no, Billy! True as God I didn't!

DUGAN: (Aside to INSPECTOR.) Let's leave them alone, they'll talk. (MRS. WORTHINGTON, INSPECTOR, DUGAN and O'MARA exit door R.)

GOLDIE: (Still holding EEL'S arms.) Why, I'd rather die than snitch.

EEL: (Jerking away and going R.) How about two years ago?

GOLDIE: I didn't even then when you left me dying. They framed you while I was in the hospital.

EEL: Who?

GOLDIE: Dugan and his—

EEL: Sh!!! Oh if I could only believe you, kid.

GOLDIE: Look at me, Billy. Do you think I'd snitch?

EEL: (Looks at her, then pushes her head roughly back.) No, I can't believe you did it, kid. (EEL takes GOLDIE in his arms.)

GOLDIE: (Sobbingly.) I'm so glad to see you again.

EEL: Me, too, kid. Gee, your head feels as natural on my shoulder as a piece of pie on a prize-fighter's knife. (EEL takes GOLDIE from his shoulder and says inquiringly.) But what are you doing here?

GOLDIE: (Drying her tears.) Bein' held on suspicion, but they can't get met I'm protected. Dugan's got to—

EEL: Nix on the crackin', don't shoot your trap, they're leavin' us together for a stall. Talk about something else. (EEL turns R. and GOLDIE grabs his hand.) Do you still love me?

GOLDIE: Always.

EEL: Will you marry me?

GOLDIE: If you want me to.

EEL: You know I do. (Looks around suspiciously.) Say, if I beat this rap (DUGAN comes, on door R., and stands at upper end of desk), let's get spliced and go out West, turn over a new leaf, and begin life all over again, far away from the subway world where the sun of happiness is always clouded and the ace of joy is coppered. What do you say?

GOLDIE: Gee! them's the kindest words you've ever said to me. (Then lightly.) And I'll march down the aisle with you, with my hair in a braid.

EEL: Great!! Gee, I wonder if we could make our get-away now. (Both start for door C., but DUGAN, who has come down behind them, stops them.)

DUGAN: How do you do! Would you like to take a little trip out in the air with me?

GOLDIE: Say, I'd rather be home with the headache, than at the Movies with a guy like you. (Crosses L.) (INSPECTOR enters door R. going behind desk.)

INSPECTOR: Well, have you got anything to say to me before I lock you up for the night?

EEL: Nothin', except that it's a frame-up, and we defy you to go through with it.

INSPECTOR: Take 'em down.

DUGAN: (Above door L.) Come on. (EEL starts for door L.)

GOLDIE: Good-night, Inspector.

INSPECTOR: Good-night.

EEL: (Turning at door L.) Same from me, Inspector.

INSPECTOR: Good-night, Bradley. (DUGAN shoves the EEL roughly off.

GOLDIE circles around and switches in front of DUGAN.) By the way, Goldie, what's the number of your flat on East Broadway?

GOLDIE: (Hesitatingly at door L.) 327, Inspector.

INSPECTOR: Thanks.

GOLDIE: (Impudently.) You're welcome. (Exit door L. followed by DUGAN.) (O'MARA locks door after them.)

INSPECTOR: (Calling O'MARA.) O'Mara!

O'MARA: (At door L.) Yes, sir.

INSPECTOR: I want a wire installed at 327 East Broadway.

O'MARA: (In front of desk.) Goldie's flat?

INSPECTOR: Yes. I'm leaving it to you to see that the orders are carried out to the letter.

O'MARA: Yes, sir, to-morrow.

INSPECTOR: To-night, at once. I'm going to turn them loose. You understand?

O'MARA: (Looks puzzled, then face brightens.) I understand.

DARK CHANGE

SCENE II

STREET SCENE, IN EAST BROADWAY

Showing flat house with stoop. Time: The same evening. A small boy enters L. with bottle of milk, goes up steps door C., rings bell, clicker sounds, and he exits door C. MAGGIE enters door C. She is an East side janitress. She has a tin pail on her arm around which is wrapped newspaper. She walks off L. PERKINS and BROOKY are heard off R.)

PERKINS: (Entering R. briskly.) Come on, Brooky, don't be so slow.

BROOKY: (Straggling in after PERKINS.) I say, old chap, this sort of work is most laborious. This flitting from one tram to another, and being jostled and ordered to "step lively" by vulgar guards, and running, yes actually running. It's not only bad taste, old man, but positively undignified. (Dusting shoes with handkerchief, L., PERKINS is up in vestibule of door C.)

PERKINS: If you want to supply your paper with live news, you've got to keep hustling.

BROOKY: Very true, but it seems such a waste of energy.

PERKINS: (Coming down to BROOKY.) No energy is wasted that is productive of flaring headlines. Now take that note pad I gave you, and get your pencil busy with a description of this neighborhood. (Goes R. making notes.)

BROOKY: (Taking paper and pencil from pockets after a search for them.) This is more like being a Scotland Yarder than a reporter.

PERKINS: A Scotland Yarder!

BROOKY: I should say detective.

PERKINS: (Coming L.) Let me tell you something, Brooky. The reporters and newspapers unravel more cases than the police.

BROOKY: I dare say you do. You're so damned inquisitive.

PERKINS: It isn't inquisitiveness, my boy, it's just being on the level with the public.

BROOKY: (Laughing.) You know, some great man said, "The public be damned."

PERKINS: He wasn't a great man, he was an ignorant man. The public will stand for just so much, then look out; let your mind wander back to the history of the French Revolution. An infuriated public is the most ferocious blood-lapping animal in the earth's jungle.

BROOKY: Perky, I adore your descriptive talents.

PERKINS: (Going up into vestibule and ringing bell.) You make me sick.

BROOKY: But surely you're not going to enter that apartment house unannounced?

PERKINS: No, I'll tell them a couple of reporters want some news, then you'll hear language no paper can print.

BROOKY: Why, are they all foreigners?

PERKINS: Say, Brooky, you're a perfect ass.

BROOKY: No, my dear fellow, none of us are perfect.

PERKINS: (Coming down out of vestibule to BROOKY.) Now listen, I told you that I had inside information that the EEL and GOLDIE were to be released, that's why I hustled you over here. I could have come alone, but I let you in on a big scoop for your paper.

BROOKY: Righto, old chap, righto; but what bothers me is, what's it all about?

PERKINS: It's about time you got next to yourself.

BROOKY: Another impossible metaphor, my dear fellow; how can one get next to one's self without being twins?

PERKINS: Brooky, Englishmen as a rule are thick, but you are a density of thickness that is impenetrable.

BROOKY: Yes, I know I am a rare sort.

PERKINS: Now, we haven't time to argue a lot of piffle. The girl isn't in yet, there's no answer to my ring, so let's stroll around and come back later. (Exit R.)

BROOKY: (Not seeing that PERKINS has gone.) Righto! old man, we'll stroll, for if there's anything that I like, its having a nice little—(Seeing that PERKINS is gone.) Perkins! you said stroll. Don't run, don't run, it's so damned undignified. (Exit R.) (Enter L., O'MARA dressed in citizen's clothes. He looks at number on house then motions off for TOM to come on. TOM comes on L., they go up into vestibule and look for names on bells. Enter Officer FLYNN, stealthily.)

FLYNN: Come on, now, you don't live there, I've had my eye on you for five minutes.

O'MARA: (Coming down from vestibule to FLYNN.) Well, keep your eye on something else, if you know what's good for you. (Takes badge out of pocket.)

FLYNN: (Surprised.) Central Officer! (Whistles and walks off R.)

O'MARA: (Returning to vestibule.) Ring any bell?

TOM: No, her flat's on the second floor, so I'll ring up the top flat. (TOM rings the bell and sound of electric door opener is heard, they both exit door C.)

(FLYNN strolls back on from R. ad MAGGIE enters from L.)

FLYNN: Hello, Maggie! been out to get the evening paper? There is not much in it.

MAGGIE: There's enough in it to quench me thirst after a hard day's work.

FLYNN: I see you've got the paper wrapped around something good.

MAGGIE: I have that, and it's meself instead of the paper'll be wrapped around it in a minute. (Light goes up in window above.)

FLYNN: I see you've got a new tenant. Is she hard on you?

MAGGIE: Divel-a-bit! She's a nice respectable dacent girl, and aisy to get along with. I never seen her with no men folks. Maybe she's a widdy, as I'd like to be.

FLYNN: A widow? What's the matter with your old man?

MAGGIE: He ain't worth powder enough to blow up a cock-roach.

FLYNN: Is he working?

MAGGIE: He ain't done a tap since the civil war.

FLYNN: That's quite a vacation.

MAGGIE: Vacation? It's a life sentence of laziness.

FLYNN: There's many a good man layin' off.

MAGGIE: No, the good men are dyin' off, it's the bums that are layin' off.

FLYNN: (Looking at house.) Well, the landlord of this house ain't particular about his tenants.

MAGGIE: Not a bit, it's been a nest for thieves ever since I came here.

FLYNN: Well, they've got to live somewhere, the jails are overcrowded.

MAGGIE: Oh, I don't mind thim, they can steal nothin' from me but me old man, and they're welcome to him without usin' a jimmy.

FLYNN: A jimmy? You're getting on to the thief slang.

MAGGIE: Why wouldn't I? That's all I hear mornin' and night from "Tommy the Rat," "Tim the Flim," and "John the Con."

FLYNN: You know all their monakers?

MAGGIE: I do that. Say, they've given me a monaker, too.

FLYNN: What do they call you?

MAGGIE: "Mag the Jag."

FLYNN: (Laughs.) Well, I must be off. (Starts off R.)

MAGGIE: (As she goes up into vestibule.) Won't you come in and have a sup of beer and a pull at the old man's pipe?

FLYNN: I can't, I've got a stationary post.

MAGGIE: Look at that now, that shows where you stand. Good-night, John.

FLYNN: Good-night, Maggie. (Exits R.) (Enter EEL and GOLDIE arm in arm, talking earnestly. As they come to steps, GOLDIE goes up and unlocks door. EEL sees FLYNN coming up on R., he lights cigarette and motions to go in. GOLDIE exits door C. FLYNN comes up to EEL, who throws the match in his face and disappears door C. as FLYNN is rubbing his eyes.)

DARK CHANGE

SCENE III

SAME NIGHT, INTERIOR OF GOLDIE'S FLAT

Living room, bedroom, and kitchen can be seen. At rise, O'MARA and TOM are installing the dictagraph, on wall L. C. TOM is standing on chair L. C. He places the instrument—then runs his hand down to wire.)

TOM: All right, Jim, hand me that picture.

O'MARA: (C. handing TOM framed picture.) Here you are, Tom.

TOM: (Hangs picture over dictagraph, gets off of chair and backs off, seeing if it's placed right.) There, that'll do, I guess.

O'MARA: Nobody would ever suspect anything's been happening here.

TOM: (Picking up bits of wire and tools from floor L. C. O'MARA puts chair TOM has been standing on, R. and brings bag C.) Pick up these pieces. Did you give the Inspector the office?

O'MARA: Twenty minutes ago.

TOM: (Putting scraps into bag.) The job took a little longer than I thought it would.

O'MARA: (Closing bag and handing it to TOM.) Yes, and we'd better get a gait on out of here, or the EEL and his girl will be walkin' in on us. (Door slams off stage.)

BOTH: What's that!

O'MARA: It must be them!

TOM: (Starts for door R.)

O'MARA: We can't go that way.

TOM: (Indicating the window L.) The fire escape, quick. (TOM crosses quickly to window L., opens it, and goes through.)

O'MARA: (Follows TOM, but stops at window L.) Wait a minute! (Goes back, turns out light, then goes through window, closing it after him.) (Footsteps begin on steps off stage as O'MARA pulls down window.) Stage is in darkness but for the moonlight that streams in through window L. Steps sound closer. Key rattles and door is unlocked. Door R. opens just a bit at first, then GOLDIE enters, followed by the EEL.)

EEL: (Holding GOLDIE back.) Wait a minute, kid, till I strike a match.

GOLDIE: Oh, never mind, Billy, I don't need one. (Gropes her way C. and turns on light. EEL stays at door R. listening to hear if they are followed.) Home again! Gee! but that guy what said "ther ain't no place like home" must have travelled some.

EEL: (Turning around.) Yep! Gee, but this is some swell dump you got here, Kid!

GOLDIE: Ain't this classy?

(The EEL hurries into bedroom and then into kitchen as though looking for some one. GOLDIE follows him, but stops at kitchen door.) What are you looking for, the ice-box?

EEL: (Coming down to C. R. of GOLDIE.) No, it ain't that.

GOLDIE: What then, lookin' for a sleeper?

EEL: No telling what they're up to. You don't think they've given us our liberty, without a string to it, do you? They're Indian givers, they are.

(Starts for door R.)

GOLDIE: Gee, Billy! I hadn't thought of that. (Goes into bedroom and lights electric light L. of bedroom off C.)

EEL: (R. C. looking at door R.) I kind of thought I saw a light through the bottom of this door, when we was coming up the stairs.

GOLDIE: (Coming down C.) Oh, it must have been the reflection of the moon. (Takes off hat and puts it on dresser in bedroom. EEL crosses room backwards to L., holding hand in moonlight to make the shadow on bottom of door. GOLDIE watches him. EEL then turns to window and GOLDIE looks under bed.)

EEL: (Excitedly.) This latch is sprung.

GOLDIE: I must have left it open, when they hiked me down to the club house.

EEL: Are you sure?

GOLDIE: SURE!

EEL: (Going down L.) Well, then, I guess we're all right for the present at least.

GOLDIE: (Coming down C. with travelling bag which she has taken off of bed.) Yes, until Dugan finds out we've been sprung, and then he'll be after us like a cat after a mouse. (Puts bag on table up R.)

EEL: We'll be on a rattler for Chi, before that. How long will it take you to pack?

GOLDIE: (Going into bedroom.) About a half hour.

EEL: That's good. If Dugan does go after us (Chuckles.), he's got to get us first.

GOLDIE: (Coming down C. with kimono which she has taken from door C. in bedroom, and is folding.) Say, Billy, I guess I'd better lock this door. (Starts for door, but his next line stops her.)

EEL: He can't break in here without a search warrant, and he can't get that before Monday. (Lying down on couch.)

GOLDIE: Well, what's he going to get it on then? (Putting kimono in bag on table R., picking up a pair of shoes from the floor near table, but the EEL's next line stops her.)

EEL: (Still on couch.) You ought to know Dugan well enough by this time. He'll get something on us, leave it to him.

GOLDIE: (Stopping thoughtfully in door C., then throwing shoes on floor near bed decisively and coming down C.) If he does, I'll turn squealer for the first time in my life.

EEL: (Jumping off of couch quickly.) Don't you do it. I could never look you square in the eyes again if you did.

GOLDIE: It ain't no worse to squeal than it is to steal.

EEL: Yes, it is, Kid, God'll forgive a thief, but he hates a squealer.

GOLDIE: Maybe you're right, Billy. Well, I guess we'd better get a move on. (Going into bedroom and getting hair brush off of dresser.) We can't get out of here any too soon to suit me. (Putting brush in bag on Table R., then smiling at EEL.)

EEL: You betcher! (Goes to mantle L. and leans against it thoughtfully.)

GOLDIE: (Coming C.) What's on your mind now?

EEL: I was just thinkin' of that first job I'd have to do when we get to Chi.

GOLDIE: What do you mean?

EEL: Gee, Goldie, I hate to go back to the old life. (Sits on sofa L.)

GOLDIE: Old life? I thought you said we was goin' to begin all over again, and live like decent, respectable people?

EEL: I know, but you've got to have money to be respectable.

GOLDIE: Well, we'll get the money.

EEL: That's what I hate about it. Having to get it that way.

GOLDIE: But Billy, I mean honestly, work for it.

EEL: (Rising and coming R.) Yes, but supposing we can't get work? And supposing we can't hold it after we do get it?

GOLDIE: If they go digging into our past, it'll be tough rowing. But there (caressing EEL.), don't let's worry till we come to the bridge. Wait until we get to Chicago. (Goes into bedroom and takes down coat which is hanging on door C.)

EEL: (Lies on couch L.) Have you got enough cale to carry us over there?

GOLDIE: (Brushing off coat at door C.) What?

EEL: I say, have you got enough money to hold us till we get to Chi?

GOLDIE: (C. looking in surprise.) Why no, Billy, I ain't got no money.

EEL: (Surprised, slowly rising from couch to sitting position.) What?

GOLDIE: I ain't got a cent. I thought you had the sugar.

EEL: Me?

GOLDIE: AIN'T you got no money neither?

EEL: (Throwing away cigarette and going R.) I ain't got enough money to buy the controlling interest in a rotten egg. (Goldie throws coat on couch.) How about that necklace?

GOLDIE: Why, Dugan's got it.

EEL: Well, how about your share?

GOLDIE: Well, he promised I was going to get five hundred out of it, but now that you're sprung, I suppose I'll have to whistle for it.

EEL: Well, I see where I have to get to work before we get to Chicago.

GOLDIE: (Turning him around quickly.) What do you mean?

EEL: Well, we've got to get to Chi, and as the railroads are very particular, somebody'll have to pay our fares. I won't be long. (Crosses L. in front of GOLDIE and gets hat and coat off of sofa. GOLDIE runs to door R., then as EEL turns:)

GOLDIE: Oh no, no, don't, please don't. We're going to be good, you said so yourself. We're going to travel the straight road.

EEL: (C. with hat and coat in hand.) But that road won't take us to Chi. (Pause.) You see, there's no other way out of it. (Starts toward door but GOLDIE stops him pleadingly.)

GOLDIE: Oh no, you musn't, you shan't. I won't go with you if you do. I won't go! I won't go! (Becomes hysterical, pounds on door, then begins to cry.)

EEL: (Putting arm around her.) There, there, don't cry. Look! (He turns her around and then puts his hat and coat in chair above door R.) (GOLDIE takes his hands in relief The EEL pats her cheek.) You see, I'll do as you say. (Crossing down C.) I'll cut it out.

GOLDIE: (Following the EEL and putting her arms around him.) I knew you would.

EEL: Oh, you did? Well, what's the next move?

GOLDIE: I don't know, Billy.

EEL: There you are. (Crosses L.) We're no better off than we were before. By Monday, Dugan'll have me back in the Tombs, maybe on a charge of murder. You know that he ain't going to rest while I'm loose.

GOLDIE: Then why not let me end it all?

EEL: Not by squealing.

GOLDIE: It will be that sooner or later.

EEL: (Coming R. slowly.) No, the best way is to let me go out and get some money. (Crossing GOLDIE and going toward hat and coat on chair R.)

GOLDIE: (Stopping him.) But, Billy, you promised me—

EEL: (Turning to GOLDIE.) I don't mean to rob anybody (Scratches head in puzzled way, then brightly, as thought strikes him), I mean to borrow it.

GOLDIE: (Joyfully.) Borrow it?

EEL: Yes, I'll knock a guy down, strip him of his leather, get his name and address, then when we get to Chicago, I'll send it back to him.

GOLDIE: (Shaking her head and smiling.) Oh no, it won't do.

EEL: Why?

GOLDIE: You might forget his address. (Going up C. into bedroom.) Now, you come and help me pack the trunk. (Stopping.) Oh Billy, come help me pull this trunk in there. (Disappearing to R. of trunk. EEL comes and takes L. end and they carry it into living room and place it C. under chandelier to open up stage. As they carry it down stage she speaks.) There are a few more things to go in.

EEL: (As they set trunk down.) I've got it.

GOLDIE: What?

EEL: I know where I can get that money.

GoLDffi: Where?

EEL: Isaacson.

GOLDIE: What Isaacson?

EEL: Why the fence on Second Ave. I'm aces with him.

GOLDIE: Yes, but what have you got to pawn?

EEL: I don't need nothing. I've thrown thousands of dollars his way in business, he'll lend me a century sure. I'll be back in fifteen minutes. (Goes to chair and gets coat and hat, then starts for door R.)

GOLDIE: Wait! (Crosses to mantel L. and gets keys from up stage end.) Here, take my keys. (Coming back to C. above trunk where EEL meets her putting on coat and hat.) To make sure, we'd better work on signals.

EEL: (Taking keys.) How do you mean?

GOLDIE: In case anything happens while you're gone, when you come back, ring the bell downstairs three times. If I don't answer, everything's O. K., come up; but if I do answer, don't come up, see?

EEL: If you don't answer, everything's all right, come up; but if you do answer, don't come up.

GOLDIE: That's it.

EEL: I got you. (Goes to door R. Opens it quickly to see if anyone is there. Closes door, footsteps are heard in hall, then going downstairs, then door slams.)

GOLDIE: (Listens intently until door slams, then begins to pack trunk. Opens trunk first. Gets jacket from couch where she has thrown it, puts it in trunk. Goes up into bedroom and gets skirt which hangs out of sight on end of dresser. Comes down C. shaking skirt. Long, low whistle stops her, then club raps.) Bull's!! (Looks up at light burning, turns it out and closes the trunk at the same time. Stands still until she sees the shadow of man's hand in the moonlight on the wall R. Frightened exclamation, then cowers on sofa. DUGAN appears at window, looks in, then raises window and enters, closing window after him. Takes gun out of pocket, then goes up into kitchen and bedroom. At door C. he sees GOLDIE, points gun at her.

DUGAN: Ah! (GOLDIE springs to her feet with frightened exclamation, and DUGAN says:) don't squawk or I'll pop sure!

GOLDIE: (Nervously.) Me squawk? What do you think I am, a school teacher?

DUGAN: (Goes to door R., opens it to see if anyone is there, closes it and locks door. Comes to C., turns on light, then puts gun in pocket. Coming L. to GOLDIE.) I don't want to frighten you.

GOLDIE: (L. nervously.) I know, but one look at you would scare some people to death.

DUGAN: Am I that homely?

GOLDIE: Homely? Why an undershot bulldog is a peacock, 'long side of you.

DUGAN: Ain't I welcome?

GOLDIE: You're about as welcome as a rainy holiday. (Sits on sofa.)

DUGAN: Say, Goldie, we've been almost more than friends in the last two years.

GOLDIE: You mean almost friends. (Rising.) Never more. Dugan, you know why I've been your go-between in the System. Because you promised to let up on the Eel.

DUGAN: I'll never let up on him. He's a crook.

GOLDIE: Well, what are you? (Turns L. away from DUGAN.)

DUGAN: Don't get sore, Goldie. You know I want you for myself. (Puts his arms around GOLDIE'S waist.)

GOLDIE: Well, you're wasting time. (Pulls savagely away from him and crosses R.)

DUGAN: (Following GOLDIE R.) Am I? I'll get you, or I'll send you both up for years.

GOLDIE: (Savagely into DUGAN's face.) Is that why you had me steal that necklace?

DUGAN: Yes, if you want to know it, I've been trying for two years to get something on you, and now I've got you.

GOLDIE: Well, suppose I squeal.

DUGAN: It's my word against yours, the word of an officer against a crook.

GOLDIE: Say, Dugan, if looks of contempt would hurt a man's feelings, I'd disable you with a squint. (DUGAN goes L., getting necklace out of pocket; GOLDIE is in panic for fear EEL will ring the bell, but she crosses and sits on trunk.)

DUGAN: Goldie, this necklace will bring four thousand dollars from a Buffalo fence, and if you'll say three words, "I love you," the price is yours. Won't you say them, Goldie? Just three words?

GOLDIE: (Thinks it over, then looks at DUGAN.) Go—to—Hell.

DUGAN: (Going L. puts back necklace and takes out red wallet, then comes C. to GOLDIE.) Well, how does this strike you? Here's twenty thousand dollars. It's all yours for the asking. Twenty thousand dollars. (Sits on trunk beside GOLDIE.)

GOLDIE: Gee, but you're doing a land office business.

DUGAN: I've got no kick coming. Why say, I can take care of you in real style. Why waste your time on the EEL? I can make more money in a week than he can steal in a year.

GOLDIE: That's because you're a better thief than he is. (Rises and goes R.)

DUGAN: I wouldn't say that. (Following GOLDIE R.) Come on, Goldie (putting his arms around her, with purse in front of her face), what's the answer?

GOLDIE: (Apparently weakening.) Twenty thousand dollars! Gee, that's a lot of money, and I could live right.

DUGAN: (Greedily, as though he has won her.) Sure you could. I'd set you up like a Queen, and between us we could milk the Tenderloin dry.

GOLDIE: But the Eel?

DUGAN: (Crossing L. and putting wallet away.) I'll attend to him! (Then to GOLDIE who has come L.) Listen to this! Ten minutes after you two were turned loose, an old man was beaten and robbed, not two blocks from here. He never came to! (GOLDIE backs R. in horror. DUGAN follows.) He died on his way to Bellevue. Do you know who the murderer is? I'm here to arrest him on the charge of murder.

GOLDIE: (In mad rage.) You lie, Dugan! Billy said you'd frame him, but you won't this time—(GOLDIE flies at DUGAN as though to scratch his eyes out, but he struggles with her and throws her to the floor L.) No, Dugan, not murder, that would mean the chair! (GOLDIE on knees pleading to DUGAN. Bell rings three times, they both start. DUGAN puzzled and surprised, and GOLDIE terror-stricken, wondering what to do. Then the thought of the bell on the wall comes. Looking at DUGAN with a forced smile and still on the floor.) Oh, I wonder who that can be? (By the last two words she is on her feet and makes a dash for the bell up L., but DUGAN reaches it firse.)

DUGAN: No, you don't. I'm wise. "If I answer, don't come up." (GOLDIE, in disgusted rage, goes down to head of couch, followed by DUGAN.) Old stuff, Goldie. Let him come, I want him. (Door slams off stage. GOLDIE starts and DUGAN goes to door R. and unlocks it. They both stand rigid. DUGAN with gun in hand, while footsteps come nearer. As door opens and EEL enters.)

GOLDIE: Look out, Billy! (DUGAN grabs EEL'S hand and throws him in the room and locks the door. While he is doing this EEL runs across room over trunk and disappears behind sofa. When DUGAN turns, he can't locate EEL and points gun up into bedroom.)

DUGAN: Hands up, Billy! Hands up! (He then locates EEL behind sofa.) I won't tell you again! Hands up! (The EEL holds hands up and appears behind sofa.) (GOLDIE is up C. behind trunk.) Goldie, frisk him clean. (GOLDIE protests.) Come on! Come on! (DUGAN points gun at EEL, and GOLDIE runs to him and goes through his pockets. She finds tobacco bag which she hands to DUGAN. He doesn't take it, and she drops it on floor.) Get to his gun pocket. Get to his gun pocket. (GOLDIE hesitates, then goes to EEL'S hip pocket, where she finds a roll of money. She tries to put it back but DUGAN sees it.) Come on, hand it over. (GOLDIE appeals to the EEL who pantomimes to do so, and she hands it to DUGAN.) This is the money he took from the man he killed. (Putting money into red wallet and returning wallet to pocket.)

EEL: Do you think I'd frisk a stiff? Let me tell you something, Dugan. (Throwing hat on floor.) You staked me two years ago in the Pen, and then tried to make me believe that Goldie was in on the frame. You lied like a yellow dog, Dugan, and you know it. Yes, I am a crook and a thief, and I've robbed a lot of people, but I'm just a little bit above you, Dugan, just a little bit above you. Because, I never took money from a woman, and that's part of your graft. (DUGAN takes out gun as though to hit EEL with it. GOLDIE grabs his arm and bites his hand and he drops the gun; Noise begins off stage. GOLDIE runs to door R. while EEL and DUGAN struggle. DUGAN throws EEL off and goes toward window L. EEL sees gun on floor R., runs and gets it, but GOLDIE prevents his shooting it. The Police break in the door at this point. One catches GOLDIE as she is running toward the window L. Another, who comes through the window, catches the EEL. The Inspector stands at door R., crowd back of him. DUGAN comes down to him.)

DUGAN: Well, Inspector, I got him. He robbed and croaked an old man. I got him with the goods on!

INSPECTOR: Let these people go! (Pointing to DUGAN.) There's your man, arrest him! (GOLDIE and the EEL are released.)

DUGAN: Inspector, you've got nothing on me.

INSPECTOR: No? (Crossing to DUGAN.) Well, there's a dictagraph in this room (GOLDIE rushes into EEL'S arms.), and we've got everything on you, you dog. You're a disgrace to all mankind. It is unclean curs like you that have bred a cancer in the department, and pointed the finger of suspicion at ten thousand honest policemen. But that cancer must be cut out, and the operation begins now. Take him away. (Policemen hand-cuff DUGAN, who struggles, then resignedly walks off, preceded and followed by police. The INSPECTOR follows them, but stops and turns at door R.) Well, Billy! (EEL and GOLDIE come C. and stand in front of trunk.)

EEL: Well, Inspector?

INSPECTOR: If you're going to live square, stick to it. (EEL takes GOLDIE'S hand.) I never want to see you at headquarters again. (EEL drops his head and GOLDIE puts her arm around him.) I won't even need you as a witness. The dictagraph has recorded all. (EEL and GOLDIE pleased.) Good-night! (INSPECTOR exits, closing door after him.)

EEL and GOLDIE: Good-night, Inspector! (They both listen until his footsteps die off, and door slams. Then EEL runs to door to listen, and GOLDIE sits dejectedly on trunk.)

GOLDIE: Well, we're broke again. (Tearfully.) We can't go West now, so there's no use packing. (The EEL goes stealthily to window L., looks out, pulls dictagraph from wall, then comes down R. of GOLDIE who is sitting on trunk and has watched him. He taps her on the shoulder, taking DUGAN'S red wallet out of pocket.)

EEL: Go right ahead and pack! (GOLDIE looks astounded, and begins to laugh.)

CURTAIN

First picture. (Both sitting on trunk counting money.)

A PERSIAN GARDEN

CHARACTERS
(Order in which they appear.)
ROSE DUDLEY STANFORD
LETTY PHIL
BETTY DOWLEH
SHEIK ABU MIRZAH NEHMID DUCKIN
MRS. SCHUYLER HAMILTON SCHUYLER
    PAUL MORGAN

SCENE
The Rose Gardens of the American Legation in Persia—the entrance to the building on left. Large Persian jardinieres on right with a large Persian Rose Tree.

OPENING NUMBER
ROSE: "The Girl in the Persian Rug." After number off stage is heard in old man's voice: "Illa au Rose aboukar."
GIRLS: (Running up.) Oh—here comes the old Sheik now. (Enter the old SHEIK ABU MIRZAH preceded by Persian servant.)
ABU: Ah—ma Rosa Persh—ma waf to be—to-morrow we marry, eh? (The SHEIK carries eartrumpet.)
ROSE: (Running from him in alarm.) Oh, don't touch me—don't—don't! (They are both yelling at each other as MRS. SCHUYLER enters first arch and sees ROSE'S actions—she is flashy—an ex-chorus girl—married to the retiring consul.)
MRS. SCHUYLER: Say, tie a can to that duet. What's the matter?
ROSE: (Crossing to her.) Oh, Mrs. Schuyler, I won't marry him—I hate him!
MRS. SCHUYLER: Oh, the poor old prune. (Crossing to ABU, garrulously.) How are you, Sheik? Our little ward, Rose, is so young and foolish! But I was just that innocent when I was in the chorus. When I came out of it, believe me, I was a different woman. (Enter Persian servant.)
SERVANT: The new consul wants to know when we are going to move out—
MRS. SCHUYLER: Not till after Rose's wedding to-morrow. (ROSE utters exclamation of rage, slaps the SHEIK'S face and exits.) I was just that emotional until I'd been married a few times—Come, Sheik—my husband won't return from Tabris till this evening—join me in a cocktail. (She illustrates drink in pantomime.)
ABU: (Understanding pantomime.) Yes! Yes! (LETTY and BETTY go up to table and chair C.)
MRS. SCHUYLER: Mousta, two cocktails on my back porch. Come, Sheik—Sheik! (Business with girls.) This way to the dog house. (Takes hold of chain on his ear trumpet and passes him in. Girls have gone off.) Oh—and, Mousta—don't put any cherries in—they take up too much room in the glass. (She exits

one way—Waiter, another.)

(MUSIC. Entrance of men.)

PAUL: (Entering with DUDLEY.) Well, there are some beautiful girls in our new Persian home—has Phil brought our things from the boat? Phil! Phil! (Phil enters with all the luggage.)

PHIL: (Meekly.) Here I am, sir.—

PAUL: (As if brushing mosquitoes away.) Oh gee! these Persian mosquitoes! (Finally kills one on his own face.)

PHIL: (Hungrily.) When are we going to have lunch, sir?

PAUL: Well, there are several little things I want you to do first. (Whacking him on one side of face.) Another mosquito.

PHIL: (Gratefully.) Oh, thank you, sir.

DUDLEY: Paul, you look as if you were mashed on that Madison girl—(Sees mosquito on PHIL's face.) Another mosquito. (Whacks him on other side of face.)

PHIL: Oh, thank you, sir—I have never seen such extreme kindness. (Both whack him this time—one on each side of face.)

PAUL: Ho! Ho! Two of them this time.

PHIL: Probably twins.

DUDLEY: I'll go in and see when the retiring consul will move out.

PAUL: All right, and I'll get a bite of luncheon awhile. (DUDLEY exits.)

PHIL: (Hungrily.) Oh—are you going to have your luncheon *alone*? (PAUL sees mosquito on PHIL—is about to kill it—PHIL falls back.) Ah—let it live—let it live.

PAUL: Now—you run in the house and take our things out of the grips.

PHIL: Is there any other little thing I can do for you?

PAUL: Not till after I've had my lunch.

PHIL: Thank you, sir! (PHIL looks a starved look at him—exits into house—stumbling over bundles.) (ROSE is heard singing off-stage chorus of "My Little Persian Rose"—enters humming.)

PAUL: (As he hears her singing.) It's Miss Madison—I know her sweet voice!

ROSE: (As she enters and sees PAUL, she stops singing, embarrassed.) Oh, I didn't know you were here. (The music continues faintly in orchestra.)

PAUL: I'm not—I'm in heaven when I hear you sing.

ROSE: Oh, I hope you don't mean my singing kills you.

PAUL: No—for *then*, I'm afraid I wouldn't be in heaven. What was that song?

ROSE: An old Persian poet taught me the words.

PAUL: (Ardently.) Oh, how I love—those words. Are you going back to America with Mr. and Mrs. Schuyler?

ROSE: (Sadly.) No, I must stay here in Persia.

PAUL: (Forgetting himself.) Hooray!

ROSE: Ah—but you don't know.

PAUL: Know what?

ROSE: Don't ask me now—good day, sir. (She courtesies and runs off.)

(Music in orchestra stops.)

PAUL: I wonder what she meant by that?

PHIL: (Rushing on.) I've taken out your things. Now, may I eat? (Persian servant enters in haste.)

SERVANT: Oh please, sir, the Sheik has drunk three cocktails, and Mrs. Schuyler says he is disgusting. Quick, get someone to take him home.

PAUL: Phil—do you hear? The Sheik's disgusting—take him home. (Servants exit.)

PHIL: (As he exits.) Is there any little thing I can do for you?

PAUL: Not just now. (PHIL exits.) The melody of that song haunts me. (He starts to hum it.) (PHIL enters with SHEIK on his shoulders—struggles to get him off. Finally exits with him. As he exits, MRS. SCHUYLER enters first arch.)

MRS. SCHUYLER: I hope he gets the old fool home, all right. (Sees PAUL.) Oho—it looks good to mother. (Business of humming same song.)

PAUL: (Turning and seeing her, with great surprise.) Agnes!

MRS. SCHUYLER: (Startled.) Mercy, where was I Agnes?

PAUL: (Crosses to MRS. SCHUYLER.) Have you forgotten—the summer I met you in Niagara Falls?

MRS. SCHUYLER: Niagara Falls? I must have been on one of my honeymoons—oh, yes—of course—Mr. Morgan. (They shake hands.) You see, I've met so many mushy men. (He sighs.) What makes you look so unhappy?

PAUL: I'm in love with a girl.

MRS. SCHUYLER: Only one? Why so economical?

PAUL: Ah—I'm afraid you don't know what real love is.

MRS. SCHUYLER: Oh, yes I do! Real love is the kind that lasts after you've heard a man sleeping right out loud. Who's the girl?

PAUL: Miss Madison.

MRS. SCHUYLER: (Surprised.) Our Rose? Not on your life. To-morrow, before we return to America, she's to marry the Abu Mirzah, and nothing can prevent it.

PAUL: (In horror.) She's being sacrificed to that old mummy—I'll kill him.

MRS. SCHUYLER: The doctors say he is so strong, nothing can kill him, except his fondness for Persian plums, and there is a mandate out inflicting death upon any man who sends him any. (ROSE enters.)

PAUL: (Crossing to her.) Oh, Miss Madison, I've just heard—

MRS. SCHUYLER: Rose—go to the grape arbor at once—I'll join you there presently. (DUDLEY enters.)

DUDLEY: Say, Paul—I—(Sees MRS. SCHUYLER—with surprise.) Lena—

MRS. SCHUYLER: Du, "Allmaechtiger Strohsach"—where was I Lena?

DUDLEY: Have you forgotten, in Germany, Unter den Linden?

MRS. SCHUYLER: Germany? Oh, the man who made love to me over a plate of frankfurters? Well—well—wie geht's! Tell me, do you think I've grown stouter since the days when I was Lena? (PAUL laughs.)

DUDLEY: Not a bit. (PAUL and ROSE laugh.)

MRS. SCHUYLER: (Seeing ROSE and PAUL in earnest conversation.)

Excuse me. (She crosses and grabs ROSE.) Rose, there's some grape juice waiting for us in the grape arbor. (She sends ROSE off.) (Boys step toward MRS. SCHUYLER.) Boys—later—when Rose has gone, you may come and crush a grape with me in the arbor. (She exits.)

PAUL: Aber nit! Dud, she's determined to keep us apart—you must help me—go and grab her, and run her off into the house.

DUDLEY: Lena—not much—she once flung a glass at my head.

PAUL: Well, then, where's Phil? (Calls.) Phil—Phil! (DUDLEY calls also. PHIL rushes on.)

PHIL: Am I going to eat?

PAUL: Quick, go and grab Mrs. Schuyler in the grape arbor.

PHIL: Grab her in the grape arbor?

PAUL: (Pushing them off.) And run her into the house. Quick. (He pushes PHIL off one way.) And you run into the house and hold her there. (Rushes DUDLEY into house.) I'll run to the grape arbor to join Rose when she's alone. (He exits.) (PHIL enters, pushing MRS. SCHUYLER toward the house. They enter from grape arbor.)

MRS. SCHUYLER: (Beating him with parasol.) The idea! What's the meaning of this? You little runt! (Pushing him off.) (Ad lib talk.) Who are you, anyhow?

PHIL: (Turning and seeing her.) Maggie!

MRS. SCHUYLER: (As before.) For the love of the Chambermaids' Union, where was I Maggie?

PHIL: Don't you remember when I was a "merry merry" with you in the "Blonde Broilers' Burlesque" troupe?

MRS. SCHUYLER: Were you one of the Blonde Broilers?

PHIL: Sure, I was the fellow that came out in the last act disguised as a bench.

MRS. SCHUYLER: (Finally remembering him.) Oh, you dear old Benchie! (They embrace.) And I used to come in and sit all over you.

PHIL: That's how I came to fall in love with you.

MRS. SCHUYLER: A man always thinks more of a woman when she sits on him.

PHIL: Do she?

MRS. SCHUYLER: She do.

PHIL: Come and sit on me now.

MRS. SCHUYLER: (Coyly.) Oh, you fascinating devil.

PHIL: Ah, go on—ah, sit on me. (Business of sitting—nearly flopping—finally getting on his knee.)

MRS. SCHUYLER: You're not the bench you used to be!

PHIL: You're not the sitter you used to be.

MRS. SCHUYLER: Remember the night you let me flop?

PHIL: I couldn't get into my part at all that night. I kept saying to myself: Phillip, be a bench, be a bench; but when I felt you near me, all the benchiness left me. When you sat on me, I put my arms about you, like this. (Does so.)

MRS. SCHUYLER: Ah—how it all comes back to me now! When you would put your arms about me, I would close my eyes and make believe it was Otis Skinner. (Business.)

PHIL: And then before all the crowd, I kissed you so. (He illustrates as PAUL enters with ROSE from arbor.)

PAUL: (Seeing PHIL and MRS. SCHUYLER.) Well—(They break apart.) I'm surprised!

MRS. SCHUYLER: (Works PHIL around to hide him first, then turns him around to PAUL.) You wouldn't be if you were as used to it as I am.

PAUL: (Aside to PHIL.) What did I tell you to do?

(PHIL seizes MRS. SCHUYLER and runs her into house—she saying: "What's the idea," etc., till off.) (Sunset falls upon scene.)

SONG—PAUL and ROSE—"My Little Persian Rose." (ROSE exits at end of song.)

PAUL: (Left alone.) I won't let her marry him. (A girl passes, crying out "Persian Plums—who will buy?")

PAUL: Persian Plums—Mrs. Schuyler said the old Sheik had such a passion for them, they might prove his death. Here! Girl—let me have a basket. (Hands her a roll of money.) There! (As he comes down with plums, the girl exits.) But she said whoever was caught sending him any would suffer the penalty of death. (Gets idea and calls off.) Phil—Phil! (Moonlight effect. As PHIL enters, anxiously, PAUL extends the basket of plums to him.)

PHIL: (Taking plums, greedily.) Oh thanks, I was starving—

PAUL: (Stopping him as he is about to eat.) Here—here—they're not for you. Quick—take them to the palace of the old Sheik Abu Mirzah.

PHIL: But I left him asleep in his bed, sir.

PAUL: Well, place them where he'll see them when he wakes, and (ominously) don't let anyone catch you with them, for the country is full of revolutionists and it might mean death.

PHIL: (Trembling.) My death! Is there any other little thing I can do for you?

PAUL: No. (Several pistol shots are heard. PHIL drops plums and starts to run into house. PAUL catches him by the hair—business.) You coward! I'm surprised! Go to the Palace of the Abu Mirzah. (He places basket in PHIL's hands.) Go!

(As PHIL backs off with plums, he bumps into a fierce looking Persian who enters. PHIL starts and has comedy exit. The Persian is the Emir Shahrud, who has disguised himself as DOWLEH the chef. DOWLEH grinds his teeth at PAUL, who runs off.)

(DOWLEH sneaks over to house mysteriously—sees someone coming, and then runs and hides behind rosebush.)

(Now, moonlight floods scene. MRS. SCHUYLER enters in evening gown with LETTY and BETTY. Waiter enters and sets two tables.)

MRS. SCHUYLER: Turn up the lights!

LETTY: Our last night in Persia.

MRS. SCHUYLER: I've ordered my "paflouka" out here. (MRS. SCHUYLER crosses to rosebush and, DOWLER jumps out at her.) Mercy—

how you scared me!

DOWLEH: Fatima!

MRS. SCHUYLER: Now, I'm a cigarette!

DOWLEH: You are cruel to me—the noble Prince of Persia, who just to be near you, disguised himself as a cook.

MRS. SCHUYLER: Prince, I eat your cooking—that's kind enough.

DOWLEH: (Business.) Yes, I love you so that one day I hear a lady say you paint your face—I put a secret poison in her food—she took one taste—in ten seconds, she die.

MRS. SCHUYLER: It serves her right for telling the truth.

DOWLEH: Come! Fly with me!

MRS. SCHUYLER: Oh Prince, I've flown so much in my days, there isn't another flap left in me. (Throws him off.) Go—serve my "paflouka!"

DOWLEH: You throw me down—very well—I will be revenged. (Grinds his teeth in her ear.) Mmmm-ha!

MRS. SCHUYLER: (With start, holding ear.) He bit me. (The girls come down as DOWLEH goes off bumping into DUDLEY, who enters in dress clothes—he swears at DUDLEY, in Persian and exits.)

DUDLEY: (To MRS. SCHUYLER.) Oh Lena—if it's you that has made him mad, I'd advise you not to taste any of his food again.

MRS. SCHUYLER: Why?

DUDLEY: I just heard *he's* under suspicion of having put poison in a lady's food, which killed her in ten seconds.

MRS. SCHUYLER: Ten seconds! Then it was true. (Waiter enters with "paftouka.") Oh my beautiful paflouka—and it smells so good.

DUDLEY: But Lena—you *daren't touch* it unless you get someone to try it first.

MRS. SCHUYLER: Will you?

DUDLEY: Excuse me. (She turns to the three—they all decline.)

MRS. SCHUYLER: Oh, if heaven would only send some unsuspecting imbecile to taste my paflouka for me—(PHIL backs on from grape arbor—looking to see if he's being followed.) Heaven has sent it hither. (She steps PHIL's way. As he bumps into her, he starts.) Hello!

PHIL: (After start.) Hello.

MRS. SCHUYLER: Why, what's the matter?

PHIL: Oh, I'm faint—for food.

MRS. SCHUYLER: (Aside to others.) Oh, it's a shame to do it. (To PHIL.) How would you like to "paflouka" with me?

PHIL: (After business.) No—before I do anything else, I must eat.

MRS. SCHUYLER: To "paflouka" is to eat.

PHIL: Well—hurry—let's do it.

MRS. SCHUYLER: (To waiter.) Now, Mousta place my "rakoush" before him.

PHIL: (As waiter places soup and roll before him.) Oh, it looks like soup.

MRS. SCHUYLER: (Crossing to him.) I always start with something hot.

PHIL: (Takes spoonful.) It is soup! (As he goes for second spoonful, they hold his hand.)

MRS. SCHUYLER: (Counting.) One—two—three—four—five—six— seven—eight—nine—ten—(Looking at him.) How do you feel?

PHIL: (Completely puzzled.) Well, I can't say I feel just full yet.

DUDLEY: Go on, take a bite of roll.

PHIL: Thank you! (He takes one bite—as he goes for second bite, DUDLEY holds his hand—as they all count ten. Looking from one to another.) Say, what is this—a prize fight?

MRS. SCHUYLER: (Looking at him closely.) (DUDLEY takes roll from PHIL.) It's all right—he still lives—I feel better now.

PHIL: I'm glad of that. (He starts to take another spoonful of soup.)

MRS. SCHUYLER: Mousta, bring my rakoush. (Just as PHIL gets spoon to mouth, MOUSTA grabs it out of his hand and crosses with soup and roll to MRS. SCHUYLER, saying to PHIL in Persian: "Rekkra milta suss.")

PHIL: Say, isn't there some mistake? I understood that was my rakoush.

MRS. SCHUYLER: No, dear boy—it's ours. (She starts to eat.)

PHIL: I guess that's what they call to paflouka.

MRS. SCHUYLER: Oh, it tastes good.

PHIL: It sounds good.

MRS. SCHUYLER: Now, Mousta, my bird and salad. (He exits.)

PHIL: I hope the bird's an ostrich. (He hears MRS. SCHUYLER drink soup.) (Enter MOUSTA—crosses with bird to MRS. SCHUYLER.)

MRS. SCHUYLER: No—place it before him.

PHIL: Yes—put it down—put it down.

MRS. SCHUYLER: No one can cook a bird like Princey.

PHIL: A bird? It looks like an insect! (He sees them approaching him as before and grabbing the bird in his hand starts to make off with it—they seize him and throw him into chair.)

PHIL: (As DUDLEY snatches bird from him.) Say, what kind of a game is this anyhow?

MRS. SCHUYLER: I'll explain. The chef is enraged at me, and as he's under suspicion of having put poison in a lady's food that killed her in ten seconds—

PHIL: (Jumping up in alarm.) Poison?

MRS. SCHUYLER: (With DUDLEY'S help setting him down again.) Yes, so we got you to try my food on—

PHIL: Oh, I see—I'm the dog.

DUDLEY: Precisely. Now go on—taste that bird.

PHIL: No, thanks—I've had enough.

ALL: (Together.) Go on—commence! (Business of making him taste bird.)

MRS. SCHUYLER: One—

PHIL: (Finishing counting for her.) Two—(To nine.) (As he reaches ten, he sneezes.)

MRS. SCHUYLER: I'm afraid to look. (Business of PHIL tasting bird, then getting idea of pretending to be poisoned, he commences to get a fit.) Help! Bring a chair! (They finally get his feet on chair.) Well, we got him on the chair anyhow.

DUDLEY: He's poisoned—

LETTY and BETTY: We've killed him.

MRS. SCHUYLER: Come on—let's beat it—(They all run off. PHIL gets up to grab all the food, when DUDLEY is heard off, calling "Lena."—He flops back with a jump to same dead position on floor. Finally gets up, grabs all the food and exits. MRS. SCHUYLER re-enters.)

MRS. SCHUYLER: He's gone and he's taken all the food with him. Quick, Mousta, clear away all these things. (Paul enters.)

PAUL: Mrs. Schuyler, I'm really in love with Rose. (DOWLEH enters now in Persian dress clothes.)

DOWLEH: Ah, Fatima—can I see you alone? (DUDLEY enters.)

DUDLEY: Oh, Lena, could I see you alone?

MRS. SCHUYLER: If any more turn up, I'll scream. (LETTY and BETTY run on, carrying a note.)

LETTY: An important letter.

MRS. SCHUYLER: (Opening it.) From my husband.

BETTY: I'm afraid it's bad news.

MRS. SCHUYLER: Bad news! P'raps he's coming home earlier than I expected. (Reads:) "Dear Becky!"

ALL THE MEN: Becky!

MRS. SCHUYLER: Yes, we met at Arverne! "I have heard of your carrying on with four old sweethearts: Had it been *one*, I would have killed him quietly and let the matter drop, but four are too many. I shall kill them all and divorce you. Expect me at ten.—Hamilton." Oh, gentlemen, this is awful—Hamilton is unlike most men—he means what he says—

PAUL: (Following.) But surely you can find a few more to help us defend ourselves.

MRS. SCHUYLER: Ah, you don't know Hamilton. When he's angry, an army couldn't withstand him.

DOWLEH: If your husband kills, I will kill him.

MRS. SCHUYLER: Ah, that doesn't worry me—but he may cut my allowance.

DUDLEY: (Following.) We *must* save you from such a fate.

MRS. SCHUYLER: Save me? You could! If there was one among you brave enough to say: "I am the only guy here ever loved your wife. Kill *me*, but don't cut her allowance."

MEN: (Going up stage.) Excuse me! (Waiter enters with straws in glass, from arbor.)

MRS. SCHUYLER: Ah—straws—the very thing—gentlemen. (Takes them out of glasses.) Come—choose—whoever has the shortest straw is to show his courage and die for me—who is it? Who is it? (PHIL enters—they see him—drop straws—and seize him.)

PAUL: Phil!

MEN: Ah! Welcome to our city. Welcome! Welcome!

PHIL: Is there any little thing I can do for you?

MRS. SCHUYLER: Yes. My husband will be here at any moment to kill these gentlemen and divorce me. You can save us all by saying you are the only old sweetheart of mine here.

PHIL: Excuse me!

MRS. SCHUYLER: Oh, Benchie! Think of your bench days when I used to sit on you—

PHIL: If you'd only sit on me now, I'd feel safer—

PAUL: Now don't be a fool. When he comes, say: "I am the only man here ever had an affair with your wife. What have you to say about it?"

ALL: (Together.) Repeat that now.

PHIL: (In terror.) I am the only man here ever had anything to do with your wife—just like that. (An automobile horn heard.)

GIRLS: Oh, here he is—(They run off. Business of men holding PHIL and finally rushing off as an enormous figure in Persian "get-up" enters.)

MRS. SCHUYLER: (Picking up PHIL.) Benchie, it's sweet and accommodating of you to die for these three gentlemen—a favor I shan't forget. (From behind the Persian giant steps a midget in swell citizen clothes)—"It's Hamilton—(Mrs. Schuyler picks him up and kisses him.) Oh, Hamilton-I'm so glad you've come. (Crossing to Persian.) And Nehmid Duckin—it is an honor to have the prime minister with us. I'll go for a stroll with you and come back when (Turning to husband) you're through with this gentleman.

NEHMID: (In deep voice.) Is he the one?

MRS. SCHUYLER: Yes—you're looking great. (Takes his arm.)

NEHMID: So are you! (In deep tones to PHIL.) And now sir, you explain. (Exits with Mrs. Schuyler.) (PHIL stands in terror, thinking a powerful foe stands behind him. In reality, it is the midget husband. PHIL tries to talk. At first he cannot.)

PHIL: (After comedy biz.) I have a wife with an affair—I mean an affair with your wife—what have you to say about it?

MR. SCHUYLER: (In piping voice.) I'm very angry. (PHIL starts—looks up to see where voice comes from—doesn't see anyone—walks and bumps into HAMILTON—rolls up his sleeves.)

PHIL: (Bravely.) What have you to say about it? (Slaps his hand over his mouth.) Don't say a word—I've been waiting for something like you to show up. (He backs HAMILTON off—his hand on his face.)

FINALE: (During this, ROSE enters in bridal costume to be wed to SHEIK. Servant enters announcing his death from eating Persian Plums.

SONG: "Who Sent These Persian Plums?"

Then, final meeting and happiness of lovers and comedy characters and picture as "My Little Persian Rose" is repeated for

CURTAIN

MY OLD KENTUCKY HOME

CHARACTERS
    OLD BLACK JOE . . . . An ex-slave, eighty years of age
    ARTHUR MAYNARD. . . . . Owner of a Kentucky Plantation
    VIOLA MAYNARD . . . . His Daughter
    CHARLIE DOOLITTLE. . . . . Her Sweetheart
    EDGAR TREMBLE. . . . . With a heart of stone
    MRS. ALICE WILSON. . . . . A frail widow
    HARVEY SLICK . . . . An adventurer
    FELIX FAKE . . . . His assistant
    CHLORINDA SOURGRASS. . . . . A lady of color
    CISSIE, LOTTIE, FANNIE, TILLIE, GOLDIE, DORA, MAGGIE, MABEL, GERTIE. . . . . Invited Guests

SCENE: Garden of ARTHUR MAYNARD'S plantation. Landscape backing. Set house at left with practical veranda (if possible). Wood wings at right. Set tree up stage at right behind which old pocketbook containing a number of greenbacks is concealed. Bench in front of tree. Pedestal up stage at left, dog-house at right.

    DISCOVERED: (At rise of curtain an invisible CHORUS is heard singing "My Old Kentucky Home." Then GOLDIE and other invited girl friends come on stage and sing a MEDLEY OF POPULAR CHORUSES. At conclusion of medley, VIOLA enters from house.)

    VIOLA: Girls, do you know why I've invited you all today?
    FANNIE: To tell us that you're engaged to be married.
    VIOLA: Nothing so fortunate. This is my father's birthday, and I've arranged a little celebration in his honor, and I want you all to participate.
    LOTTIE: We won't do a thing but enjoy ourselves.
    VIOLA: But there's one dark cloud, girls.
    (CHLORINDA enters from house.)
    TILLIE: Yes, here comes the dark cloud now.
    VIOLA: The dark cloud I refer to is Mrs. Wilson, who calls herself a widow and who has been hanging around father for the last few months in the hope that he'll make her Mrs. Maynard number two.
    DORA: The hussy!
    MAGGIE: The cat!
    VIOLA: I wouldn't care if she loved father, but I suspect that all she's after is his money.
    CHLORINDA: His mazuma.
    GERTIE: Get on to the African Jew!
    LOTTIE: Any woman that wants to fool your father has to get up early in the morning.
    VIOLA: Mrs. Wilson sometimes looks as if she stays up all night. (All girls laugh.)
    VIOLA: If she only knew that the old plantation is mortgaged up to the roof,

I guess she wouldn't be so anxious about marrying father.

VIOLA: (To CHLORINDA.) Well, Chlorinda, what brings you out here?

CHLORINDA: I jes' came out to say dat refreshments am ready in de house if de young ladies am thirsty or hungry.

(CHORUS by ladies of company, then they exit into house. VIOLA remains on stage.)

(CHARLIE DOOLITTLE enters from R. and stealing up softly behind VIOLA, puts his hands over her eyes.)

CHARLIE: Guess who it is?

VIOLA: Is it a human being?

CHARLIE: (Effeminately.) Why, I like that! Of course, it is.

VIOLA: It's Lottie.

CHARLIE: No.

VIOLA: Then it's Fanny.

CHARLIE: No.

VIOLA: Then it must be Lillie.

CHARLIE: No; you silly goose, it's Charlie.

VIOLA: (In disgust.) I thought you said it was a human being?

CHARLIE: Just for that you must sit down on the bench and give me a kiss.

VIOLA: Wait a minute till I go into the house and get a veil. The sunlight hurts my eyes. (She exits at L.)

CHARLIE: (Moving towards R.) That will just give me time to go into the grove and smoke a cigarette. (Exits.)

(Enter CHLORINDA from house. She has a green veil on, which hides her face; she sits down on bench.)

CHLORINDA: Ebery wench on dis plantation has got a fellah 'ceptin me, so I went to a fortune tellah an' she said Ah should sit on dis heah bench ebery day and ah nice fellah would come along. Well, I'se been doing it now for ovah a month an' Ah habent seen no nice fellah yet; in fact, Ah habent seen a fellah of any kind.

(Enter CHARLIE from R.)

CHARLIE: Ah, there, my sugar plum.

CHLORINDA: Ain't he jes' too sweet for anything?

CHARLIE: So you love your baby?

CHLORINDA: 'Deed I do, honey.

CHARLIE: Then lay your beautiful head on my manly breast and let me pour sweet words of love into your ear.

CHLORINDA: Go to it, kiddo. (Business of CHARLIE petting CHLORINDA.)

CHARLIE: And now, ain't you going to, give me a nice, sweet kiss, darling?

CHLORINDA: Help yourself to as many as you want.

(CHLORINDA lifts veil just enough to let CHARLIE touch her lips. He does not, however, notice that she is colored, and is busily engaged hugging and kissing her, as VIOLA enters from house; she is very much surprised.)

VIOLA: Charlie Doolittle, what does this mean? (CHLORINDA raises her veil, then laughs and runs into house.)

CHARLIE: (Discovering his error.) Why, my dear, it's all a mistake; I thought—that is to say—er—

VIOLA: I'm not surprised at your embarrassment. The idea of making love to our colored cook the minute my back is turned.

CHARLIE: If you'll just let me explain—

VIOLA: Explain nothing. I'm going to tell my father how you've insulted me. He doesn't like you, anyhow, and if he ever catches you on the premises, your life won't be worth 23 cents in Confederate money. (VIOLA exits into house.)

CHARLIE: Ain't she the exasperating creature! I declare, she's made me so peevish, I could crush a grape. The idea of telling me her father doesn't like me. Why shouldn't he like me? (ARTHUR MAYNARD appears in back-ground unnoticed by CHARLIE.) But, anyhow, I'm not afraid of her father. Why, if he were to stand before me right at this moment, I'd—

MAYNARD: (Stepping suddenly to the front.) Well, what would you do?

CHARLIE: I'd run like the devil. (Runs off stage at R.)

MAYNARD: I'm going to keep that disgusting fellow off the premises if I have to notify the dog-catcher. (Notices pedestal.) Ever since a tornado knocked that statue off its pedestal, this garden has looked rather bare, so I've put an advertisement into the newspaper, offering five hundred dollars for a suitable statue to take its place.

(Mrs. Wilson enters from R. and coughs gently to attract MR. MAYNARD'S attention.)

MAYNARD: (Turning around.) Why, Mrs. Wilson!

MRS. WILSON: Good morning, Mr. Maynard!

(Both talking at the same time.) This is indeed a surprise. I did not expect to see you as early as this. How are you feeling? Good? That's good. Lovely day, isn't it?

MAYNARD: I have often wanted to ask you, Mrs. Wilson, where is your husband?

MRS. WILSON: I don't know.

MAYNARD: What's that, you don't know where your husband is?

MRS. WILSON: No; you see, he is dead—

MAYNARD: (Laughingly.) I understand. Did he leave you much?

MRS. WILSON: Yes, nearly every night.

MAYNARD: No, no; I mean, did he leave you any property?

MRS. WILSON: Yes, five small children, and believe me, Mr. Maynard, it's hard to lose a husband when you have five children. Do you think I ought to get another?

MAYNARD: No; I think five are enough.

MRS. WILSON: I see you will have your joke.

MAYNARD: Are you fond of horses?

MRS. WILSON: I love horses.

MAYNARD: Well, come down to the stable and I'll show you some of the finest thoroughbreds you ever looked at. (They both exit Right I.)

(Enter HARVEY SLICK and FELIX FAKE at centre; HARVEY carries a heavy blackthorn walking stick.)

HARVEY: Now remember, you're a statue.

FELIX: You're a liar.

HARVEY: Don't call me a liar.

FELIX: Then don't call me a statue.

HARVEY: Don't you understand, the guy what owns this plantation offers five hundred dollars for a statue and I've come to get the money.

FELIX: But what have I got to do with all this?

HARVEY: You're the statue.

FELIX: Go on; I never was a statue in my life.

HARVEY: All you have to do is to get on that pedestal and stand perfectly still.

FELIX: Oh, I just have to stand perfectly still.

HARVEY: That's the idea. Don't move a muscle.

FELIX: But suppose a fly hops on my nose?

HARVEY: Don't notice it.

FELIX: Or suppose some bad boys throw stones at me?

HARVEY: Why, my boy, simply don't notice it.

FELIX: I don't think I want the job.

HARVEY: Why, of course you do. The figure you are to represent is called "Ajax defying the lightning."

FELIX: Oh, a jackass defying the lightning.

HARVEY: No, Ajax; but look sharp, for here comes Mr. Maynard now. Quick, jump on the pedestal.

(HARVEY hands stick to FELIX, who quickly jumps on pedestal and poses in funny position, as Maynard enters from right.)

MAYNARD: (To HARVEY.) Well, sir, what can I do for you?

HARVEY: You advertised for a statue, I believe.

MAYNARD: I did, sir.

HARVEY: Well, I think I've got just what you want—"a jackass defying the lightning."

MAYNARD: What's that?

HARVEY: Excuse me, I mean "Ajax." (Aside, and pointing to FELIX.) That son of a gun has got me talking that way now.

MAYNARD: I'll be pleased to look at your statue.

HARVEY: (Pointing to FELIX on pedestal.) Here it is, sir.

MAYNARD: (After surveying it critically.) What material is the statue made of?

HARVEY: Brass—pure brass.

MAYNARD: I think the statue will suit me except that the nose is a bit too long.

HARVEY: Well, you can easily take off a piece with a hammer and chisel.

MAYNARD: Why, so I can. But here's another objection. Suppose thieves come around some night and steal the statue?

HARVEY: All you have to do is to bore a hole through one of its legs, pass a chain through it and fasten to the pedestal. (FELIX works up this situation by comic mugging.)

MAYNARD: A very good idea. How much do you want for the statue?

HARVEY: Five hundred dollars.

MAYNARD: That's a lot of money, but I think I shall buy it anyhow.

HARVEY: Well, just hand over the five hundred, and the statue is yours. (MAYNARD and HARVEY move to a position in front of the statue. MAYNARD takes a roll of bills from his pocket and in handling them, drops one. As he bends forward to pick it up, FELIX pokes him with the stick, knocking him over frontwards. MAYNARD thinks HARVEY has kicked him.)

MAYNARD: (To Harvey.) What do you mean by kicking me, sir?

HARVEY: Why, I didn't kick you.

MAYNARD: If I hadn't set my heart on owning the statue, I'd call the deal off right now.

HARVEY: (Starting to get a bit angry.) I tell you I didn't kick you.

MAYNARD: Well, don't do it again. Here's your money. (MAYNARD hands HARVEY roll of bills, who counts it and lets the last bill fall on stage. In stooping to pick it up, FELIX pokes HARVEY, causing him to fall over frontwards. HARVEY thinks MAYNARD has kicked him.)

HARVEY: (To MAYNARD.) A joke's a joke, but this is going entirely too far.

MAYNARD: What on earth are you talking about?

HARVEY: You just kicked me.

MAYNARD: I didn't.

HARVEY: You did.

MAYNARD: I didn't.

FELIX: Shut up.

MAYNARD and HARVEY: (Both talking together.)

Don't tell me to shut up. I didn't tell you to shut up. Well, somebody did.

HARVEY: I'm awful thirsty.

MAYNARD: I'll go into the house and get you a glass of wine.

FELIX: Well, hurry up about it.

MAYNARD: (Thinking HARVEY spoke.) I never heard such impudence in all my life. Why, the idea!

(Exits into house.)

FELIX: Yes, the idea.

HARVEY: Well, I got the old fool's money all right.

FELIX: Where's my share?

HARVEY: (Laughing.) Now, who ever heard of a statue having mo-non-ey.

FELIX: But you promised me half of the five hundred dollars.

HARVEY: Well, suppose I did; you don't expect me to keep my word, do you? You'd be a pretty looking sight, carrying two hundred and fifty dollars around with you. Why, I'd have to lay for you in some dark alley and take it away from you. I want you to understand that I'm the wise guy of this combination and if you want any of my money, you've got to take it away from me. (HARVEY has taken a position just in front of FELIX, who is still on the pedestal. FELIX slips his hand slyly into HARVEY'S pocket and takes all the money.)

HARVEY: (Moving to centre exit.) Well, so long, Felix, so long, and remember, Felix, that money is the root of all evil.

(HARVEY exits.)

FELIX: (Holding up roll of bills.) Well, I've extracted some of the root all right, all right. (FELIX exits at right.)

(Big SINGING NUMBER by VIOLA and ladies of company.)

(Then, MR. MAYNARD enters from the house.)

GOLDIE: In behalf of all your friends who are assembled here today, Mr. Maynard, I want to congratulate you on your birthday anniversary.

MAYNARD: Ah, thank you, ladies, I appreciate your good wishes very much.

DORA: I hope you will live to be a hundred years old.

MAYNARD: (Laughing.) I hope so—but why should the Lord take me for a hundred when he can get me at 70?

(OLD BLACK JOE comes ambling in from Right to melody of "Old Black Joe.")

MAYNARD: Well, Old Black Joe, how are you feeling today?

JOE: Well, Massa, I'se got rheumatiz in the lef' shoulder—an' de lumbago in mah back—an' I don' hear very well—an' ma teeth am troubling me some—an' mah eyes is going back on me—an' mah stomach ain't as good as it used to be—but otherwise, Massa, I'se feelin' as sound as a nut.

MAYNARD: What can I do for you, Old Black Joe?

JOE: Massa, my mind ain't as clear like it used ter be, but der's one thing I ain't never forgotten, and dat is your birthday university, so I'd feel powerful flattered if you would accept these few flowers what I picked myself. (Hands MAYNARD small bouquet.)

MAYNARD: Of all the many gifts I will receive to-day, Old Black Joe, there is none that I will treasure more highly than these flowers.

JOE: Ah, thank you, Massa, thank you.

(OLD BLACK JOE exits to melody of "Old Black Joe.")

GOLDIE: I never could understand, Mr. Maynard, why you always make such a fuss about that nigger, Old Black Joe.

MAYNARD: Old Black Joe may have a black skin, but he's got a white heart and I'll cherish and protect him as long as I have a roof over my head.

GOLDIE: One would think that he had done you some great favor, Mr. Maynard.

MAYNARD: He more than did me a favor. He once saved my life.

CHORUS OF GIRLS: Tell us about it.

MAYNARD: (To melodramatic music.) It was during the days of '61, when brother fought against brother and the Blue was striving to overpower the Grey. On this very plantation, while hardly more than a lad, I was attacked and badly wounded and would have fallen into the hands of the enemy if it had not been for

Old Black Joe, who, at the risk of his own life, carried me to a place of safety and nursed me back to health again.

CHORUS OF LADIES: Three cheers for Old Black Joe.

(SONG by Ladies—all exit.)

(Enter CHARLIE at centre.)

CHARLIE: I'm crazy about Viola, but I know she will never marry me unless her father gives his consent. If I only knew a way to win him over. Ah, here comes Chlorinda. Perhaps she can help me.

(Enter CHLORINDA from house.)

CHARLIE: Hello, Chlorinda.

CHLORINDA: Miss Sourgrass, if you please.

CHARLIE: What's the matter with Chlorinda?

CHLORINDA: I only allows gentlemen I'se well acquainted with to call me Chlorinda.

CHARLIE: Well then, Miss Sourgrass, do you want to earn a dollar?

CHLORINDA: What's the matter with it?

CHARLIE: There's nothing the matter with it. You see, I'm in love with Viola Maynard, but her father doesn't like me. Now, if you can fix things up so her father will accept me as a son-in-law, I will give you a dollar.

CHLORINDA: Jes leave it to me and in half an hour he'll be so tickled to see you that he'll put his arms around your neck and kiss you.

CHARLIE: That will be splendid.

CHLORINDA: The dollar, please.

CHARLIE: I never pay in advance.

CHLORINDA: No dollar, no kisses.

CHARLIE: (Handing her a dollar.) Oh, very well, but see that you do as you promise.

CHLORINDA: Leave it to me.

(CHARLIE exits at right.)

(MR. MAYNARD enters from house.)

CHLORINDA: Did you hear what happened to Charlie Doolittle?

MAYNARD: I suppose he took a pinch of snuff and blew his brains out.

CHLORINDA: Goodness no; guess again.

MAYNARD: No, I won't. I'm not at all interested in that addlepated, monkey-faced nincompoop. He's after my daughter, but he shall never marry her. Why, if wives could be supported for fifty cents a year, that empty-headed specimen of vacuous mentality couldn't even keep a cock-roach from starving.

CHLORINDA: Don't say dat, massa, for Charlie's uncle has jes' died an' left him fifty thousand dollars.

MAYNARD: (Very much astonished.) How much did you say?

CHLORINDA: Five hundred thousand dollars.

MAYNARD: Five hundred thousand dollars?

CHLORINDA: Yes, sah; five million dollars?

MAYNARD: I always did like Charlie.

CHLORINDA: But you jes' said—

MAYNARD: Never mind what I just said. I was only joking. Here's a dollar to keep your mouth shut.

(MAYNARD hands CHLORINDA a dollar.)

CHLORINDA: Yes, sah.

MAYNARD: I consider Charlie Doolittle an exceptionally bright young man, and even if he didn't have a dollar in the world I would still consider him an excellent match for my daughter.

CHLORINDA: But you jes' said he couldn't even support a cock-roach.

MAYNARD: Never mind about that. Here's another dollar. (Hands CHLORINDA another dollar.) And now, if you see Charlie Doolittle, tell him I want to see him right away.

CHLORINDA: Yes, sah. (She exits at right.)

MAYNARD: (Looking at empty pedestal.) I wonder what became of the statue? I guess Chlorinda carried it into the barn because it looks like rain. (Enter CHARLIE from right. He coughs to attract MAYNARD'S attention.)

CHARLIE: Are you very angry at me, Mr. Maynard?

MAYNARD: Angry at you, Charlie? Why, how can you only imagine such a thing? Have a cigar.

CHARLIE: (Accepting the cigar with misgivings.) It isn't loaded with dynamite, is it?

MAYNARD: Certainly not. I give you the cigar because I like you, Charlie, and I always have liked you.

CHARLIE: It's very kind of you to say that (During these speeches, FELIX has sneaked back on the pedestal, still carrying the blackthorn stick.)

MAYNARD: You have only to say the word and you can have anything I've got.

CHARLIE: Can I have your daughter?

MAYNARD: Why certainly, Charlie. Just say the word and she's yours.

CHARLIE: It all seems like a dream. (Business of FELIX hitting MAYNARD on hat with stick and smashing it in. MAYNARD thinks CHARLIE did it.)

MAYNARD: Now see here, Charlie, as my future son-in-law, I want you to feel perfectly at home here, but there's such a thing as carrying things too far.

CHARLIE: Why, Mr. Maynard, what do you mean?

MAYNARD: I saw you smash my hat just now, Charlie.

CHARLIE: I didn't smash your hat.

MAYNARD: You didn't smash my hat?

CHARLIE: No; I didn't smash your hat.

MAYNARD: Well, somebody did. However, as I was about to remark, you have but to name the day and I'll give my daughter a wedding that will—(FELIX smashes CHARLIE'S hat with stick. CHARLIE thinks MAYNARD did it.)

CHARLIE: Now, see here, Mr. Maynard, I may have straw-colored hair and wear a number fourteen collar, but I object—I very seriously object to having anybody crush my hat.

MAYNARD: I didn't crush your hat.

CHARLIE: I saw you.

MAYNARD: (Getting very angry and shaking fist in CHARLIE'S face.) You say you saw me crush your hat?

CHARLIE: (Backing water.) Well, I thought I saw you.

MAYNARD: (Mollified once more.) Well, that's different. However, it really isn't worth talking about. You know that all I want in this world is to see you happy.

CHARLIE: Then perhaps you can lend me fifty dollars.

MAYNARD: Lend you fifty dollars? Why certainly. Here you are. (Hands CHARLIE the money.) No doubt, you'll be able to pay me back when you receive the money that was left you in the will.

CHARLIE: What will?

MAYNARD: Why, the will of your uncle.

CHARLIE: What uncle?

MAYNARD: What uncle? Why, your millionaire uncle who just died and left you all his money.

CHARLIE: I never had a millionaire uncle and nobody has left me a penny.

MAYNARD: (Wiping perspiration off his face.) What; then you are not a rich man?

CHARLIE: Rich; why, that fifty dollars you just gave me is every penny I've got in this world.

MAYNARD: (Getting excited.) Oh you fraud, you deceiver, you disgraceful beggar; I've a great mind to—(Raises fist as if to strike CHARLIE.)

CHARLIE: (Rushing off at right.) Assistance. Assistance!

(HARVEY comes in at centre and stands in background ground; FELIX is still on pedestal.)

MAYNARD: There is only one way to keep that disgusting dude off the premises. I'll get a savage dog if it costs me a thousand dollars. (Exits into house.)

HARVEY: (To FELIX, who steps off pedestal.) You hear that?

FELIX: Hear what?

HARVEY: He wants a savage dog.

FELIX: Well, suppose he does?

HARVEY: You're the dog.

FELIX: What?

HARVEY: You're the dog.

FELIX: Say, what's tbe matter with you anyhow? First I was a statue and now I'm a dog. Next I suppose I'll be an automobile or a bag of peanuts.

HARVEY: That's all right. Pass yourself off as the dog and we'll divide the thousand dollars between us.

FELIX: Yes, you'll get nine hundred and ninety-nine and I'll get the balance.

HARVEY: Nonsense; I'll only take what is right.

FELIX: And I'll have to take what is left.

HARVEY: For the love of Mike be reasonable. This is the chance of a lifetime.

FELIX: I'll impersonate the dog if you get me something to eat.

HARVEY: What do you want to eat for?

FELIX: I'm starving.

HARVEY: All right, it's a bargain. You impersonate the savage dog and I'll see that you're well fed. (Both exit at centre.)

(Enter MRS. WILSON, from right.)

MRS. WILSON: I must force a proposal of marriage out of Mr. Maynard today yet. It's true I don't love him, but he's got lots of money, and money is everything in this world.

(Enter CHLORINDA from house, crying.)

MRS. WILSON: Why Chlorinda, what's the matter?

CHLORINDA: I'se just been down to the cemetery.

MRS. WILSON: Well, you ought to laugh.

CHLORINDA: Why, why should I laugh?

MRS. WILSON: It's the people who are in the cemetery and cannot get out who ought to be crying.

CHLORINDA: Dat's all very well, Mrs. Wilson, but I jes' copied some of de inscriptions off de tombstones, and I tells you I feels awful mournful about it.

MRS. WILSON: I don't see why you should feel sad, Chlorinda.

CHLORINDA: You don't? Well, jes' listen to some of dese. (Reads from a stack of cards, one tombstone inscription being written on each card.)

"Here lies the body of Michael Burke, who lost his life while dodging work."

"I loved my mother, I hated to leave her, but what can you do with the typhoid fever? "

"Mamma loves Papa, and Papa loves women; Mamma saw Papa with two girls in swimmin'."

"Here lies the mother of 28; there might have been more, but now it's too late."

"Shed a few tears for Matty Mack, a trolley car hit her a slap in the back."

"Here lies my poor wife much lamented. She's happy and—well, I am contented."

"Here lies the body of Martin Brown. He was blown in the air and he never came down."

"Willie Greene, sad regrets—aged 9—cigarettes."

(Enter MR. MAYNARD from house.)

MAYNARD: Won't you step inside the house, Mrs. Wilson—I mean Alice—and have a glass of birthday punch with the other ladies?

MRS. WILSON: Delighted, I'm sure. (Exits into house.)

CHLORINDA: Won't I get punch, too?

MAYNARD: Yes, if you don't get back to your work, you'll get a punch in the jaw in about another minute.

MAYNARD: I hope some one comes along soon with a savage dog. I'd rather go to Charlie Doolittle's funeral than to a picnic. (Looks off toward house.) Ah, there is Mrs. Wilson. How beautiful she is. I think this is my golden chance to propose to her. (Exits into house.)

(Enter HARVEY at centre, pulling FELIX in by chain fastened around his neck. FELIX now wears a dog's head and body.)

HARVEY: (Aside to FELIX.) Now remember, all you have got to do is to act like a savage dog, and after I collect the money from Mr. Maynard, you'll get yours.

FELIX: (Removing dog's head.) I hope I don't get it where I've got this collar.

HARVEY: Oh, you'll get it all right.

FELIX: (Starting to leave stage.) I'm going home.

HARVEY: (Catching him by chain.) Here, here, where are you going?

FELIX: I don't like the way you say, "Oh, you'll get it."

HARVEY: Oh, that's all right. And now whatever you do, act like a dog.

(FELIX tries to nip HARVEY'S leg, but he springs aside and says.) Delighted. Why, you're commencing to feel like a dog already.

FELIX: When do I get something to eat?

HARVEY: Very shortly now.

(Sees MAYNARD coming from house.) Quick, put on your dog's head, for here comes Mr. Maynard.

(Enter MAYNARD.)

MAYNARD: (To HARVEY.) Well, sir, and what can I do for you?

HARVEY: Your servant told me you were looking for a ferocious dog and I think I have an animal that will just suit you.

MAYNARD: Yes, I do want a savage dog, and if you have such a beast we can do business together.

FELIX: (Aside.) Now, I'm a beast.

(HARVEY kicks at FELIX to get him to shut up.)

HARVEY: (Pointing to FELIX.) This animal is so ferocious that if anyone should come across his path at night when he is unchained he would tear him limb from limb.

MAYNARD: (Noticing FELIX.) Is this the dog?

HARVEY: (Rubbing his hands.) Yes, sir, and if you searched the world over, you couldn't find a more savage high-bred animal. He is full of animation.

MAYNARD: (Scratching himself.) I think he is full of fleas. But, tell me, what do you ask for him?

HARVEY: One thousand dollars.

MAYNARD: That's a lot of money.

HARVEY: Not for this dog.

MAYNARD: Perhaps I ought to explain to you what I want the dog for.

HARVEY: I daresay you feel lonely for a companion.

MAYNARD: No, sir; I want a dog for my daughter, sir, to keep off a worthless, good-for-nothing dude who comes pestering around here after her because he knows that her father has a lot of money, and thinks that if he marries his daughter he can move to Easy Street.

HARVEY: I see; he is looking for a soft snap.

MAYNARD: That's it, but I'll fool him. I want a dog that will chew him up into pieces if he ever dares to set his foot inside my garden gate again.

HARVEY: My dog will suit you exactly.

MAYNARD: But a thousand dollars is an awful lot of money.

HARVEY: Not for this animal. In the first place, you never have to feed him.

MAYNARD: What's that! You mean to say that this dog goes without food?

HARVEY: That's the idea exactly.

(FELIX shows signs of disgust. He can work up some funny business by taking off his mask whenever HARVEY and MAYNARD are talking together and quickly slipping it on again when he thinks their attention is directed towards him.)

MAYNARD: Why, it's preposterous. You don't suppose I would keep a dog around the house and never feed him?

HARVEY: I tell you this dog never eats.

MAYNARD: Why, that's cruelty to animals!

HARVEY: Well, if you feel that way about it, you might go out into an empty lot and get some rusty tomato cans and a few pieces of scrap iron and feed those to him.

MAYNARD: Does he enjoy such things?

HARVEY: Certainly he does. In fact, if you were to put a choice piece of juicy tenderloin steak before him right now that dog wouldn't touch it.

MAYNARD: A most remarkable animal.

FELIX: (Taking off his dog mask, aside.) I'm going home.

HARVEY: (Aside, to FELIX.) Shut up or you'll spoil everything.

(FELIX makes a grab for MAYNARD'S leg.)

MAYNARD: Help! Help! Your dog is killing me.

HARVEY: Don't get frightened, Mr. Maynard, he is perfectly domesticated and will eat off your hand.

MAYNARD: Yes; he'll eat off my leg, too, if I'm not careful.

HARVEY: (To FELIX.) Lie down, Otto, lie down, I say. (Kicks FELIX, who lets go of MAYNARD'S leg.)

MAYNARD: (Going quickly out of harm's way, yet delighted.) Just the dog I want—a fine animal. I am sure with him around that Charlie Doolittle won't dare to show his face on the premises.

HARVEY: Better buy him while you have the chance.

MAYNARD: (Taking roll of bills from pocket and counting out the money.) I think I will. Here's the thousand dollars.

HARVEY: And now the dog is yours.

(MAYNARD fastens dog to exterior of dog-house.)

MAYNARD: I hope I have better luck with him than I had with my other dogs.

HARVEY: Why, what do you mean?

FELIX: (In back-ground.) Yes, please explain yourself.

MAYNARD: (Chuckling.) Well, you see my neighbors ain't very fond of dogs and as fast as I get one they either poison him or shoot him.

FELIX: (In back-ground.) I can see my finish.

HARVEY: Well, it won't make any difference with this dog. You can fill him full of bullets and he won't even feel it.

FELIX: (Aside.) No, I'll be dead.

HARVEY: (Continuing.) And as for poisoned meat, why, he would rather have Paris green or strychnine on his meat than salt.

MAYNARD: (Chuckling.) Certainly a remarkable animal. And now, if you will excuse me a minute, I will go into the house and tell my daughter about the dog. (He exits into house.)

HARVEY: (Gleefully.) The scheme worked beautifully and I am just a thousand dollars ahead.

FELIX: (Indignantly.) What do you mean by telling him that I eat tin cans and scrap iron?

HARVEY: Why, that was only a little joke on my part.

FELIX: Oh, it was a joke, was it? And suppose the neighbors fire their pistols at me and riddle me with bullets, what then?

HARVEY: Why, simply don't notice it. Anyhow, don't complain to me, you're the dog, not I, and if the neighbors kill you, that's not my funeral.

FELIX: I can see myself in dog heaven already. And how about my share of the money?

HARVEY: The what?

FELIX: The money. The dough, the mazuma.

HARVEY: The money? Since when do dogs carry money? Ha, ha! That's a good joke. A very good joke. (Exits at R. 2.)

MAYNARD: (Re-enters from house.) And now to see if I can't make friends with the dog.

(FELIX barks furiously at MAYNARD as soon as he comes near.)

MAYNARD: He is just the animal to keep Viola's lover away. I will call her out, and show her the dog. (Calls off to house.) Oh, Viola! (Dog snaps at MAYNARD as latter passes him.)

VIOLA: (From the doorstep of house.) What do you want, father?

MAYNARD: I want to show you the new dog I bought. (Dog barks furiously.) See if you can make friends with him.

(VIOLA approaches FELIX, who leans his head affectionately against her and puts his arm around her waist.)

VIOLA: He seems to like me all right, father.

MAYNARD: I cannot understand it.

VIOLA: Perhaps he doesn't like men.

FELIX: (Aside.) No; I ain't that kind of a dog.

VIOLA: I wonder if the dog is hungry?

MAYNARD: I'll go into the house and get him a bone. (Exits into house.)

(FELIX starts rubbing his dog's head against VIOLA'S hip. She screams and exits into house.)

(CHARLIE DOOLITTLE enters from Right.)

CHARLIE: I haven't seen Viola for half an hour, so I think I'll serenade her. (Starts in singing chorus of song, "Only One Girl in This World for Me.")

(FELIX howls accompaniment. CHARLIE sees dog, who tries to grab him.)

CHARLIE: I'll get a pistol and shoot the beast.

FELIX: Gee, but he's got a nasty disposition!

CHARLIE: I'll return in two minutes. (Exits at right.)

FELIX: (Unfastening catch that holds him to dog-house.) And I will be gone in one minute. (Exits at Centre.)

(MR. MAYNARD and VIOLA enter from house.)

MAYNARD: Viola, I am worried.

VIOLA: What's the matter, father?

MAYNARD: I am afraid that Old Black Joe's mind is beginning to weaken. Sometimes he sits for hours babbling about the old plantation as it existed in the days of '61.

VIOLA: How strange!

MAYNARD: Only last week a celebrated doctor assured me that if Old Black Joe could but gaze once more on the old plantation as it looked before the War, his mental powers would come back to him as sharp and clear as ever.

VIOLA: I have an idea.

CHARLIE: (Appearing suddenly from Right.) Well, pickle it, because it's going to be a hard Winter.

(MAYNARD starts to chase CHARLIE, who quickly exits.)

MAYNARD: (To VIOLA.) What is your idea, daughter?

VIOLA: I propose that all the girls dress themselves as pickaninnies and indulge in the sports and pastimes of the South before the War, so that Old Black Joe will think he is once more among the scenes of his boyhood days.

MAYNARD: A great idea—and we'll put it into execution at once.

(A PICKANINNY NUMBER BY THE GIRLS LED BY VIOLA. When the pickaninny number is over, "Old Black Joe." ENTIRE COMPANY DRESSES THE STAGE and forms itself into picturesque groupings. Selections by a colored quartette can also be appropriately introduced.)

(Song, "Old Black Joe," by OLD BLACK JOE, company joining in the chorus.)

JOE: Bless me, am I dreaming, or do I see once more de old plantation?

MAYNARD: (Cordially.) The very same, Joe, the very same.

JOE: Why, it seems, Massa, as if a heavy load is lifting from mah mind and de memory of things dat I'se forgotten dese fifty years am coming back to me.

VIOLA: Three cheers for Old Black Joe! (Entire company gives cheers.)

MAYNARD: And now, ladies and gentlemen, on the occasion of my birthday, I also have the honor to announce that Mrs. Wilson has this day consented to become my wife.

(MRS. WILSON steps forward from house and bows to assembled guests in a triumphant way, the guests coldly return her bow.)

(EDGAR TREMBLE enters from Centre.)

MAYNARD: What can I do for you, Mr. Tremble?

TREMBLE: Just one thing, and that is to give me the money you owe me. The mortgage I hold on your plantation for $50,000 is due today and, unless you hand over the money right away, I'll turn you out bag and baggage.

MAYNARD: (Pleadingly.) Won't you give me a few days longer to try and raise the money?

TREMBLE: Not a day, not an hour. I must have the money at once or out you go.

MAYNARD: (Wringing his hands.) I am a ruined man! (Turning to MRS. WILSON.) But at least I will have the consolation of a true and loving companion. (MAYNARD reaches out for her hand, but she draws it away.) Why, what does this mean, Alice?

MRS. WILSON: I fear, Mr. Maynard, that I was never cut out to be a poor man's wife, so I ask you to release me from my engagement. (Walks off stage at Right accompanied by the hisses of the guests.)

TREMBLE: (To MAYNARD.) As you evidently haven't got the $50,000 to pay the mortgage, the plantation becomes mine and I now order you all off the premises.

OLD BLACK JOE: Not so fast.

TREMBLE: (To Joe.) What do you mean by butting in, you black devil? (Sarcastically.) Perhaps you've got the $50,000 to pay the mortgage?

OLD BLACK JOE: No, sah, ain't got no money, but somethin' in mah memory tells me dat I know where some money is hidden.

MAYNARD: (In surprise.) Why, what do you mean, Old Black Joe?

VIOLA: Yes, explain yourself.

OLD BLACK JOE: Well, sah, jes' after de War broke out your father went and hid $50,000 where de Union soldiers couldn't find it.

MAYNARD: (Imploringly.) Can't you remember where the money was hid, Joe?

OLD BLACK JOE: Let me think, Massa, let me think.

VIOLA: Yes, Joe, try and remember.

OLD BLACK JOE: (With a sudden burst of light in his eyes.) I remembers now. He hid the money in dat old tree over dere.

(VIOLA rushes over to tree accompanied by several of the guests.)

TREMBLE: I hope you don't place any faith in the silly fairy stories of this doddering old nigger.

VIOLA: (Pulling an old and worn pocketbook from behind the trunk of the tree.) Here it is! Father, here it is! (She runs to her father and hands him the pocketbook. He eagerly takes out the contents, a big roll of bank bills, and hastily counts them.)

MAYNARD: It's fifty thousand dollars and the old plantation is saved, thanks to Old Black Joe! (To JOE.) Let me grasp your hand. (Shakes OLD BLACK JOE by the hand.)

CHARLIE: (Who has sneaked on the scene from R. 2. To JOE.) Yes, give us your flipper, Joe.

HARVEY: (Who suddenly appears on the scene and shakes JOE'S hand.) It's all right, Joe; you wait for me after the show and I'll buy you some horseradish ice cream and a fried cigarette sandwich.

MAYNARD: Now that the plantation remains, I invite you one and all to join me in a Fried 'Possum and Sweet Potato Dinner.

FELIX: (Who also appears on the scene, carrying his dog's head in his hand.) Thank heavens, I'll get something to eat at last.

CHORUS OF VOICES: Three cheers for Mr. Maynard!

MAYNARD: And don't forget Old Black Joe, for it was through him that I have been able to save

"My OLD KENTUCKY HOME."

(Final Chorus by entire company.)

CURTAIN

GLOSSARY

ACT IN ONE.—An act playing in One (which see).

AD LIB.—Ad libitum—To talk extemporaneously so as to pad a scene or heighten laughter.

AGENT, VAUDEVILLE.—The business agent for an act.

APRON.—That part of the stage lying between the footlights and the curtain line.

ARGOT.—Slang; particularly, stage terms.

ASIDE.—A speech spoken within the sight and hearing of other actors, but which they, as characters in the act, do not "hear."

AUDIENCE-LEFT.—Reverse of stage-left (which see).

AUDIENCE-RIGHT.—Reverse of stage-right (which see).

BACK OF THE HOUSE.—Back stage; the stage back of the curtain.

BACKING.—A drop, wing, or flat used to mask the working stage when a scenery-door or window is opened.

BACKING, INTERIOR.—Backing that represents an interior.

BACKING, EXTERIOR.—Backing that represents an exterior.

BARE STAGE.—Stage unset with scenery.

BIG-TIME.—Circuits playing two shows a day.

BIT, A.—A successful little stage scene complete in itself. A small part in an act.

BOOK OF A MUSICAL COMEDY.—The plot, dialogue, etc., to differentiate these from lyrics and music.

BOOK AN ACT, TO.—To place on a manager's books for playing contracts; to secure a route.

BOOKING MANAGER.—One who books acts for theatres.

BOOSTER.—See "PLUGGER."

BORDER.—A strip of painted canvas hung above the stage in front of the border-lights to mask the stage-rigging.

BORDER-LIGHT.—Different colored electric bulbs set in a tin trough and suspended over the stage to light the stage and scenery.

BOX SET.—A set of scenery made of "flats" (which see) lashed together to form a room whose fourth wall has been removed.

BREAKING-IN AN ACT.—Playing an act until it runs smoothly.

BUNCH-LIGHT.—Electric bulbs set in a tin box mounted on a movable standard to cast any light—moonlight, for instance— through windows or on drops or backings.

BUSINESS, or BUS., or BIZ.—Any movement an actor makes on the stage, when done to drive the spoken words home, or "get over" a meaning without words.

CENTRE-DOOR FANCY.—An interior set containing an ornamental arch and fitted with fine draperies.

CHOOSER.—One who steals some part of another performer's act for his own use.

CLIMAX.—The highest point of interest in a series of words or events—the "culmination, height, acme, apex." (Murray.)

CLOSE-IN, TO.—To drop curtain.

COMEDY.—A light and more or less humorous play which ends happily; laughable and pleasing incidents.

COMPLICATION.—The definite clash of interests which produces the struggle on the outcome of which the plot hinges.

CRISIS.—The decisive, or turning, point in a play when things must come to a change, for better or worse.

CUE.—A word or an action regarded as the signal for some other speech or action by another actor, or for lights to change, or something to happen during the course of an act.

CURTAIN.—Because the curtain is dropped at the end of an act—the finish.

DIE.—When a performer or his act fails to win applause, he or the act is said to "die."

DIMMER.—An electrical apparatus to regulate the degree of light given by the footlights and the border-lights.

DRAPERY, GRAND.—An unmovable Border just in front of the Olio and above Working Drapery.

DRAPERY, WORKING.—The first Border; see "BORDER."

DROP.—A curtain of canvas painted with some scene and running full across the stage opening.

DUMB ACT, or SIGHT ACT.—Acts that do not use words; acrobats and the like.

EXPOSITION.—That part of the play which conveys the information necessary for the audience to possess so that they may understand the foundations of the plot or action.

EXTERIOR BACKING.—See "BACKING, EXTERIOR."

EXTRA MAN, or WOMAN.—A person used for parts that do not require speech; not a regular member of the company.

FANCY INTERIOR.—The same as "Centre-door Fancy" (which see).

FARCE.—A play full of extravagantly ludicrous situations.

FIRST ENTRANCE.—Entrance to One (which see).

FLASH-BACK.—When a straight-man turns a laugh which a comedian has won, into a laugh for himself (see chapter on "The Two-Act").

FLAT.—A wooden frame covered with a canvas painted to match other flats in a box set.

FLIPPER.—Scenery extension—particularly used to contain curtained entrance to One, and generally set at right angles to the proscenium arch (which see).

FLIRTATION ACT.—An act presented by a man and a woman playing lover-like scenes.

FLY-GALLERY.—The balcony between the stage and the grid iron, from where the scenery is worked.

FLYMEN.—The men assigned to the fly-gallery.

FOUR.—The stage space six or more feet behind the rear boundaries of Three.

FRONT OF THE HOUSE.—The auditorium in front of the curtain.

FULL STAGE.—Same as Four.

GAG.—Any joke or pun. See "POINT."

GENRE.—Kind, style, type.

GET OVER, TO.—To make a speech or entire act a success.

GLASS-CRASH.—A basket filled with broken glass, used to imitate the noise of breaking a window and the like.

GO BIG.—When a performer, act, song, gag, etc., wins much applause it is said to "go big."

GRAND DRAPERY.—See "DRAPERY, GRAND."

GRIDIRON.—An iron network above the stage on which is hung the rigging by which the scenery is worked.

GRIP.—The man who sets scenery or grips it.

HAND, TO GET A.—To receive applause.

HOUSE CURTAIN.—The curtain running flat against the proscenium arch; it is raised at the beginning and lowered at the end of the performance; sometimes use to "close-in" on an act.

INTERIOR BACKING.—See "BACKING, INTERIOR."

JOG.—A short flat used to vary a set by being placed between regulation flats to form angles or corners in a room.

LASH-LINE.—Used on flats to join them tightly together.

LEAD-SHEET.—A musical notation giving a melody of a popular song; a skeleton of a song.

LEGITIMATE.—Used to designate the stage, actors, theatres, etc., that present the full-evening play.

MELODRAMA.—A sensational drama, full of incident and making a violent appeal to the emotions.

MUGGING.—A contortion of the features to win laughter, irrespective of its consistency with the lines or actions.

OLIO.—A drop curtain full across the stage, working flat against the tormentors (which see). It is used as a background for acts in One, and often to close-in on acts playing in Two, Three and Four.

ONE.—That part of the stage lying between the tormentors and the line drawn between the bases of the proscenium arch.

OPEN SET.—A scene composed of a rear drop and matching wings, and not "boxed"—that is, not completely enclosed. See "BOX SET."

PALACE SET.—Palace scene.

PART.—Noun: the manuscript of one character's speeches and business; the character taken by an actor. Verb: to take, or play, a character.

PLAY UP, TO.—To pitch the key of a scene high; to play with rush and emphasis.

PLUGGER.—A booster, a singer who sings new songs to make them popular.

POINT.—The laugh-line of a gag (see "GAG"), or the funny observation of a monologue.

PRODUCE, TO.—To mount a manuscript on the stage.

PRODUCER.—One who produces plays, playlets, and other acts.

PROPERTIES.—Furniture, dishes, telephones, the what-not employed to lend reality—scenery excepted. Stage accessories.

PROPERTY-MAN.—The man who takes care of the properties.

PROPS.—Property-man; also short for properties.

PROSCENIUM ARCH.—The arch through which the audience views the stage.

RIGGING, STAGE.—The ropes, pulleys, etc., by which the scenery is worked.

RIPPLE-LAMP.—A clock-actuated mechanism fitted with ripple-glass and attached to the spot-light to cast wave-effects, etc., on or through the drops.

ROUTE.—A series of playing dates. To "route" is to "book" acts.

ROUTINE.—Arrangement. A specific arrangement of the parts of a state offering, as a "monologue routine," or a "dance routine."

SCENARIO.—The story of the play in outline.

SET.—Noun: a room or other scene set on the stage. Verb: to erect the wings, drops, and flats to form a scene.

SET OF LINES.—Rigging to be tied to drops and other scenery to lift them up into the flies.

SIGHT ACT.—See "DUMB ACT."

SINGLE MAN—SINGLE WOMAN.—A man or woman playing alone; a monologist, solo singer, etc.

SLAP-STICK BUSINESS.—Business that wins laughs by use of physical methods.

SMALL-TIME, THE.—The circuits playing three or more shows a day.

SOUND-EFFECTS.—The noise of cocoanut shells imitating horses' hoof-beats, the sound of waves mechanically made, and the like.

SPOT-LIGHT.—An arc-light with lenses to concentrate the light into a spot to follow the characters around the stage.

STAGE-DRACE.—An implement used with stage-screws to clamp flats firmly to the floor.

STAGE-CENTRE.—The centre of the stage.

STAGE-LEFT.—The audience's right.

STAGE-MANAGER.—One who manages the "working" of a show behind the scenes; usually the stage-carpenter.

STAGE-RIGGING.—See "RIGGING, STAGE."

STAGE-RIGHT.—The audience's left.

STRIKE, TO.—To clear the stage of scenery.

STRIP-LIGHT.—Electric bulbs contained in short tin troughs, hung behind doors, etc., to illuminate the backings.

TAB.—The contraction of "tabloid," as burlesque tab, musical comedy tab.

TALKING SINGLE.—A one-person act using stories, gags, etc.

THREE.—The stage space six or more feet behind the rear boundaries of Two.

TIME.—Playing engagements. See "BIG-TIME," "SMALL-TIME."

TORMENTORS.—Movable first wings behind which the Olio runs, fronting the audience.

TRAP.—A section of the stage floor cut for an entrance to the scene from below.

TRY-OUT.—The first presentation of an act for trial before an audience with a view to booking.

TWO.—The stage space between the Olio and the set of wings six or more feet behind the Olio.

TWO-A-DAY.—Stage argot for vaudeville.

WING.—A double frame of wood covered with painted canvas and used in open sets as a flat is used in box sets; so constructed that it stands alone as a book will when its covers are opened at right angles.

WOOD-CRASH.—An appliance so constructed that when the handle is turned a noise like a man falling downstairs, or the crash of a fight, is produced.

WOOD-SET.—The scenery used to form a forest or woods.

WORKING DRAPERY.—See "DRAPERY, WORKING."

WORK OPPOSITE ANOTHER, TO.—To play a character whose speeches are nearly all with the other.

Echo Library
www.echo-library.com

Echo Library uses advanced digital print-on-demand technology to build and preserve an exciting world class collection of rare and out-of-print books, making them readily available for everyone to enjoy.

Situated just yards from Teddington Lock on the River Thames, Echo Library was founded in 2005 by Tom Cherrington, a specialist dealer in rare and antiquarian books with a passion for literature.

Please visit our website for a complete catalogue of our books, which includes foreign language titles.

The Right to Read
Echo Library actively supports the Royal National Institute for the Blind's Right to Read initiative by publishing a comprehensive range of Large Print (16 point Tiresias font as recommended by the RNIB) and Clear Print (13 point Tiresias font) titles for those who find standard print difficult to read.

Customer Service
If there is a serious error in the text or layout please send details to feedback@echo-library.com and we will supply a corrected copy. If there is a printing fault or the book is damaged please refer to your supplier.

DESIGNLINESMAGAZINE.COM

Jim Caruk
   editorial@renoanddecor.com